CRIME

INTERNATIONAL PERSPECTIVES, SOCIOECONOMIC FACTORS AND PSYCHOLOGICAL IMPLICATIONS

LAW, CRIME AND LAW ENFORCEMENT

CRIME

INTERNATIONAL PERSPECTIVES, SOCIOECONOMIC FACTORS AND PSYCHOLOGICAL IMPLICATIONS

MICHAEL HARRY PEARSON
EDITOR

nova publishers

New York

For permission to use material from this book please contact us:
Telephone 631-231-7269; Fax 631-231-8175
Web Site: http://www.novapublishers.com

NOTICE TO THE READER

The Publisher has taken reasonable care in the preparation of this book, but makes no expressed or implied warranty of any kind and assumes no responsibility for any errors or omissions. No liability is assumed for incidental or consequential damages in connection with or arising out of information contained in this book. The Publisher shall not be liable for any special, consequential, or exemplary damages resulting, in whole or in part, from the readers' use of, or reliance upon, this material. Any parts of this book based on government reports are so indicated and copyright is claimed for those parts to the extent applicable to compilations of such works.

Independent verification should be sought for any data, advice or recommendations contained in this book. In addition, no responsibility is assumed by the publisher for any injury and/or damage to persons or property arising from any methods, products, instructions, ideas or otherwise contained in this publication.

This publication is designed to provide accurate and authoritative information with regard to the subject matter covered herein. It is sold with the clear understanding that the Publisher is not engaged in rendering legal or any other professional services. If legal or any other expert assistance is required, the services of a competent person should be sought. FROM A DECLARATION OF PARTICIPANTS JOINTLY ADOPTED BY A COMMITTEE OF THE AMERICAN BAR ASSOCIATION AND A COMMITTEE OF PUBLISHERS.

Additional color graphics may be available in the e-book version of this book.

Library of Congress Cataloging-in-Publication Data

Crime : international perspectives, socioeconomic factors and psychological implications / editor, Michael Harry Pearson.
  pages cm
 Includes index.
 ISBN 978-1-62948-657-4 (hardcover)
 1. Crime. 2. Crime--Economic aspects. 3. Crime--Psychological aspects. I. Pearson, Michael Harry, editor of compilation.
 HV6025.C717 2014
 364--dc23
                        2013043717

Published by Nova Science Publishers, Inc. † New York

CONTENTS

PREFACE

In this book, the authors discuss crime issues from an international perspective, with a focus on socioeconomic factors and psychological implications. Topics include a qualitative analysis of contemporary Australian prison exit issues including prisoner re-entry and prisoner reintegration; offender profiling; hate crime in the U.S. and its relevant factors; stories of rape victims struggles and survival; a European examination of youth sexual aggression and victimization; positive psychology, offender rehabilitation and restorative justice; the effects of crime on marriages, divorce and births to single mothers in bordering states of Mexico; a comparison of geospatial data concerning crime in China and in the U.S.; prosecution of while collar criminals; and the question of whether stigmatized minorities are over-represented in delinquency in France.

Chapter 1 - The problems concerned with prisoner re-entry, prisoner reintegration and prison exit and the relationship with pro-criminal behaviours has been a topical issue confronting the behavioural science literature since the inception of the study of crime and deviance. Penologists, criminologists, and forensic psychologists have long pondered the questions, why do ex-prisoners return to prison' and what are the real issues that affect prisoners exiting prison'. This study utilised a semi-structured interview to probe insights and perceptions from individuals who had personally experienced the process of going from a confined prisoner to free member of society. The methodological approach was taken in order to gain firsthand snap-shots of the actual issues confronting an exiting prison population. These interviews were subject to a thematic content analysis, revealing that the exiting prison population experienced a range of Negative Post-Release issues including: Accommodation, Employment, Finances, Substance Abuse, and Social Anxiety. It was also found that the prison experience brought together immediate family relationships. The most profound finding of this study was that these issues did not occur in isolation, rather these issues co-existed and merged to form complex clusters of overlapping issues. The overall finding of this study revealed that there are significant issues that confront ex-prisoners exiting prison and that there is a real need for custodial programs focusing on prisoner exit and for community aftercare to assist individual prisoner's reassimilation back into society.

Chapter 2 - The area of Offender Profiling generates a lot of interest in both the academic field and the everyday world as a result of a few highly prolific cases (e.g., Jack the Ripper, Boston Strangler). Historically, profiling has been based on intuition and experience, but as the field has matured, the need to be more scientific in approach has led to the development of empirically driven models/typologies of offender behaviour based. Different approaches have attempted to define, and operationalize offender profiling based on the individual principles inherent in each approach.

Briefly, the Criminal Investigative approach to profiling initially relied upon the investigative experience and observation of FBI agents who soon started publishing on the topic. However, in more recent years, large databases containing information on serial and violent crime/criminals has allowed for more empirical approaches to emerge. The Clinical approach, on the other hand, adopts a model of offender profiling that centers on the concept of motives. Finally, and most recently, the Statistical approach has aimed to provide a testable scientific framework for identifying and inferring offender characteristics/motives.

However, none of these approaches alone can explain the complexities of offending behaviour. The Criminal Investigative approach brings with it a multitude of experience from investigators; the Clinical brings an abundance of medical and privileged client-based knowledge; while the Statistical approach aims to provide more objective measures and examination of offending behaviour. Without the experience, knowledge, and information offered by the first two approaches, the ability to know which variables to look for or code for would be lost. However, the latter Statistical approach allows practitioner-based knowledge to be integrated with the objective examination of offending patterns and correlated findings. Therefore, the way forward should seek to integrate all of the approaches. Together, the approaches strengthen each other and give weight and support to one another. More importantly, they help strengthen the field of offender profiling as a whole.

In this chapter, an overview and critique of the offender profiling literature; its underlying assumptions; and the relationship between the crime scene actions and the offender characteristics will be presented. In addition, each of the approaches to offender profiling that have developed over its short empirical history will be described and critiqued.

Chapter 3 - The term "hate crime," which refers to a crime that involves "the manifest evidence of prejudice" (Hate Crimes Statistics Act, 1990), was first introduced in the United States in the late 1960s by the 1964 Federal Civil Rights Law and still occurs in the U.S., even around the world. This review examines the phenomenon of hate crimes in the United States and reveals that the incidence of anti-racial hate crimes varied among different racial groups; that anti-religious hate crimes were committed toward Jews and Muslims more than to others; and that anti-sexual orientation hate crimes focused on male homosexuals more than others. Other findings revealed that anti-religious hate crimes were more likely to be directed against property, whereas anti-racial and anti-sex orientation hate crimes were more likely to be directed against people, suggesting that the nature of these hate crimes are different. In addition, Whites displayed both higher ingroup favoritism and higher outgroup hatred (especially toward Blacks), but AIANs and Asians displayed lower ingroup favoritism that may be due to greater ingroup heterogeneity. It is postulated that, at the macro-level, a national climate of respecting outgroups may influence normative pressures against expressing hate-related aggression. At the micro-level, some relevant individual difference variables of offenders have been identified: the awareness of mortality salience, outgroup-directed emotion (anger, fear-anxiety, and disgust), aggressiveness, personality (SDO and RWA), and certain socio-demographic variables (i.e. gender, age, hate group membership). Although hate crime victims were usually strangers to the offenders, they were sometimes acquaintances. Possible solutions to hate crimes include "law enforcement" to interdict the expression of outgroup hatred and "education" about mutual tolerance and respect for diversity by implementing the recommended elements of the contact hypothesis.

Chapter 4 - Gender based violence features as one of the most pressing human rights, social and public health challenge throughout the world. Rape is one of the attributes and manifestations of such gender based violence. Rape is worldwide epidemic known for dehumanizing victims in multiple ways. This paper explains rape through the lens of victimology. The paper is qualitative in nature and based on empirical data taken from a research project. The purpose of this study is to identify the factors associated with rape and focus on psychological consequences of rape on the victims. The study also explores the victim recovery process and victim assistance programs available in Bangladesh to reintegrate and rehabilitate them. Qualitative approach was followed in doing so. The findings show that gender inequality, power relations, masculinity, propensity of revenge, ill sexual behavior etc. act as influencing factors behind the rape incidents. The study also indicates that psychological effects of being raped are worse than physical injuries. Rape results both short term and long term harm in the life of rape victims. Depression, post traumatic stress disorders, poor self-esteem, destructive behavior, self blame, distrust others are the common effects were found in rape victims. Moreover, victims' personality, life cycle, family and community support, the way they are treated by police, court or hospital services are mentioned by the respondents as important and significant factors affecting rape victims' coping capacities. However, the study concludes that victim recovery process could minimize the trauma of rape victims through crisis intervention along with victim assistance programs. Hence, more government and non-government interventions and community awareness are necessary to address and redress the rape crime and rape victims.

Chapter 5 - During the period 2010–2013 an EU research project – "Youth Sexual Aggression and Victimization" (Y-SAV) – has investigated the problem of sexual aggression towards young people (12–25 years). The first aim of the project was to create a knowledge base of studies on the prevalence, incidence and risk factors of sexual aggression as well as legal and public health responses, covering all 27 EU states. The collection of these data shows that there seems to be a great variety between different regions and cultures in Europe. The awareness of the problem, the reporting of rape, the legal, research and policy standards vary. In general it can be stated that the attention to the problem is proportional to the incidence, i.e. that the countries that have most rape reports per capita also have most research and policies on the issue. The relation between attention to the problem and the amount of police reports also works in the opposite direction; with more awareness more victims turn to the legal system (and other institutions) for assistance.

The prevalence research on national levels indicates that the risk for a young person of being sexually abused seems to be relatively high in all European countries. A problem in making comparisons between countries has been the use of different methods and criteria. Therefore, another aim of the project was to create a standard set of indicators and standards for prevalence studies that will, in the future, make it possible to compare the extent of youth sexual aggression in different countries. A third aim of the Y-SAV project was to establish an international interdisciplinary network for exchange on best practices, state responses and legal rules to prevent youth sexual victimization. This article concentrates on the governmental issues and concludes that legal harmonization would be difficult to obtain, but that some legal standards, e.g. a rape law based on non-consent, would improve the teenagers´ situation. A discussion within the European community about the age of consent, which varies from 13 to 18 years, could be a way to get the sexual victimization of teenagers on the agenda.

Chapter 6 - Traditionally, criminologists have used psychology to understand and reduce violence by focusing on the negative traits that lead people to crime. This approach is encapsulated in the Risk Need Responsivity (RNR) model of rehabilitation, which is now being challenged at practical, policy, political and financial levels internationally. The Good Lives Model (GLM) was recently developed as an alternative approach focusing on nurturing the offender's personal strengths and goals. This paper takes the next step in deepening the relationship between rehabilitation theory and restorative justice. The authors use the perspectives and tools of positive psychology and the GLM to provide a fresh critical analysis of restorative practices, which have recently received much attention by policy makers and politicians. What can restorative justice learn from positive psychology? Is there anything to be gained from this relationship for rehabilitation theories? How can the victim and the community be brought into the rehabilitation debate?

Chapter 7 - Crime and drug-related violence in Mexico have resulted in job losses, decreases in incomes, business closures, a drop in tourism, and the migration of thousands of individuals trying to escape the violence. The purpose of this chapter is to determine the effects of this crime on marriages, divorces, births to single mothers, and the percent of births to teen mothers in Mexico. Using a spatial model and a panel dataset, it was found that the effects of crime transcend state borders. In particular, states with higher birth rates to single mothers and higher percents of births to teen mothers were found bordering those states with high crime rates. Furthermore, states with high birth rates to single mothers tended to have bordering states with low birth rates to single mothers. Given these additional spatial effects of crime, the true social costs of crime to Mexico may far exceed initial estimates, justifying the use of more resources in the fight against crime and drug-related violence.

Chapter 8 - The use of geographic information systems (GIS) based crime mapping to analyze disseminate information about crime rates, locations and characteristics has been a growing trend and has recently become widespread enough that a comparison between major countries on several continents is possible. While comparisons between nations that are advanced users of GIS like the USA, United Kingdom, Canada and Germany is easy crime data is just starting to become available in a geocoded format in China. A comparison of crime data between China and the USA is therefore feasible. Increasingly web-based data portals are the means for researchers, law enforcement professionals and the general public to understand the pattern and occurrence of crime in their communities and nations and can be used for international comparisons as well. The rapid evolution of regional and local crime data in China and USAwill also be discussed. In particular geospatial data related to crime incident locations, patterns and characteristics will be discussed. One important focus will be the precision and accuracy of the available geospatial data.

Chapter 9 - Defense lawyers in white-collar crime cases tend to take charge over information management at an early stage. It is difficult to overstate the importance of theory to understand white-collar crime lawyers and attorney-client relationships. Important theories include agency theory with principal and agent, transaction cost theory of cooperation, neutralization theory about guilt, attribution theory for explanations, conspiracy theory of external causes, resource-based theory for knowledge access, and stages of growth theory for relationship.

Chapter 10 – The authors address the question of whether minorities are over-represented in delinquency in France, based on an exhaustive database of all the juveniles below 19 years old convicted for serious crimes (liable to imprisonment according to the French Law) in the period 1985-2005 in Isère (about 1 million inhabitants), one of the French Departments. Serious crimes have a higher clearance rate than petty crimes and are thus less biased by police differential selection because authors are actively searched.

Since neither religion nor ethnic traits are available in French legal documents, it is not possible to trace back the offenders' geographic, religious or ethnic origin accurately. Following the practice of the INSEE (the French National Institute of Statistics and Economic Studies) the authors use the birthplace of the parents as a proxy to differentiate between juveniles that belong to stigmatized minorities – which in France are mostly African and Turkish immigrants and their offspring – from those of European origin. The author's bare data are consistent with the widespread opinion that stigmatized minorities are over-represented in crime: they represent about 50% of the convicted juveniles in the author's database, while in the same period their proportion in Isère slowly declined from 25% to less than 20% of the juvenile population.

The authors explore whether this apparent over-representation remains upon restricting comparisons to populations with similar socioeconomic status. According to the author's estimations based on the parents' status, the overwhelming majority of offenders (all origins taken together) live in urban areas, below the poverty threshold. Based on detailed census data of the same period in Isère the authors estimate that among the poor urban juveniles, minorities represent roughly half of the population. Thus, within the juvenile sub-populations of similar socioeconomic status, there is no evidence of minority over-representation among those convicted of serious crimes.

In: Crime
Editor: Michael Harry Pearson

ISBN: 978-1-62948-657-4
© 2014 Nova Science Publishers, Inc.

Chapter 1

GETTING OUT AND FALLING BACK: A QUALITATIVE ANALYSIS OF CONTEMPORARY AUSTRALIAN PRISON EXIT ISSUES

Marc A. Renton

Bond University, Queensland, Australia

In loving memory of my father
Douglas Mark Renton
16 April 1942 - 27 August 2013

ABSTRACT

The problems concerned with prisoner re-entry, prisoner reintegration and prison exit and the relationship with pro-criminal behaviours has been a topical issue confronting the behavioural science literature since the inception of the study of crime and deviance. Penologists, criminologists, and forensic psychologists have long pondered the questions, why do ex-prisoners return to prison' and what are the real issues that affect prisoners exiting prison'. This study utilised a semi-structured interview to probe insights and perceptions from individuals who had personally experienced the process of going from a confined prisoner to free member of society. The methodological approach was taken in order to gain firsthand snap-shots of the actual issues confronting an exiting prison population. These interviews were subject to a thematic content analysis, revealing that the exiting prison population experienced a range of Negative Post-Release issues including: Accommodation, Employment, Finances, Substance Abuse, and Social Anxiety. It was also found that the prison experience brought together immediate family relationships. The most profound finding of this study was that these issues did not occur in isolation, rather these issues co-existed and merged to form complex clusters of overlapping issues. The overall finding of this study revealed that there are significant issues that confront ex-prisoners exiting prison and that there is a real need for custodial programs focusing on prisoner exit and for community aftercare to assist individual prisoner's reassimilation back into society.

PREAMBLE

> Getting them out to a farm with no fences that is a good start. Wearing normal clothes, you know, civilian clothes as they call it. ... Some courses ... [consisting of] outside people coming into the prison. ... It is important to get them guys who haven't been to jail in you know, because they categorise this and that, you know if they want [you] to get well [and inevitably we are the] ... people that are going to ... be [back] in society. (Male participant of this study, aged 30).

Before embarking on a discussion about the main subject matter of this study — issues surrounding the re-entry of prisoners into the community — it is instructive to engage in a broader examination of the role of prisons in contemporary society. This preamble does not aspire to present an overview of corrections, nor does it introduce the topic of prisoner exit. Instead it provides some select (albeit lengthy) reflections into the correctional experience: ranging from judicial officers, prison ministers, corrective services, and the United Nations to provide a background to the questions posed by this present research.

Prisons, despite significant costs and enduring problems, are an essential component of society. While some empirical evidence suggests that they do in fact reduce offending rates (Weatherburn, Hua, & Moffatt, 2006, 2009; Moffatt, Weatherburn, & Donnelly, 2005) there is a need to question their place in contemporary societies. To this end the observations by Judge Dennis Challeen (1986, p. v) raise important considerations about those whom we send to prison:

> We want them to have self worth. So we destroy their self worth. We want them to be responsible. So we take away their responsibility. We want them to be a part of our community. So we isolate them from our community. We want them to be positive and constructive. So we degrade them and make them useless. We want them to be non-violent. So we put them where there is violence all around them. We want them to be kind and loving people. So we subject them to hate and cruelty. We want them to quit being the tough guy. So we put them where the tough guy is respected. We want them to quit hanging out with losers. So we put all the losers in the state under one roof. We want them to quit exploiting us. So we put them where they can exploit each other. We want them to take control of their own lives, their own problems, and quite being a parasite. So we make them totally dependent upon us.

Challeen poses the paradoxes inherent in incarceration where the expenditure of up to $75,000 per prisoner per year in most Australian jurisdictions (Productivity Commission, 2010) seems to be misspent. Instead we should be asking what is the best way to equip prisoners to lead productive and crime free lives upon their release from custody — a query taken up by Ron Nichols, the International President of Prison Fellowship (ABC Radio National, 2010):

> I think we have to as a society ask ourselves the question, 'what do we expect in terms of outcomes of justice'? Because the outcomes currently do not serve justice. Upwards of 60 percent of the people who are in prison today have either been there before or will reoffend after their release. So it is not working and it leaves victims unsatisfied, it leaves the community less safe because folks often come out of prison being more educated in the ways of crime and that is not serving the cause of justice.

These telling statements and certainly the recidivism figure that approaches two-thirds must surely direct our attention to the need to improve the release or re-entry circumstances for all prisoners. Yet, recently the Queensland Corrective Services Department (Queensland Government, 2009, p. 1) by their own admission stated:

> International research consistently identifies that prisoners typically face a range of barriers to successful reintegration following release from custody. The immediate post-release period has been identified as a high-risk period for recidivism, homelessness, drug overdose and suicide. For many offenders, a return to crime becomes a 'quick-fix' solution to obstacles and difficulties encountered during this time, particularly in relation to establishing safe and affordable accommodation, living independently and being financially responsible for any dependents.

This statement accords with key elements of the Standard Minimum Rules for the Treatment of Prisoners (United Nations, 1977, pp. 255-6) which outlines the obligations that exist for assisting incarcerated prisoners to reassimilate back into the community:

> Before the completion of the sentence, it is desirable that the necessary steps be taken to ensure for the prisoner a gradual return to life in society. This aim may be achieved, depending on the case, by a pre-release regime organised in the same institution or in another appropriate institution, or by release on trial under some kind of supervision which must not be entrusted to the police but should be combined with effective social aid. ... The treatment of prisoners should emphasize not their exclusion from the community, but their continuing part in it. Community agencies should, therefore, be enlisted wherever possible to assist the staff of the institution in the task of social rehabilitation of the prisoners. There should be in connection with every institution social workers charged with the duty of maintaining and improving all desirable relations of a prisoner with his family and with valuable social agencies. Steps should be taken to safeguard, to the maximum extent compatible with the law and the sentence, the rights relating to civil interests, social security rights and other social benefits of prisoners.

The questions posed in the present study draw on those observations made in the quoted sources above. The key issue is: 'What difficulties do prisoners face in the transition from being a prisoner to member of the community?' In doing so the thesis acknowledges the symbolism and practical need for places of incarceration; it also however notes the somewhat fractured aims of prisons such as those raised by Justice Challeen; it deliberately focuses on the claims by Nichols about how justice can best be served for those both in and outside of the prison walls; and it examines whether the lofty ideals espoused in those quotes from QCS and the UN are being realised in contemporary Australian penitentiaries.

INTRODUCTION

The problems concerned with prisoner re-entry, prisoner reintegration and prison exit and the relationship with pro-criminal behaviours has been a topical issue confronting the behavioural science literature since the inception of the study of crime and deviance. Penologists, criminologists, and forensic psychologists have long pondered the questions, 'why do ex-prisoners return to prison' and 'what are the real issues that affect prisoners exiting prison'. The process of releasing prisoners into the community is known, among other terms, as 'prison exit' and there has been some policy, program and research attention paid to this process within the social science literature.

Indeed there are said to be four key problematic areas in prison exit: Employment and Finances; Accommodation; Substance Abuse; and Family Issues. Considerable empirical and evaluation evidence shows that ex-prisoners who struggle with these issue areas have a greater likelihood to reoffend and therefore return to custodial facilities. The public safety implications of these issues, if not adequately addressed, are profound (Travis, Crayton & Mukamal, 2009), as are the sheer costs in the criminal justice system for releasing prisoners who are not adequately equipped for their prison exit back into 'life on the outside' of prison.

While there is some literature that addresses prison exit problems, predominately these insights have been captured quantitatively, there is a relative paucity of research that delves beneath the surface of those broad categorical areas: money, housing, interpersonal relationships and drug and alcohol use. In particular, there is very little in the way of research in Australia on these factors. One recent study by Willis and Moore (2008) did examine the prison exit process at the Australian national level, however, their study focused exclusively on indigenous prisoners, and found that there were specific factors for recently-released indigenous inmates.

The current study therefore endeavours to fill the lacuna in the prison exit literature by adopting a focus on Australia, on non-indigenous inmates and applies a qualitative methodological approach. This type of research aspires to delve deeper into the experiences of those recently released. Additionally, this research is designed to gain a more rich and descriptive understanding of the prison exit issues. Furthermore, this study endeavours to investigate the perceived problems confronting prisoners, from the ex-prisoners' perspective, when they had previously exited the prison environment and gone back into the community.

The rationale for this current study came about via a conversation that this author had with an ex-prisoner – 'Barry' (not his real name). Barry had been released from prison for approximately 18 months, had found accommodation, employment, and recently had purchased a motor vehicle. Barry claimed that he went to an office of the Royal Automotive Club of Queensland (RACQ) and applied for motor vehicle insurance and was refused because he had a conviction for robbery within the previous five years. Barry's story was verified by accessing the RACQ's (2010) online insurance guidelines that specifically require 'details of any criminal acts … committed during the past 5 years … in relation to Fraud, Theft or Burglary, Drugs, Arson, Criminal, Malicious or Wilful Damage'. Barry further claimed that he had experienced other issues since he had exited prison. Barry's experience raised a critical question, 'what are the difficulties that prisoners exiting encounter?' and this study sets out to explore these issues.

LITERATURE ON PRISONER EXIT ISSUES

Overview of Australian Penal System

It has been suggested that Australia is a nation built on a transported convict penal system (Anderson, 1998; Farrington, 2009; Findlay, Odgers & Yeo, 2009). Transporting prisoners to penal colonies dates back to England at the beginning of the 17th century (Abbott, 1985; DEWHA, 2008). The first Caucasian settlers to arrive in Australia were English prisoners, acting as a workforce, to carve out a settlement in the Australian wilderness (Donnachie, 1986; Farrington, 2009). Six transport ships, with a total of 730 prisoners, landed at Botany Bay, New South Wales in 1788 (Farrington, 2009). This was the beginning of the Australian prison system with the last transportation arrived in Fremantle, Western Australia in 1868 (DEWHA, 2008).

The 'separate system' laid the foundation of what we know as prison in this modern day, when in 1847 at Port Arthur, Tasmania the first Separate System Prison (SSP) in Australia received its initial prisoners. An SSP is constructed with individual cells to segregate, confine, and house individual prisoners. The ideology of the SSP revolves around the notion of behavioural modification in an attempt to reshape prisoners' disposition to criminal behaviour, via isolation, and thus removing all diverting stimulus (DEWHA, 2008). Therefore, whilst prisoners are segregated from each other; they are unable to learn new criminal skills. Another goal of the SSP was based on the late 1700s penal reformer John Howard's (Farrington, 2009) solitude model; which argued silence and solitude will force the prisoner to reflect upon their offending behaviours and lead them to repentance (DEWHA, 2008; Farrington, 2009; Nilsson, 2003).

In 1850 the Long Bay Penitentiary, Sydney, New South Wales was opened with the aim of rehabilitation prisoners. Long Bay was designed on the SSP model and many Australian prisons followed the SSP and rehabilitation mould for approximately the follow 125 years. However, in 1975, at Long Bay Penitentiary, a new wave of SSPs in Australia began with the opening of Katingal (Matthews, 2007). The Katingal experiment was a mixture of isolation and sensory deprivation with the goal of correcting or exerting restricted punitive and coercing control over high risk, unmanageable, and dangerous prisoners (Matthews, 2007). Referring to Katingal, Lucas (1976) a psychiatrist, argued that the very nature of long term solitary confinement and social isolation can amount to form of mental torture.

The Katingal experiment was replicated in 1980 at Pentridge Prison's Jika Jika High-Security Unit (JJHSU) in Victoria with devastating consequences. The environmental and segregated nature of the architectural design of the JJHSU led to the death of five prisoners after they barricaded themselves inside one of the JJHSU's units and set it alight (Carlton, 2007; Minogue, 2010). In Australia the SSP trend continues with the Woodford Correctional Centre's Maximum Security Unit (MSU) opening in 1997, now there are four MSU's in Queensland; New South Wales has the Goulburn Correctional Centre High Risk Management Unit; South Australia has the Yatla Correctional Centre X-Wing; and Victoria has Barwon Correctional Centre Acacia Unit (Brown, 2008). The Queensland Kennedy Report (1988) endeavoured to shift the prison objective from punitive environments and established correctional environments in Queensland.

Kennedy (1988; King, 2007) made 65 findings and 80 recommendations into how the correctional system should be set up. Finding 14 stated, — Prisons should be called Correctional Centres - and finding 15 stated — Prison Officers and Probation and Parole Officers should be called Correctional Officers‖ (p. ii; Kennedy, 1988). Kennedy (1988) also made recommendations, which have now been implemented, focusing on educational and therapeutic rehabilitation programs being available to all prisoners. Kennedy (1988) also championed a cause to move away from SSP styled prison towards Podular Direct Supervision Prisons PDSP (Tartaro, 2006). A PDSP is characterised by a proactive supervision stratagem and a standardized physical environment (Tartaro, 2006). In Queensland, this shift began with the opening of the Sir David Longland, Lotus Glenn, and Borallon Correctional Centres, and continues across the nation to this present day.

The Australian prison population is an ever increasing one and it has expanded at an enormous rate since the first 730 prisoners landed at Botany Bay, New South Wales in 1788 (Farrington, 2009; Finlay, Odgers & Yeo, 2009). As at September 2010, there were approximately 86, 023 adults subject to a corrections order (ABS, 2010), who were imprisoned or subjected to a community corrections order in Australia. Of this figure, 29, 361 were held in custody either on remand (i.e., and convicted and/or un-sentenced) or serving custodial sentences (ABS, 2010). Over half (56%) of those prisoners had been in prison before (ABS, 2010), and approximately 95% of these prisoners will eventually be released from prison again (Owens, 2009). Unfortunately, the precise daily prison release figures are not published for Australian jurisdictions.

Annually, on the 30 June census data for prisoners is captured (ABS, 2010; Walker, 1989). Included in the census data are details inclusive of age, offence-type, sentence length, gender, type of custody (i.e., open or secure prison facility), and aboriginality (ABS, 2010; Walker, 1989). These types of demographics have been referred to as the 'stock' of prisoners (Walker, 1989), and are important when examining who makes up the prison environment. This data demonstrates that there is an over representation of Aboriginal prisoners compared with non-Aboriginal prisoners, that secure custody correctional centres accommodation house approximately 3.5 times more prisoners than open custody facilities, and that approximately 93% of the Australian prison population is male (Productivity Commission, 2010).

Over a ten year period; for example, there has been a significant increase in the imprisonment rates for offences such as assault, sexual assault, stealing, government security, and drug offences (ABS, 2001, 2010; Carcach & Grant, 2000). It is also noted that nationally the prison population has almost doubled between 1991 and 2009 (ABS, 2001, 2010) and that this growth is beyond the national population growth per 100 000 (Biles, 2009).

Prisoner Exit Operationalised

Defining the concept of prisoner exit was extremely difficult. Predominately, the behavioural sciences literature relies upon notions of 'prisoner re-entry' (see Lynch & Sabol, 2001; Sieter & Kadela, 2003; Travis & Petersilia, 2001) or 'prisoner reintegration' (see Pettus & Severson, 2006), which for the purpose of this study would be misleading. The term re-entry can give an impression that preparatory steps have been taken to assist the prisoner back into the community. Likewise, the term reintegration can imply that prison releases will be gradual and will work towards phasing prisoners back into the community. Whereas the term prison exit involves a concept of immediate change or either environment or mindset; therefore prison exit is operationalised, —the psychological and physical assimilation that prisoners go through from being a 'confined' prisoner to a 'free' member of the community'.

Prison Exit Issues

Planning for prison exit is not a new concept, and prisons or their contemporary counterparts 'correctional centres' have long understood that exiting prisoners confront specific obstacles on their way back into society (Pettus & Severson, 2006; Queensland Government, 2009). It has been suggested that ex-prisoners face difficulties in the areas of stigma associated with being imprisoned, financial problems, identity issues, and personal relationships (Clear, Rose, & Ryder, 2001; Pettus & Severson, 2006; Tiburco, 2008). However, the behavioural science literature has more broadly and consistently identified the dominant prison exit issues as: (1) Employment and Finances (Freudenberg, 2006; Lucken & Ponte, 2008; McDonough & Burrell, 2008); (2) Accommodation (Baldry, McDonald, Maplestone, & Peeters, 2004, 2006; Hall, 2009); (3) Family Issues (Farrington, Coid, & Murray, 2009; Meek, 2007); and (4) Substance Abuse (Bird & Hutchinson, 2002; Burrows et al., 2000). This paper will now individually examine these issues.

Employment and Finances

In many Australian jurisdictions, as a part of the Sentence Management or Case Management process, prisoners are required to actively participate in intervention programs to address, what has been termed, offending behaviour (King, 2007; Mulligan, 2007). Another limb of this process is that prisoners engage in employment available at their respective prisons (Baer et al., 2006; Mulligan, 2007). The type of work available to prisoners range from industrial (e.g., constructing furniture, bakery, and assembling and packing) to centre support (King, 2007; Mulligan, 2007). These employment opportunities assist in reducing the overall operational costs of running the prison (Mulligan, 2007). Remuneration is extremely low and ranges, in Queensland at least, from a minimum of $1.26 to a maximum of $4.11 per day (Mulligan, 2007). When taking into account that prisoners must manage this income to provide hygiene products and to maintain contact with the outside community, there is little realistic opportunity for prisoners to save meaningful finances to assist in their return to the community.

As prisoners move from the highly structured daily routine of prison life and into the community, employment provides three primary functions. Firstly, employment generates an income so that ex-prisoners can obtain basic needs such as food, clothing, & shelter (Baer, et al., 2006; Freudenberg, 2006). Secondly, employment elevates the pressure to generate an income via pro-criminal activities (Baer at al., 2006; Carter, 2009; Freudenberg, 2006; Lucken & Ponte, 2008; McDonough & Burrell, 2008). Thirdly, employment replaces a regimented prison routine and provides a lifestyle structure with the potential to reduce the enticement to engage in substance abuse related behaviours (Freudenberg, 2006). Researchers have successfully demonstrated, via a post-prison release sample, that as the level of vocational training and the level of pay and job quality increases, the level of re-imprisonment or confirmed criminal recidivism decreases (Lucken & Ponte, 2008; McDonough & Burrell, 2008). To understand this construct such as the fact that employment and job satisfaction equates to a reduction in recidivism, it is ideal to explore the socioeconomic field of what jobs are obtainable to a released prisoner population.

It is suggested that the job market is a highly competitive market. Compounding this issue, for people leaving prison, is the need to compete with others for employment with the added burden of having criminal convictions taint their ability of obtaining meaningful employment (Baer at al., 2006; Freudenberg, 2006; Lichtenberger, 2006; Rakis, 2005). It could be this very concern that drives ex-prisoners toward the low-income, low-education and low-wage end of the employment market (Freudenberg, 2006; Rakis, 2005). Other confounding variables must be considered within this complex mix, for example, prisoners usually have poor educational qualifications, they generally come from a low socioeconomic background (Raphael, 2010; Raphael & Stoll, 2004), have a high proportion of mental health issues, and have substance abuse issues (Makkai & Payne, 2003), all of which work together to limit their opportunity to enter the job market.

State sanctioned (i.e., parliamentary) discrimination is another obstacle to gaining employment. Legislative enactments can either directly or indirectly prevent ex-prisoners with certain types of convictions from gaining employment in prescribed industries (Lucken & Ponte, 2008; Owens, 2009). Certain legislations skilfully sidestep the application of discrimination by positing terms like 'applicants must pass a character test' (see Health Practitioners (Professional Standards) (QLD) Act 1999; Liquor Act (QLD) 1992; etc). This creates a system of having a skilled worker released from prison prohibited from meaningful employment and reduces classes of ex-prisoners from becoming productive members of the community (Freudenberg, 2006; SEETRC, 1996). The public safety implications of similar policies are obvious; they remove employment opportunities from ex-prisoners and provide a perceived incentive to engage in pro-criminal activities to generate finances.

Accommodation

There are two general and distinct stages of housing to prisoners and ex-prisoners. The first stage is pre-arrest or pre-incarceration accommodation and the second stage is the post-release stage. Both of these stages can be further broken down into subdivisions applicable to the individual circumstances of the prisoner. These circumstances include if the prisoner was living alone or with friends, family, partner, or others (Baldry et al., 2006). In addition, type of accommodation, for example, house, apartment, caravan, shelter, or being homeless are other complex issues that affect the prison exit process (Baldry et al., 2006).

The underlying difference between these two stages is that at the pre arrest or pre-incarceration stage the offender is in a situation relevant to accommodation and this is distinct from the post-release stage, as the ex prisoner is usually confronted with seeking suitable housing. Homelessness appears to be a key factor for individuals exiting prison (Baldry et al., 2006; Freudenberg, 2006). There is an elevated risk for the homeless being imprisoned, as opposed to those with stable accommodation, and once imprisoned a loss of housing can be a consequence (Baldry et al., 2004; Freudenberg, 2006). Short terms of imprisonment include the propensity of having disadvantageous effects on accommodation stability (Freudenberg, 2006). In some communities, prisons become major suppliers of homeless shelters. A study conducted in New York City (NYC) into the demographics of homeless shelters (Freudenberg, 2006), found that above 30% of NYC's homeless shelters were made up of single adults that have recently exited prison. Furthermore, one study (Baldry et al., 2004) demonstrated that there was a rise in homelessness in a post-prison release population, with

18% of prisoners reporting to being homeless pre-incarceration as compared to 21% being homeless post-incarceration. There is also a link between homelessness, in a prison exit population, and criminal recidivism (Baldry, et al., 2006; Benda, 1983; Conway, 1999; McCarthy & Hagen, 1991).

Internationally, the social science literature has consistently indicated that a vital factor of social integration of ex-prisoners is both suitable and stable accommodation (Baldry, et al., 2003; Conway, 1999; McCarthy & Hagen, 1991). However, it is noted that there is a paucity of research related to exiting prisoners and accommodation issues (Baldry, et al., 2006). As a predicative recidivism indicator, lack of stable accommodation has been positively correlated with a return to pro-criminal behaviours and a subsequent return to custody (Baldry, et al., 2004, 2006; Benda, 1983; Yoshikawa et al., 2007). Frequent accommodation shifts post release (i.e., more than twice in a three month time period), and subsequent transient styled behaviours, have been suggestive of elevated substance abuse behaviours (Baldry et al., 2004). Yet prisoners are released back into the community without suitable accommodation and little support of gaining and maintaining suitable accommodation (Baldry et al., 2004; Ramsay, 1986).

Family Problems

When examining the family structure of prisoners it is well established that convicted parents usually have offspring that go on to live pro-criminal lifestyles (Farrington, Coid, & Murray, 2009). The issue of intergenerational transmission of convictions is beyond the scope of this study, however, worthy of noting. It is debatable, however, it is suggested that at the point of detention the typical family unit (i.e., husband, wife, & children) are thrown into turmoil and these relationships, and parenting skills erode via this forced separation (LaValle, 1995; Weymouth & Telesco, 1998; Wittbold, 1997). The subject of post release family problems falls within the realms of relationship issues and is gauged in respect of how the prison experience affects the family unit (Raney, Magaletta & Hubbert, 2005; Meek, 2007). There is a myriad of variables that contribute to family issues.

At the point of detention, both prisoners and family members report feelings of isolated and this level of isolation has been reported to increase the longer the prisoner is incarcerated (Light & Campbell, 2006; Weymouth & Telesco, 1998). There is also evidence of communication breakdowns between prisoner and family, with the added notion of not knowing what and how to share with one another (Danes, 2008; Weymouth & Telesco, 1998). The issue of communication breakdown can be a creature of imprisonment, with access to loved ones being limited and highly monitored via the process of visitation, phone calls, and censored mail (Danes, 2008; Farrington, 2009; King, 2007; Mulligan, 2007).

It appears that the primary source of support for ex-prisoners upon release is the family unit (Martinez, 2006). There is a lack of suitable studies which delve into how family dynamics affect prisoner exit. There is however, some studies demonstrating the importance of family relationships and family support playing vital roles in successful prison exit (Martinez, 2006). Released prisoners usually rely on family members for financial support, accommodation, and emotional support (Naser & La Vigne, 2006). It was concluded in these studies that a lack of a realistic family support highly correlated with a return to pro-criminal behaviours and a return to prison (Martinez, 2006).

Substance Abuse

There is an overwhelming body of evidenced demonstrating a positive correlation or link between substance abuse and pro-criminal behaviour (see Gillespie, 2004; Goldstein, 1998; Leukefeld, Araujo & Farabee, 1997; Makkai & Payne, 2003; Menard, Mihalic & Huizinga, 2001; Nelles et al., 2000; Ogloff & Davis, 2005; Parker & Auerhahn, 1998; Wodak, 2005). Additionally, it is well documented in the behavioural scientific literature that substance abuse or a substance related diagnosis is a valid and reliable predictor for recidivism or re-offending (Ogloff & Davis, 2005; Yoshikawa et al., 2007). However, Putnins (2003) found that substance abuse before imprisonment is not a reliable predictor of criminal recidivism. Contextually, and for the purpose of this study, post-prison and prison exit issues that effect substance abuse and any subsequent behaviours will be explored. For the purpose of clarity, post prison substance abuse is a reliable predictor of rearrest and re-imprisonment (Payne, 2007).

When examining the overall impact of substance abuse and career offenders, Makkai & Payne (2003) found that 51% of offenders attributed substance abuse as the root cause of their criminality. Furthermore, 62% of prisoners reported that they were under the influence of drugs or alcohol when they committed their most recent offences (Makkai & Payne, 2003). The Drug Use Monitoring in Australia (DUMA) project validated self report drug use with urine analysis and found that 79.5% of respondents who self reported drug use (i.e., up to 30-days prior to arrest) returned a positive urine analysis test to either cocaine, heroin, or methylamphetamine (Makkai & McGregor, 2002). A United Kingdom based study (Burrows, Clarke, Davison, Tarling & Webb, 2000) demonstrated via self-report, that 66% of prisoners had used drugs up to 30-days before imprisonment; half of this sample was offered aftercare in the community, however, only 11% had a fixed appointment; and until community assistance is supplied, ex-prisoners are likely to engaging in pro-criminal behaviour and be returned to prison.

There is also the elevated risk of death resulting from fatal drug overdose for the exiting prison population (Bird & Hutchinson, 2003; Farrell & Marsden, 2008; Shewan, Hammersley, Oliver & McPherson, 2000). There is now a quite persuasive body of empirical evidence gathering and pointing towards higher drug-related mortality rates amongst the prison exit population (Bird & Hutchinson, 2003; Farrell & Marsden, 2008; Shewan et al., 2000). A remarkable statistic (Bird & Hutchinson, 2003) points to drug related death rates of prisoners exiting prison was three times higher than custodial suicides and seven time higher in the immediate two week postrelease stage than any other times at liberty (i.e., for male ex-prisoners aged 15-35 years). It has been said that 59% of post-prison deaths are attributed to fatal drug overdoses (Farrell & Marsden, 2008; Shewan et al., 2000). The evidence of drug related mortality when juxtaposed with ex-prisoners preconceptions of how they believe they are coping with their individual substance abuse shows no association. In one study (Baldry et al., 2004) it was found most prisoners with substance abuse histories reported that their substance use was not problematic, however, when these ex-prisoners were followed into the community they increasingly reported substance abuse related difficulties. This study showed that the more time the substance abusing ex-prisoner was in the community the more problematic their substance abuse issues became (Baldry et al., 2004).

METHODOLOGY AND RESULTS

Method

It is noted from the outset that this study was exploratory in nature and as such required careful consideration when developing a methodological strategy. In order to centre how individual ex-prisoners depict meaning of their lives post release (Moustakas, 1994), this study was designed around individual interviews with volunteer participants who have previously experienced prison release. The overall research design incorporated a qualitative methodological approach. The application of qualitative data collection enabled the researcher to explore a wide range of substantive prison exit problems, whilst allowing the researcher to delve into a rich description of the prison exit process (Anderson, 2010; Guion & Flowers, 2005; Hancock, 2002). This strength of qualitative data gathering extended well beyond a quantitative methodological approach, which would have had the potential to constrict the data collection phase, as opposed, to extending it (Anderson, 2010).

There are specific strengths in employing qualitative data collection and interpretation methodologies in exploratory research. The flexibility of an interviewing approach enabled the researcher to closely engage individual participants and draw out more sensitive information (Guion & Flowers, 2005). During this process the direction of data gathering could be continually adapted as the researcher became more familiar and understood the unique issues confronting the participant pool (Anderson, 2010). Importantly, this approach moved data collection beyond researcher preconceptions of what the actual prison exit issues were and were not, and gathered data accordingly (Bryman, Bresnen, Beardsworth & Keil, 1988; Creswell, 1998).

The interviews were semi-structured in design, therefore permitting a detailed examination of individual respondent experiences and teasing out sensitive information (Haigh, 2007; Johnson, 2000). The direction of the interview was dependant on interviewee response, with the researcher using prompts to redirect the route of investigation, in accordance with a conversational natured interview (Bryman, 2004). This approach was employed in an attempt to capture the participants' explanations in a flexible and reactive manner (Haigh, 2007).

Participants

The participants comprised (N = 20) residents at Mirikai — a 40-bed residential drug and alcohol rehabilitation centre operated by the Gold Coast Drug Council in Queensland, Australia. Mirikai was deemed suitable as the recruitment site because this facility is involved in the Queensland Drug Court diversion program, and as such deals with post-release issues. All residents had ongoing substance abuse issues and were under treatment for drug use problems. These residents were sampled because of the link between substance abuse and criminal behaviour and the inevitable potential for re-incarceration (Gillespie, 2004; Goldstein, 1998; Leukefeld, Araujo & Farabee, 1997; Makkai & Payne, 2003; Menard, Mihalic & Huizinga, 2001; Nelles et al., 2000; Ogloff & Davis, 2005; Parker & Auerhahn, 1998; Wodak, 2005). However, it should be noted that less than one-third of residents at this facility have been incarcerated previously and as such a screening procedure was utilised. Only those who had been incarcerated in the past for a period of at least three months were eligible for inclusion in the sample.

There were 16 male and 4 female volunteers in this study. Participants' ages overall ranged from 20 to 50 years (M = 28.5; SD = 7.47), with the range for females being slightly narrower (28 to 36 years). The educational levels achieved by the participants ranged from completion of Year 8 to Year 12 (M = 9.8; SD = 2.67); however, one participant only attended a special requirement school, whilst another was in the second year of a Bachelor of Law degree. Their longest custodial sentence ranged from 3 months to 6 years and 3 months (M = 21.23; SD = 23.11). The number of times that individual participants were sent to prison ranged from one to 20 times (M = 3.75; SD = 4.38). Generally their last offence was non-violent, with 13 males and 2 females being last imprisoned for property, drugs or regulatory type offences. Violence was measured by the application of the criteria set forth in the Australian Standard Offence Classification (ABS, 2008) matrix and compared with the Violent Offenders Schedule within the Penalties and Sentences Act (QLD) 1992. The type of convictions that this sample were imprisoned for included break and entering, burglary, weapon possession, drug possession, stealing, breaches of domestic violence orders, unlawful use of motor vehicle, fraud, drug manufacturing, drug trafficking, assaults, going armed in public to cause fear, and armed robbery.

Procedure

There were three strategies for recruitment. Initially, the researcher visited the rehabilitation facility and strategically placed recruitment posters throughout the centre. In the second instance the researcher again visited the facility and gave a formal presentation about the research project in order to give residents the opportunity to ask questions about what would and would not be required of them. The final recruitment step involved the researcher attending the facility and waiting in interview rooms, at notified times, for potential volunteer participants. Participants who volunteered to be interviewed were given a written explanatory statement outlining the reason the research was being undertaken and what was involved. The participants were asked if they were willing to having their responses digitally-recorded and were asked to complete a consent form if they agreed. Participation in the study was completely voluntary and no incentives were offered.

Each volunteer was interviewed for approximately one hour using the semi-structured interview schedule. The interview questions centred on specific issues drawn from the literature, namely employment/finance, accommodation, and family issues. It was envisaged, based on the sample being drawn from a drug and alcohol treatment centre, that substance abuse issues would reveal themselves without prompting, and thus no specific questioning concerning this issue was raised. These questions addressed times that the participant had previously been released from prison. The interview data were transcribed and assigned a numerical referent to ensure that all response data was rendered anonymous (noting of course that the interviews themselves were confidential given that they were face-to-face). In addition, for the purpose of this thesis, respondents were additionally assigned random male and female names so that their individual insights can be further discussed contextually within the body of this study. These data were then cleaned, in order to give grammatical structure from verbal conversation to transcribed interview. It is noted that the conversations made sense when they were face to face, however, when transcribed, lacked the nuances of verbal communication and appeared somewhat fragmented. Therefore, contextual alterations were made, adding and in some instances removing words to give the interview narratives grammatical meaning.

Given that the research design was exploratory and qualitative, a thematic content analysis was conducted to glean themes from the transcribed interviews. There were two limbs to this level of analysis. The first step, however, was to isolate the responses to the specific topic areas, namely employment, finance, accommodation, substance abuse and family issues. This approach produced broad themes, and initially, specific focus centred on positive and negative interview accounts. The second step delved deeper into the narratives and fleshed out more salient issues. This was accomplished by fragmenting these themes (i.e., positive & negative), discarding and obvious extraneous data (i.e., information that was not relevant to this study, for example, 'my lawyer did not follow my instructions' and 'I wanted a job as prison librarian'), and searching for sub-issues. This approach allowed for a more precise understanding of themes of both an independent individual interview and themes running across/between interviews. This tactic produced more discrete issues within the aforementioned categories, and produced others outside of this range. It is noted that, producing categories and allocating them to data groups involves a level of interpretation of the data under examination (Atkinson & Delemont, 2005; Darlington & Scott, 2002; Haigh, 2007; Stringer & Dwyer, 2005). Thus, any themes produced from this procedure are simply researcher's interpretations of respondent accounts and are therefore subjective in nature. The first analytic process was to extract all responses regarding the four key issues drawn from the literature and these are presented first in the results section below.

Results

The thematic content analysis was able to reduce the interview narratives down to three dominate descriptive levels. These themes included Negative, Positive and Pleas for Improvement; and further sub-issues clustered within these primary themes. In respect to these results, it is noted that the interview schedule focused on accommodation and employment, finances, and family issues.

Within the Negative (descriptive) Theme, five prevailing issues emerged: (1) Accommodation issues focused on participant difficulties in locating suitable and stable accommodation immediately after their release from prison, and also focused accommodation type. (2) Employment issues revolved around an inability to secure meaningful employment with the stigma of previously being imprisoned coupled with the added shame of having criminal convictions. (3) Finance issues revealed a lack of financial resources to meet the everyday basic necessities of life (i.e., food, clothing, shelter, transportation, etc). (4) Government Funded Drug Use involved a belief that the federal government should fund the acquisition of illicit drugs for the consumption of ex-prisoners. and (5) Social Anxiety issues exposed difficulties that a prison exit population have when engaging with members of the wider community – social anxiety was an unexpected finding as no specific interview questions were asked in respect to emotional state. Importantly, it was found that if a participant experienced difficulties in one of these areas, then they were more likely to experience difficulties in multiple of these areas. It appears that these problematic areas do not occur in isolation, rather they cluster and co-occur together.

Within the Positive (descriptive) Theme two main sub-issues emerged: (1) Family Cohesion issue revealed that the immediate family group was drawn closer together via the prison experience. and (2) Jail House Role Models issue exposed a belief that fellow prisons play a vital role in equipping ex-prisoners for their lives in the community.

There was another grouping that also emerged outside of the positive and negative themes. Pleas for Improvement, which consisted of two principle descriptive sub-issues: (1) Gradual Release issues exposed a perceived need for prisoners to be slowly reintegrated into the community via stages of less restriction and community based supervision. and (2) Follow Up Aftercare issues revealed a need to have community agencies providing support for exiting prisoners in the community. Table 1 displays by gender, the constructs of the thematic content analysis and the areas that each individual participants of this study self-reported. Table 1 demonstrates that each participant experienced a range of post-release issues. This paper will now more clearly explain and discuss, in detail, the overall results of this study. It is reiterated that the reported names in this paper are not the actual names of any participant of this study.

Table 1. Results of the Thematic Content Analysis by Participant, Genter and Constuct

HOW PARTICIPANTS FELL INTO THE OVERALL THEMES EMERGING FROM STUDY										
ID		NEGATIVE RESULTS					POSITIVE RESULTS		PLEAS FOR IMPROVEMENT	
Participant	Gender	Accom	Employ	Finance	Gov Funded Drug Use	Social Anxiety	Family Cohesion	Jail House Role Models	Gradual Release	After Care
1	Male	–	–	–	–	–	✓	✓	✓	✓
2	Male	✓	–	✓	–	✓	✓	–	✓	✓
3	Male	–	✓	✓	–	–	✓	–	–	✓
4	Male	✓	✓	✓	✓	✓	✓	–	✓	✓
5	Male	✓	✓	✓	–	✓	✓	–	✓	✓
6	Female	–	✓	–	–	✓	✓	✓	✓	✓
7	Male	✓	✓	✓	✓	–	✓	–	–	✓
8	Male	–	✓	✓	✓	–	✓	✓	–	–
9	Female	–	–	–	–	✓	✓	–	✓	✓
10	Female	✓	✓	✓	–	✓	–	–	✓	✓
11	Male	✓	✓	✓	–	–	✓	✓	–	✓
12	Male	–	✓	✓	–	✓	✓	–	✓	✓
13	Male	✓	✓	✓	–	–	–	–	–	✓
14	Male	✓	✓	✓	✓	–	–	✓	✓	✓
15	Male	✓	✓	✓	✓	✓	–	–	–	✓
16	Female	–	✓	✓	✓	–	✓	–	–	–
17	Male	✓	✓	✓	–	–	–	–	✓	✓
18	Male	–	✓	–	–	✓	✓	✓	✓	✓
19	Male	✓	✓	✓	✓	–	✓	✓	✓	✓
20	Male	✓	✓	✓	✓	–	–	–	✓	✓

DISCUSSION

Section One: Negative Themes

This section will present and discuss, in detail, each of the five negative sub issues outlined in the aforementioned results section: 'accommodation', 'employment', 'finances', 'government funded drug use', and 'social anxiety'. It is noted that the questioning schedule did not incorporate questions concerned with government funded drug use and social anxiety issues. Excerpts from the interview narratives will be provided in order to justify theme description, sub-theme allocation into the negative grouping, and also to contextualise the following discussions.

Accommodation

Accommodation was an area of interest and was included in the interview schedule. Participants in this study generally had relatively stable accommodation circumstances prior to going to prison — they lived with family or in their own homes (buying or renting). On release however they reported that their accommodation became characterised by instability where the situation of 'couch-surfing' or 'sleeping rough' became the norm. They also reported significant difficulties in securing accommodation ranging from not knowing how to search for housing, having sufficient money to pay bonds, and having to wait on lengthy public housing lists.

CASE STUDY 1.1: HANK'S ACCOUNT OF POST INCARCERATION ACCOMMODATION

Hank is a 22 year old man, who has been imprisoned 4 times, with his longest custodial sentence being 8 months imprisonment. Hank has been imprisoned in New South Wales and in Queensland and is a non-violent ex-prisoner convicted of property offences such as break and entering. Hank is the father of one daughter. Hank was concerned with the time that it took for him to find suitable and stable accommodation when he was released from prison.

I didn't have stable accommodation. I was just staying wherever. Yeah couch surfing, yeah that was about it yeah. It was hectic. I would go here, use drugs, end up crashing or end up going out for the night and I'd crash at somebody's lounge or I'd crash in my car. … I didn't really have much control on where I went the next day. I just rode with whatever happened, and just went with it.

I put my name [down] for housing and all that and I got that bit of half-way when I walked out of the jail gate. I got into that accommodation and I ended up moving in with this hairdresser and I was staying there for a while to finish off my parole. And I didn't even know that hairdresser from a bar of soap and she felt sorry for me. And it wasn't a relationship type of thing. It was that she felt sorry for me. I was just lucky that she felt sorry for me and she was an old lady. And most people would not have that opportunity.

So after they were finished in that half-way [house] where were they going to go? They help you put in the applications for housing, but then there is [a] waiting [list] for housing. But you are expected to find somewhere to go after your time is finished. And I think you get two and a half months there [in a half-way house] and you have to fucken move on and find your own place.

Hank's account of his post-incarceration accommodation demonstrates a key finding from the present study that many ex-prisoners receive short-term assistance via halfway house schemes on exit from prison. This situation however is short-lived, and as Hank noted this period is not long enough to enable them to be able to search and source suitable and stable housing. Indeed, Hank felt that he was just 'thrown out' of prison and forced to deal with his non-accommodation status. Those released from custody then tend to go through an extended period of 'couch-surfing' or 'sleeping rough' in the bush or in their motor vehicles if they are fortunate enough to have one.

Probably had my car been going, I probably would have lived in my car in the bush maybe.

These experiences were certainly repeated by other participants in this study. One male said that he, "Sort of couch surfed between family and friends and mates. Because I didn't have the necessary help to be put straight into accommodation or a unit or a house or anything like that" and another said that he stayed at, "anyone's house until they got sick of me and then I'd moved onto the next one — just couches". Furthermore this experience was seen as degrading, exhausting and frustrating by those who had to endure it where one said that, "sleeping on park benches and people's front yards is not fun — it's fucken shit". They also raised the dangers of engaging in this kind of transient accommodation for they were more exposed to theft of their property or violence when sleeping in multiple-tenanted housing or sleeping rough in their cars or in parks. Finally, it was evident that this transient housing cycle was usually as short-lived as the halfway house accommodation sourced at their time of release for participants reported how they soon ran out of friends or their family members were not prepared to house them for longer periods of time.

The other major aspect of accommodation as reported by participants was the lack of assistance given and the sheer enormity of the difficulties they faced in trying to secure accommodation. As Hank indicated, he received only minimal help in completing applications forms for public housing but these applications rarely yielded definite offers. Others too complained about the lack of assistance stating that they, "*didn't have the necessary help to be put straight into accommodation or a unit or a house or anything like that*".

These experiences of obtaining only short-term housing in halfway facilities, lengthy periods of living with friends or family or sleeping rough, and the overall lack of assistance generally accord with the post-release literature. Thus findings about accommodation issues in this study reflect previous research and support the notion that homelessness is a key factor for individuals exiting prison (Baldry et al., 2006; Freudenberg, 2006) where it has been noted that there is a rise in homelessness brought about by an episode of imprisonment in the order of 3% (Baldry et al., 2004). Given the qualitative data yielded in the present study it is suggested that this may be a gross underestimate given that the common experience is at least one of a substantial period of transient accommodation following release.

Employment

Employment was an area of interest and was included in the interview schedule. Participants in this study were generally employed prior to going to prison — enabling them to support themselves (i.e., pay rent, purchase food and clothing). However, on release they reported that they experienced difficulties finding employment and that this was characterised be criminal background checks, absences in résumé details, and a competitive job market not sympathetic to ex-prisoners.

CASE STUDY 1.2: ALBERT'S ACCOUNT OF POST INCARCERATION EMPLOYMENT

Albert is a 28 year old man, who has been imprisoned 3 times, with his longest custodial sentence being 12 months imprisonment. Albert was imprisoned in Queensland and is a non-violent ex-prisoner, convicted of property offences such as break and entering. Albert has no children. Albert described his employment history pre-incarceration and contrasted these accounts with his post-release experiences and discussed his inability to obtain meaningful employment post-conviction and postincarceration.

[Pre-Incarceration] I could jump straight into a job. I was a lot younger too and I was more willing to do things you know. I didn't have the criminal mind too, you know, want to play up. I was more willing, actually to do the right thing rather than play up. I just found it a lot easier. People were more willing to take me on. I was getting offered apprenticeships.

[Post-Incarceration employment] was on and off. Like a lot of people wouldn't take me on, cause they would do criminal [history] checks and all those sorts of things. And half of them wouldn't trust me, cause a lot of it was dealing with money or clients or stuff. There was no trust from a lot of people. It was really hard for me. I ended up going to Boys Town to get employment and that was sort of a last resort. And that sort of helped a bit, but I'd have to find it myself. [For example, I applied at] a pharmaceutical place in Brisbane. They've got to do criminal [history] checks because we were working with tablets and stuff like that. As soon as they did the criminal [history] check … as soon as they found [out my criminal history] … there was no chance. And that was through a job agency. Your confidence goes down and you sort [of] give up a bit on trying to get employment. That made it really difficult for me.

In most communities, employment is a core value that entails able-bodied citizens to engage in employment, contribute to society (i.e., pay taxes), and to pay their own way (McDonough & Burrell, 2008). However, for a postrelease prison population, no matter how pure an individual's intention, to gain employment and contribute to society can be a very daunting task. Albert's account of post incarceration employment provides a fitting example of the stress that is placed on ex-prisoners when re-entering the workforce. Albert's description was not isolated and reflected an issue that was consistent across interview narratives.

The fundamental issues were an inability of securing meaningful employment with the additional stigma of previously being known as an ex-prisoner combined with the added shame of having criminal convictions (Baer at al., 2006; Carter, 2009; Freudenberg, 2006; Lichtenberger, 2006; Rakis, 2005; Tiburco, 2008). Importantly, it was found that most of the participants in this study had stable employment prior to being imprisoned. This is an interesting finding, in that it debunks a notion that offenders are habitual and crime is their main source of income (Lucken & Ponte, 2008; McDonough & Burrell, 2008). Participants in this study consistently provided contrasts between pre-incarceration employment being a time that they were able to find and secure employment with the difficulties that they experienced by being unemployed post-release.

> Well you lose you job when you go [to prison] … I can image that people that did do any sort of [jail] time would lose their job, you know they are not going to expect to walk out walk in with a job, [their] same job. … I used to be a rigger, but for the last five years I haven't worked.

Another overwhelming issue for these participants was an inability to overcome their criminal history when entering the job market (Carter, 2009; Rakis, 2005). Many participants reported that they would apply for employment only to be turned down after an employee ran a criminal background check. On male said, "*I've had no work since I got out. … I don't know, people see your fucken [criminal] record and what you have done, and they don't want fucken nothing to do with you. … I applied for jobs, I applied for [a job as a] bakery worker and all that, cabinet making and they don't want nothing to do with you*". Generally, employers are more unwilling to employ ex-prisoners than any other underprivileged group (Carter, 2009). This appeared to have a negative effect on self-esteem and would cause some of the participants to stop seeking employment and return to pro criminal behaviours to support themselves. Importantly participants reported high stress levels linked to being willing to obtain employment, but not being able to so based on a discrimination of previously being imprisoned.

The post-prison employment findings of this study are consistent with Senate Employment, Education and Training References Committee (SEETRC, 1996) observations about exiting prisoners and the workforce. The SEETRC (1996) found that exiting prisoners, often with positive outlooks and useful work skills, cannot find employment or partake in further education because there is no community support to assist them to do so. The consequence of nil assistance in gaining employment and gaining further skills, causes many to reoffend and be subsequently returned to prison (SEETRC, 1996). When examining these issues Chairman John Tierney (SEETRC, 1996) said, "this is an outrageous waste of skills, time and money".

Finances

Finance was an area of interest and was included in the interview schedule. The finance issue can be viewed as an extension of the employment issues. Participants in this study were generally employed and had a stable income prior to going to prison. Upon release, they had no savings and no finances to assist them at the exit stage of their sentence. Generally, these participants could not financially meet everyday living costs of being a member of the community. All found that they immediately had to resort to government welfare assistance and seek friends and family for financial support. Others reoffended to provide an income.

CASE STUDY 1.3: BRENDON'S ACCOUNT OF POST INCARCERATION FINANCES

Brendan is 33 year old man who has been to prison three times, with his longest custodial sentence being 12-months imprisonment. Brendan has been imprisoned in Victoria, and Queensland for various non-violent offences, including drug supply and fraud. Brendan has a 12-year old son. Brendan described his financial situation after release from prison as.

My financial situation, like most people, unless they have got parents that have got money was pretty bad. I think that I got out with a half a cheque and had to live on that for two weeks. … I think at the time [it] was a couple of hundred bucks, two hundred and fifty bucks. And then I had to pay rent and buy food. Yeah it's not a really good situation that they do for people [these] days. It [is] pretty much the same as far as I know. They give you a cheque when you get out and expect you to be able to find accommodation, get yourself new clothes. [What] if you have lost a lot of your stuff? So the financial situation for a lot of people wouldn't be too crash hot.

As I said I had work, I was working before I went to jail, so I was pretty dependant on myself. Once I got out of jail I had a little bit of money to last me a long amount of time, it just wasn't really enough. As for housing, you have to be on the dole for probably three to six months before they will give you assistance to getting your own bond to your own flat. I think that it was a lot easier before I went to jail because I had all the time in the world to do my own thing and work and I had my own money. When I got out of jail there was nothing there to help me except a half a dole cheque.

Human beings require, what has been termed, the Basic Necessities of Life that are required to sustain and support life. These include simple things like food, water, clothing, & shelter. It is noted that in all Australian jurisdictions that it is a legal and moral obligation governed by a duty of care and statute to supply persons under care the basic necessities of life. Failure to do so can result in criminal prosecution. In this fast paced contemporary society these basic necessities of life cost money.

Brendon's account of post incarceration finances revealed that he struggled to support himself. This issue ran parallel for the other participants in this study. It was found that when they were released from prison they lacked financial support to supply themselves with these basic necessities of life. Many struggled being released and immediately lived on Commonwealth Government assistance (i.e., Centrelink Benefits; Centrelink, n.d.), one male spoke of these benefits, "*well your dole, you get a full cheque ... straight away and that doesn't take long when you buy your necessities you know, food, hygiene stuff, clothing for yourself you know, new shoes, smokes, phone credit, there goes your cheque and you don't get any money again*". Others resorted to family and crime, one felame stated, "*I was pretty screwed. I had to rely on Mum and Dad. I was on Centrelink benefits and crime a little bit*".

The Commonwealth Government Allowance Scheme that directly applies to ex-prisoners who have recently exited prison, is a one off Crisis Payment of approximately $240 (Centrelink, n.d.). This scheme provides that a recently released prisoner can apply to Centrelink for a crisis payment within 7-days of release from prison, provided that the ex-prisoner can prove that they have been incarcerated for at least 14 consecutive days (Centrelink, n.d.). Conversely, this payment is only half of the normal job seeking benefit payment (i.e., New Start Allowance; Centrelink, n.d.) and fails to take into account the individual merits or circumstances of the exiting ex-prisoner. For example, persons on the New Start Allowance can apply when they have been fired from employment; however, these individuals confront different obstacles as opposed to ex-prisoners.

Ex-prisoners, usually immediately need to find clothing, seek accommodation requiring the payment of a bond, connection of electricity, establishing a telephone account, food, hygiene products, and transportation. These are just a basic list of needs that confront an exiting prison population. The findings that ex-prisoners struggle with financial issues when they exit prison, appear to provide ex-prisoners with an incentive to engage in pro-criminal behaviours, or at the very least provide ex-prisoners with a plethora of excuses to return to crime.

Government Funded Drug Use

Government Funded Drug Use was not an area of interest and was not included in the interview schedule. As previously noted all participants in this study had substance abuse histories and were under treatment for substance abuse issues. Generally, participants prescribed to self-reported titles such as 'drug addict' or 'alcoholic' and felt that it was their respective substance abuse issues that led them to prison in the first instance. The prison experience appeared to do nothing to elevate substance dependence and most participants felt that the government held an obligation to fund their respective substance abuse issues.

CASE STUDY 1.4: KIM'S ACCOUNT OF GOVERNMENT FUNDED DRUG USE

Kim is a 28 year old woman who has been to prison only once. Kim was sentenced to a 6-month custodial sentence, and served this sentence in Queensland. This sentence was in relation to the dangerous operation of a motor vehicle. Kim is the single mother of a young boy. Kim has described that after she was released she spent her Commonwealth Welfare Payment on drugs for her own use and this initial purchase continued her cycle of substance abuse.

> I was pretty screwed. I had to rely on Mum and Dad. I was on Centrelink benefits and crime a little bit. I think [that] I got an EBT [card] for a hundred and forty five dollars. Hundred and forty five dollars and went and spent that on drugs and kept [my drug use] going from there.

The Government Funded Drug Use theme can be considered as an extension or subdivision of the Post-Incarceration Finances theme and represented a lack of available funds to support a drug related lifestyle. In spite of a variety of substance abuse intervention programs, ex-prisoners with histories of substance abuse have comparatively low long-term recovery rates (Tiburco, 2008). These relatively low substance abuse recovery rates, combined with the stigma of previous criminal and substance abuse histories, can cause the exit process for these ex-prisoners to be clouded with feelings of hopelessness (Tiburco, 2008). Throughout the interview narratives were indications that these exiting prisoners felt lost, had feelings of poor self esteem and felt that they needed to resort back to what they knew to cope with these feelings – 'drug use'.

Kim's account of Government Funded Drug Use was not an isolated incident. Several participants stated that when they collected their Commonwealth Government Allowance (i.e., Crisis Payment; Centrelink, n.d.,) all that they wanted to do was immediately spend the entirety of their Crisis Payment on drugs:

Crisis payment whatever it is, I [took that money and] went and got on [drugs].

It was just money from Centrelink. … I got that and went and got drugs.

[With my] crisis payment that was the first thing that I went and did. That's like two hundred and twenty bucks. And that was gone that day on gear [which is drugs].

I was on Centrelink [benefits]. … I spent it on drugs and shit.

There was no finance, [only a] Centrelink payment. … The dole cheque [all] … went on drugs.

These participants were questioned on what they thought their Crisis Support Payment was meant to be spent on. All participants acknowledged that this allowance was to be used for food, clothing, accommodation, etc. However, there appeared to be a sub-issue of an entitlement to spend their Crisis Payment on getting 'high', and purchasing drugs and alcohol. When pressed for a rational why they thought spending their Crisis Payment on drugs and alcohol was acceptable, many participants responded with comments like, "I'm a drug addict". It appeared that these participants were blaming the government for criminalising narcotics. An overriding justification for these participant's pro-criminal behaviours was they would stop offending if the Commonwealth Government either: (a) supplied them with drugs and alcohol; or (b) gave them money so that they could obtain drugs and alcohol.

These accounts are clear, almost half of the participant pool freely offered accounts that immediately after they were release from prison they spent all of their available funds obtaining either drugs or alcohol. The engagement, immediately after release from prison, in substance abusing behaviours demonstrates mala-fide intentions and an inability to lead substance free and subsequent crime free lifestyles in the community.

Kim's account was that she went to Centrelink, obtained her Crisis Payment, immediately obtained drugs and proceeded to continue her drug use and sink deeper into her substance addiction. It is well documented that substance abuse is a criminogenic and predictive indicator of pro-criminal behaviours and criminal recidivism. Not only is this group at an elevated risk of drug related death (i.e., drug overdose; Bird & Hutchinson, 2003; Shewan,

Hammersley, Oliver & McPherson, 2000), drug related infections (i.e., abscesses; Nelles et al., 2000), and drug related disease (i.e., Hepatitis C, HIV; Nelles et al., 2000), this group is at an elevated risk of being rearrested and reimprisoned.

Societal Anxiety

Social Anxiety was not an area of interest and was not included in the interview schedule. Participants in this study generally functioned well and had relatively good communication and interaction skills with members of the community prior to going to prison. Upon release, however, they reported that they experienced significant difficulties interacting and communication with members of the general community. These difficulties reportedly manifested themselves in the form of social anxiety – revolving around crowds, interacting with sale assistants in stores, and basic communication skills.

CASE STUDY 1.5: EMILY'S ACCOUNT OF SOCIETAL ANXIETY

Emily is a 36 year old woman who has been to prison twenty times, with her longest custodial sentence being 5-years imprisonment. Emily has been imprisoned in New South Wales, Victoria, and Queensland for various violent and non-violent offences, including drug trafficking, going armed in public to cause fear, assaults and property offences such as break and entering. Emily is the mother of three children. Emily has described that after her release from prison she felt anxious around people and crowds, and that this anxiety led her to re-offend.

I would have gotten used to being around the members of society again. Learnt how to catch trains again [and] buses. Get over all of that anxiety of walking down the street. I got released from Sydney once, really good, all good, but then [I] got released and had to go into the city and catch the train back to Queensland. … I was too scared to go and ask for a train ticket. I didn't want to go in and talk to these normal people. I should, I should have. I had been in there [prison] talking to [correctional] officers and store people for long enough, but instead I went up the [Kings] Cross and got on. And sabotaged myself and went back to using [drugs]. Because I didn't want to, I don't know, I was too scared to go in [to buy my ticket]. You just don't think that you are going to fit in out here. That's happened to me a few times too.

Well when you leave jail you are so pumped up and full of good vibes and you go walking down the street and people are so negative. And when you go up to talk to people … [they] seem to just bring you down and you get this anxiety, do you know what I mean? You get this glow when you leave jail, I don't know I always do and most of my friends do [also], [and] they are pretty happy and strong people. And you get out there and it doesn't take long for society to bring them down to this level. And they get all of this anxiety because they are so strong and they are around all of their people [in prison] to deal with [it] and they get out into the community and they are just lost. And yeah they get, and I see them, the glow just disappears.

Emily's account of Societal Anxiety revealed that whilst she was incarcerated, she was able to interact with correctional staff and other prisoners, and that she reported no experiences of anxiety whilst in custody. It was not until she was out in the wider community that her social anxiety issues emerged. Emily's description was not isolated when it came to reporting feelings of social anxiety. Emily gave a report that she could not approach a ticket counter to purchase transportation from New South Wales to Queensland; which was a condition of her release upon parole. Instead, Emily violated her parole order and reported that this violation came about because she was fearful of interacting with 'normal people'. The consequences of social anxiety, in Emily's account, led her to resort back to substance abuse related behaviours, and an eventual return to prison.

Other participants in this study reported similar difficulties and feeling of social anxiety when attending shops, interacting with shop attendants, and when finding themselves in crowds of people. These feeling of social anxiety emerged with an undercurrent of paranoia. A number of participants were concerned that people were looking at them. Across a proportion of interviews, participants reported to encountering a combination or mixture of anxiety related difficulties connected with shopping outings, crowds and paranoia. One male stated, "A bit of paranoia, it was for me. I was always in a hat and sunnies you know, just too many people … crowds, yeah social anxiety". Another stated:

> For me, I found when I have just gotten out of … [a] high security jail, that first initial period, say, I don't know the first two, three weeks, its like I'm very, I don't know, I feel funny when I walk into shops to buy something [and I feel] like people are looking at me, stuff like that. … Well I have gone into buy clothes, normally I would just buy what I want, go in and try it on … pay for it and go. But [now] I would walk in [and] just grab it off the rack and get out of there as quick as I can. I don't know, I just think [and I feel] paranoid [and that] people are looking at me.

Other participants reported that they felt anxious about not having a clear release plan and not knowing what they would do or where they would go, once released into the community. One female participant, who had served numerous terms of imprisonment and had been released numerous times, said that her level of anxiety upon release would cause her to tremble:

> I'm anxious every time I get out [of prison]. … My anxiety goes thought the fucken roof. … When I'm free, when I walk out of those gates, I get my shit and then it's like what am I going to do now. Then the anxiety goes whooooo. Because what am I going to do? … I'm fucken shaking like a fucken leaf because I'm scared of what I'm going to do.

Emily disclosed that she knew other ex-prisoners who experience a general level of social anxiety when engaging with general members of the community. Emily revealed that when most prisoners are released, they are 'full of good vibes' and that anxiety related to communicating with 'negative' members of the general community diminishes these feelings of wellbeing. This account implied that the impacts of these negative interactions (i.e., with general members of the community) is a catalyst to ex-prisoners losing their way in the community.

The Social Anxiety issue was a difficult theme to interpret, and the following questions arise: did the prison experience contribute to these reported accounts of anxiety? Do these participants normally experience varying levels of social anxiety? Is the diathesis stress model at play? Briefly, the diathesis stress model is a theory that explores causes of psychopathology (Monroe & Simons, 1991). The premise here is that stress triggers a diathesis, which intern manifests a predisposition, perhaps genetic in nature, into an incidence of psychopathology (Monroe & Simons, 1991). In the context of this study did the participants that reported experiencing social anxiety have a predisposition to anxiety and the stress of exiting prison caused a manifestation of social anxiety? These questions are difficult to answer, are beyond the scope of this thesis, and are suggested areas of further research.

Section Two: Positive Themes

This section aspires to present and discuss, in detail, both of the two positive sub-issues: 'family cohesion' and 'jail house role models' outlined in the results section. This section will follow the same format as the negative discussion section and provides excerpts from the interview narratives in order to justify theme description, justify sub-issue allocation into the Positive Grouping, and also to contextualise the following discussions.

Family Cohesion

Family Issues was an area of interest and was included in the interview schedule. However, it was not anticipated that the prison experience would unit prisoners and their respective families. Participants in this study generally came from dysfunctional families and reported that there were varying levels of animosity between their immediate families (mother, father, brothers, and sisters) prior to being incarcerated. However, it was found that during the prison experience, for varying reasons, the family unit became solidified, gathered around the incarcerated member, and generally these relationships became closer.

CASE STUDY 2.1: JOHN'S ACCOUNT OF FAMILY COHESION

John is a 22 year old man who has been to prison twice, with his longest custodial sentence being 6-months imprisonment. John was imprisoned in Queensland for various non-violent property offences, including break and entering. John has no children. John said that his prison experience has brought his family closer together and that there has been a significant positive shift in his relationships with all family members post-release. John disclosed that his pre-incarceration family relations were.

> Not really good. I really didn't speak [to] them that much. They didn't really make any effort to see me or they just wanted to criticise me for doing the wrong thing. [But now] my relationship with my mother and brother is starting to get better. It wasn't that great when I started to get in trouble with the law. Because [now] I'm showing them that I want to change and get back on top of my life. I talk to my Mum nearly everyday on the phone and now she is willing to let me go move [in]to her house.

Most of the interview narratives revealed that the prison experience bonded the immediate family (i.e., mother, father, brother, sister, and children) closer together. A consistent finding within and between interview narratives was that prior to being imprisoned the relationships between participant and their immediate family were strained, not functioning well, and a large proportion of these participants stated that these relationships had become estranged. Dominant explanations for these strain relationships focused on individual involvement in pro-criminal and pro-substance abuse behaviours.

John's Account of Family Cohesion is a fitting example of the principal descriptive accounts given by other participants into how these estranged relationships began to be re-established. Predominately, these accounts revolved around conscious and concerted efforts made by these participants to demonstrate to family members that they are striving to abstain from their previous criminal and substance abusing lifestyles and live a law abiding life:

> Well we didn't used to speak; they were over cops turning up [at home] every week and the house getting raided [by the police] all [of] the time. And seeing me getting taken away [by the police] all the time. … Yeah they [family relationships] are all right now. Because I am trying to change my life. For starters trying to do [drug and alcohol] rehab[ilitation] and just trying [to] get away from that whole [criminal and drug related] lifestyle that I used to have. So they have got a bit more trust in me now.

Conversely, the bonding of family relationships did not extend past the immediate family. The interview narratives demonstrated that romantic relationships (i.e., husband/wife, boy/girlfriend, lover, sexual partner), in the main, did not extend past the prison episode. There appeared to be three fundamental reasons why the romantic relationships deteriorated to the point of nil-repair. Firstly, the non-incarcerated partner could not remain monogamous to their relationship; secondly, the non-incarcerated partner continued to engage in pro-criminal and pro-substance abuse behaviours; and thirdly, the strain of separation, via incarceration, hindered communication between the couple to a point that they both grew apart. Some participants revealed that when they were imprisoned that they felt isolated from their romantic partner, and that this isolation caused severe communication breakdowns. Other participants revealed that because of the way visitation areas are monitored, that their phone calls are recorded, and that their mail is read; there was no opportunity to privately communicate with there romantic partners.

Jail House Role Models

Jail House Role Models was an expected finding of this study. Participants in this study generally believed that what they had learnt from their fellow prisoners was more therapeutic and equipped then far better than the programs offered by corrective services. It was generally revealed that positive modelling and positive reinforcement from other prisoners assisted in the prison exit process.

CASE STUDY 2.2: WAYNE'S ACCOUNT OF JAIL HOUSE ROLE MODELS

Wayne is a 24 year old man who has been to prison only once. Wayne was sentenced to 3-months imprisonment and served the entirety of this sentence, plus an additional 6-months on remand. This sentence was served in Queensland. Wayne was imprisoned for a breach of a domestic violence order. Wayne is the father of a two-year old boy. Wayne disclosed that it was the other prison inmates that he met whilst in prison that had a positive therapeutic/rehabilitative effect up him, and caused him to mature and redirect his life. Wayne described this as.

> Jail sort of changes you, I don't know if it is a male perspective or getting taught by older men, but they sort of train you to snap out of childish behaviours and stuff like that. Because they teach ya, if they see good in ya and good qualities in ya, they take the time out to spend with you to teach ya ways and methods of working things out on the outside. Well that's [what] happened with me anyway.

> Well employment was pretty hard before that because I was using and drinking all of the time. Not really thinking about keeping my stuff together or keeping my shit together to do that type of thing, because I wasn't in the right frame of mind. But after going to prison and getting amongst it, I thought that they were pretty amazing men. [They] taught me things, and means, and ways how to get ready for when I get out [of prison] again. They just pushed me to get a job and get on the straight and narrow and support my family, and work and earn money … to survive I guess. I guess [it makes you] smarter and [I] grew up I think. Jail changes people, and most people change from it, and learn from it and take the advise.

Criminologists and penologists alike have suggested that the prison environment is a university of crime, where prisoners learn more complicated criminal behaviours and develop strong criminal networks (Petersilia, 2003; Pettus & Severson, 2006). This notion is based on North American behavioural scientist Albert Bandura's (1977) Social Learning Theory (SLT). SLT posits behaviours being learnt (e.g., substance abuse, pro-criminal acts) based on environmental exposure, modelling or mimicking the behaviours of others (Allen, 2007; Bandura, 1969; Ormrod, 1999). Therefore, learning has the potential to be hazardous, extremely laborious, and lacking in understanding if it were depended on the effects of an individuals sole actions (Allen, 2007; Bandura, 1977). Providentially, human behaviour is mostly learned vicariously and observationally via modelling others (Bandura, 1977; Brandon, Herzog, Irvin, & Gwaltney, 2004). This type of modelling serves to form cognitive impressions or maps that guide and even propel future actions (Allen, 2007; Bandura, 1977; Brandon et al., 2004; Ormrod, 1999). Thus, learning can become a symbiotic relationship between the environment and the learner (Allen, 2007).

SLT can be used as an explanation for pro-criminal and deviant behaviours (Akers & Jensen, 2005; Brandon et al., 2004). Importantly, it is acknowledged that pro-criminal and deviant behaviours, in many cases, are situational and contextually specific, in that behaviours exhibited in one situation may not be appropriate in another (Allen, 2007). Crimonogenic development opportunities can direct an understanding of an environment and how antisocial behaviours can affect the individuals within that environment (Akers &

Jensen, 2005; Allen, 2007). Fundamental to Bandura's (1977) SLT is the notion that people learn what is and what is not collectively tolerable within their respective environments, and are ultimately products of these environments (Brandon et al., 2004). If a culture, say a prison environment, promotes poor communication, dishonesty, unethical behaviours, and a lack of transparency, then individuals within this culture may not tolerate individuals with disagreeing values (Allen, 2007).

SLT provides a sound elucidation of the attainment, continuation, and modification of pro-criminal and deviant behaviours embracing social, nonsocial, and environmental characteristics to advance motivation and manage pro-criminal behaviours and to endorse and undercut conformity (Akers & Jensen, 2005). Simply put the same social learning forces operate in contexts of social make-up, interaction, and circumstances, produces either conforming or deviant behaviour (Akers & Jensen, 2005). From a corrective perspective, SLT encompasses the idea of individuals learning behaviours from modelling others in their surroundings; these models have the potential to assist or obstruct desistance behaviour development schemes dependent on environmental contexts once prisoners return to the community (Allen, 2007; Akers & Jensen, 2005).

Brown and Ross (2010) present a rather compelling argument about using ex-prisoners that have ceased engaging in pro-criminal behaviours as a modelling strategy (i.e., intervention tool) to teach other to cease their individual offending. This approach ties Desistance Theory with Social Learning Theory (outlined above) to bring about change in offending attitude. Furthermore, Bandura's (1977) Social Learning Theory (SLT) provides a basis for Wayne's explanation of how Jail House Role Models have had positive effect upon his life. Wayne's account revealed, prior to going to prison, he lacked an understanding what is and what is not acceptable community behaviours. Wayne gave a description that his fellow prisoners took the time to encourage him to redirect his life, and from this experience he matured. Wayne stated that based on his interaction with his fellow prisoner that he is now motivated to work, support his family, lead a crime and drug free life, and be a productive member of the community.

Section Three: Pleas for Improvement Themes

Two of the most dominant themes of this study concerned pleas from ex-prisoners for prison exit policy and practice reform. An overwhelming majority of the participants in this study stated that there are two primary areas in need of change in order to assist prisoners exiting prison. Both of these areas are unique from one another. Firstly, the reimplementation of 'gradual release' programs to phase prisoners back into their respective communities. Secondly, post-prison 'follow up aftercare' to address immediate needs that confront an exiting prisoner. In the same format as the Negative and Positive Discussion sections, excerpts from the interview narratives will be provided in order to justify theme description, sub-issue allocation into the pleas for improvement grouping, and also to contextualise the following discussion.

Gradual Release

Participants generally found that by releasing them directly from secure custody into the community that they were commonly unable to reassimilate back into society. Most participants recommended that a gradual phasing back, via levels of less restriction and supervision, would greatly assist them to 'fit' back into their respective communities.

CASE STUDY 3.1: PAUL'S ACCOUNT OF GRADUAL RELEASE

Paul is a 39 year old man who has been to prison three times, with his longest custodial sentence being 4-years. Paul has been imprisoned in Queensland for various violent and non-violent offences, including armed robbery and property offences such as break and entering. Paul has no children. Paul has described that policy and practice change is required to assist ex-prisoners exiting prison, and outlines that gradual release is the best option. Paul said:

> [Leave of Absence] programs you know. Get them used to going out to [and] finding employment. … [The] Release to Work [program] you know was a good thing too. … For example, I was on it [the Release to Work Program] a few years ago and it got me out of jail to work [and] to find employment and I found employment and I saved money up slowly you know. I had a structured accommodation to live in, supplied by corrective services. And they helped me sort of get used to [a] working [routine]. Being self [sufficient], probably becoming more responsible for myself. … Make them [prisoners] feel responsible you know. Gave them somewhere to go to you know, [something] to aim for, instead of getting out to nothing.

Participants consistently stated that they require a gradual reintroduction from the prison environment back into the community. They stated that at post-release they struggled to reassimilate from a highly structured and regimented prison based routine to having no daily structure in the community. A highly structured and regimented prison routine includes set times throughout the day that significant happenings occur. For example, being confined inside and outside of a cell, having meals prepared and distributed three times a day, sports and exercise, visitation, library book carts, and even medical appointments.

Participants generally revealed that open custody accommodation should be more frequently utilised to assist an individual prisoner's gradual reintroduction back into the community. In Australia, there are in excess of three times more prisoners accommodated in secure correctional centres as opposed to open security correctional centres. Participants in this study voiced a real concern about releasing ex-prisoners from secure correctional centres straight back into the community:

> By integrating people through the system for a start. … I don't think that people should be getting released from Maximum Security facilities. You know after two, three … anything over 18-months. I suppose that is not a good thing to be doing [releasing ex-prisoners from maximum security prisons straight out onto the street].

> Give [th]em [something] like integration back onto the outside [of prison]. Like [when I was in] the Brisbane Youth Detention Centre. They have got this little house that they put you into when you have about one month to go. And they put you into there and you stay

there until you get out ... and you have to cook your own feeds and all that. [It] reintegrate[s] you back into the community.

Participants also suggested corrective services reintroduce day leave style programs, where prisoners are given leave from prison to go home to mix with family members, go shopping, and to participate in other community events. On male participant spoke of a leave of absence program:

> Leave of Absence ... is [when] you are given [a] specific time, like say a couple of days or a week when you are supervised and you go home and then you come back to jail. During that time you are out there [in the community], you are reintegrating back into society.

Furthermore, participants wanted to see the reintroduction of the Release to Work (RTW) program, where prisoners are given supervised release into the community to seek and engage in meaningful employment. Paul's account of gradual release emphasised the benefits of the RTW program. Paul indicated that the RTW program assisted him in saving finances for his eventual release from prison; it also enabled him to establish both a work ethic and work routine, and increased his level of self-esteem via giving him a sense of responsibility. Other participants gave similar accounts that the RTW program assisted them greatly with employment, finance, and reintegrating back into the wider community.

Follow Up Aftercare

The most consistent finding of this study was that an overwhelming percentage (90%) voiced a concern that when they exited prison there was a lack of follow up community care. Nearly all of the participants in this study revealed that there was a lack of community based aftercare to assist them with issues that they were confronting in the community soon after release from custody.

CASE STUDY 3.2: DOUG'S ACCOUNT OF FOLLOW UP AFTERCARE

Doug is a 33 year old man who has been to prison three times, with his longest custodial sentence being 12-months imprisonment. Doug has been imprisoned in Queensland and Victoria for various non-violent property offences, including drug supply and break and entering. Doug is the father of a 12 year old boy. Doug disclosed that after he was released from prison, he felt abandoned and that there was a complete lack of community after care and community support to assist him with difficult prison exit issues that he was confronting. Doug said.

> I think that the government should take a bit more notice of people that have been sent to jail and [especially when they] get out. Cause they do say that there are things out there to help you get back into the community, but [there is] not really anybody that follows it up. There is not really a big follow up. Housing, they tell you that they will help you get a house, and accommodation and work and you don't ever hear back from them. ... As you

are leaving jail there is someone that comes around and says their there to help you and to get you back into society. But there is not ever a follow up on that, not on my occasions anyway.

When I got out all my stuff had gone, and there was nobody there to help me. They [corrective services] were promising [that they would help me]. The people at the jail said that they are here to help me. They [said that they] are going to help me get accommodation, they are gonna make sure that I was doing the right thing. But when I got out there was nothing, there was no one who asked me for my phone number to see if I was OK. Yeah the[y] ... really need to take a look at how they are doing their rehabilitation. And if they are going to help somebody [then] they really have to be connected, they have to put in a big effort. A big effort to make sure that person, ... [once] they've gone in and seen [that person] and told them they are gonna help [them]. [That] it's followed up, and if it is not followed up it is pretty likely that people are going to go back to jail. They should actually go around to the person's house and see if they are living in a stable place. Make sure that they are living with [suitable] people ... [that they] are able to get along with. Not getting themselves back into crime or bad things with drugs. Make sure that they've got enough food to last them for two weeks. Make sure that they are not about to get back into crime because they have got nothing [and are struggling financially]. They should really make more [of an] effort to help them [ex-prisoners] get back into employment and not just giving them a [phone] number to call, [connect them with something] like a job club. Get people to come in twice a week maybe or a couple of times [a week] and they should follow [ex-prisoners] up to see how they are doing.

Doug's account of follow up aftercare demonstrated that he felt abandoned by the prison system, coupled with a notion that he was 'kicked-out' of prison and left to fend for himself. Doug expressed concerns that whilst he was still imprisoned he was promised post-prison support and after he was released he found that there was no assistance available. This issue was compounded upon release from prison that all of his personal possessions had gone missing and that he had no where to live. Doug relayed that he found himself lost in a changed community and that there were no immediate services that he could call upon that deal specifically with ex-prisoners and their unique post-release issues.

Doug's account of abandonment was not an isolated description. Many participants in this study experienced similar difficulties. These difficulties ranged from not being able to locate support agencies that could assist with issues like emergency accommodation, clothing, food, and even locating medical assistance and mental health practitioners.

The amount of support you get when you get out [is next to nothing]. Well you are given this baseline of parole and told you have to provide clean urine [tests] and this that and the other. But there is no support in between your next parole date or the next time that you go and see your parole officer. There is no [specific] stuff to help you work on the [prison exit] issues. Inside [prison] the courses seem to be alright. But I think that there needs to be some sort of continuation for when you get out [of prison]. Some support or something ... instead of being left to your own devices, because you just want to get back to the same thing that you were doing before, [committing crime and using drugs]. Actually the prison system could help you [a lot more in the community].

Many participants disclosed that they attend intervention programs in custody, but the program ended in prison. It was revealed that the intervention programs would be more beneficial and effective if these programs incorporated a community aftercare component to give practical applications of the taught subject material. It is suggested that this approach would equip exiting prisoners with better coping skills and points of contact once they reach the community.

Doug's account was consistently mimicked between interview narratives and offers both insight and strategies that corrective services and or other community based agencies can implement to assist the prison exiting population. An overriding idea was community corrections and or other community based agencies periodically check in with recently released prisoners to ask them how they are coping, ensuring that they have the basic necessities of life, and to check on substance abuse issues.

> Instead of just chucking them out [of prison] ... and saying here you go deal with it. ... There should be a prison network agency for jobs to help them [find employment in the community]. They should follow you up [after release] and see if you have [enough] money, if you need food, if they need clothes, and if they have a got a [drug] habit.

> I think that there needs to be more, like a lot of people get out and they have no where to go, like more help with housing, jobs, finance, budgeting, support networks, making sure that people have those support networks.

It appears that the lack of follow up aftercare, as described firsthand by the participants in this study, contributes significantly to the negative issues outlined in study (i.e., Post-Incarceration Accommodation; Post-Incarceration Employment; Post-Incarceration Finances; Government Funded Drug Use; and Social Anxiety). It is suggested that the negative impacts of these issues could be significantly reduced by proving post prison support and community aftercare. In 1996, the Senate Employment, Education and Training References Committee (SEETRC, 1996) drew a similar conclusion and recommended that:

> ... each State and Territory, with the assistance of the Commonwealth government, immediately establish, in relevant community-based prisoner support organisations, liaison officers for ex-offenders to work in conjunction with parole, education, training, employment and other relevant agencies to achieve a sound transition for ex-offenders from prison into the community, in accordance with the requirements of the jurisdiction's 'through-care' strategy. (p. 74).

Despite this SEETRC recommendation, not one participant in this study stated that there was adequate post-prison follow up care, other than reporting to a community corrections officer (i.e., a parole officer).

LIMITATIONS

Like all studies there are clearly limitations to the present research, with several identified here and each of these issues are discussed in turn below. The first significant limitation is that the participants of this study were all recruited at a single rehabilitation centre and therefore there are potential questions about their representativeness to an exiting prison population. However, it should be noted that all participants have been incarcerated and therefore have first-hand prison exit experiences and it is difficult to recruit former inmates via general community sampling. The rehabilitation centre directly deals with ex-prisoners because of its relationship with the local Drug Court Diversion Program and this made this an ideal recruitment venue because of the known links between substance abuse and pro-criminal behaviours. This also meant that the participant pool was relatively homogeneous (Collins, Onwuegbuzie & Jiao, 2007; Handwerker & Wozniak, 1997) thus increasing the robustness of the findings of this study (Collins, Onwuegbuzie & Jiao, 2007; Green, 2001).

The nature of this study involved the use of a digital recording device, and the participants were informed that the interviews were going to be recorded. The researcher noted that during the interviews that the participants seemed hyperaware of this presence and use of the recording device and this caused answers to appear guarded. In addition, some of the participants gave very short answers and further in-depth probing was required to elicit full and meaningful answers. It did appear that the presence of the recording device brought about a level of uncomfortableness with the participants in this study. It is suggested for further research to have multiple interviews with the participants in order to build a rapport between researcher and participant and to promote a level of comfort for recorded interviews. Other strategies might include having a second person to act as note-taker with the digital recording device being located further away.

The nature of this study involved asking ex-prisoners about previous experiences that they encountered as they exited prison. The limitation here was with multiple episodes of prison exit and that the participants were telescoping back in time to when they previously exited prison and in some cases in between episodes of prison release. It should also be acknowledged that the participants were in the throes of recovering from drug use and undergoing intensive residential treatment. Telescoping bias occurs when participants are asked to reflect upon distant past events and they report that events occurred more recently than they actual did occur (Luks & Brady, 2003). When combined with a social desirability bias, responses can heavily lean either towards positive or negative accounts and participant can appear more certain of these accounts because of the telescoping effect (Lam & Buehler, 2009; Luks & Brady, 2003). The actual episode of prison exit, at times become clouded, and it was difficult to ascertain whether or not the participant was giving responses leaning towards their most negative or most positive experiences dependant on questioning. As a suggestion for future research, a sample of ex-prisoners should be semi-longitudinally followed as they exit the physical prison and into the community for a period of time. If this approach was taken, then the researcher would be gathering 'live' data as it was happening and would provide for a more robust qualitative methodological approach.

CONCLUSION

In summary, this study has presented insights into the psychological and physical assimilation issues that prisoners go through from being a 'confined' prisoner to a 'free' member of the community. The interview narratives of exprisoners supported national and international behavioural science literature that when ex-prisoners leave prison they face real and daunting obstacles whilst attempting to take their place back into society. The responses given to interview prompts by participants indicated that accommodation, employment and finances are problematic for a prison exit population. Another area that appeared problematic was social anxiety. Many participants consistently stated that when they were released they struggled to function outside of the highly structured and regimented prison routine, and many suffered social anxiety performing simple tasks like going shopping and interacting with members of the general community.

It was noted that for the vast majority of the participants in this study that these negative issues did not occur in isolation, they did co-exist with other negative issues to create a more problematic set of negative circumstances. The public safety implications of the negative descriptive findings of this study are profound, and those charged with confining and releasing prisoners (i.e., corrective services) need to pay urgent attention to these particular areas.

The interview narratives revealed a plea from ex-prisoners for correctional system change and prison exit policy reform. These changes included a move away from releasing ex-prisoners from secure correctional environments, and taking a uniformed approach towards gradually reintegrating prisoners back into their respective communities. It was suggested that this could be achieved in a variety of ways including, pushing long term prisoners into open security correctional environments, expanding the use of day leave, utilising release to work and home detention programs. Furthermore, an overall lack of follow up community aftercare was a theme that continually and persistently repeated itself throughout all interviews. The type of aftercare requested included assistance in finding accommodation, gaining employment, obtaining clothing, food, and hygiene products, and ultimately assisting them re-establishing their lives back in the community.

The findings of this study present, qualitatively, an in-depth understanding of the issues that confront a prison exit population, however, it is noted that much more research in this area is required to shed light on the overall issues. This could be achieved by conducting in-depth interviews with prisoners before they are released from prison, and then following these individuals into the community as they experience these issues first hand. Focus could be applied to the social anxiety, gradual release, and community follow up aftercare issues outlined in this thesis to reveal why these areas are so problematic to this population.

The findings of this study demonstrate that there are a cluster of negative aspects in being released from prison, which far outweigh the positive. Significant work needs to be done to better equip prisoners for their release back into the community. Suggested areas include external experts attending correctional centres to teach and instruct prisoners about potential issues that they may face as they exit prison; educating prisoners about practical daily life skills (i.e., cook, cleaning, co-inhabiting in civilian living, interaction with members of the general public); and via the introduction and application of individually based transition programs. These types of programs need to incorporate both custodial and community based support components. Without establishing community support agencies, with the sole aim of assisting exiting prisoners, these problematic issues will remain. These support agencies need to liaise with corrective services, parole authorities, other community agencies, and the individual prisoner's social networks to provide holistic aftercare.

In conclusion, this author argues that if changes are not made to the assistance provided to exiting prisoners then recidivism rates will remain at 60 percent and beyond. Furthermore, given the increase in prisoner numbers in Australia in the last 20 years – a doubling from 15,000 to 30,000 – then there will be more people on the street without recourse to housing, jobs, financial assistance and who are suffering high levels of social anxiety. Ultimately, the aim of releasing prisoners only to have them return to custody will be a continuing case of 'getting out and falling back'.

REFERENCES

Abbott, G. J. (1985). The Botany Bay decision. *Journal of Australian Studies*, Vol. 16, 21-41.

Akers, R. L., & Jensen, G. F. (2005). Social Learning Theory and Crime: A Progress Report. *Advances in Criminological Theory*, Vol. 15, 1-61.

Allen, S. J. (2007). Adult learning theory and leadership development, *Leadership Review*, Vol. 7, 26-37.

Anderson, C. (2010). Presenting and evaluating qualitative research, *American Journal of Pharmaceutical Education,* Vol. 74(8), 1-7.

Anderson, C. (1998). Unfree labour and its discontents: Transportation from Mauritius to Australia, 1820-1850. *Australian Studies*, Vol. 13(1), 116-133.

Atkinson, P., & Delamont, S. (2005). Analytic Perspectives. In N. Denzin & Y. Lincoln (Eds.), *The Sage Handbook of Qualitative Research* (3rd Ed.). Sage Publications: Thousand Oaks. pp. 821-840.

ABC (Australian Broadcasting Commission). (2010). Getting out of prison, Radio National, retrieved 14 December 2010, <*http://www.abc.net.au/rn/programs*>.

ABS (Australian Bureau of Statistics). (2008). Australian standard offence classification (ASOC) Australia (2nd Ed.), Canberra: Commonwealth of Australian, retrieved 14th December 2010, <*http://www.ausstats.abs.gov.au/ausstats/subscriber.nsf/0/181552DD 634CCCCCA2574970016EE08/$File/12340_2008%20(second%20edition).pdf*>.

ABS (Australian Bureau of Statistics). (2001). Prisoners in Australia, Canberra: Commonwealth of Australian, retrieved 14th December 2010, <*http://www.ausstats.abs. gov.au/ausstats/subscriber.nsf/0/3D05115F FD321B3ECA256B870082E837/$File/45170 _2001.pdf*>.

ABS (Australian Bureau of Statistics). (2010). Prisoners in Australia, Canberra: Commonwealth of Australian, retrieved 14th December 2010, <*http://www.abs.gov.au/ ausstats/abs@.nsf/mf/4517.0*>.

Baer, D., Bhati, A., Brooks, L., Castro, J., La Vigne, N., Mallik-Kane, K., Naser, R., Osborne, J., Roman, C., Roman, J., Rossman, S., Solomon, A., Visher, C., & Winterfield, L. (2006). *Understanding the challenges of prisoner reentry: Research findings from the Urban Institute's prisoner reentry portfolio.* Urban Institute Justice Policy Center.

Baldry, E., McDonald, D., Maplestone, P., & Peeters, M. (2004). The role of housing in preventing re-offending. *AHURI Research & Policy Bulletin*, Vol. 36, 1-6.

Baldry, E., McDonald, D., Maplestone, P., & Peeters, M. (2006). Ex-Prisoners, homelessness and the state of Australia. *Australian and New Zealand Journal of Criminology*, Vol. 39(1), 20-33.

Bandura, A. (1969). Social-learning theory of identification processes. In D. A. Goslin (Ed.), *Handbook of socialization theory and research*, Chicago: Rand McNally.

Bandura, A. (1977). Self-efficacy: Towards a unifying theory of behavioural change. *Psychologial Review*, Vol. 84, 191-215.

Benda, B. (1983). Predictors of arrest and service use among the homeless: Logit analyses. *Psychosocial Rehabilitation Journal*, Vol. 17(2), 145–161.

Biles, D. (2009). Corrections. In H. Heyes, & T. Prenzler (Eds.*), An introduction to crime and criminology* (2nd Ed). Frenchs Forest: Pearson Prentice Hall.

Bird, S. M., & Hutchinson, S. J. (2002). Male drugs-related deaths in the fortnight after release from prison: Scotland, 1996–99. *Addiction*, Vol. 98, 185–190.

Brandon, T. H., Herzog, T. A., Irvin, J. E., & Gwaltney, C. J. (2004). Cognitive and social learning models of drug dependence: Implications for the assessment of tobacco dependence in adolescents, *Addiction*, Vol. 99, 51-77.

Brown, D. (2008). *The effect of terrorism and terrorist trials on Australian prison regimes.* The Crime and Justice research Network University of New South Wales, 61-76.

Brown, M., & Ross, S. (2010). Mentoring, social capital and desistance: A study of women released from prison. *The Australian and New Zealand Journal of Criminology*, Vol. 43(1), 31–50.

Bryman, A., M. Bresnen, A. Beardsworth, and T. Keil (1988). Qualitative research and the study of leadership. *Human Relations*, Vol. 41(1), 13-30.

Bryman, A. (2004). Social research methods. (2nd Ed.). Oxford: Oxford University Press.

Burrows, J., Clarke, A., Davison, T., Tarling, R., & Webb, S. (2000). *Research findings no. 109: The nature and effectiveness of drugs through care for released prisoners.* London: Home Office.

Carcach, C., & Grant, A. (2000). Imprisonment in Australia: The offence composition of Australian correctional populations, 1988 and 1998. *Trends and Issues in Crime and Criminal Justice*, No. 164. Australian Institute of Criminology.

Carlton, B. (2007). *Imprisoning resistance: life and death in an Australian supermax.* Sydney: Institute of Criminology Press.

Carter, F. C. (2009). Career development strategies for clients with criminal histories. *Career Planning and Adult Development Journal,* 188-196.

Centrelink. (n.d.). Crisis payment for released prisoners. Canberra: Australian Government, retrieved 14 December 2010, <*http://www.centrelink.gov.au/internet/internet.nsf /filestores/ch012_0612/$file/ch012_0612en.pdf*>.

Challeen, D. A. (1986*). Making it right: A common sense approach to criminal justice.* Aberdeen: Melius and Peterson Publishing.

Clear, T. R., Rose, D. R., & Ryder, J. A. (2001). Incarceration and the community: The problem of removing and returning offenders. *Crime & Delinquency*, 47(3), 335-351.

Collins, K. M. T., Onwuegbuzie, A. J., & Jiao, Q. G. (2007). A mixed methods investigation of mixed methods sampling designs in social and health science research. *Journal of Mixed Methods Research,* Vol. 1(3), 267-294.

Conway, J. (1999). *Housing needs of prisoners and their families in Queensland: Issues paper.* Brisbane: Queensland Department of Housing.

Creswell, J. W. (1998). *Qualitative inquiry and research design: Choosing among five traditions.* London: Sage Publications Ltd.

Danes, K. (2008). *Families behind bars: Stories of injustice, endurance and hope.* Sydney: New Holland.

Darlington, Y., & Scott, D. (2002). Qualitative Research in Practice: Stories from the field. *Crows Nest*: Allen & Unwin.

DEWHA (Department of the Environment, Water, Heritage and the Arts). (2008). Australian convict sites world heritage nomination. Canberra: Commonwealth of Australian, retrieved 14 December 2010, <http://www.environment.gov.au/heritage/places/world/convictsites/index.html>.

Donnachie, I. (1986). The convicts of 1830: Scottish criminals transported to New South Wales. *Scottish Historical Review*, Vol. 65(1) 34-47.

Farrell, M., & Marsden, J. (2008). Acute risk of drug-related death among newly released prisoners in England and Wales. *Addiction*, 103, 251–255.

Farrington, K. (2009). Maximum security: Inside stories from the world's toughest prisons. *Melbourne: Ice Water Press*.

Farrington, D. P., Coid, J. W., & Murray, J. (2009). Family factors in the intergenerational transmission of offending. *Criminal Behaviour and Mental Health*, Vol. 19, 109–124.

Findlay, M., Odgers, S., & Yeo, S. (2009). Punishment and penalty. In M. Finlay, S. Odgers, & S. Yeo (Eds.), *Australian Criminal Justice* (4th Ed.). Melbourne: Oxford University Press.

Freudenberg, N. (2006). Coming home from jail: A review of health and social problems facing U.S. jail populations and of opportunities for reentry interventions. *American Jails*, 9-24.

Gillespie, W. (2004). The context of imprisonment. In S. Stanko, W. Gillespie, & G. Crews (Eds.), *Living in prison: A history of the correctional system with an insider's view*. Westport: Greenwood Press.

Goldstein, P. (1998). The drugs/violence nexus: A tripartite conceptual framework. In J. Inciardi, & K McElrath (Eds.), *The American drug scene*. Los Angeles: Roxbury.

Green, E. C. (2001). Can qualitative research produce reliable quantitative findings? *Field Methods*, Vol. 13(1), 3–19.

Guion, L. A., & Flowers, L. (2005). Using qualitative research in planning and evaluating extension programs, University of Florida, retrieved on 9 November 2010, *http://edis.ifas.ufl.edu*.

Haigh, Y. (2007). Why they desist: Understanding the life worlds of young people involved in crime. Institute of Restorative Justice and Penal Reform, Murdoch University, retrieved 14th December 2010, <http://www.cscr.murdoch.edu.au/_docs/whytheydesist.pdf>.

Hall, S. (2009*). Indiana implements a faith and character based housing program, Corrections Today*, 62-68.

Hancock, B. (2002). Trent focus for research and development in primary health care: An Introduction to Qualitative Research. *Trent Focus*.

Handwerker, W. P., & Wozniak. D. F. (1997). Sampling strategies for the collection of cultural data: An extension of Boas's answer to Galton's problem. *Current Anthropology*, Vol. 38, 869-75.

Health Practitioners (Professional Standards) (QLD) Act 1999.

Johnson, H. (2000). Key findings from the drug use careers of female offenders study. *Trends and Issues in Crime and Criminal Justice*. Australian Institute of Criminology.

Kennedy, J. (1988). *Reports of the Commission of Review into Corrective Services in Queensland*.

King, T. (2007). *Boggo Road and beyond*. Brisbane: Watson Ferguson & Company.

Lam, K. C. H., & Buehler, R. (2009). Trips down memory lane: Recall direction affects the subjective distance of past events. *Personality and Social Psychology Bulletin*, Vol. 35(2), 230-243.

LaValle, J. J. (1995). *Coping when a parent is in jai*. Rosen: New York.

Leukefeld, C., Araujo, G., & Farabee, D. (1997). Drugs, crime and HIV. *Substance Use and Misuse*, Vol. 32, 749-756.

Lichtenberger, E. (2006). Where do ex-offenders find jobs? An industrial profile of the employers of ex-offenders in Virginia. *The Journal of Correctional Education*, Vol. 57(4), 297-311.

Light, R., & Campbell, B. (2006). Prisoners' families: Still forgotten victims? *Journal of Social Welfare & Family Law*, Vol. 28(2), 297–308.

Liquor Act (QLD) 1992.

Lucas, W.E. (1976). Solitary confinement: Isolation as coercion to conform. *Australian and New Zealand Journal of Criminology, Vol. 9*, 153-167.

Lucken, K., & Ponte, L. M. (2008). A just measure for forgiveness: Reforming occupational licensing regulations for ex-offenders using BFOQ analysis. *Law and Policy, Vol. 30*(1), 46-72.

Luks, S., & Brady, H. E. (2003). Defining welfare spells: Coping with problems of survey responses and administrative data. *Evaluation Review*, Vol. 27(3), 395-420.

Lynch, J. P., & Sabol, W. J. (2001). Prisoner reentry in perspective. *Crime policy report*, Urban Institute Justice Policy Centre.

Magaletta, P. R., & Herbst, D. P. (2001). Fathering from prison: Common struggles and successful solutions. *Psychotherapy*, Vol. 38, 88-96.

Makkai, T., & McGregor, K. (2002). Drug use monitoring in Australia (DUMA): 2002 annual report on drug use among police detainees. *Research and Public Policy Series No. 47*. Australian Institute of Criminology.

Makkai. T., & Payne, J. (2003). Drugs and crime: A study of incarcerated male offenders. Research and Public Safety Series No 52. Australian Institute of Criminology.

Martinez, D. J. (2006). Informal helping mechanisms: Conceptual issues in family support of reentry of former prisoners. *Journal of Offender Rehabilitation*, Vol. 44(1), 23-37.

Matthews, B. (2006). Intractable. Sydney: Macmillan.

McCarthy, B., & Hagen, J. (1991). Homelessness: A criminogenic situation*? British Journal of Criminology,* Vol. 31(4), 393–410.

McDonough, J., & Burrell, W. D. (2008). Offender workforce development: A new (and better?) approach to an old challenge. *Federal Probation*, Vol. 72(2), 71-76.

Meek, R. (2007). Parenting education for young fathers in prison. *Child and Family Social Work,* Vol. 12, 239–247.

Menard, S., Mihalic, S., & Huizinga, D. (2001). Drugs and crime revisited. *Justice Quarterly,* Vol. 18, 269-299.

Minogue, C. (2010). Inside my skull: Personal responsibility and the moral lessons learnt. *Zadok Perspectives*, 1-6.

Moffatt, S., Weatherburn, D., & Donnelly, N. (2005). What caused the recent drop in property crime? (No. 85*). Sydney: NSW Bureau of Crime Statistics and Research.*

Monroe, S. M., & Simons, A. D. (1991). Diathesis stress theories in the context of life stress research implications for the depressive disorders. *Psychological Bulletin*, Vol. 110(3), 406-425.

Moustakas, C. (1994). *Phenomenological Research Methods*. London: Sage Publications.

Mulligan, L. (2007). *Justice behind bars: Understanding the Queensland prison system.* Brisbane: Prisoners' Legal Services Publishing.

Naser, R. L., & La Vigne, N. G. (2006). Family support in the prisoner reentry process: Expectations and realities. *Journal of Offender Rehabilitation*, Vol. 43(1), 93-106.

Nelles, J., Hirsbrunner, H., Fuhrer, A., Dobler-Mikola, A., & Harding, T. (2000). Reduction of drug and HIV related harm in prison: Breaking taboos and applying public health principles. In D. Shewan, & J. B. Davies (Eds.), *Drug use and prisons: An international perspective.* Sydney: Harwood Academic Publishers.

Nilsson, R. (2003) The Swedish prison system in historical perspective: A story of successful failure? *Journal of Scandinavian Studies in Criminology and Crime Prevention*, Vol. 4, 1-20.

Ogloff, J., & Davis, M. (2005). Assessing risk for violence in the Australian context. In D. Chappell, & P. Wilson (Eds.), Issues in: *Australian crime and criminal justice.* Chatswood: LexisNexis Butterworths.

Ormrod, J.E. (1999). *Human learning* (3rd Ed.). Upper Saddle River: Prentice Hall.

Owens, C. D. (2009). Social symbols, stigma, and the labor market experiences of former prisoners. *The Journal of Correctional Education*, 60(4), 316-342.

Parker, R., & Auerhahn, K. (1998). Alcohol, drugs, and violence. *Annual Review of Sociology*, 24, 291-311.

Payne, J. (2007). Recidivism in Australia: Findings and future research. *Research and Public Policy Series No. 80*. Australian Institute of Criminology.

Penalties and Sentences Act (QLD) 1992.

Petersilia, J. (2003). *When prisoners come home*. New York: Oxford University Press.

Pettus, C. A., & Severson, M. (2006). Paving the way for effective reentry practice: The critical role and function of the boundary spanner, *The Prison Journal*, Vol. 86(2), 206-229.

Productivity Commission (2010). Report on Government Services 2010, Volume 1: Early Childhood, Education and Training; Justice; Emergency Management. Steering Committee for the Review of Government Service Provision, retrieved 14 December 2010, *<http://www.pc.gov.au/__data/assets/pdf_file/0005/93902/rogs-2010 volume1. pdf>*.

Putnins, A. (2003). Substance use and prediction of young offender recidivism. *Drug and alcohol review,* Vol. 22(4), 401–408.

Queensland Government (2009). Transitions: Release preparation program, Fact Sheet, Queensland Corrective Services, 1-2, retrieved 14 December 2010, *<http://www. correctiveservices.qld.gov.au/Publications/Corporate_Publications/Program_Factsheets /Transitions_staff.pdf>*.

RACQ (Royal Automotive Club of Queensland). (2010). Motor vehicle insurance police guidelines, retrieved 14th December 2005, *<http://www.racq.com.au/__data/assets/pdf_ file/0003/52626/Motor_Vehicle_PDS_RCMV2_10-09_02.pdf>*.

Rakis, J. (2005). *Improving the employment rates of ex-prisoners under parole.* Federal Probation, Vol. 69(1), 7-12.

Ramsay, M. (1986). Housing for the homeless ex-offender: Key findings from a literature review. *Research Bulletin*, Vol. 20, 57–60.

Raney, V. K., Magaletta, P., & Hubbert, T. A. (2005). Perception of helpfulness among participants in a prison-based residential substance abuse treatment program. *Journal of Offender Rehabilitation*, Vol. 42(2), 25-34.

Raphael, S. (2010). *Incarceration and prisoner reentry in the United States.* Discussion Paper no. 1375-10, Institute for Research on Poverty.

Raphael, S., & Stoll, M. A. (2004). The effect of prison releases on regional crime rates. *Brookings-Wharton Papers on Urban Affairs*, 207-255.

SEETRC (Senate Employment, Education and Training References Committee). (1996). Report of the inquiry into education and training in correctional facilities. Canberra: Parliament House.

Shewan, D., Hammersley, R., Oliver, J., & McPherson, S. (2000). Fatal drug overdose after liberation from prison: A retrospective study of female ex-prisoners from Strathclyde Region (Scotland). *Addiction Research,* Vol. 8(3), 267-278.

Sieter, R. P., & Kadela, K. R. (2003). Prisoner reentry: What works, what does not, and what is promising. *Crime & Delinquency*, Vol. 49(3), 360-388.

Stringer, E., & Dwyer, R. (2005). Action Research in Human Services. New Jersey: Pearson.

Tartaro, C. (2006). Watered down: Partial implementation of the new generation jail philosophy. *The Prison Journal*, Vol. 86(3), 284-300.

Travis, J., Crayton, A., & Mukamal, D.A. (2009). A new era in inmate reentry, *Corrections Today,* 38-41.

Travis J., & Petersilia, J. (2001). Reentry reconsidered: A new look at an old question. *Crime & Delinquency,* Vol. 47(3), 291-313.

Tiburco, N. J. (2008). Long-Term recovery from heroin use among female ex offenders: Marisol's story. *Substance Use & Misuse*, Vol. 43, 1950–1970.

United Nations. (1977). *Human rights in the administration of justice: Protection of persons subjected to detention or imprisonment.* Adopted by the First United Nations Congress on the Prevention of Crime and the Treatment of Offenders, held at Geneva in 1955, and approved by the Economic and Social Council by its resolution 663 C (XXIV) of July 1957 and 2086 (LXII) of 13 May 1977.

Walker, J. (1989). Prison sentences in Australia: Estimates of the characteristics of offenders sentenced to prison in 1987-88. *Trends and Issues in Crime and Criminal Justice*, No. 20. Australian Institute of Criminology.

Weatherburn, D., Hua, J., & Moffatt, S. (2006). How much crime does prison stop? The incapacitation effect of prison on burglary. (No. 93). *Sydney: NSW Bureau of Crime Statistics and Research.*

Weatherburn,D., Hua, J., & Moffatt, S. (2009). Rates of participation in burglary and motor vehicle theft: Estimates and implications for policy. (No. 130). *Sydney: NSW Bureau of Crime Statistics and Research.*

Weymouth, T. D. (1998). *Outsiders looking in: How to keep from going crazy when someone you love goes to jail.* Fresno: Linc.

Willis, M., & Moore, J. P. (2008). Reintegration of Indigenous prisoners. *Trends and Issues in Crime and Criminal Justice, No. 364.* Australian Institute of Criminology.

Wittbold, M. K. (1997). *Lets talk about when your parent is in jail.* Rosen: New York.

Wodak, A. (2005). *Drugs, crime and crime reduction.* In D. Chappell, & P.

Wilson (Eds.), Issues in: *Australian crime and criminal justice.* Chatswood: LexisNexis Butterworths.

Yoshikawa, K., Taylor, P. J., Yamagami, A., Okada, T., Ando, K., Taruya, T., Matsumoto, T., & Kikuchi, A. (2007). Violent recidivism among mentally disordered offenders in Japan. *Criminal Behaviour and Mental Health,* Vol. 17, 137–151.

In: Crime
Editor: Michael Harry Pearson

ISBN: 978-1-62948-657-4
© 2014 Nova Science Publishers, Inc.

Chapter 2

OFFENDER PROFILING: A REVIEW AND CRITIQUE OF THE APPROACHES AND MAJOR ASSUMPTIONS

Shannon Vettor, Jessica Woodhams and Anthony R. Beech*
University of Birmingham, West Midlands, UK

ABSTRACT

The area of Offender Profiling generates a lot of interest in both the academic field and the everyday world as a result of a few highly prolific cases (e.g., Jack the Ripper, Boston Strangler). Historically, profiling has been based on intuition and experience, but as the field has matured, the need to be more scientific in approach has led to the development of empirically driven models/typologies of offender behaviour based. Different approaches have attempted to define, and operationalize offender profiling based on the individual principles inherent in each approach.

Briefly, the Criminal Investigative approach to profiling initially relied upon the investigative experience and observation of FBI agents who soon started publishing on the topic. However, in more recent years, large databases containing information on serial and violent crime/criminals has allowed for more empirical approaches to emerge (Snook, Luther, House, Bennell, & Taylor, 2012). The Clinical approach, on the other hand, adopts a model of offender profiling that centers on the concept of motives. Finally, and most recently, the Statistical approach has aimed to provide a testable scientific framework for identifying and inferring offender characteristics/motives.

However, none of these approaches alone can explain the complexities of offending behaviour. The Criminal Investigative approach brings with it a multitude of experience from investigators; the Clinical brings an abundance of medical and privileged client-based knowledge; while the Statistical approach aims to provide more objective measures and examination of offending behaviour. Without the experience, knowledge, and information offered by the first two approaches, the ability to know which variables to look for or code for would be lost. However, the latter Statistical approach allows practitioner-based knowledge to be integrated with the objective examination of offending patterns and correlated findings. Therefore, the way forward should seek to

---

* Shannon Vettor email: slvettor@gmail.com

integrate all of the approaches (Alison, West, & Goodwill, 2004; Alison, Goodwill, Almond, van den Heuvel, & Winter, 2010). Together, the approaches strengthen each other and give weight and support to one another. More importantly, they help strengthen the field of offender profiling as a whole.

In this chapter, an overview and critique of the offender profiling literature; its underlying assumptions; and the relationship between the crime scene actions and the offender characteristics will be presented. In addition, each of the approaches to offender profiling that have developed over its short empirical history will be described and critiqued.

INTRODUCTION

Offender profiling, while not a new phenomenon, only started developing as an area of research interest when the FBI Academy in Quantico started publicising their techniques in the 1970's (e.g., Douglas, Ressler, Burgess, & Hartman, 1986), which resulted in offender profiling becoming more widely known (Canter, 2004). Currently, the term offender profiling relates to the analysis of crime scene behaviours in order to generate both offender characteristics and investigative suggestions to aid in the generation, prioritisation, and identification of relevant suspects (Rainbow, 2007).

Reiser (1982) has described profiling as "an arcane art, in which psycho-diagnostic assessment and psychobiography are combined with case evidence and probabilities from similar cases to draw a picture of a likely offender" (p. 261). This method provides possible descriptions of potential perpetrators of crime based on the analysis of the offence, the manner in which the offence is committed, and by the determination of personality aspects of the offender and characteristics from their crime scene actions before, during and after the offence (Blau, 1994). The underlying rationale is that behaviour will reflect personality, and by examining behaviour exhibited during the perpetration of a crime, an investigator can determine the likely characteristics of the person responsible for the offence (Douglas et al., 1986).

The ability to make such inferences requires both consistency in offending behaviour and distinctiveness. Simply expressed, offender profiling is represented by Canter's (2011) "profiling equation", (or the "A → C equation"), where the inferences, (represented by the arrow) are derived from offence-related actions (i.e., the crime location, time, victimology, etc.) which are informative about the characteristics of the offender (Canter, 2004; 2011). The inferences developed are made with the intent to aid law enforcement personnel in their investigations (Holmes & De Burger, 1988).

MAJOR ASSUMPTIONS OF OFFENDER PROFILING

There are two assumptions that must be met if inferences about an offender's characteristics are to be derived from crime scene actions. The first is the *Behavioural Consistency* assumption, which implies that an offender will show similar behaviours across their offences (Canter, 1995a; Green, Booth, & Biderman, 1976). The second is the *Homology* assumption, which states that if two perpetrators exhibit similar crime scene behaviour, they will also possess similar characteristics (Alison, Bennell, Mokros, & Ormerod, 2002; Mokros & Alison, 2002).

These two assumptions are used to validate the "profiling equation" (Canter, 2011). In order for reliable inferences to be made about an offender, their crime-scene behaviours should be consistent across their crimes. These actions then provide information about the potential characteristics of the offender, with offenders exhibiting similar crime actions possessing similar characteristic (Canter, 2004; 2011). If these assumptions are invalid, the practice of offender profiling not only becomes inaccurate, but the advice given to a criminal investigation would be misleading, resulting in both human and financial costs (Alison et al., 2002; Gudjonsson & Copson, 1997).

The Behavioural Consistency Assumption

With regards to *behavioural consistency*, the body of supporting research comes from the area of case linkage (Bennell & Jones, 2005; Woodhams & Grant, 2006), comparative case analysis (Bennell & Canter, 2002), or linkage analysis (Hazelwood & Warren, 2003). These different terms refer to a form of behavioural analysis based on the behavioural similarity and distinctiveness of the offence. It is used to identify a series of crimes committed by the same offender (Woodhams, Hollin, & Bull, 2007), often when there is a lack of physical evidence (e.g., DNA) to identify the offender (Davies, 1991). Research from this area supports the assumption that some offenders behave consistently within crime types, including sexual assault (e.g., Grubin, Kelly, & Brunsdon, 2001; Knight, Warren, Reboussin, & Soley, 1998), homicide (e.g., Salfati & Bateman, 2005; Santtila, Laukkanen, Zappala, & Bosco, 2008; Santtila, Pakkanen, et al., 2008), burglary (e.g., Bennell & Canter, 2002; Bennell & Jones, 2005; Goodwill & Alison, 2007; Green et al., 1976; Tonkin, Santtila, & Bull, 2012), robbery (e.g., Woodhams & Toye, 2007), and arson (e.g., Fritzon, Canter, & Wilton, 2001; Santtila, Fritzon, & Tamelander, 2005).

Common features exist between linkage analysis and offender profiling, and some consider linkage analysis to be another type of offender profiling. The main similarity is that both share the underlying assumption of offender *behavioural consistency*; the hypothesis that offenders will display in their behaviour consistency across a series of offences (Canter, 1995b; Woodhams, Bull, & Hollin, 2007). The possibility of linking a series of crimes can be beneficial and helpful for the police as it allows for the collection of information across different crimes, the potential of increasing evidence against an offender, the combining of separate investigations utilising more effective police resources and lastly, the production of similar fact evidence in legal proceedings (Grubin et al., 2001; Hazelwood & Warren, 2003; Labuschagne, 2006). There is growing potential for the utility of linkage analysis in investigating less serious crimes (e.g., robbery), beyond its current success with investigating stranger rape or murder, or other more serious crimes (Woodhams et al., 2007).

The Homology Assumption

The concept of *homology* was borrowed and adapted from comparative biology (Owen, 2007). The term was originally defined by Richard Owen as "the same organ in different animals under every variety of form and function" (Owen, 1843; p. 379), is based on structure, not function. It refers to structures in different species that have a common evolutionary ancestry; even if they no longer serve the same purpose or have the same appearance (Owen, 2007). Its adapted use in offender profiling lies in the concept of similarity between crime scene actions (loosely analogous to structure) and the characteristics that give rise to the actions (loosely analogous to ancestry). Like the arms of a human, the foreleg of a dog, the wing of a bird, and the fin of a fish can all be traced back to a specific original limb in a prehistoric vertebrate, the homologous behaviours exhibited in a crime can be linked back to a similar characteristic possessed across different offenders. The mapping of the biological sense of *homology* and the use of the term within offender profiling is not completely harmonious. However, it is unclear whether the use of the term [by Alison et al., 2002] was meant to be a direct translation to offender profiling, or used as a distinct (although tenuously similar) concept specific to offender profiling.

While studies have shown that offenders (of various types) exhibit *behavioural consistency* across crimes (e.g., Bennell & Jones, 2005; Grubin et al., 2001; Woodhams et al., 2007), there has been little conclusive support for the assumption of *homology*. A few studies have examined the relationship between background characteristics and offence behaviour, which to some extent support the *homology* assumption (i.e., bivariate relationships have been found; Canter & Fritzon, 1998; Davies, Wittebrood, & Jackson, 1998; House, 1997). In a study of 210 solved stranger rapists, Davies et al. (1998) identified that a rapist's criminal background could be predicted from his offence behaviour. Taking precautions not to leave fingerprints (e.g., wearing gloves) was linked with having a prior custodial sentence, most likely for burglary. As well, an offender who took this precaution was more likely to be a repeat or serial offender, whereas, when no such precaution was taken, they were three times more likely to be a one-off sexual offender. Semen destruction indicated a fourfold increase in the offender having been convicted for prior sexual offences. Theft from the victim and forced entry were other indicators of prior convictions for burglary. Making references to the police during the offence and the use of extreme violence against the victim were an indication of prior convictions for violence. As these findings, Davies et al. concluded the most promising models were those that predicted whether the offender had prior convictions for burglary, prior convictions for violent offences, and whether the offence was more likely to be a one-off occurrence rather than committed by a serial sexual offender.

Although Davies et al. demonstrated that some specific crime scene actions were linked to particular offender characteristics, their analysis has been criticised for being little more than predicting associated base rates (Mokros & Alison, 2002). House (1997) investigated the inverse of the *homology* assumption; that is, that rapists with different crime scene behaviours should have different criminal histories. He categorised rapists as criminal, intimate, aggressive, or sadistic and, in direct opposition to the *homology* assumption, he found a high degree of similarity in criminality across the four types. Canter and Fritzon (1998) looked at the crime scene behaviours from 175 UK arsons and found mixed results. For three of the four thematic classifications of arson (i.e., instrumental-person, expressive-object, and expressive-person), there were no conclusive differences between the background characteristics. The instrumental-object arsons and the expressive-object arsons were the only two to have positive relations with offender characteristics; the former with younger offenders and the latter with being a serial arsonist. Doan and Snook (2008) had similar limited results using a sample of Canadian arsonists who were categorised according to Canter and Fritzon's themes. Approximately 56% of the comparisons between background characteristics and the different thematic classifications of arson violated the *homology* assumption. They suggest the discouraging findings could, in part, be due to sample differences (UK versus Canadian) and the lack of verification of the arson themes proposed by Canter and Fritzon.

In the same study, Doan and Snook also looked at a sample of robberies classifying them as Cowboys, Bandits, and Robin's Men, in accordance with Alison, Rockett, Deprez, and Watts (2000). The majority of the robberies were classified as Cowboys or Bandits, with the comparisons between the background characteristics of these two groups yielding little support for the *homology* assumption Woodhams and Toye (2007) also found no support for the *homology* assumption in their study of commercial robberies. They examined whether the commercial robbers could be clustered according to characteristics of the offences, and whether the background information of these groupings would significantly differ. The analysis produced three clusters of robbers based on their crime scene behaviour. However, these three groups did not significantly differ according to offender age, ethnicity, employment, previous convictions, or distance travelled from home to offence.

In Mokros and Alison's study (2002), the crime scene behaviour, socio-demographic characteristics, and criminal histories of a sample of 100 British male stranger rapists were examined. Using correlational analysis, they tested for similarities between offenders' behaviour and their characteristics. However, they also found no evidence to support the *homology* assumption. This indicates that the process of drawing inferences about background characteristics from crime scene actions is not a simple *if A then C* principle. Mokros and Alison argue that the *homology* assumption, as a simple behaviour-to-characteristics model, fails because it is too simplistic and neglects the moderating influence of a third factor; namely, the situation.

In support of this assumption, Goodwill and Alison (2007) have shown that the incorporation of context (e.g., the level of planning or aggression used) allows for the prediction of rapists' characteristics (i.e. such as age) from their crime scene information (i.e., victim age). Alison et al. (2002) suggest that without further acknowledgement of the situational influence, a link between offender characteristics and crime scene actions is unlikely to be found. Thus, until this happens, any advice to police investigations should remain confined to the prioritisation of suspects, as this relies more on *behavioural consistency*.

In a novel study based on domestic burglaries, Tonkin, Bond, and Woodhams (2009) found support for both the *behavioural consistency* and *homology* assumption. Their results showed the deprivation of an offender's residence and employment status was associated with the expensiveness of their footwear worn during the crime. In other words, the more expensive an offender's footwear is, the greater the deprivation of their residence and the more likely they are to be unemployed. Age and gender did not relate reliably to the price of footwear worn by the offender. In pragmatic terms, Tonkin et al.'s results suggest that expensive footwear (based on impressions left at the crime scene) are related to unemployed offenders who live in areas of deprivation.

The assumption of *behavioural consistency* is not dependent upon the assumption of *homology* being met or of it being valid; as consistent behaviour across actions does not necessitate the sameness or similarity of characteristics across offenders (Alison et al., 2002). That said behavioural consistency is *necessary* for offender profiling to work. Put differently, the offender's actions have to remain consistent for similarities to be found between their personal characteristics and behaviour (Mokros & Alison, 2002). However, the assumption of behavioural consistency would be valid if the assumption of homology is found to be valid, due to the implication that similar characteristics imply a consistency of behaviours across actions (Mokros & Alison, 2002). Yet, for offender profiling to be considered a legitimate, and importantly, a useful form of behavioural analysis, both of these assumptions must be met and found to be valid (Alison et al., 2002), as they underpin all forms of profiling.

SITUATIONAL CONTEXT AND OFFENDER PROFILING

Offender Profiling has been largely based upon personality and trait approaches, which see the basic units of personality, and therefore, behaviour, as largely non-situational and based on context-free dispositional constructs (Alison et al., 2002; Davies et al., 1997; Pervin, 2002). There is evidence that behaviour can be predicted across situations based on scores of basic trait dimensions, often cited in employment and job performance literature (Hogan, 1991; Hogan & Ones, 1997). One explanation is that once self-schemas become well organised, through our experiences, we selectively respond to information in ways congruent with our expectations and self-views (Fiske & Taylor, 1991). With regards to longitudinal stability, there is moderate support for the stability of temperamental characteristics observed in childhood and personality in young adulthood (Caspi & Silva, 1995), even connections with childhood temperament – measured as early as age 3- and criminal behaviour (Block, Block, & Keyes, 1988; Caspi, 2000; Raine, Reyonds, Venables, Mednick, & Farrington, 1998). However, there is greater support for stability of personality throughout adulthood (Alwin, Cohen, & Newcomb, 1991; Glenn, 1980; Pervin, 2002). As we age we become more consistent and less likely to change, but there still remains the potential *to* change (Roberts & Del Vecchio, 2000). People unconsciously filter experiences, elicit responses from others, and choose certain life paths which are consistent with their personality, so even the person-environment interactions can be seen to support a level of continuity in personality, as well as allowing for the potential for change (Caspi & Roberts, 2001).

The relationship from crime scene aspects to offender characteristics is not as straight forward as it initially appeared to be (Goodwill & Alison, 2007; Mokros & Alison, 2002). The lack of substantial support for the assumption of homology, and the imperfect support found for behavioural consistency is evidence of this – there are other influencing factors not being considered or included in this relationship. A better definition of offender profiling might be "the application of psychological theory and behavioural evidence analysis to the investigation and reconstruction of physical evidence that relates to a particular offender's crime scene characteristics, victimology, motivation and behaviour patterns" (Gee & Belofastov, 2007; p. 62). However, even this definition leaves out key aspects of information that many profiles overlook – offender perception and offence context. The influence of such factors is recognised in models of personality (e.g., Mischel and Shoda's [1995] CAPS model).

Traditional personality functioning is seen as more of a static consistent model, while more current conceptions of personality and behaviour, see behaviour as more dynamic and conditional on the individual *and* the specific situations in which they find themselves (Shoda, Mischel, & Wright, 1994). The debate is whether people show consistency in their behaviour across situations because of inherent internal personality traits (the person side of the debate), or whether behavioural consistency is affected by the situation, is not inherent in the person, and therefore is contextually variable (the situation side of the debate) (Pervin, 2002). While this debate has not completely dissipated, there has been some headway in an attempt to reconcile the two camps. Allport, Cattell, and Eysenck (founding influences of personality psychology) all recognise to some degree the importance of the situation and the variability of individual behaviour. Allport (1961) acknowledged that our personality dispositions are never completely consistent, but also empathised that we do exhibit relatively enduring patterns of thoughts, feelings, and behaviour (Roberts & Caspi, 2001). Personality interactionists believe the more important question is *"how* do characteristics of the person interact with characteristics of the situation"(Pervin, 2002, p. 78) which allows for the multiple factors that contribute to the exhibition of behaviour (Ahadi & Diener, 1989), and for the interaction between both the internal personal traits, and the influence of the situation on a person's behaviour.

The link between A and C represents a complex and challenging set of variables and circumstances that work to modulate criminal behaviour – a relationship largely ignored in the current pool of literature. The original idea that the way a person thinks directs the person's behaviour (Douglas et al., 1986) does not account for the multitude of other variables that are present at any given moment which influence behaviour. No two offenders are exactly alike; they do not do the very same thing in the very same way or for the very same reasons throughout their offences. Although, if the situation in which the offender's crimes are committed are similar, and have the same or similar psychological meaning for them, it would follow that behavioural consistency in this circumstance would be expected (Mischel & Shoda, 1995; Shoda et al., 1994). Even when the same discernible behaviour is observed there can be several different reasons for why and how this behaviour was brought about – similar acts can occur for different reasons, and different acts can happen to serve similar purposes (Douglas et al., 1986). If this is true, there are implications for offender profiling. While no professional will argue against the fact that people do not respond *exactly* the same way in exactly the same situations, this does not mean there are not consistencies within a person's response. Looking at overarching behavioural domains, personality psychology has found there is variation in the consistency of non-criminal behaviour (Funder & Colvin, 1991; Furr & Funder, 2004), concurrently studies looking at criminal behaviours, such as Grubin et al. (2001) and Bennell and Canter (2002), have also found this. Thus, while there will be variations across people's behaviours, and more specifically in the ways offenders commit their crimes, there will also be many significant similarities. When considering the differences and similarities among people, and offenders, given similar characteristics and backgrounds, similar thought processes, and similar situations, we could expect a similar *degree* and *level* of responses and behaviours to occur, both across offenders, and within a single offender.

In an attempt to integrate the approaches to personality theory, and understand the stable intra-individual patterns of variability inherent in an individual's behaviour across situations more dynamic conceptualisations of trait theory have been developed. One such model is Mischel and Shoda (1995; 1998) cognitive-affective processing system (CAPS)[1]. CAPS

---

[1] The CAPS model has been the focus in much Offender Profiling discussions (e.g., Alison et al., 2002; Markson, Woodhams, & Bond, 2010; Sorochinski & Salfati, 2010; Woodhams, 2012).

places the conception of personality within the social world in order to contextualise the individual and allow the examination of the reciprocal interaction between person-environment (Mischel & Shoda, 2008). Person variables, such as how people construe/encode situations and themselves, are important, but these are components of a dynamic and interconnected organised system of relationships, that interacts with the social-psychological situations (Mischel & Shoda, 2008). CAPS theory assumes that people differ in the ease with which cognitive and affective mental representations or units, CAUs, become active, but also that individual differences reflect the accessibility of CAUs as well as the distinctive organisation of relationships among them (this is the stable structure of the personality system) (Mischel & Shoda, 2008). The CAUs are comprised of constructs, expectations, and beliefs of how the person sees themselves, people and events around them, and the situations they encounter. They encompass the affects, the feelings, emotions and affective responses, as well as, the desired outcomes and goals of the individual. The potential behaviours and the *if...then* scripts and strategies for attaining outcomes, and one's own behaviour and internal states are also a part of the CAUs (Mendoza-Denton & Mischel, 2007). The CAPS theory postulates that the meanings of situations will vary and have different impacts between people, as well as within an individual, and on different occasions (Eaton, South, & Krueger, 2009). This means that different situations will activate different CAUs; producing an *if.....then* behavioural contingency. Therefore, when the situations (the *ifs*) change, so will the *thens* (Mischel & Shoda, 2008). CAPS theory highlights three points: 1) personality systems are understood in terms of their cognitive-affective units, as well as, the coherent organisation of those units; 2) this system functions and interacts with the social environment. Lastly, 3) people will behave in variable and distinctive manners which characterise that individual (Cervone, 2005).

The CAPS model is one paradigm for theoretically testing and supporting the assumptions of offender profiling as it allows for both behavioural consistency within the individual, even cross-situationally. In addition, it provides logical underpinning for the hypotheses of behavioural distinctiveness and similarities across crime types and between offenders.

CRITIQUE OF OFFENDER PROFILING LITERATURE

An area in which offender profiling has been subject to critical evaluations is in terms of the body of literature on this topic. Reviews have concluded that common sense rationales are abundant, especially those articles written pre-1990, those with a more clinical orientation, or those authored by law enforcement professionals (Snook, Eastwood, Gendreau, Goggin, & Cullen, 2007). Typologies of offenders have been a major product coming out of the profiling literature. The development of a typology, or classification, of categories of offenders within specific crime types allows, in theory, for the assignment of a crime scene to a specific category that will have a corresponding category of offender that exhibits those specific categories of crime scene characteristics with known characteristics. The premise behind typologies and basic profiling is that each offender type within the typology is defined by the occurrence of characteristics, behaviours, and crime-related variables that are representative of it. Within each type the same characteristics co-occur regularly with each other, and they do not co-occur with the specific characteristics of any other type of offender (Sarangi & Youngs, 2006). The idea being that each offender within a type will share the same, or similar, characteristics, behaviours, and crime-related variables.

Dowden, Bennell, and Bloomfield's (2007) systematic review of the offender profiling literature identified at least 132 published articles related to offender profiling since the mid-1970s. What they found was a rapid increase in the amount of offender profiling research, as well as an increase in the statistical sophistication (e.g., none, descriptive, or inferential) of the research. It was also found that there was an increase in the amount of studies being published in peer-reviewed journals, although the majority of these published articles were discussion pieces, basic assumptions, literature reviews, or experiential studies, all of which provided little or no statistical analyses. Despite this observation, Dowden et al.'s review shows there's been an advancement of academic peer-reviewed offender profiling research (both in volume and statistical sophistication). Even with the advancements in the offender profiling research, there is still a need for further empirical testing of the assumptions underpinning profiling (Snook et al., 2007).

TYPOLOGICAL APPROACHES TO OFFENDER PROFILING

The various approaches to profiling are commonly grouped into three schools of thought: a criminal investigative approach, a clinical practitioner approach, and a scientific statistical approach (Alison et al., 2010; Muller, 2000). For the current chapter, the criminal investigative approach will be further partitioned into the pragmatic and theory-led approaches. The emphasis of this chapter will be on these four approaches of offender profiling as their explicit aim and focus is on predicting personal characteristics, not always the case with other forms of behavioural investigative advice (e.g., linkage analysis; geographical profiling; equivocal death analysis), and will centre around sexual aggressors of adult women (e.g., rape and sexual murder).

Pragmatic Criminal Investigative Approach to Offender Profiling

In the USA, the FBI provides behavioural-based investigative and operational support through the National Centre for the Analysis of Violent Crime's (NCAVC) Behavioural Analysis Unit (BAU). The BAU assists law enforcement agencies by their review and assessment of a criminal act, by interpreting the offender's behaviour during the crime, and the interactions between the offender and the victim during the commission of the crime and as expressed in the crime scene (FBI, 2008). One of the more well-known examples of a classification system for offenders is that of the Organised/Disorganised typology of serial killers outlined by Ressler, Burgess and Douglas (1988). This classification system was originally developed to examine lust and sexual sadistic murderers, in which ultimate sexual satisfaction is achieved through the brutal and sadistic killing of the victim (Arrigo & Purcell, 2001). Developed through the review of case records, direct observations, and investigative interviews with of a sample of thirty-six men who were representative of this group of sexually oriented murderers, this dichotomy has since been applied to non-sadistic, non-serial sexual homicides and also types of arson (Ressler et al., 1988).

According to the typology at the basic level, the organised murderer is believed to lead an orderly life, which is reflected in the crimes he commits. He has an average to above average intelligence, which is displayed in the evidence of planning of his offences; he will bring and take with them a weapon of choice, and will exert control over his victim by use of restraints, and he will be socially competent. The disorganised murderer will have average to below-average intelligence, be socially incompetent, will display little if any planning of the offence, and will leave the body in open view; their crime scene will show an overall sense of disorder. Two further categories of "mixed" and "sadistic" were later developed by Douglas, Burgess, and Ressler (1992). The mixed category contains elements from both the organised and disorganised categories, while the sadistic category described those offenders who derive pleasure and gratification from causing suffering and pain, through torture and humiliating their victims. While only recently empirically tested, and found unreliable (see Canter, Alison, Alison, & Wentink, 2004), the organised/disorganised dichotomy has been widely used and praised in police investigations across the USA and other countries worldwide (Snook, Cullen, Bennell, Taylor, & Gendreau, 2008).

Another typology of serial murder put forward by Holmes and Holmes (1998) was a development of an earlier typology of Holmes and De Burger (1988). Holmes and Holmes' typology outlined five classifications of serial murderers, developed through the examination of 110 known serial murderers, through court transcripts, interview data, case studies, clinical reports and biographical accounts. The five types in their classification were: 1) the Visionary killer, 2) the Mission killer, 3) the Hedonistic-Thrill killer, 4) the Hedonistic-Lust killer, and 5) the Power/Control Oriented killer. The visionary killer murders because they are told to by the visions or voices they see and hear. Their offences tend to be chaotic and disordered. While the mission murderer kills those individuals they have judged as unworthy or undesirable. Their offences are swift, with no pre-mortem or post-mortem activities. The hedonistic-thrill killer murders for the pleasure and excitement of the kill, which is often a long process. Whereas, the hedonistic-lust killer kills for the sexual gratification, both while the victim is alive and after they have been killed. Both subtypes of the hedonistic killer plan and organise their offences. These killings focus on sexual gratification and sadistic acts. The fifth type of killer, the power or control killer is motivated by the need for power and dominance over another person, and they gain greater gratification the longer the offence goes on (Canter & Wentink, 2004). Holmes and Holmes' types are not mutually exclusive, although they claim that each offender's behaviour will have a dominate theme that would relate to their background characteristics and from this they would be able to be classified into a distinct category (Canter & Wentink, 2004). While, the Holmes and Holmes classification system may use different variables and words to describe the crimes and offenders, it is largely influenced by the original FBI organised/disorganised typology (Canter, Alison, Alison, & Wentink, 2004).

Knight and Prentky (1990) classification model of sexual offenders is primarily based on the motivation of the offender and takes into account that many offenders may not fit into a discreet number of limited categories. Their classification model, The Massachusetts Treatment Center Rape Classification System (MTC:R3), is based on the assumption that while sex offenders are a heterogeneous group, there will be some similarities in those offenders who commit sexual assaults (Knight, 1999; Robertiello & Terry, 2007). Based on the examination of clinical and criminal files, standardised tests, clinical interviews, and self-report measures, The MTC: R3 includes four typologies: the opportunistic offender (low/high social competence) whose offences are impulsive and unplanned predatory acts, with immediate sexual gratification as the motivating factor; the pervasively angry offender, who is motivated by anger and hatred, and will use violence regardless of victim resistance; and the vindictive offender (low/high social competence) motivated by power, control, and hatred, who is likely to physically harm, humiliate, and degrade his/her victims. The sexual offenders are subdivided into non-sadistic (low/high social competence) and the sadistic (fantasy/nonfantasy), both are preoccupied with sex and aggression, as well as physical inadequacy (Goodwill, Alison, & Beech, 2009; Robertiello & Terry, 2007). The MTC: R3 has been found to be a valid and reliable classification system for studying and classifying sexual offenders (Fargo, 2007; Knight, 1999), and a valuable framework in devising and providing treatment programmes for offenders (Canter, Bennell, Alison, & Reddy, 2003; Knight, 1999).

Ressler et al. (1988) have outlined the stages of generating a criminal profile used by the FBI. Stage one, *profiling inputs*, is about gathering and studying all the information that is relevant to solving the crime (e.g., crime scene information, victimology, forensic information, police reports, photos). Any information that deals with possible suspects should not be examined or included; as such information may unconsciously prejudice the profile and distort the impartiality and objectivity of the profile. Stage two is the *decision process models* in which all the profiling inputs are organised and arranged into significant patterns. It is during this stage that aspects of the type of homicide (e.g., single, double, triple, mass, spree, serial), the primary objective of the offender (e.g., whether homicide was primary or secondary motivation), the victim risk level (e.g., victim age, life style), and the risk of apprehension for the offender are being evaluated. The levels of escalation, the amount of time for the committing of the crime and location factors are also assessed during this stage. Stage three, *crime assessment*, involves the profiler reconstructing the sequences of events of the crime to establish just how certain things happened, how the people involved interacted with each other and to determine which category the crime fits into, organised vs. disorganised. The offender's motivation is considered at this stage and combined with the overall assessment of the crime scene. The fourth stage is the generation of the *criminal profile*. The background information, physical characteristics, habits, beliefs and values, pre-offending behaviour will be included and commented on based on the crime scene information provided. It is at this stage that investigative recommendations might also be made. The fifth stage in profile generation is the application of the profile to the *investigation*. The criminal profile is written into a report, provided to the agency and added into the investigation. The profiler will re-evaluate the profile if or when new information becomes available. In the sixth and final stage, *apprehension*, the profile is evaluated for its accuracy and success at identifying the suspect.

Critique of the Pragmatic Criminal Investigative Approach

The original profiling conducted by the FBI, based on 36 interviews, was shaped by intuition, educated guesswork, and the agent's experience in criminal investigations (Holmes & De Burger, 1988). The typologies were not quantitatively tested nor based on stringent methodological research and researchers have subsequently found deficiencies within the profiles the FBI agents were producing (Alison & Canter, 1999; Muller, 2000).

The organised/disorganised dichotomy was based on a very small sample of interviewed sexual murderers and lacked any comparison or control group (Coleman & Norris, 2000). Canter et al. (2004) points out that the interviews relied on retrospective self-reports from the offenders which can be very inaccurate as they relied on the offender's memory about specific points in time and on 'trust' that the offender did not lie about their experiences and offences. In addition, no comparison group was used, thereby calling into question whether any of the variables are actually *specific* to adulthood sexual murder perpetration. As well, the majority of the sample used by Ressler, Burgess and Douglas did not experience social deviance in the early years of their lives, which has been found frequently in the backgrounds of sexual homicide perpetrators (Meloy, 2000), meaning that any conclusion drawn using this dichotomy will not be generalizable across any other sample or study. The original sample of men were identified as either organised or disorganised, not based on any scientific research or theoretical underpinning, but on the combination of experience and intuition of the officers involved in conducting the study (Muller, 2000). This intuitive separation was done a priori, before any statistical tests were used to analysis the differences between the two groups, which some argue led to a self-fulfilling prophecy, rather than a valid behavioural dichotomy (Kocsis, Irwin, & Hayes, 1998).

Canter (1994) also criticised this classification as the boundaries between the two distinctive typologies of serial murders are often blurred and non-distinct – many offenders would be a hybrid of more than one type (Canter et al., 2004). Neither group is particularly rich in detail, nor does the typology address key issues relating to the offender's identity, nor lend to the apprehension of the offender as they often leave the investigator with some abstract notion of the offender and the crime (Keppel & Walter, 1999). No published literature exists detailing just how these typologies are to be used in the evaluation of a crime scene nor for the purposes of developing a profile (Palermo & Kocsis, 2005).The inability to confidently and consistently assign offenders to one or the other type of offender affects the ability to draw concrete conclusions about the offender's characteristics, thereby, questioning the pragmatic utility of this classification system.

Holmes and Holmes' serial murder typology has also come under scrutiny. Hicks and Sales (2006) have questioned the reliability and validity of the four main types as there is no indication of any theoretical or empirical derivation. Canter and Wentink (2004) had five major criticisms of Holmes and Holmes' serial murder typology. The first criticism is the lack of any systematic account of how the interviews with 110 serial murders were conducted, and how these interviews led to their classification system. Secondly, there has been no direct empirical testing of the five typologies (until Canter and Wentink's study) and therefore no verification of co-occurrence of any type. The terminology used to describe each typology is not fully described (i.e. act-focused versus process-focused) leading to uncertainty as to under what conditions and offender or offence should be assigned to one type or another. A further criticism was the overlap of features between the five typologies (i.e. controlled crime scene, body movement, specific victim were listed for both lust and power/control killer). The fifth criticism, is based around the inherent assumptions of a typology which Holmes and Holmes' typology fails to adhere to: "with each type, the characteristics that define that specific type are likely to co-occur with one another with regularity...and specific characteristics of one type are assumed not to co-occur with any frequency with the specified characteristics of another type" (Canter & Wentink, p. 493). Upon testing the five types using a multidimensional approach they found little evidence to support the distinction between the serial murders based on Holmes and Holmes' 1989 typology.

Knight and Prentky's classification is also not without its potential limitations. The interpretation and classification of the offender into one of the types in the MTC: R3 is partly subjective and based on the interpreter's experience, skill, and intuition, potentially leading to unreliability (Goodwill et al., 2009). There are also concerns surrounding the generalizability to a wider population as the typologies were developed using only those offenders held within the MTC, which are a sample of "sexually dangerous" offenders and therefore not representative of other samples of sexual offenders (Barbaree, Seto, Serin, Amos, & Preston, 1994).

The publication of an FBI profiling methodology, described in both in Douglas et al. (1986) and Ressler et al.'s (1988), has been criticised for lack of description about how they constructed their typologies (e.g., organised/disorganised) (Beauregard & Proulx, 2002; Canter et al., 2004), the typical occurrence of many of the organised features in most serial murders (Canter et al., 2004), and for its lack of theoretical backing (Canter, 1994; Muller, 2000). Muller (2000) also points out, the FBI methodology falls short of being scientific based on its lack of falsifiability (the ability of a theory to be tested – verified or falsified) and ability to propose hypotheses that are empirically testable. As much of the early FBI methodology was based on their experience and intuition, was not part of the public domain, and focused on perceived fantasies and sexual motivations, it was hard to empirically test. Despite its critics, the FBI model of profiling still remains influential (Canter et al., 2004; Hicks & Sales, 2006).

Theory-Led Approach to Offender Profiling

While the original profiling and reports produced by the FBI might have been more experience-led, other endeavours incorporated theory, by trying to address the behaviours, motivational continuum and the effects of learning on the offender (e.g., Fisher & Beech, 2007). These tried to address the criticism of the pragmatic approach of not being scientific (falsifiable) by producing and submitting their works into the criminal investigative approach to be peer-reviewed. Sex and aggression have been two categories of motivating factors that have been used to categorise rape (Cohen, Garfalo, Boucher, & Seghorn, 1971; Cohen, Seghorn, & Calamas, 1969). Groth, Burgess, and Holmstrom (1977) and Groth and Birnbaum (1979) also argue that power and anger are primary non-sexual motivations for rape. Each of these occur in a variety of different forms throughout the rape literature. For example, anger and aggression may be evident in different forms of hostility, or destructive acts, such as verbal violence, gratuitous violence, tearing the victim's clothing, and acts meant to humiliate the victim (Canter et al., 2003; Canter & Heritage, 1990). Offenders driven primarily by sex may be preoccupied with sexual fantasies and sexual gratification or pleasure (Mann & Hollin, 2007). Power as a motivation may be expressed through behaviours that demonstrate the offender's control over the victim and control of the offence. These may include the use of various levels of coercion, the binding or gagging of the victim, and actions that suggest pre-planning and preparation (Canter et al., 2003). Sadistic aggression may be the extreme forms of these motivations.

The heterogeneity of the motivations behind sex offending has led to the development of various typologies (Groth et al., 1977; Knight & Prentky, 1990) in which offending behaviours are interconnected with explanations of the intentions, motivations, and inferred offender characteristics (Canter, 1996). Groth et al.'s (1977, 1979) anger, power, and sadistic typology of rapists is one such categorisation. The Anger rapists' offences are characterised by physical brutality, with excessive amounts of violence and force (Palermo, 2003), while the sexual component is used as a means to express and discharge the offender's built up feelings of anger and rage. Often the sexual acts are viewed with disgust by the offender and are used to punish the victim (Pardue & Arrigo, 2008). The offender will often use a violent blitz attack, striking, beating and tearing at their victim. Alternatively, the offender will try to gain the trust of the victim using a confidence-style approach, talking to them and then suddenly attacking the victim. The rape is not usually fantasised about beforehand, and the attacks tend to be of short duration and impulsive or spontaneous, triggered by some upsetting event involving a significant (female) figure in the offender's life. The anger rapist uses sex as their weapon and is fuelled by the motive of revenge (Groth & Birnbaum, 1979; Groth et al., 1977).

For the power rapist, the desire of the offender is to possess their victim sexually, not physically harm them. Often, the sexual acts become a way for the offender to compensate for their feelings of inadequacy, and becomes a way for the offender to express their level of mastery, strength, control, authority, identity and capability (Groth & Birnbaum, 1979). The amount of force used is only that to accomplish the sexual assault and gain control over the victim. Often this is done using verbal threats, intimidation with a weapon or physical force when needed. The victims of power rapists are often held for longer periods and repeatedly assaulted while held captive, further enforcing the idea of power and dominance over the victim.

The sexual attacks of the power rapists are often fantasised about beforehand, with the offender imaging the victim initially resisting and then in spite of themselves, becoming less resistant and more receptive, and even gratefully submitting, to the offender's sexual prowess and embrace (Groth et al., 1977). The fantasised excitement, anxiety and anticipated pleasure is never fully realised for the offender and the offender is disappointed and finds little sexual satisfaction from the actual assault. The disappointment in the offence often leads to an escalation of violence used during the attacks as the offender becomes more desperate to achieve the fantasised experience that escapes them (Groth & Birnbaum, 1979). The victims of power rapist tend to be approximately the same age as the offender or younger and where choice is based on availability, accessibility, and vulnerability (Palermo & Kocsis, 2005).

In the third type, the sadistic rapist, sexuality becomes fused with aggression in a manner that transforms anger and power into something that becomes erotic, although interconnected and often at the extremes of the various motivations and corresponding behaviours (Canter et al., 2003). The offender finds the maltreatment of their victim gratifying, and derives pleasure in their torment, anguish, distress, helplessness and suffering (Groth et al., 1977; Hazelwood & Burgess, 1987). Bondage, torture and various bizarre and ritualistic actions are the focus of the attacks, accompanied by explicitly abusive acts (e.g., biting, burning with cigarettes) and in extreme cases mutilation of specific areas of the victim's body (e.g., breasts, genitalia, buttocks) all of which play a part in his masturbatory fantasies. In addition, foreign objects may be used to penetrate the victim sexually. The excitement for the sadistic rapist comes from the infliction of pain upon their victim, which is meticulously planned beforehand. This type of rapist stalks, abducts, abuses, and even murders their victims, taking precautions against detection (Groth & Birnbaum, 1979). The infliction of pain can provide gratification, or can act as a necessary step to other forms of sexual activity. The sadistic rapist's excitement increases with the level of aggression they use, and the more powerful they feel. Typically, there is an increase in the aggression from one offence to the next, even though the attacks themselves may have many similar aspects. These individuals are usually able to hide their offending, and are often described as quite personable, likeable and friendly (Dietz, Hazelwood, & Warren, 1990; Groth & Birnbaum, 1979).

The original 1977 rapist typology of Groth, Burgess, and Holmstrom was reviewed and modified by Keppel and Walter (1999) which now includes four types of sexual murder (see Table 1.1):

Table 1.1. Keppel and Walter's Classification of Sexual Murder by Motivation, Victim Selection, and Level of Planning

	Motivation	Victim Selection	Weapon Selection and Use	Level of Planning	Offender Characteristics
Power Reassurance	Sexual gratification	Specific; may be acquaintance	Escalation of weapon selection and use	Planned rape; unplanned murder	Mid 20's; criminal history (sexual offences); socially isolated; unmarried; troubled military service; use of porn
Power Assertive	Power, control, dominance	Stranger	Knife; rope; Brought to scene and used	Planned rape, unplanned murder	Early 20's; heavy use of alcohol and drugs; criminal history (burglary, theft); unsuccessful relationship history; social isolated; troubled Military service; antisocial; use of porn
Anger Retaliatory	Anger	Specific; symbolic of person they seek to take revenge on	Fists; blunt objects; knives	Planned rape; planned murder	Mid to late 20's; unsuccessful relationship history; criminal history (violent offences)
Anger Excitation (sadistic)	Sadistic sexual gratification	Specific; symbolic of offender's fantasies	Ropes; ligatures; knives; specialised tools of torture	Planned rape; planned murder	Variable age; potentially married; unmarked military service; use of porn; potential drug use

1) *Power Reassurance*, represents a planned, single rape of the victim with an unplanned death resulting because the victim resists the offender's attempts of sexual seduction. The sexual offence is a means for the rapist to express his sexual competence and when this fails, the subsequent killing permits him to sexually explore further and re-affirm his sexual

competence by allowing him to carry out sexual acts that he was unable to while the victim was alive. Often the victim is someone that the offender watches, or they may be a casual acquaintance (e.g., neighbour) (Keppel & Walter, 1999).

2) *Power Assertive*, this is a planned rape with little concern shown for the victim. The killing of the victim is unplanned, often resulting from an increase in physical aggression used to control the victim. The sexual assault serves as a basis to assert the perpetrator's masculinity and dominance over the victim (Keppel & Walter, 1999; Pardue & Arrigo, 2008). Often there are multiple ante mortem rapes of the victim. The resulting death of the victim represents for the offender the success of asserting their power and control. The victim will often be a stranger and was chosen based on opportunity and surprise. The offender will spend very little time with the victim once death has been achieved (Keppel & Walter, 1999).

3) *Anger Retaliatory*, the rape and murder are both planned with the murder involving overkill. This attack is perpetrated out of vengeance, and the victim is symbolic of the person the offender is seeking to take revenge upon (Keppel & Walter, 1999).

4) *Anger Excitation (Sadistic)*, these sexual attacks and subsequent murder are planned. The infliction of pain, mutilation, and the terrorising of the victim is for the gratification of the offender; all serving to feed the offender's appetite for killing. There is prolonged contact with the victim which can last hours or even days. The victim is chosen based on the offender's fantasies (Keppel & Walter, 1999).

Critique of the Theory-Led Approach

While the above approaches highlight possible motivations for sexual offending, such as power, anger and sadistic pleasure, attributed from the crime scene analysis, the classification lacks empirical support and evidence (Fisher & Beech, 2007). To be able to infer statistical associations there needs to be in place a system of analysis and measurement. This is where the classifications within this approach fall down – they provide descriptions of abstract concepts (e.g., anger; power), but do not provide a concrete way of measuring them (Cheshire, 2004). The original typology developed by Groth et al. (1977) was not developed to specifically categorise an offender into one type or another, but as an explanation of the different facets of a sexual offender. Nor were the types mutually exclusive or consistent, again making it extremely hard to operationalize the different types. There is considerable overlap between the different types of Keppel and Walter's typology with regards to type of crime scene (e.g., organised versus disorganised), whether the offender has previous criminal histories, or had served in the military, their use of a weapon during their offence, and whether they have or had emotional or relational problems (Hicks & Sales, 2006). Therefore, the ability to draw conclusive inferences about the offender from the information from the crime scene is not feasible.

While, the descriptions provided within this approach attempt to incorporate theory around motivations and possible links with personality disorders, they are often still based on individual experience and knowledge of those developing the classifications, and as such are subject to the same limitations as the 'Early Investigative approach', as well as those of the Clinical approach outlined below.

Clinical Approach to Offender Profiling

This approach to profiling is heavily reliant on clinical judgment, training, knowledge, experience, and/or intuition, with the methods used varying according to the individual practitioner (Alison et al., 2010). The primary focus is on the specific details of each particular case. Profilers of this approach see each case as unique and believe they should be treated as such (Boon, 1997). As a result, this individualistic clinical approach leaves very few models to assess its scientific merit (Muller, 2000).

The psychodynamic approach to profiling is based on the clinical experience of the practitioner (Turco, 1990). Turco's four-step model was based around the notion that all violent behaviour was a manifestation of the mother-child struggle, where female victims were representations of all the negative elements of the mother. In the first step, the profiler considers the crime in its entirety, looking for the underlying psychodynamic processes. In the second step, the crime scene is assessed for any signs of a neurological or brain disorder. Thirdly, the profiler is required to analyse the crime scene in terms of the separation-individuation phase of the offender. Lastly, in an attempt to construct and compose a profile of the unknown offender, the demographic characteristics of the offender and victim are analysed.

In an attempt to set out a more systematic approach to profiling, in collaboration, Copson, Badcock, Boon and Britton (1997) compared their individual methodology and produced a "series of steps and set[s] of features, principles and dangers which...other clinical profilers might care to subscribe to" (p. 14). What developed out of this meeting was a 10-step procedural model (see Table 1.2), with the centrepiece of the model being the inference of motive, which is seen as the key to understanding the offender. The inferred motive "allows the importation of factors from relevant literature as starting points for the development of suggested offender characteristics" (p. 15).

The *principles* of clinical profiling as described by Copson et al. (1997, p. 16) instruct that "each piece of advice should be:

(1) *Custom made*: the advice should not rely on the recycling of some kind of generic violent anti-social criminal stereotype;

(2) *Interactive:* at a range of levels of sophistication, depending on the officers' understanding of the psychological concepts at issue; and

(3) *Reflexive:* the advice should be dynamic, in so far as every element has a knock-on effect on every other element, and evolving, in that new information must lead to reconsideration not only of the element(s) of advice directly affected but of the construct as a whole." (p. 16).

Inherent in the principles and approach of clinical profiling are the subsequent dangers. The desire to please may lead to an undermining of objectivity, while the close interaction between the profiler and officer should be avoided in order to avoid any allegations that the profile was developed to fit an already known suspect. As well, it is imperative that all data and information be recorded, even though this is an extremely difficult and time-consuming process. Related to this point, is the failure to produce a summary document of the amassed information, thereby leaving the profile vulnerable to potential misinterpretation (Copson et al., 1997). While, Copson et al. (1997) lay out a model to follow, it does not identify a systematic process for the derivation of inferences as this is dependent on the individual clinician. What they provide instead is a set of principles and dangers, which have relevance in providing behavioural investigative advice.

Table 1.2. Ten Step Procedural Model

Steps	
1	Receive briefing
2	Request case material (depending on the nature of the case
3	Visit crime scene
4	Infer reconstruction of events
	• WHO (in minute detail)
	• HOW (in minute detail)
	• TO WHOM (in minute detail)
5	Infer motive
6	Allows importation of factors from relevant literature
7	Develop psychological constructs (relating back to what/how/to whom)
8	Introduce demographics and social factors
9	Generate a range of elements of advice with probability markers as appropriate
10	Discuss with investigating officer
11	Produce report

A descriptive example of the clinical approach, as applied to sexual murderers, is provided in the work of Clarke and Carter (2000). They identified four types of sexual murderers through their work with a sample of UK sexual offenders in a specialised treatment centre in Brixton Prison in London, UK. Their profiles for types of sexual murderer were as follows:

1) *Sexually motivated murderer*, engages in sophisticated and detailed masturbatory fantasies of killing unknown but specifically targeted victims, and who can be clearly seen as the sadistic type with a primary motivation to kill;
2) *Sexually triggered murderer*, who commits an aggressive, yet controlled murder, where killing is used as a means to keep the victim quiet and to avoid later detection.
3) *Grievance motivated murderer*, who commits an aggressive and uncontrolled murder but who has no prior intent to kill, yet does so because of something the victim does or says during the assault. Extreme violence and/or humiliation against the victim, usually taking a sexual theme (e.g., mutilation to the genitals), will be evident, suggesting a loss of control.
4) *Neuropsychological dysfunction sexual murderer*, which was developed around the unclear motivations of one offender who exhibited clear neuropsychological deficits, and does not necessarily depict a group of sexual offenders.

Critique of the Clinical Approach

In the same manner that the pragmatic approach relies on practical experience, knowledge, and intuition, so too does the clinical approach. This approach is primarily based on the individual clinician's experience and knowledge gained through working with individual clients, and the application of this to drawing conclusions or inferences from crime scene information. Copson et al. (1997), and to some extent Turco (1990), provide the building blocks of providing investigative advice, yet they fail to explicitly provide guidance on *how* one would actually produce a profile. The difficulty is how "to judge when and how a clinician's tacit knowledge gets translated into formalized, explicit, and falsifiable knowledge, as well as how this knowledge subsequently leads to the generation of useful offender profiles" (Alison et al., 2010, p.118). This is a limitation born directly out of the fact that the inferences in practitioner-driven profiling are made through the knowledge and experiences of the particular clinician (Alison, Goodwill, & Alison, 2005). This not only effects the ability to compare this approach with other approaches but also the ability to compare within the clinical approach itself (e.g., between practitioners).

Another issue with this approach, as well as the pragmatic/theory led approaches, is related to the Barnum[2] or the Forer effect[3] (Forer, 1949). People often assume the description provided of the sexual offender is based on psychological assessments that may have been done, even if an assessment has not been provided with the description, and because of this are more inclined to accept it (Snook et al., 2008). Many of the profiles provided by these approaches are ambiguous and appear to describe any suspect (Alison, Smith, Eastman, & Rainbow, 2003; Alison, Smith, & Morgan, 2003). Related to this personal validation effect, is the suggestion that exposure to ambiguous descriptions may increase the faith in psychological assessment methods and the positive perceptions of the individual clinician's views, even if the method is not valid or the profiler is not actually skilled (Snook et al., 2008). The ambiguous nature of many of the profiles can also be seen to support a confirmation bias[4], in which those using the profile may 'notice' or look for information contained within the profile that confirms their preconceptions or hypotheses. This has obvious implications if a criminal is then later apprehended, as any ambiguous information contained within the profile, may appear to retrospectively describe them (Snook et al., 2008).

Statistical Approach to Offender Profiling

The statistical/research approach to criminal profiling was pioneered by Canter (e.g., Canter et al., 2003; Canter & Heritage, 1990; Canter, Hughes, & Kirby, 1998; Canter & Ioannou, 2004). The statistical approach, which asserts to be grounded in scientific methodology, is based on the multivariate analysis of the behavioural and other crime scene information to infer the characteristics, and psychological process, of unknown offenders (Ainsworth, 2001). The predictions are derived from the analysis of the characteristics and crime scene information of offenders who have previously committed crimes and who have been apprehended, and applying these results to those unknown offenders being investigated (Snook et al., 2008).

---

[2] "The phenomenon whereby people willingly accept personality interpretations comprised of vague statements with a high base-rate occurrence in the general population" (Snyder, Jae Shenkel, & Lowery, 1977, p. 104).

[3] Tendency for people to judge general, universally valid statements about personality as specific to themselves (Snook et al., 2008).

[4] See Wason, P.C. (1960). On the failure to eliminate hypotheses in a conceptual task. *The Quarterly Journal of Experimental Psychology, 12*, 129-140.

One of the earliest statistical based studies was carried out by Canter and Heritage (1990) in their development of a five-facet empirical classification for profiling sexual offenders. Information on the crime scene behaviour of 27 sexual offenders responsible for 66 assaults were analysed to develop a model. A method based on Facet Theory and using a type of Multidimensional Scaling procedure (MDS) known as Smallest Space Analysis (SSA) (Lingoes, 1973; 1979) (see Shye, Elizur, & Hoffman, 1994, for in-depth review of this technique) was used to identify five facets of sexual offending based on the offenders' behaviours during the commission of their offences.

"...Facet theory is a structural theory. In essence, it provides an approach to defining behavioural constructs and to testing hypotheses concerning the correspondence between behavioural definitions and empirical observations on variables representative of a construct" (Dancer, 1990, p. 367). Facets are sets of attributes, sharing semantic or perceptual properties, representing the underlying conceptual or semantic components of "some larger behavioural universe" (Dancer, 1990, p 367). For facets to be meaningful, they must "characterise various aspects of the content universe, they must represent conceptually distinct attributes of variables, and ... [they] must be mutually exclusive and jointly exhaustive in the context of a particular universe" (Dancer, 1990, p. 368). Non-metric multidimensional scaling (MDS) is used as a structural method to visually conceptualise the structure of a content universe and the empirical structure of observations in that universe (Dancer, 1990). SSA, a non-metric statistical analysis, represents the relationship of every variable to every other variable as distances and points in a Euclidean space, with greater similarity between variables resulting in their closer proximity in the corresponding geometric space. The closer two points are in the space, the more likely the variables co-occur. SSA attempts to find the space with the minimum number of dimensions which preserves the rank order of relations (Guttman & Greenbaum, 1998). The distribution of points on an SSA plot becomes more specific as the distance between the points increases; generally, behaviours get more specific as they are located farther from the centre of the plot and farther away from other points. An SSA plot with a tight clustering of points indicates a higher correlation between those points, and that the offending behaviours are more likely to co-occur with all the other behaviours. A plot with points towards the outer area of the space indicates behaviours, which are less likely to co-occur with all the other behaviours in the dataset. The advantage of SSA, and non-metric MDS, is that no assumptions about the underlying transformation function are made (Steyvers, 2002), and it can be used with ordinal or categorical data (Jaworska & Chupetlovska-Anastasova, 2009).

The early work of Canter and Heritage (1990), and the five facets found (intimacy, sexuality, violence, impersonal and criminality) was important as a first attempt to investigate the relationship between offender behaviours and their characteristics distinct from their inferred motives, which was a main criticism of the FBI and Clinical approaches. Since Canter's early work in the 1990's there have been several more authors (e.g., Beauregard & Proulx, 2002; Canter et al., 1998; Kocsis, Cooksey, & Irwin, 2002; Lundrigan & Canter, 2001; Porter & Alison, 2004; Porter, Woodworth, Earle, Drugge, & Boer, 2003; Santtila, Hakkanen, Canter, & Elfgren, 2003; Youngs, 2004) producing academically peer-reviewed research into many aspects of offender profiling.

More recently, Canter (1994) found that rapists' behaviour could be defined in terms of the role the victim plays for the offender (e.g., person, victim/object, or vehicle) in his analysis of 105 cases of rape. This finding was based on the underlying interpersonal interactions between the offender and the victim, which he maintains is distinct from any motivational factors. Building on this theme of victim role, Canter et al. (2003) suggested that rape could be classified by theme as well as by the severity and type of victim violation (e.g., personal, physical, and sexual). The four themes of classification were: 1) hostility, in which the offender uses aggression and violence to demean/humiliate victim; 2) control, where behaviours are utilised to immobilise the victim; 3) theft, when the offender uses the opportunity for some instrumental gain; and 4) involvement, where the offender attempts to form a pseudo-relationship with the victim. However, it should be noted that almost one-third of the rapes could not be classified as belonging to one theme, and so a fifth mixed group was created.

Another study looking at the classification of sexual offenders was that of Beech, Oliver, Fisher and Beckett (2005) in their evaluation of the Sex Offender Treatment Programme (SOTP). They classified a sample of 170 sexual offenders (112 rapists and 58 sexual murderers) into three groups according to the main motivation for their offending using MCMI-III personality profiles. The grievance motivated offender was impulsive and vengeful and blamed others for their actions. They had low insight and were highly suspicious and resentful of others. The sexually motivated offenders planned and fantasised about their offence beforehand, chose their victims and tended to believe that men were entitled to have sex. They tended not to be particularly impulsive, hostile or aggressive and used violence for instrumental purposes (e.g., to avoid detection). The sadistically motivated offender, which consisted of sexual murderers only, was fascinated and aroused by sexual violence, such as death and/or torture. They planned their offences, which often involved strangulation, mutilation and post-mortem sexual activity.

Ter Beek, Van Den Eshof and Mali (2010) investigated the offending and characteristics of a sample of Dutch rapists. Their objective was to develop a statistical model that would be able to indicate the probability of predicting basic offender characteristics (spatial behaviour, criminal history, and living situation) from observable crime characteristics, consisting of modus operandi, victim-offender interaction, and violence. They looked at groupings of separate crime scene variables (method of approach, verbal behaviour, sexual behaviour, use of violence) and single offender characteristics (spatial behaviour-distance travelled, living situation, previous convictions), and found that their models for 'distance' and 'violence convictions' were promising. For example, they found that if the offender stole an item from the victim, if he was intoxicated, if they strangled and/or demeaned the victim, if the victim had been forced to disrobe themselves, and/or if the offender performed cunnilingus on the victim, the probability that the offender had previous conviction for violence increased. This 'violence convictions' model predicted the likelihood of previous violent convictions in 71.1% of the case when 11 crime scene variables were taken into consideration. The study in general supports the claim that crime characteristics can be used to indicate probable offender characteristics. Although, these findings need to be interpreted with caution as the prediction of previous sexual assault convictions, for example, was only slightly better than chance.

Critique of Statistical Approach

While Alison and Canter (1999) were highly critical of the FBI and clinical approaches of profiling, labelling them 'intuitive' the statistical approach is not without its critics as well.

Copson et al. (1997) make the point that statistics alone do not predict the future, and extrapolation from them does not support the notion that the past will be identical to the future, nor do they inherently support the underlying assumption that similar people will do things, such as committing crime, in similar ways. The use of statistics does not guarantee the inferences drawn will be valid or reliable, as these are assuming the data, itself, are consisting of relevant and significant components, and that the statistics applied are appropriate (Copson et al., 1997).

Sturidsson et al. (2006) attempted to replicate Canter and Heritage's (1990) study and their development of five theoretical elements of sexual offence behaviours using a sample of 146 unsolved, single victim, single perpetrator sexual assault cases collected in Sweden. The motivational dimensions initially presented by Canter and Heritage using multi-dimensional scaling (MDS) were not replicated. The lack of replication could be due to the differences between Sturidsson et al.'s sample and Canter and Heritage's. Also, Sturidsson et al.'s sample were all single offence sexual offenders, whereas, some of Canter and Heritage's sample were repeat sexual offenders, which is a problem in itself, as any apparent structure could be due to the consistency of these serial offenders. However, it should be noted that upon review, Goodwill, Alison, and Humann (2009) found that Sturidsson et al.'s use of MDS was incorrect as they had used the ALSCAL procedure in SPSS, which produces a dissimilarity matrix, as opposed to using the PROXSCAL procedure, which produces a similarity matrix. This would have resulted in the variables of high frequency being positioned around the periphery of the plot, while low frequency variables were clustered more centrally, meaning the objects which are positioned closer together are more dissimilar – which is inconsistent with other MDS studies (e.g., Alison & Stein, 2001; Canter & Heritage, 1999; Canter et al., 2004; Canter et al., 2003; Mokros & Alison, 2002), where the opposite solution is utilised.

Questions have been raised as to the use of MDS, itself, as a statistical research method, because replication across several studies (Canter & Heritage, 1990; House, 1997; Kocsis et al., 2002) using similar variables has not been successful. Highly correlated variables tend to distort MDS, with these clustering in the central area of the plots and less correlated variables being pushed outwards, making meaningful interpretation of the plot problematic. As well, the inclusion of too few variables, upon visual inspection of the graph and a latent dimension, makes determining rapist behaviour less apparent (Sturidsson et al., 2006). The interpretations of the behavioural themes from the plots, where the dividing lines are drawn, are both subjective and dependent on the individual researcher/profiler (Goodwill et al., 2009). MDS has been cited as being affected by cultural differences (Kocsis et al., 2002), the selection and quality of data included in the analysis, as well as how the raw data were recorded and coded (Sturidsson et al., 2006). The sample or data used in the analysis, and generalised into models, are based on a set of known offenders, and therefore, may not be representative of all offenders (Wilson & Alison, 2004).

CRITIQUE OF OFFENDER PROFILING IN GENERAL

Each of the approaches to offender profiling has its inherent strengths and weaknesses, which have been outlined above. That said there are more general critiques of offender profiling that are consistent across the different approaches. Two of the main areas of critical evaluation are the pragmatic use and validity of profiles, and the quality of data used in profile development.

Pragmatic Use and Validity

There are a number of general drawbacks within offender profiling research as a whole. Two important concepts that need to be considered are 1) the validity of the profile, the accuracy of predicting the characteristics of unknown offenders, and 2) the utility of the information contained within the profile, whether it can be used pragmatically by investigators (Kocsis & Palermo, 2007). There have only been a handful of studies which have directly attempted to test the validity and accuracy of profiles and the abilities of profilers as compared to non-profiling groups (e.g., Copson, 1995; Kocsis, 2004; Kocsis, Irwin, Hayes, & Nunn, 2000; Pinizzott & Finkel, 1990). Kocsis and colleagues have concluded from these studies that the profiler groups are more accurate than the comparison groups (typically composed of students, police officers, or psychologists). However, Bennell, Jones, Taylor, and Snook (2006) critic these claims since they pertain not to "absolute" accuracy of the predictions made by profilers, but to the relative accuracy of predictions made by the different groups. So while, it may look like the profilers are more accurate in their predictions, they are still only found to be accurate approximately 45% of the time (Bennell et al., 2006). Bennell et al. argue that this level of accuracy is not high enough to be investigatively useful, as half of the information provided was not useful, and there is no minimum useful accuracy level set. Some of these studies also suffer from internal and external validity problems. The sample of professional profilers used is quite often low (Dowden et al., 2007; Kocsis, 2003) and may not be representative. As well, there is a lack of an objective and tested criteria against which to test a sample of actual profiles (Homant & Kennedy, 1998) as many of the studies testing the accuracy and validity of profiles are artificial in nature (Dowden et al., 2007; Kocsis, 2003), limiting their external validity.

The FBI claim to have tested the validity of profiles compiled by their Behavioural Science Unit in an internal report, with the finding of an 80% degree of accuracy. Yet, this report has never been made public and is only known as it is mentioned in Pinizzott's (1984) work. As this document has not been made public, or made available for scrutiny, the claims of accuracy cannot be verified. There are also many examples of profiles in true-crime stories or biographies in which claims of profiling accuracy are made, although the ability to confirm the validity of the profiling techniques used or the profilers themselves is limited, as a large number of these true-crime biographies are written by profilers themselves (e.g. 'The Jigsaw Man' and 'Picking up the Pieces' by Paul Britton).

There is mixed support for the accuracy of offender profiles, as well as for their usefulness as an investigative tool. Some studies show that investigating officers utilise profiles because they believe they work, and are useful in identifying and prioritising suspects (Copson, 1995; Jackson, van Koppen, & Herbrink, 1993). For those officers that do not necessarily believe that profiles are useful, yet still use them, this could be because they feel there is nothing lost by using all available investigative techniques (Snook et al., 2008). A study by Alison et al. (2003) raises concern when it comes to assessing the perceived accuracy and usefulness of offender profiles. They found in two separate studies that the majority of police officers and forensic professionals rated both fabricated and genuine profiles as at least somewhat (75%) accurate despite being given distinctly different descriptions of the criminal. Most participants also rated the profile as useful. This relates back to the *perceived* accuracy and utility of offender profiles mentioned earlier in this chapter, and how if the profile is perceived to be accurate this is linked with it being considered as useful as well.

Quality of Data

The quality of data used in profiling research is often limited by what is available, how it can be coded and how rich and/or robust they are. Many studies have limited sample sizes due to the nature of the data collection. Much of the research in this area is conducted by academics that collaborate with law enforcement agencies. With the sharing of data between law enforcement and academia there are many data protection issues which must be addressed. Even after access has been granted, the quality of the data still must be taken into consideration. These data can only be as good as what is available to the officers at the time of the investigation. What is collected is often inaccurate and not in a form that is conducive for empirical research (Mokros & Alison, 2002). The data from law enforcement agencies may vary as a result of disparities in collection protocols across different agencies (e.g., no systematic guidelines for information collection; time constraints), thus lowering internal validity. The evidence is collected for the purpose of a police investigation, not for research purposes, and often with little contextual grounding (Alison, Snook, & Stein, 2001). Without the ability to generalise, and extend the results obtained from studies and make predictions about the larger population of offenders, the application of the results becomes more limited. For example, the original FBI organised/disorganised dichotomy may have been accurate in so much as it explained some of the facets of the 36 individual sexual offenders on which it was based, but it severely lacked any external validity. This means the dichotomy may fail to accurately predict behaviours or characteristics of offenders who were not included in the original sample. A similar argument can be made with Groth et al.'s (1977), or Clarke and Carter's (2000) or Canter and Heritage's (1990) classifications. Although, the information and knowledge coming out of these classifications, and others, has been invaluable in progressing offender profiling and our understanding of offending behaviours and offenders.

Equally, the main advantage in using evidence collected during an investigation is that it represents *naturally* occurring behaviours exhibited by an actual offender; not a controlled subject in a controlled laboratory (Alison et al., 2001). At present, the effective utilisation of the data requires careful consideration of the biases potentially inherent, and any conclusions drawn from research must keep these limitations in mind when making generalisations (Alison, et al., 2003).

DIRECTIONS FOR OFFENDER PROFILING

There has been a shift in the offender profiling paradigm in an attempt to address some of the limitations and criticism raised. One such change has been the replacing of the term 'Offender Profiler' with 'Behavioural Investigative Advise(r)' (BIA) – an indication of the evolution and recognition of the range of input and contributions psychologists might provide during criminal investigations (Rainbow, 2008). BIAs can provide not only profiling advice, but investigative support and recommendations which are grounded in behavioural sciences, investigative knowledge, and in theory. They are a professional group of individuals with vast experience of serious crime and the knowledge to integrate their behavioural advice into an investigation (Rainbow, 2007). They have the potential to contribute to many aspects of the investigative process. While, BIA still does involve what is typically considered to be offender profiling (e.g., crime scene assessment), it also involves providing investigative suggestions, linking of crimes, suspect prioritisation, investigative interviewing, risk assessment, media advice, and familial DNA prioritisation (Rainbow & Gregory, 2009). This broader definition recognises the wider range of evidence-based methods by which psychologists might provide advice with regards to various aspects of a criminal investigation (Alison, McLean, & Almond, 2007). The advice provided is for the increased understanding of an event and for informing and prioritising investigative decision making and actions (Rainbow & Gregory, 2009).

There have been some efforts made with regards to the regulation of the practice of giving and using behavioural and psychological advice. The Association of chief Police Officers (ACPO) implemented a set of working conditions for BIAs, a process to audit and evaluate the behavioural advice provided to investigators, and guidelines for the accurate management of information, enabling evidence-based strategic development, priority setting, resilience, and a clear application process for BIAs (Rainbow, 2008). This system allows for the detailed monitoring of behavioural investigative advice being provided to major crime investigations. This is important as BIAs are not all the same; they have different areas of expertise, and provide a range of services depending on their individual competencies (Rainbow, 2008). BIA represents a more integrated multidisciplinary approach which not only adds to the clinical understanding of offences, but also contributes to investigations (Alison et al., 2010).

There are limitations with regards to the admissibility of BIA as expert evidence in court proceedings as the process and standards of BIA fall short of the admissibility standards due to the heterogeneous nature of profiling and the variation in BIAs' qualifications and specific knowledge (Meyer, 2007). Although steps have begun to provide a clear, transparent, and documented system of the type of knowledge and core competencies, and achievements required for BIAs to fulfil and assess their role successfully (Rainbow, 2008). This more current field widens the scope of the potentially pragmatic application of psychology to criminal investigations through scientifically based, replicable, transparent knowledge and research (Alison et al., 2010).

CONCLUSION

So, *is offender profiling effective?* This is an important question when one considers the faith put in profiles, and the status offender profiling can be given in forensic investigations (Snook et al., 2008). While, some of the preceding studies may have limited results, they show there is the possibility of inferring some offender characteristics from crime scene behaviour and providing (albeit limited) support to the underlying assumptions of offender profiling. The area of offender profiling generates a lot of interest in both the academic field and the everyday world as a result of a few highly prolific cases (e.g., Jack the Ripper, Boston strangler). Historically profiling has been based on 'intuition' and experience, but as the field of offender profiling has matured the need to be more scientific in approach has led to the development of models/typologies of offender behaviour based around the findings of empirical studies.

Different approaches have attempted to define, and operationalize offender profiling based on the individual principles inherent in the approach. The Criminal Investigative approach initially relied heavily on intuition and experience of the FBI agents and who researchers who started publishing in the area of profiling. Although, the development of large databases and systems containing information on serial and violent crime/criminals, such as the FBI's Violent Criminal Apprehension Program (ViCAP) (Collins, Johnson, Choy, Davidson, & MacKay, 1998; Howlett, Hanfland, & Ressler, 1986) and the Violent Crime Linkage System (ViCLAS) in Canada (RCMP; Collins et al., 1998), has allowed for the utilisation of a lot of information and data, and the drawing upon of many of the same theories and models that many in the academic field and other areas of investigative psychology use (Snook et al., 2012). The Clinical approach developed a model of offender profiling centered on the concept of motives. While, the Statistical approach aimed to provide a testable psychological and scientific framework for inferring characteristics.

None of the approaches alone explain the complexities of offending. The FBI/Pragmatic approaches bring with them a multitude of investigative experience; the Clinical an abundance of medical and intimate client-based knowledge; while the Statistical approach provides a means in which to more objectively measure and examine offending behaviour. Without the experience, knowledge, and information that is engrained and gathered in the first two approaches, the ability to know which variables to look for or code for would be lost. While the latter statistical approach, allows for the removal of the individual, the individual opinions and biases, and for an objective examination of the patterns and findings. Therefore, the way forward should seek to integrate all of the approaches (Alison, West, & Goodwill, 2004; Alison et al., 2010). Together the approaches strengthen each other and give weight and support to each other and more importantly, offender profiling as a whole.

REFERENCES

Ahadi, S., & Diener, E. (1989). Multiple determinants and effect size. *Journal of Personality and Social Psychology, 56,* 398-406.

Ainsworth, P. B. (2001). *Offender profiling and crime analysis.* Devon: Willan Publishing

Alison, L., Bennell, C., Mokros, A., & Ormerod, D. (2002). The personality paradox in offender profiling: A theoretical review of the processes involved in deriving background characteristics from crime scene actions. *Psychology, Public Policy and Law, 8,* 115-135.

Alison, L., & Canter, D. (1999). *Profiling in policy and practice.* Dartmouth: Aldershot.

Alison, L., Goodwill, A. M., & Alison, E. (2005). The madjenko, mascav and eve case: A study in linking and suspect prioritisation. In L. J. Alison (Ed.), *The forensic psychologists casebook: A practical guide in preparing reports on violent and sexual offences.* London: Willian.

Alison, L., Goodwill, A., Almond, L., van den Heuvel, C., & Winter, J. (2010). Pragmatic solutions to offender profiling and behavioural investigative advice. *Legal and Criminological Psychology,15,* 115-132.

Alison, L.J., Rockett, W., Deprez, S., & Watts, S. (2000). Bandits, cowboys and robin's men: The facets of armed robbery.. In D.V. Canter & L.J. Alison (Eds.), *Profiling property crimes* (pp. 75-106). Aldershot, England: Ashgate Publishing.

Alison, L., Smith, M. D., Eastman, O., & Rainbow, L. (2003). Toulimn's philosophy of argument and its relevance to offender profiling. *Psychology, Crime, and Law, 9,* 173-183.

Alison, L., Smith, M. D., & Morgan, K. (2003). Interpreting the accuracy of offender profiles. *Psychology, Crime, & Law, 9,* 185-195.

Alison, L., Snook, B., & Stein, K. (2001). Unobtrusive measurement: Using police information for forensic research. *Qualitative Research, 1,* 241-254.

Alison, L.J., & Stein, K.J. (2001). Vicious circles: Accounts of stranger sexual assault reflect abusive variants of conventional interactions. *The Journal of Forensic Psychiatry, 12,* 515-538.

Alison, L.J., West, A., & Goodwill, A.M. (2004). The academic and the practitioner: Pragmatists views of offender profiling. Psychology, Public Policy & Law, 10, 71-101.

Allport, G.W. (1961). *Pattern and growth in personality.* New York: Holt.

Alwin, D.F., Cohen, R.L., & Newcomb, T.M. (1991). *Political attitudes over the life span: The Bennington women after fifty years.* Madison, WI: University of Wisconsin Press.

Arrigo, B.A., & Purcell, C.E. (2001). Explaining paraphilias and lust murder: Toward an integrated model. *International Journal of Offender Therapy and Comparative Criminology, 45,* 6-31.

Barbaree, H.E., Seto, M.C., Serin, R.C., Amos, N.L., & Preston, D.L. (1994). Comparisons between sexual and nonsexual rapist subtypes: Sexual arousal to rape, offense precursors, and offense characteristics. *Criminal Justice and Behavior, 21,* 95-114.

Beech, A. R., Oliver, C., Fisher, D., & Beckett, R. (2005). *STEP 4: The sex offender treatment programme in prison: Addressing the offending behaviour of rapists and sexual murderers.*

Beauregard, E., & Proulx, J. (2002). Profiles in the offending process of nonserial sexual murderers. *International Journal of Offender Therapy and Comparative Criminology, 46,* 386-399.

Bennell, C., & Canter, D. (2002). Linking commercial burglaries by modus operandi: Tests using regression and ROC analysis. *Science & Justice, 42,* 153-164.

Bennell, C., & Jones, N. (2005). Between a ROC and a hard place. *International Journal of Investigative Psychology and Offender Profiling, 2,* 23-41.

Bennell, C., Jones, N., Taylor, P.J., & Snook, B. (2006). Validities and abilities in criminal profiling: A critique of the studies conducted by Richard Kocsis and his colleagues. *International Journal of Offender Therapy and Comparative Criminology, 50,* 344-360.

Blau, T. H. (1994). *Psychological services for law enforcement.* New York: Wiley.

Block, J., Block, J.H., & Keyes, S. (1988). Longitudinally foretelling drug usage in adolescence: Early childhood personality and environmental precursors. *Child Development, 59,* 336-355.

Boon, J. (1997). The contribution of personality theories to psychological profiling. In J.L. Jackson, & D.A. Bekerian (Eds.). *Offender profiling: Theory, research, and practice* (pp. 44-59). Hoboken, NJ: John Wiley & Sons Inc.

Canter, D. (1994). *Criminal shadows*. London: Harper Collins.

Canter, D. (1995a). Psychology of offender profiling. In R. Bull & D. Carson (Eds.), *Handbook of psychology in legal contexts* (pp. 343-355). Chichester, UK: John Wiley and Sons.

Canter, D. (1995b). *Criminal shadows*. London: Harper Collins.

Canter, D. (1996). *Psychology in action.* Brookfield, VT: Dartmouth.

Canter, D. (2004). Offender profiling and investigative psychology. *Journal of Investigative Psychology and Offender Profiling, 1*, 1-15.

Canter, D. (2011). Resolving the offender "profiling equations" and the emergence of an investigative psychology. *Current Directions in Psychological Sciences, 20,* 293-320.

Canter, D., Alison, L., Alison, E., & Wentink, N. (2004). The organized/disorganized typology of serial murder. *Psychology, Public Policy and Law, 10,* 293-320.

Canter, D.V., Bennell, C., Alison, L.J., & Reddy, S. (2003). Differentiating sex offences: A behaviorally based thematic classification of stranger rapes. *Behavioral Sciences and the Law, 21,* 157-174.

Canter, D.V., & Fritzon, K. (1998). Differentiating arsonists: A model of fire-setting actions and characteristics. *Legal and Criminological Psychology, 3,* 73-96.

Canter, D., & Heritage, R. (1990). A multivariate model of sexual offence behavior: Developments in 'offender profiling'. *The Journal of Forensic Psychiatry, 1,* 185-212.

Canter, D., Hughes, D., & Kirby, S. (1998). Paedophilia: pathology, criminality, or both? The development of a multivariate model of offence behaviour in child sexual abuse. *The Journal of Forensic Psychiatry, 9,* 532-555

Canter, D., & Ioannou, M. (2004). A multivariate model of stalking behaviours. *Behaiormetrika, 31,* 1-18.

Canter, D.V., & Wentink, N. (2004). An empirical test of Holmes and Holmes's serial murder typology. *Criminal Justice and Behavior, 31,* 489-515.

Caspi, A. (2000). The child is father of the man: Personality continuities from childhood to adulthood. *Journal of Personalty & Social Psychology, 78,* 158-172.

Caspi, A., & Roberts, B.W. (2001). Personality development across the life course: The argument for change and continuity. *Psychological Inquiry, 12,* 49-66.

Caspi, A., & Silva, P.A. (1995). Temperamental qualities at age 3 predict personality traits in young adulthood: Longitudinal evidence from a birth cohort. *Child Development, 66,* 486-498.

Cervone, D. (2005). Personality architecture: Within-person structures and processes. *Annual Review of Psychology, 56,* 432-452.

Chesire, J.D. (2004). Review, critique, and synthesis of personality theory in motivation to sexually assault. *Aggression and Violent Behaviour, 9,* 633-644.

Clarke, J., & Carter, A. J. (2000). Relapse prevention with sexual murderers. In D. R. Laws, S. M. Hudson & T. Ward (Eds.), *Remaking relapse prevention with sex offenders* (pp. 389-401). London: Sage.

Cohen, L.J., Garfalo, R.F., Boucher, R., & Seghorn, T. (1971). The psychology of rapists. *Seminars in Psychiatry, 3,* 307-327.

Cohen, M.L., Seghorn, T., & Calmas, W. (1969). Sociometric study of sex offenders. *Journal of Abnormal Psychology, 74,* 249-255.

Coleman, C., & Norris, C. (2000). *Introducing criminology.* Devon: William Publishing.

Collins, P.I., Johnson, G.F., Choy, A., Davidson, K.T., & MacKay, R.E. (1998). Advances in violent crime analysis and law enforcement: The Canadian violent crime linkage analysis system. *Journal of Government Information, 25,* 277-284.

Copson, G. (1995). *Coals to Newcastle? Police use of offender profiling.* London: Home Office Police Research Group.

Copson, G., Badcock, R., Boon, J., & Britton, P. (1997). Editorial: Articulating a systematic approach to clinical crime profiling. *Criminal Behaviour and Mental Health, 7,* 13-17.

Dancer, L.S. (1990). Introduction to facet theory and its applications. *Applied Psychology: An International Review, 39,* 365-377.

Davies, A. (1991). The use of DNA profiling and behavioural science in the investigation of sexual offences. *Medicine, Science and Law, 31,* 95-101.

Davies, A., Wittebrood, K., & Jackson, J. L. (1998). *Predicting the criminal record of a stranger rapist (Special interest series paper 12).* London: Home Office, Policing and Reducing Crime Unit.

Dietz, P.E., Hazelwood, R.R., & Warren, J. (1990). The sexually sadistic criminal and his offenses. *The Bulletin of the American Academy of Psychiatry and the Law, 18,* 163-178.

Doan, B., & Snook, B. (2008). A failure to find empirical support for the homology assumption in criminal profiling. *Journal of Police and Criminal Psychology, 23,* 61-70.

Douglas, J., Burgess, A., Burgess, A., & Ressler, R. (1992). *Crime classification manual.* Lexington, MA: Lexington Books.

Douglas, J., Ressler, R., Burgess, A. W., & Hartman, C. (1986). Criminal profiling from crime scene analysis. *Behavioral Sciences & the Law, 4,* 401-421.

Dowden, C., Bennell, C., & Bloomfield, S. (2007). Advances in offender profiling: A systematic review of the profiling literature published over the past three decades. *Journal of Police and Criminal Psychology, 22,* 44-56.

Eaton, N., South, S.C., & Krueger, R.F. (2009). The cognitive-affective processing system(CAPS) approach to personality and the concept of personality disorder: Integratingclinical and social-cognitive research. *Journal of Research in Personality, 43,* 208 -217.

FBI. (2008, 30 September 2008). Investigative Programs Critical Incident Response Group. Retrieved 23 October, 2008, from *http://www.fbi.gov/hq/isd/cirg/ncavc.htm*

Fisher, D., & Beech, A.R. (2007). Identification of motivations for sexual murder. In J. Proulx, E. Beauregard, M. Cusson, & A. Nicole (Eds.), *Sexual murderers: A comparative analysis and new perspectives* (pp. 175-190). Chichester, UK: John Wiley & Sons Ltd.

Fiske, S.T., & Taylor, S. (1991). *Social cognition.* New York: McGraw-Hill.

Forer, B.R. (1949). The fallacy of personal validation: A classroom demonstration of gullibility. *The Journal of Abnormal and Social Psychology. 44,* 118-123.

Fritzon, K., Canter, D., & Wilton, Z. (2001). The application of an action system model to destructive behaviour: The examples of arson and terrorism. *Behavioral Sciences & the Law, 19,* 657-690.

Funder, D.C., & Colvin, C.R. (1991) Explorations in behavioural consistency: Properties of person, situations, and behaviours. *Journal of Personality and Social Psychology, 60,* 773-794.

Furr, R.M., & Funder, D.C. (2004). Situational similarity and behavioural consistency: Subjective, objective, variable-centered, and person-centered approaches. *Journal of Research in Personality, 38,* 421-447.

Gee, D., & Belofastov, A. (2007). Profiling Sexual Fantasy: Fantasy in Sexual Offending and the Implications for Criminal Profiling. In R. N. Kocsis (Ed.), *Criminal profiling: International theory, research and practice* (pp. 49-71). Totowa, NJ: Humana Press Inc.

Glenn, N.D. (1980). Values, attitudes, and beliefs. In O.G. Brim, Jr. & J. Kagan (eds). *Constancy and change in human development* (pp. 596-640). Cambridge, MA: Harvard University Press.

Goodwill, A. M., & Alison, L. (2007). When is profiling possible? Offence planning and aggression as moderators in predicting offender age from victim age in stranger rape. *Behavioral Sciences & the Law, 25,* 823-840.

Goodwill, A.M., Alison, L., & Beech., A.R. (2009). What works in offender profiling? A comparison of typological, thematic, and multivariate models. *Behavioral Sciences & the Law, 27,* 507-529.

Goodwill, A.M., Alison, L., & Humann, M. (2009). Multidimensional scaling and the analysis of sexual offence behaviour: A reply to Sturidsson et al. *Psychology, Crime & Law, 15,* 517-524.

Green, E.J., Booth, C.E., & Biderman, M.D. (1976). Cluster analysis of burglary M/O's. *Journal of Police Science and Administration, 4,* 382-388.

Groth, A. N., & Birnbaum, H. J. (1979). *Men who rape: The psychology of the offender.* New York: Plenum Press.

Groth, A. N., Burgess, A. W., & Holmstrom, L. L. (1977). Rape: Power, anger, and sexuality. *The American Journal of Psychiatry, 134,* 1239-1243.

Grubin, D., Kelly, P., & Brunsdon, C. (2001). *Linking serious sexual assault through behavior.* London: Home Office, Research Development and Statistics Directorate.

Gudjonsson, G.H., & Copson, G. (1997). The role of the expert in criminal investigation. In J.L. Jackson & D.A. Bekerain (Eds), *Offender profiling: theory, research and practice* (pp. 61-76). West Sussex, England: John Wiley & Sons.

Guttman, R. & Greenbaum, C.W. (1998). Facet theory: Its development and current status. *European Psychologist, 3,* 13-36.

Hazelwood, R.R., & Burgess, A.W. (1987). An introduction to the serial rapist research by the FBI. *FBI Law Enforcement Bulletin, 56,* 16-24.

Hazelwood, R., & Warren, J. (2003). Linkage analysis: Modus operandi, ritual and signature in serial sexual crime. *Aggression and Violent Behavior, 8,* 587-598.

Hicks, S. J., & Sales, B. D. (2006). *Criminal profiling: Developing an effective science and practice.* Washington, D.C.: American Psychological Association.

Hogan, R. (1991). Personality and personality measurement. In M. D. Dunnette & L. M. Hough (Eds.), *Handbook of industrial and organizational psychology* (pp. 327–396). Palo Alto, CA: Consulting Psychologists Press

Hogan, J., & Ones, D.S. (1997). Conscientiousness and integrity at work. In R. Hogan, J.Johnson, & S. Briggs (Eds), *Handbook of personality psychology* (pp. 849-870). San Diego, CA: Academic Press.

Holmes, R. M., & De Burger, J. (1988). *Serial murder.* London: Sage Publications.

Holmes, R.M., & Holmes, S.T. (1998). *Serial murder* (2nd ed.). Thousand Oaks, CA: Sage.

Homant, R. J., & Kennedy, D. B. (1998). Psychological aspects of crime scene profiling: Validity research. *Criminal Justice and Behavior, 25*, 319-343.

House, J. C. (1997). Towards a practical application of offender profiling: The RNC's criminal suspect prioritization system. In J. L. Jackson & D. A. Bekerain (Eds.), *Offender profiling: Theory, research and practice* (pp. 177-190). Chichester, England: Wiley.

Howlett, J.B., Hanfland, K.A., & Ressler, R.K. (1986). The Violent Criminal Apprehension Program: A progress report. *Law Enforcement Bulletin, 14.*

Keppel, R. D., & Walter, R. (1999). Profiling killers: A revised classification model for understanding sexual murder. *International Journal of Offender Therapy and Comparative Criminology, 43*, 417-437.

Knight, R.A. (1999). Validation of a typology for rapists. *Journal of Interpersonal Violence, 14*, 303-330.

Knight, R.A., & Prentky, R.A. (1987). The developmental antecedents and adult adaptations of rapist subtypes. *Criminal Justice and Behavior, 14*, 403-426.

Knight, R.A., & Prentky, R.A. (1990). Classifying sexual offenders: The development and corroboration of taxonomic models. In W.L. Marshall, D.R. Laws, & H.E. Barbaree (Eds) *Handbook of sexual assault: Issues, theories, and treatment of the offender* (pp. 23-52). New York, NY: Plenum Press.

Knight, R. A., Warren, J. I., Reboussin, R., & Soley, B. (1998). Predicting rapist type from crime-scene variables. *Criminal Justice and Behavior, 25*, 46-80.

Kocsis, R.N. (2003). Criminal psychological profiling: Validities and abilities. *International Journal of Offender Therapy and Comparative Criminology, 47*, 126-144.

Kocsis, R. N. (2004). Psychological profiling of serial arson offenses: An assessment of skills and accuracy. *Criminal Justice and Behavior, 31*, 341-361.

Kocsis, R.N., Cooksey, R.W., & Irwin, H.J. (2002). Psychological profiling of offender characteristics from crime behaviors in serial rape offences. *International Journal of Offender Therapy and Comparative Criminology, 46*, 144-169.

Kocsis, R. N., Irwin, H. J., & Hayes, A. F. (1998). Organised and disorganised criminal behaviour syndromes in arsonists: A validation study of a psychological profiling concept. *Australian and New Zealand Journal of Psychiatry, Psychology, and Law, 5, 117-131.*

Kocsis, R. N., Irwin, H. J., Hayes, A. F., & Nunn, R. (2000). Expertise in psychological profiling: A comparative assessment. *Journal of Interpersonal Violence, 15*, 311-331.

Kocsis, R. N., & Palermo, G. B. (2007). Contemporary problems in criminal profiling. In R. N. Kocsis (Ed.), *Criminal profiling: International theory, research, and practice* (pp. 327-345). Totowa, New Jersey: Humana Press.

Jackson, J. L., van Koppen, P. J., & Herbrink, J. C. M. (1993). *Does the service meet the needs? An evaluation of consumer satisfaction with specific profile analysis and investigative advice as offered by the Scientific Research Advisory Unit of the National Criminal Intelligence Division (CRI).* The Netherlands: Netherlands Institute for the Study of Criminality and Law Enforcement (NISCALE).

Jaworska, N., & Chupetlovska-Anastasova, A. (2009). A review of multidimensional scaling (MDS) and its utility in various psychological domains. *Tutorials in Quantitative Methods for Psychology, 5,* 1-10.

Labuschange, G. (2006). The use of linkage analysis as evidence in the conviction of the Newcastle serial murderer, South Africa. *Journal of Investigative Psychology and Offender Profiling, 3*, 183-191.

Lingoes, J. (1973). *The Guttman-Lingoes nonmetric program series.* Ann Arbor, MI: Mathesis.

Lingoes, J. (1979). *Geometric representation of relational data.* Ann Arbor, MI: Mathesis Press.

Lundrigan, S., & Canter, D. (2001). A multivariate analysis of serial murderers' disposal site location choice. *Journal of Environmental Psychology, 21,* 423-432.

Mann, R. E., & Hollin, C. R. (2007). Sexual offenders' explanations for their offending. *Journal of Sexual Aggression, 13,* 3-9.

Markson, L., Woodhams, J., & Bond, J.W. (2010). Linking serial residential burglary: comparing the utility of modus operandi behaviours, geographical proximity, and temporal proximity. *Journal of Investigative Psychology and Offender Profiling, 7,* 91-107.

Meloy, J.R. (2000). The nature and dynamics of sexual homicide: An integrative review. *Aggression and Behavior, 5,* 1-22.

Mendoza-Denton, R., & Mischel, W. (2007). Integrating system approaches to culture and personality: The cultural cognitive-affective processing system.In S. Kitayama & D. Cohen (Eds.), *Handbook of Cultural Psychology* (pp. 175-195). New York, NY: The Guildford Press.

Meyer, C. B. (2007). Criminal profiling as expert evidence? An international case law perspective. In R. Kocsis (Ed.), Criminal profiling: International theory, research, and practice (pp. 207–247). Totowa, NJ: Humana Press.

Mischel, W. (1968). *Personality and assessment.* New York: Wiley.

Mischel, W., & Shoda, Y. (1995). A cognitive-affective system theory of personality: Reconceptualising situations, dispositions, dynamics, and invariance in personality structure. *Psychological Review, 102,* 246-268.

Mischel, W., & Shoda, Y. (1998). Reconciling processing dynamics and personality dispositions. *Annual Review of Psychology, 49,* 229-258.

Mischel, W., & Shoda, Y. (2008). Toward a unified theory of personality: Integrating dispositions and processing dynamics with the cognitive-affective processing system. In O.P John, R.W. Robins, & L.A. Pervin (Eds). *Handbook of personality: Theory and research* (pg 208-241). New York, NY: Guildford Press.

Mokros, A., & Alison, L. J. (2002). Is offender profiling possible? Testing the predicted homology of crime scene actions and background characteristics in a sample of rapists. *Legal and Criminological Psychology, 7,* 25-43.

Muller, D. A. (2000). Criminal profiling: Real science or just wishful thinking? *Homicide Studies, 4,* 234-264.

Owen, R. (1843). *Lectures on the comparative anatomy and physiology of the invertebrate animals.* London, England: Longman, Brown, Green, Longmans.

Owen, R. (2007). *On the Nature of Limbs: A discourse,* edited by R. Amundson (with a preface by B.K. Hall and introductory essays by R. Amundson, K. Padian, M.P. Windsor and J. Coggon). Chicago: University of Chicago Press.

Palermo, G.B, & Kocsis, R.N. (2005). *Offender profiling: An introduction to the sociopsychological analysis of violent crime.* Springfield, Ill: Charles C. Thomas Publisher Ltd.

Pardue, A., & Arrigo, B.A. (2008). Power, anger, and sadistic rapists. *International Journal of Offender Therapy and Comparative Criminology, 52,* 378-400.

Pervin, L. A. (2002). *Current controversies and issues in personality* (Third ed.): John Wiley & Sons Inc.

Pinizzott, A. J. (1984). Forensic psychology: Criminal personality profiling. *Journal of Police Science & Administration, 12,* 32-40.

Pinizzott, A. J., & Finkel, N. J. (1990). Criminal personality profiling: An outcome and process study. *Law and Human Behavior, 14,* 215-233.

Porter, L., & Alison, L.J. (2004). Behavioural coherence in violent group activity: An interpersonal model of sexually violent gang behaviour. *Aggressive Behavior, 30,* 449-468.

Porter, S., Woodworth, M., Earle, J., Drugge, J., & Boer, D. (2003). Characteristics of sexual homicides committed by psychopathic and nonpsychopathic offenders. *Law and Human Behavior, 27,* 459-470.

Rainbow, L. (2007). The role of behavioural science in criminal investigations. *Forensic Update, 88,* 44-48.

Rainbow, L. (2008). Taming the beast: The UK approach to the management of behavioural investigative advice. *Journal of Police and Criminal Psychology, 23,* 90-97.

Rainbow, L., & Gregory, A. (2009). Behavioural investigative advice: A contemporary view. *The Journal of Homicide and Major Incident Investigation, 5,* 71-82.

Raine, A., Reynolds, C., Venables, P.H., Mednick, S.A., & Farrington, D.P. (1998). Fearlessness, stimulation-seekingm and large body size at age 3 years as early predispositions to childhood aggression at age 11 years. *Archives of General Psychiatry, 55,* 745-751.

Ressler, R., Burgess, A., & Douglas, J. (1988). *Sexual homicide: Patterns and motives.* New York: The Free Press.

Robertiello, G., & Terry, K.J. (2007). Can we profile sex offenders? A review of sex offenders typologies. *Aggression and Violent Behaviour, 12,* 508-518.

Roberts, B.W., & Del Vecchio, W.F. (2000). The rank-order consistency of personality traits from childhood to old age: A quantitative review of longitudinal studies. *Psychological Bulletin, 132,* 1-25.

Roberts, B.W., & Caspi, A. (2001). Personality development and the person-situation debate: It's déjà vu all over again. *Psychological Inquiry, 12,* 104-109.

Salfati, G.C., & Bateman, A.L. (2005). Serial homicide: An investigation of behavioural consistency. *Journal of Investigative Psychology and Offender Profiling, 2,* 121-144.

Santtila, P., Fritzon, K., & Tamelander, A. L. (2005). Linking arson incidents on the basis of crime scene behavior. *Journal of Police and Criminal Psychology, 19,* 1–16.

Santtila, P., Hakkanen, H., Canter, D., & Elfgren, T. (2003). Classifying homicide offenders and predicting their characteristics from crime scene behaviour. *Scandinavian Journal of Psychology, 44,* 107-118.

Santtila, P., Laukkanen, M., Zappala, A., & Bosco, D. (2008). Distance travelled and offence characteristics in homicide, rape, and robbery against business. *Legal and Criminological Psychology, 13,* 345-356.

Santtila, P., Pakkanen, T., Zappala, A., Bosco, D., Valkama, M., & Mokros, A. (2008).Behavioural crime linking in serial homicide. *Psychology, Crime and Law, 14*, 245-265.

Sarangi, S., & Youngs, D. (2006). Spatial Patterns of Indian Serial Burglars with Relevance to Geographical Profiling. *Journal of Investigative Psychology and Offender Profiling, 3*, 105-115.

Shoda, Y., Mischel, W., & Wright, J. C. (1994). Intraindividual stability in the organization and patterning of behavior: Incorporating psychological situations into the idiographic analysis of personality. *Journal of Personality and Social Psychology, 67*, 674–687.

Shye, S., Elizur, D., & Hoffman, M. (1994). *Introduction to facet theory*. London: Sage Publications.

Snook, B., Cullen, R.M., Bennell, C., Taylor, P.J., & Gendreau, P. (2008). The criminal profiling illusion: What's behind the smoke and mirrors? *Criminal Justice and Behavior, 35*, 1257-1276.

Snook, B., Eastwood, J., Gendreau, P., Goggin, C., & Cullen, R. M. (2007). Taking stock of criminal profiling: A narrative review and meta-analysis. *Criminal Justice and Behavior, 34*, 437-453.

Snook, B., Luther, K., House, J. C., & Bennell, C., & Taylor, P. J. (2012). Violent crime linkage analysis system: A test of inter-rater reliability. *Criminal Justice and Behavior, 39*, 607-619

Sorochinski, M., & Salfati, G.C. (2010). The consistency of inconsistency in serial homicide: Patterns of behavioural change across series. *Journal of Investigative Psychology and Offender Profiling, 7,* 109-136.

Steyvers, M. (2002). Multidimensional scaling. In: *Encyclopedia of cognitive science.* London, UK: Nature Publishing Group.

Sturidsson, K., Langstrom, N., Grann, M., Sjostedt, G., Asgard, U., & Aghede, E. M. (2006). Using multidimensional scaling for the analysis of sexual offence behaviour: A replication and some cautionary notes. *Psychology, Crime, and Law, 12*, 221-230.

Ter Beek, M., Van Den Eshof, P., & Mali, B. (2010). Statistical modelling in the investigation of stranger rape. *Journal of Investigative Psychology and Offender Profiling, 7,* 31-47.

Tonkin, M., Bond, J.W., & Woodhams, J. (2009). Fashion conscious burglars? Testing the principles of offender profiling with footwear impressions recovered at domestic burglaries. *Psychology, Crime & Law, 15*, 327-345.

Tonkin, M., Santtila, P., & Bull, R. (2012). The linking of burglary crimes using offender behaviour: Testing research cross-nationally and exploring methodology. *Legal and Criminological Psychology, 17,* 276-293.

Turco, R.N. (1990). Psychological profiling. *International Journal of Offender Therapy and Comparative Criminology, 34,* 147-154.

Woodhams, J. (2012). Offender profiling and crime linkage. In G. Davies, & A. Beech (eds), *Forensic psychology: Crime, justice, law, interventions (2nd edition)* (pp.171-188). Chichester, UK: John Wiley & Sons Ltd.

Woodhams, J., Bull, R., & Hollin, C. R. (2007). Case linkage: Identifying crimes committed by the same offender. In R. N. Kocsis (Ed.), *Criminal profiling: International theory, research and practice* (pp. 117-133). Totowa, NJ: Humana Press Inc.

Woodhams, J. & Grant, T. (2006). Developing a categorization system for rapists' speech. *Psychology, Crime and Law, 12,* 245-260.

Woodhams, J., Hollin, C.R., & Bull, R. (2007). The psychology of linking crimes: A review of the evidence. *Legal and Criminological Psychology, 12,* 233-249.

Woodhams, J., & Toye, K. (2007). An empirical test of the assumptions of case linkage and offender profiling with serial commercial robberies. *Psychology, Public Policy, and Law, 13,* 59-85.

Youngs, D. (2004). Personality correlates of offence style. *Journal of Investigative Psychology and Offender Profiling, 1,* 99-119.

In: Crime
Editor: Michael Harry Pearson

ISBN: 978-1-62948-657-4
© 2014 Nova Science Publishers, Inc.

Chapter 3

HATE CRIME AND ITS RELEVANT FACTORS

Wen Cheng

National Sun Yet-sen University, Kaohsiung, Taiwan (R. O. C.)

ABSTRACT

The term "hate crime," which refers to a crime that involves "the manifest evidence of prejudice" (Hate Crimes Statistics Act, 1990), was first introduced in the United States in the late 1960s by the 1964 Federal Civil Rights Law and still occurs in the U.S., even around the world. This review examines the phenomenon of hate crimes in the United States and reveals that the incidence of anti-racial hate crimes varied among different racial groups; that anti-religious hate crimes were committed toward Jews and Muslims more than to others; and that anti-sexual orientation hate crimes focused on male homosexuals more than others. Other findings revealed that anti-religious hate crimes were more likely to be directed against property, whereas anti-racial and anti-sex orientation hate crimes were more likely to be directed against people, suggesting that the nature of these hate crimes are different. In addition, Whites displayed both higher ingroup favoritism and higher outgroup hatred (especially toward Blacks), but AIANs and Asians displayed lower ingroup favoritism that may be due to greater ingroup heterogeneity. It is postulated that, at the macro-level, a national climate of respecting outgroups may influence normative pressures against expressing hate-related aggression. At the micro-level, some relevant individual difference variables of offenders have been identified: the awareness of mortality salience, outgroup-directed emotion (anger, fear-anxiety, and disgust), aggressiveness, personality (SDO and RWA), and certain socio-demographic variables (i.e. gender, age, hate group membership). Although hate crime victims were usually strangers to the offenders, they were sometimes acquaintances. Possible solutions to hate crimes include "law enforcement" to interdict the expression of outgroup hatred and "education" about mutual tolerance and respect for diversity by implementing the recommended elements of the contact hypothesis.

HATE CRIME IN THE UNITED STATES AND ITS RELEVANT FACTORS

On October 7th, 1998, a man saw a scarecrow strung to a fence at a Laramie ranch so he did not pay much attention. When he walked close by, he figured out the scarecrow was actually a college boy. The boy was Matthew Shepard, who died of his severe head injuries on October 12th, 1998, five days after he was hospitalized. The police believed that the killers set out to rob the boy in the beginning but then decided to "teach him a lesson" after learning he was gay (Hulse, 2009).

The term "hate crime," which refers to a crime that involves "the manifest evidence of prejudice" (Hate Crimes Statistics Act, 1990), was first introduced in the United States in the late 1960s by the 1964 Federal Civil Rights Law. Interestingly, hate crimes can be traced back thousands of years in human history. Incidents involving hate crimes include the persecution of Christians in the Roman Empire in the first three centuries; the Crusades, which took place from 1096 to 1291; the Armenian genocide by the Ottoman Empire in the early 19th century; and the Holocaust during World War II. In recent years, the ethnic cleansing in Bosnia and the massacre in Rwanda were also instances involving hate crimes. In addition to the historical events mentioned above, hate crimes have also been known to happen in more mundane and interpersonal settings.

The United States is known as a "melting pot" because of the diversity of its people. Although this diversity offers opportunity for much intergroup contact and tolerance, prejudice and discrimination are serious problems that still exist in the United States. The government has noted the phenomenon of hate crimes since the 1960s and has formulated legislation to prevent them, although the term "hate crime" was not commonly used until the 1980s (Byford, 2003).

The History of Hate Crime Laws

Hate crime generally refers to the crime that leads offenders to target victims because of the victims' *real* or *perceived* group membership, such as race, religion, sexual orientation, gender, gender identity, ethnicity/nationality, disability, political affiliation (Stotzer, 2007). The first hate crime case investigated by the Federal Bureau of Investigation (FBI) occurred in the early 1920s and involved the Ku Klux Klan. The major perpetrator, Edward Young Clarke, was an entrepreneur in Louisiana who had been recruited by William Simmons (the founder of the second Ku Klux Klan movement). In 1920, Edward Young Clarke started increasing membership in the Klan by recruiting what eventually became over one million members. This allowed the Ku Klux Klan to become a much more powerful group. They kidnapped, tortured, and even killed people who were of a different race or religion; moreover, thousands of people were threatened and terrified, actions that caught the FBI's attention. Although hate crime laws did not yet exist at the time, Edward Young Clarke was eventually arrested by violating the Mann Act for transporting his mistress across state lines in 1924 (*A Byte Out of FBI History*, 2004).

The 1964 Federal Civil Rights Law, 18 U.S.C. § 245(b)(2), was the first law in America involving hate crimes. The 1964 Federal Civil Rights Law affirmed individuals' rights to engage in six types of federally-protected activities, including attending school, applying for jobs, using any facility of interstate commerce, participating in public activities, patronizing a public place/facility, voting, or serving as a juror in a state court. Anyone who intimidated, interfered with, or injured another person who was engaging in, or was attempting to engage in, any of the six federally protected activities, because of their "race, color, religion or national origin," was defined as a hate crime offender by the 1964 Federal Civil Rights Law (United States Department of Justice, 2008).

Twenty-five years later, one of the largest crime bills in U.S. history—the Violent Crime Control and Law Enforcement Act, was sent to the United States Sentencing Commission in 1994. This Act was passed and enacted in 28 U.S.C. § 994 note Sec. 280003 by the United States Sentencing Commission (http://www.ussc.gov/) in 1995, and it required greater penalties for violent crimes, including hate crimes, which were based on the actual or perceived race, color, religion, national origin, ethnicity, or gender of the victims. However, this Act only increased the penalties for hate crimes but did not eliminate the restriction stated in the 1964 Federal Civil Rights Law, which required that the victims must be engaged in a federally protected activity when such violations occur (Legal Information Institute, n.d.).

However, three years after the enactment of the Violent Crime Control and Law Enforcement Act, Matthew Shepard was murdered on October 12th, 1998. His grieving mother then devoted herself to fighting for gay rights. Eleven years after Shepard's death, on October 28, 2009, President Obama finally signed the Matthew Shepard and James Byrd, Jr.[1] Hate Crimes Prevention Act. This Act expanded the existing U.S. hate crime laws to include crimes motivated by victims' actual or perceived gender, gender identity, sexual orientation, or disability. Most importantly, the Act dropped the prerequisites in the 1964 Federal Civil Right Law and the 1995 Violent Crime Control and Law Enforcement Act which required victims to be engaged in one of the six federally protected activities (United States Department of Justice, 2009).

To date, U.S. hate crime laws have been developed to protect the rights of people from different walks of life. Despite these laws, however, hate crimes still persist. The goal of this chapter is to achieve a better understanding of hate crimes in order to help ameliorate this corrosive social problem. Accordingly, the present chapter addresses the following issues:

1) What are hate crimes and what can be learned from them?
2) Who are the perpetrators of hate crimes and why do they commit them?
3) Who are the victims of hate crimes and what are the influences of hate crimes on the victims?
4) Why do hate crimes occur? And finally,
5) What factors can help to reduce the occurrence of hate crime?

By exploring the above issues, hope we can gain more insights regarding the phenomena of hate crimes in the U.S. Because the U.S. society has become more diverse, maintaining peaceful intergroup relations has become crucial for ensuring social stability.

---

[1] James Byrd, Jr. (May 2, 1949 – June 7, 1998) was an African-American who was tortured to death in Jasper, Texas by three white males with jail records on June 7, 1998, because of his skin color.

WHAT ARE HATE CRIMES AND WHAT CAN BE LEARNED FROM THEM?

Stereotyping is the cognitive aspect of inter-group bias; prejudice is its affective aspect; and discrimination is its behavioral aspect (Fiske, 2004). Hate crimes, which are extreme cases of discrimination, involve acts of anti-outgroup violence that violate federal laws. Therefore, Howard Ehrlich, the director of the Prejudice Institute, has defined hate crimes as ". . . acts motivated by prejudice . . . [which] lead to oppression." (Ehrlich, 2009).

Since 1990, the FBI's Uniformed Crime Report (UCR) Program has committed itself to assessing and monitoring hate crimes in the United States.[2] The UCR Program has collected a great deal of informative data on hate crimes. However, they only have reported the raw data (number of cases) across the nation without providing any additional statistical analyses. My colleagues and I have statistically analyzed the data collected by the FBI between 1996 and 2008 to see the changes and trends in hate crimes over a 13-year period in the United States (Cheng, Ickes, & Kenworthy, 2013). The first problem faced when analyzing the raw data collected by the FBI is that the number of hate crime incidents would usually be small if the victims' group (or the offenders' group) has a small population; on the other hand, if one subgroup population is much larger than others, its number of hate crime incidents may be correspondingly higher as well. Therefore, we used the adjusted case numbers represent how many hate crime incidents occurred per 10 million victims/offenders[3], which should be more meaningful when comparing and interpreting the differences among different groups. Following I will briefly describe our findings (Cheng, Ickes, & Kenworthy) according to the three types of hate crimes that occur most often in FBI's UCR data, anti-race, anti-religion, and anti-sexual orientation.

Anti-Race Hate Crimes

The data from the FBI's UCR program included the offenders' race (White, Black, American Indian/Alaskan Native [AIAN], Asian/Pacific Islander, and multi-racial group) and the types of anti-race hate crimes (anti-White, anti-Black, anti-AIAN, anti-Asian/Pacific Islander, and anti-multi-racial group) that were committed. The findings revealed that the offenders' race was significantly associated with the victims' perceived race across the 13 years. Specifically, Whites consistently committed more hate crimes against Blacks compared

---

[2] The FBI uses a broader definition of hate crime, defining it as crime "based solely on race, religion, ethnicity/national origin, sexual orientation, or disability" (FBI, 1996). Thus, the data collected by FBI have included anti-sexual orientation and anti-disability hate crimes since 1996, twelve years before the federal laws were enacted in 2008.

[3] If only the victims' subgroups were known, the hate crime incidents were divided by the size of victims' subgroup populations and then multiplied by 10,000,000 so that the adjusted numbers not only represent the concept of the specific hate crime rate but also meet the assumptions of the chi-square test, which requires each cell to contain at least five cases. If each cell were multiplied by a larger number (e.g., 100 million), it would have over-estimated the probability of detecting statistical differences among them. According to the same rationale, the hate crime incidents were divided by the size of offenders' subgroup populations and then multiplied 10,000,000 when the offenders' subgroups were known. However, if both of victims' and offenders' subgroups were identified, the numbers of hate crime incidents were adjusted for both of these variables. The populations of subgroups were accessed in the government reports from the U.S Census Bureau (FBI, Hate Crime Statistics, 1996-2008).

to other racial groups, and Blacks also consistently committed more hate crimes against Whites, whereas both AIANs and Asians consistently committed more hate crimes against their own racial group compared with other racial groups. In the case of AIANs, it could be argued that AIANS commit relatively more hate crimes toward AIANs than toward other racial groups because they tend to live in relative isolation from other racial groups. In the case if Asians, however, the same argument does not seem to apply. Nevertheless, in general, one would expect all groups to display ingroup favoritism and outgroup discrimination, which would lead us to expect that individuals should be more likely to commit hate crimes toward outgoups, rather than toward their ingroup. The results, however, did not turn out this way for AIANs or for Asians.

According to Social Identity Theory (Turner & Tajfel, 1986), "ingroup favoritism" should occur when individuals categorize themselves as group members. When group membership is identified and internalized as an aspect of the self-concept, and when there are important comparisons between the individuals' ingroup and outgroup, individuals should be more likely to display favoritism toward members of their ingroup (Turner & Tajfel, 1979; 1986). Apart from the tendency for most AIANs to live in relative isolation from other racial groups (making outgroup hate crimes much less likely), a second possible explanation for AIANs committing racial hate crimes against their own ingroup could be that they may not have seen their victims as members of their ingroup in those particular settings.

There are 562 federally recognized tribal governments in the United States (USINFO, 2005). Because each one has a relatively small population, the U.S. government, which is primarily composed of White officers[4], has combined and recognized these tribes as one unified racial group—American Indian/Alaskan Native. However, given the widely varying habits and customs that exist among these tribes, what kind of identification occurs when they meet each other? In other words, do they identify each other as part of the unified AIAN group, or as members of their own unique tribe? If they identify each other as members of their own tribe more strongly than members of the AIAN group, then ingroup favoritism towards their own tribe is more likely to occur.

This same interpretation might also apply to Asians in the U.S. Asians committed relatively many "ingroup" hate crimes against other Asians in 1996, 1998, 1999, 2003, 2004, 2005, 2006, 2007, and 2008, but the question here is whether they strongly identify themselves as Asians or as members of their nation of origin (Cambodia, Japan, Korea, China, Vietnam, etc.). There has been a long history of conflicts between different Asian nations. They include, for example, a series of Sino-Japanese Wars, the wars between North and South Korea, and the Taiwanese independence movement. Although people would see these as "ingroup conflicts," they may be more accurately identified as "outgroup conflicts" by people from different Asian (or AIAN) cultures. In other words, there may be greater heterogeneity of Asians and AIANs than of Blacks and Whites in the U.S., and this greater heterogeneity might account in part for what might be misperceived to be a higher level of ingroup hate crimes on the part of Asians and AIANS.

The greater heterogeneity within AIAN and Asian cultures, however, might not fully explain why they were more likely to commit hate crimes against members of their own group. Social comparison theory (Festinger, 1954) and social identity theory (Turner &

---

[4] This could be seen as an example of "outgroup homogeneity bias" where outgroups are seen as more homogeneous (Quattrone & Jones, 1980).

Tajfel, 1986) offer another, potentially complementary, explanation. It has been proposed that "social comparison" is a central aspect of "social identity theory" because the comparisons that people make between ingroup (or self) and outgroup (or other) enable them to better understand and evaluate themselves (Hogg, 2005). According to Festinger's (1954) social comparison theory, people tend to compare themselves to similar others and to emphasize any differences between them. Therefore, AIANs and Asians could form their social identities by comparing their subgroup against other subgroups within the broader AIAN and Asian categories. On the other hand, White Americans may encounter fewer racial identity problems because they are the majority and have been solving their "ingroup conflicts" in the country far longer than other racial groups have (although regional discriminations may not vanish totally), and the same might be true of Blacks.

A final explanation is suggested by system justification theory. Jost and Banaji (1994) defined system justification as the "process by which existing social arrangements are legitimized, even at the expense of personal and group interest" (p. 2). In other words, system justification theory proposes that people have a general ideological motive to justify the existing social order, especially at an implicit, non-conscious level of awareness. This motive presumably exists in disadvantaged groups as well as in advantaged ones, and is sometimes even strongest among the members of disadvantaged groups who suffer the most from the status quo. Jost, Banaji, and Nosek (2004) studied the differences of racial attitudes between Black and White respondents. They found that Whites displayed a larger percentage of implicit (78.4%) rather than explicit ingroup favoritism (51.1%), whereas Blacks were found to display more explicit (65.4%) rather than implicit ingroup favoritism (40.1%). If implicit ingroup favoritism is weaker in AIANs and Asians than in Whites in the U.S., it might result in a lower level of restraint on ingroup hate crime among AIANs and Asians, consistent with the idea of system justification theory that minority group members who suffer from the status quo may often act to support it.

In summary, Blacks were more likely to be targets of racial hate crimes than were Whites. On the other hand, Whites were more likely to commit racial hate crimes than were Asians. Specifically, Blacks were targeted by Whites and Whites were targeted by Blacks more often than expected, whereas AIANs and Asian were more likely to commit hate crimes against their own racial groups. These phenomena may be due to relatively segregated living arrangements, to system justification, or to the heterogeneity within certain groups. Nevertheless, the trend of the data over time is encouraging. The overall racial hate crime rate has decreased significantly from 1996 to 2008 ($r = -.883$, $p < .001$), as has the occurrence rate of each specific racial hate crime (anti-White: $r = -.915$, $p < .001$, anti-Black: $r = -.889$, $p < .001$; and anti-Asian: $r = -.815$, $p < .001$, see Figure 1).

Anti-Religion Hate Crimes

The FBI crime data document seven types of anti-religious hate crimes: anti-Jewish, anti-Catholic, anti-Protestant, anti-Islamic, anti-other religious group, anti-atheism/agnosticism /etc., and anti-multi-religions. The findings revealed differences of this type that varied across the 13-year period. In addition, Jews were consistently more likely to become victims of religious hate crimes compared with other religious groups. Before 2001, every other religious group was significantly less likely than Jews to be targeted by religious hate crime offenders. However, in 2001, the year of the September 11 attacks, Muslims became targeted more than all other religious groups, including Jews, whereas by 2007 and 2008, anti-Islamic religious hate crimes no longer exceeded the average of overall religious hate crimes, whereas anti-Jewish religious hate crime was still higher than the average, and all others were lower than the average rates (see Figures 2 and 3).

Anti-Race by Year

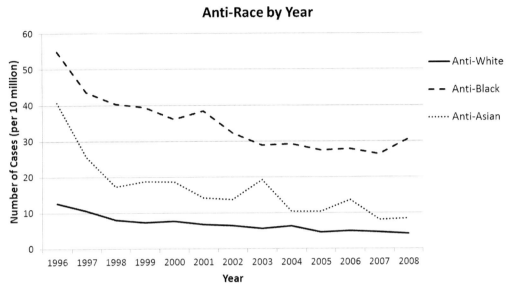

From Cheng, Ickes, & Kenworthy, 2013.

Figure 1. The trends of the adjusted numbers of cases of each anti-racial hate crime from 1996 to 2008.

Religious Hate Crime

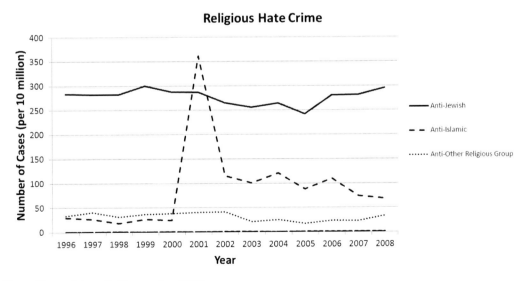

From Cheng, Ickes, & Kenworthy, 2013.

Figure 2. The trends of the adjusted numbers of cases of each anti-religious hate crime from 1996 to 2008.

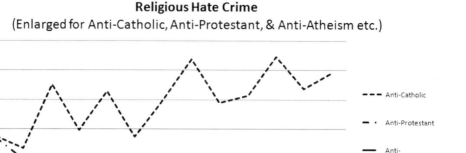

From Cheng, Ickes, & Kenworthy, 2013.

Figure 3. The trends of the adjusted numbers of cases of each anti-religious hate crime (enlarged for anti-Catholic, anti-Protestant, and anti-Atheism, etc.) from 1996 to 2008.

Anti-Jewish hate crime is an old story that is rooted in Western culture and religion. Today, as in the past, most of the anti-religious hate crimes committed are those against Jewish individuals. Although anti-Islamic hate crime rates have gradually decreased since the terrorist attacks in 2001 ($r = -.769$, $p < .05$), anti-Jewish hate crime rates remain high and unchanged in the period from 1996 through 2008 ($r = -.254$, ns). Overall, religious hate crime rates (if we exclude anti-Islamic crimes because of their temporary and dramatic increase in 2001) reveal no significant change from 1996 to 2008 ($r = -.400$, ns).

Anti-Sexual Orientation Hate Crimes

There are three types of anti-sexual orientation hate crimes reported by the FBI: anti-homosexual, anti-heterosexual, and anti-bisexual. The findings revealed that homosexuals were consistently more likely to become victims of sexual orientation hate crimes compared with other the sexual orientation groups (heterosexuals and bisexuals; see Figures 4, 5, and 6). Moreover, after separating anti-homosexual hate crime into anti-male homosexual and anti-female homosexual hate crimes, while adjusting for the subgroup populations, it was found that the number of anti-male homosexual hate crimes was significantly higher than that of anti-female homosexual hate crimes (see Figure 7).[5]

---

[5] Notice that anti-male homosexual hate crime dropped dramatically in 2005. Around 2005, the major news regarding homosexual issues was that Massachusetts' second convention to amend the Commonwealth's Constitution to disallow same-sex marriage but permit civil unions was defeated (The New York Times, 2005). The event actually started at the end of 2003, when the Massachusetts Supreme Judicial Court claimed that state's ban on same-sex marriage was unconstitutional (Burge, 2003), but it was in full swing in 2005. The marked decline in anti-male homosexual hate crimes during this time may be relevant to the friendly environment around 2005. However, there is no direct evidence for this interpretation.

This last finding is consistent with the findings reported by Falomir-Pichastor and Mugny (2009) and Keiller (2010). Falomir-Pichastor and Mugny (2009) found that heterosexual women possessed more positive attitudes toward homosexuality than did heterosexual men, and that the gender self-esteem of heterosexual men (but not heterosexual women) was negatively correlated with sexual prejudice toward homosexuals. Interestingly, this effect was stronger for men who were motivated to maintain psychological distance from homosexual men. In addition, the extent to which participants were given information about male homosexuality as a biological factor was manipulated in their study.

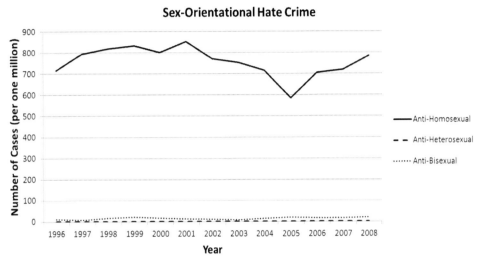

From Cheng, Ickes, & Kenworthy, 2013.

Figure 4. The trends of the adjusted numbers of cases of each anti-sexual orientation hate from 1996 to 2008.

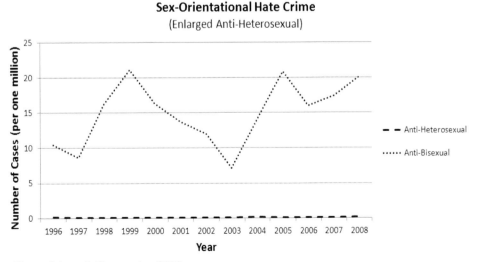

From Cheng, Ickes, & Kenworthy, 2013.

Figure 5. The trends of the adjusted numbers of cases of each anti-sexual orientation hate crime (enlarged for anti-heterosexual) from 1996 to 2008.

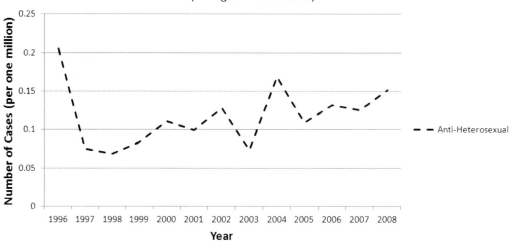

From Cheng, Ickes, & Kenworthy, 2013.

Figure 6. The trends of the adjusted numbers of cases of each anti-sexual orientation hate crime (enlarged for anti-bisexual) from 1996 to 2008.

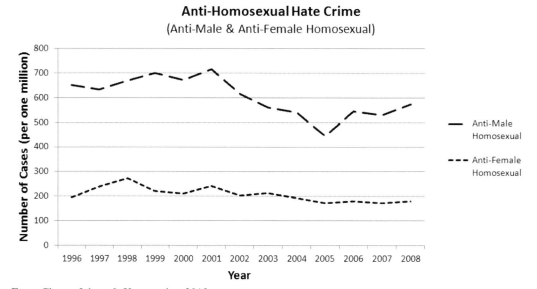

From Cheng, Ickes, & Kenworthy, 2013.

Figure 7. The trends of the adjusted numbers of cases of anti-male and anti-female homosexual orientation hate crime from 1996 to 2008.

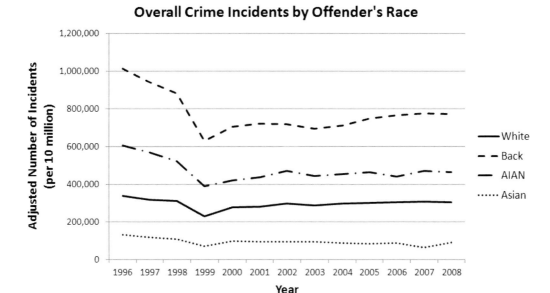

From Cheng, Ickes, & Kenworthy, 2013.

Figure 8. Adjusted numbers of incidents of overall crimes by offender' race.

Participants were either told that they were biologically different from heterosexual males (difference condition), that they were not biologically different from heterosexual men (no difference condition), or they were given no information about this issue (control condition). The results showed that, in the control group and the no difference condition, male participants' gender self-esteem was still negatively associated with their attitude toward gay men. On the other hand, the link between heterosexual men's gender self-esteem and attitude toward gay men was weakened when they were given information about the existence of biological differences between homosexual and heterosexual men (difference condition).

Moreover, in his conceptually related study, Keiller (2010) examined the "masculine ideology" of male undergraduate students. He also found that conformity to traditional masculine norms was negatively linked to men's attitudes toward gay men but not towards lesbians. National hate crime reports from 2000 to 2003 revealed that 76.4% of hate crime offenders were male (Harlow, 2005). Therefore, it is possible that the higher rate of anti-male homosexual attitudes was due to the presence of more male hate crime offenders with masculine ideology.

In summary, anti-homosexual crimes were committed significantly more than were any other anti-sexual orientation hate crimes. In addition, within anti-homosexual hate crimes, the incidence of anti-male homosexual offenses was significantly greater than that of anti-female homosexual offenses. The data revealed that gay men were targeted by anti-sexual orientation offenders about 4 to 5 times more than lesbian women in the current analyses. The data also showed that, overall, anti-sexual orientation hate crime rates have not changed much from 1996 to 2008 ($r = -.327$, ns).

TYPES OF HATE CRIMES CROSS-CATEGORIZED BY TYPES OF OFFENSES

According to the FBI reports, there are three primary subtypes of hate crime offenses: crimes against persons, crimes against property, and crimes against society. Although crimes against society are rare in the FBI hate crime reports, crimes against persons and against property are the two most commonly observed subtypes of hate crimes. While examining the incidence of these two subtypes (against persons and against property) across the categories of anti-race, anti-religion, and anti-sexual orientation hate crimes, it was found that the general rate of crimes against persons was about 65%, and the rate of crimes against property was about 35% across the 13-year span. However, anti-racial hate crimes and anti-sexual orientation hate crimes were more likely to be directed against persons, whereas anti-religious hate crimes were more likely to be directed against property, compared to the expected values (Cheng, Ickes, & Kenworthy, 2013).

In the data included in the FBI's Uniformed Crime Report, intimidation, simple assault, and aggravated assault were the three subtypes of crimes against persons that occurred most often (about 99%), while destruction/damage/vandalism, larceny-theft, burglary, and robbery were the four subtypes of crimes against property that were committed most often (about 97%). Overall, hate crimes against persons were more likely to take the form of intimidation (52%), and less likely to take the form of aggravated assaults (18%). Anti-religious hate crimes were particularly likely to reveal this pattern. On the other hand, anti-sexual orientation hate crimes were more likely to take the form of simple assaults but were less likely to take the form of intimidation, whereas anti-racial hate crimes were more likely to take the form of aggravated assaults but were less likely to take the form of intimidation, compared with the overall hate crime patterns. However, aggravated assaults have increased in anti-sexual orientation hate crimes but have decreased in anti-racial hate crimes since 2006 (for the details, please refer to Cheng, Ickes, & Kenworthy, 2013). These latter findings suggest that anti-sexual orientation hate crimes have become more severe whereas anti-racial hate crimes have decreased its severity in recent years.

When comparing the four subtypes of crimes against property (destruction/damage/ vandalism, larceny-theft, burglary, and robbery) within each target category of hate crime (anti-race, anti-religion, and anti-sexual orientation), it was found that hate crimes against property generally were committed as destruction/damage/vandalism (86%) far more often than crimes in the other three categories (larceny-theft: 6%, burglary: 4%, and robbery: 4%). Qualifying this difference only slightly, anti-religious hate crimes were the most likely to be committed through destruction/damage/vandalism compared with the overall rates, whereas anti-sexual orientation hate crimes were a little more likely to be committed through robbery compared with the overall rates. In addition, anti-racial hate crimes have been more likely to be committed through larceny-theft and burglary than have anti-religious and anti-sexual orientation hate crimes since 1999 (for the details, please refer to Cheng, Ickes, & Kenworthy, 2013).

Why are anti-religious offenses more likely to be directed towards property, whereas anti-racial and anti-sexual orientation offenses are more likely to be directed toward people? Although there has not been much relevant literature about this phenomenon, it could be proposed that when anti-religious offenders conduct hate crimes against victims, they intend to convey a strongly negative attitude against the specific religion and to "send a message" that this religion is vulnerable, rather than to express aggression toward specific individuals who practice the religion. In other words, when offenders commit religious hate crimes, they are trying to show their dislike of the religion or the higher power associated with that religion, rather than targeting individual members of the religion. This view, if correct, would help to explain why religious hate crime offenses typically involve destroying, damaging, or vandalizing property, as a way of rejecting the religion or the higher power associated with it. On the other hand, because race and sexual orientation are considered to be inherent features or characteristics of individual persons, committing hate crimes of this type more typically involves assault and intimidation as a way of displaying hatred of the targets' physical features, their behavior, or lifestyles (Dasgupta, DeSteno, Williams, & Hunsinger, 2009).

While examining crimes against people and property in greater detail, it became evident that hate crimes involving race and sexual orientation were more severe than anti-religious hate crimes. Compared to the overall expected rate, anti-religious hate crimes were more likely to be committed by intimidating people or by destroying, damaging, or vandalizing property. On the other hand, hate crimes involving sexual orientation and race were more likely to involve simple and aggravated assault, respectively. However, these trends have changed since 2006 such that anti-racial hate crimes have begun to involve more intimidation but less aggravated assaults compared with the overall hate crime patterns, whereas anti-sexual orientation hate crimes have begun to show higher numbers of cases of aggravated assaults than do the overall patterns.

In summary, there are differences in the subtypes of hate crimes depending on the nature of the target group, which seem to imply that animosity toward different "objects" of hatred (religious tenets, personal characteristics, lifestyle preferences) are expressed in different ways.

THE INCIDENCE OF HATE CRIMES COMPARED WITH OTHER CRIMES: A COMPARISON BY RACE

Are hate crimes committed at similar rates as other crimes by perpetrators of different races? If the hate crimes are not, by nature, different from other crimes, the rates of hate crimes—when compared with the overall crime rates—should be similar among racial groups. Although similar rates do not guarantee that hate crimes are the same as other crimes, differences across racial groups would indicate that hate crimes are different from other crimes, at least in respect to the offender's race.

The adjusted numbers of overall crimes and hate crimes only across offender's race are presented in Figure 8 and Figure 9. Then, after controlling for the general crime rates (i.e., computing indexes of the adjusted number of hate crimes divided by the adjusted number of general crimes, which was the proportion of hate crimes in relation to general crimes after controlling for the subgroup populations), significant differences in homogeneity were found among the four categories of racial perpetrators (Figure 10). The results reveal that Whites consistently had relatively higher hate crime rates as compared to Blacks, and Asians also had relatively higher hate crimes rates compared to Blacks and AIANs.

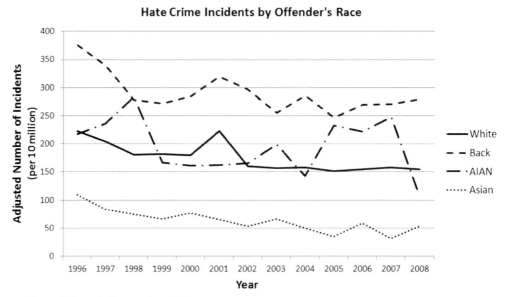

From Cheng, Ickes, & Kenworthy, 2013.

Figure 9. Adjusted numbers of incidents of hate crimes by offender' race.

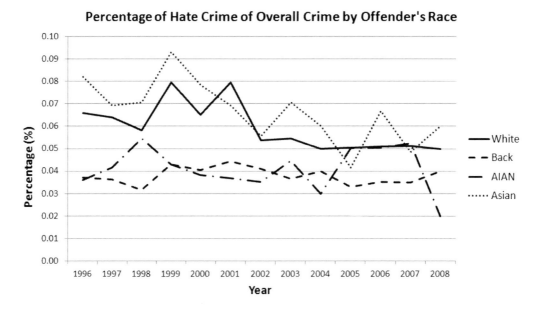

Figure 10. Percentage of hate crimes of overall crimes by offender' race.

According to system justification theory (Jost & Banaji, 1994), Whites may commit relatively more hate crimes because of their dominant position in U.S. society and their greater motivation to preserve the status quo. Why then did Asians also have a higher hate crime rate compared with Blacks and AIANs? Perhaps, as noted in a previous section, it is because Asians perpetrate more racial hate crimes against what are broadly defined as "Asian" ingroups; approximately 60% of Asian hate crimes were anti-racial hate crimes. These data suggest that the relatively higher rates of anti-Asian hate crimes by Asian perpetrators may reflect traditional animosities toward members of other Asian cultures. However, they may also reflect the fact that Asian perpetrators committed lower rates of all crimes, a fact that accentuated the rates of anti-Asian hate crimes in relative terms (see Figure 8).

WHO ARE THE PERPETRATORS OF HATE CRIMES AND WHY DO THEY COMMIT THEM?

In the FBI UCR reports, only data on the offenders' race are provided—not other information that would help us to develop "perpetrator profiles." It is, however, vitally important to know who the perpetrators are and why they commit hate crimes. By knowing this, we not only can help hate crime investigators to focus on possible suspects, but also can better understand the causes of hate crime and find ways to reduce its incidence. It is therefore important to review the available information about factors that may help us to develop "perpetrator profiles" for hate crime offenders. The potential elements of these profiles that are examined here include sociodemographic variables, mortality salience, aggression, emotion, and potential personality predictors.

Elements of Potential Perpetrator Profiles

Sociodemographic Variables

Craig and Waldo (1996) investigated people's *perceptions* regarding the perpetrators of hate crimes. They found that non-white respondents were significantly more likely than white respondents to answer that the typical offenders of hate crimes were "white males." Thus, they concluded that the individuals' perceptions of hate crime perpetrators were associated with their own racial designation. However, according to the previous analyses reported in this paper, this perception may in part reflect the reality that Whites commit more hate crimes toward other racial groups (especially toward Blacks) than toward members of their own racial group. Moreover, according to the present analyses, Whites also had higher *relative* hate crime rates when compared to other racial groups.

In another study, Levin and McDevitt (1993) collaborated with the State Attorney's Office to study hate crime incidents in the State of Illinois. They found that typical offenders were male, aged 14 to 24, and without a prior criminal record. These finding are consistent with these of Finn and McNeil (1987) who reported that half of the hate crime perpetrators arrested were adolescents and young adults between the ages of 16 and 25. Similarly, the Anti-Defamation League (ADL, 1991) reported that about 70-80% of anti-Semitic perpetrators were under 21 years old. Overall, these studies have revealed that of hate crime offenders are usually adolescents and young adults.

Social stereotypes suggest that members of certain hate crime groups (e.g. neo-Nazis, skinheads) should be particularly likely to become active (and repeated) hate crime offenders. To test this idea, Dunbar (2002) investigated 1,459 hate crime cases in the Los Angeles area from 1994 to 1995 and found that less than 5% of hate crime offences were committed by hate group members. On the other hand, Crevecoeur (2007) reported a much higher incidence in a study of 327 arrested hate crime offenders in the Los Angeles areas in 2003. She found that 130 (39.8%)[6] of the 327 offenders were probable hate group members (47 as "defined" and 83 as "possible" hate group members). In terms of absolute case numbers, however, organized hate crime members do not commit more violent hate crimes than non-members do.

Nevertheless, Dunbar (2003) studied 58 convicted hate crime offenders and found that hate crime offenders who scored high on the Bias Motivation Profile (BMP; a combined measure of a history of bias-motivated aggression, membership in a hate crime group, articulated hate speech during the commission of the crime, and the possession of hate iconography such as books, music, body tattoos, or neo-Nazi garb) were more likely to commit instrumental (deliberate and planned) aggression toward victims than were other offenders who were low on the BMP. This finding suggests that although hate group members do not commit more hate crimes than non-hate group members, they do commit hate crimes with greater premeditation.

It should also be noted that, compared with non-bias crimes, hate crimes are more likely to involve multiple perpetrators (Dunbar, 2003; Herek et al., 2002). Combining this finding with the previous findings that hate crime offenders are more likely to be young males, "peer influences" may also need to be considered. Franklin (2000) and McDevitt, Levin, and Bennet (2002) found that peer influence affects the relationship between prejudice and hate crimes. Although some offenders who participate in gang- or group-perpetrated hate crimes possess strongly prejudiced attitudes toward the outgroups whose members they victimize, other offenders may have only mildly prejudiced attitudes, or even no real prejudice at all. Many of the hate crime offenses that occur in these cases are presumably the product of peer pressure.

In sum, hate crime offenders are more likely to be young males; and compared with non-bias crimes, hate crimes are more likely to be committed by multiple offenders. And although hate group members do not appear to commit a disproportionate percentage of hate crimes, the ones they do commit are more likely to involve premeditated acts of instrumental aggression.

Mortality Salience

As noted in the previous section, the concept of mortality salience is central to terror management theory (TMT; Greenberg, Pyszczynski, & Solomon, 1986). Niesta, Fritsche, and Jonas (2008) stated that, from TMT's perspective, realizing one's mortality increase one's existential anxiety. In order to reduce existential anxiety, individuals engage in ingroup favoritism and outgroup derogation as a means of increasing their self-esteem and perceptions of control, reducing their uncertainty, and seeking the promise of death transcendence and symbolic immortality through group membership.

With regard to the predicted ingroup favoritism predicted by TMT, Ochsmann and Mathy (1994) found that individuals preferred to sit by others of the same nationality when their mortality was salient. With regard to the predicted outgroup derogation, Greenberg et al.

---

[6] Obviously, the percentage of hate group members in Crevecoeur's (2007) study was considerably higher than it was in Dunbar's (2002) study. The major reason for this difference was that Crevecoeur's (2007) data were cases of "arrested offenders" whereas Dunbar (2002) estimated the incidence of hate crimes regardless of whether the offenders were arrested or not. This difference implies that hate group members commit more hate crimes of greater severity and are therefore more likely to be arrested.

(1990) found that Christian college students evaluated Jewish college students more negatively when their mortality was salient. Similarly, McGregor et al. (1998) demonstrated that increasing students' mortality salience also increased their hostility and aggression toward those with political beliefs that were opposite to their own (i.e., by requiring them to eat more hot sauce). Moreover, Pyszczynski et al. (2006) found that mortality salience increased support for violent military interventions and the willingness to sacrifice life for political and religious ideology, and Hirschberger and Ein-Dor (2006) found that mortality salience increased violent resistance against unwanted political interventions.

Aggression

It has been shown repeatedly that having an aggressive personality significantly predicts violent crimes (Ferguson, Cruz, Martinez, Rueda, Ferguson, & Negy, 2008). There are two types of aggression: reactive aggression and proactive aggression (Crick & Dodge, 1996; Dodge, 1991). Reactive aggression, which is also known as expressive aggression, is usually a response to provocations or threats. It tends to be emotional and impulsive, and it includes a high level of autonomic arousal as well as a low level of behavioral control. On the other hand, proactive aggression, which is also known as instrumental aggression, is deliberate and planned. It is characterized by a low level of autonomic arousal combined with a high level of behavioral control (Nouvion, Cherek, Lane, Tcheremissine, & Lieving, 2007).

Dunbar (2003) has pointed out that reactive and proactive aggression could be differentially implicated in two major types of bias-motivated crimes. He argues that hate crimes with reactive aggression are usually defensive and committed without planning. As an example of this type of hate crime, Green, Strolovitch, and Wong (1997) proposed the "defended neighborhoods" hypothesis, in which hate crimes with reactive aggression occur following a perceiving threat from the denigrated outgroup to the offender's ingroup. In contrast, Dunbar (2003) argues that hate crimes with proactive aggression are premeditated and deliberate. Crimes of this type may reflect the offenders' greater ideological resolve and stronger level of social dominance.

In other words, whereas reactively aggressive hate crimes are more protective, proactively aggressive hate crimes are more predatory (Dunbar, 2003). The offenders who display reactive aggression may commit hate crimes because of a loss of control or impulsiveness. In contrast, the offenders who display proactive aggression may do so in order to actively display their hatred of the outgroup. Cornell et al. (1996) proposed that most criminal aggression is reactive and expressive. On the other hand, Salfati and Canter (1999) proposed that proactive aggression may be an indicator of a pathological ability to use aggression to achieve a goal. Offering a further qualification, Fisher (2007) reported that reactive aggression was more common in anti-racial hate crimes, whereas proactive aggression was more common in anti-sexual orientation hate crimes.

Craing (2002) proposed that aggression in the context of hate crimes serves two functions: a symbolic function and an instrumental function. In its symbolic function, aggression in the context of hate crimes serves as an expression of the hate, and offenders are motivated to commit hate crimes in response to the victims' symbolic status. It does not matter whether the victims identify themselves as a targeted social group; it only matters whether that group is despised by the offenders.

In contrast, the instrumental function of aggression in hate crimes is to create a new and different atmosphere within the community. When the hate crime occurs, it not only affects the victims and the offenders; it also influences both the victims' group (even other minority groups) and the offenders' group. The hate crime incident(s) may threaten the rest of the victims' group members or even other minority groups, which may cause some of them move out of the community, close their businesses, etc. Instrumental aggression also influences the rest of people in the offenders' own social group. They may feel pressure to behave in different ways when encountering people from the victims' social group (Craing, 2002).

Nevertheless, there are similarities between the symbolic function of hate crime aggression and reactive aggression, because they both serve as a way to express the offenders' hatred for the victims. On the other hand, the instrumental function of hate crime aggression and proactive aggression are also similar in respect to the goal of sending a threatening message to the targeted groups.

Emotion

Fiske (2004) noted that some people become extremely biased when they perceive threats toward their in-group. One of the consequences of perceiving threats is increased emotional reactivity. Christie (2006) and Niesta, Fritsche, and Jonas (2008) both stated that anxiety is central in mortality salience and its worldview defense in TMT. The core relational theme of this fear–anxiety is the sense of danger or threat, which is distinguished by an impaired use of emotion-focused coping (Smith, Haynes, Lazarus, & Pope, 1993). Lerner, Gonzalez, Small, and Fischhoff (2003) examined how emotion specifically affects people's responses to terrorism. They found that people who experienced anger are more likely to support a vengeful policy and less likely to support a conciliatory-contact policy, compared with those who experienced fear.

According to Shay (1994), fear can sometimes evoke anger as well. Shay (1994) proposed that one way to deal with intense fear is to focus on anger that can increase individuals' sense of perceived control and safety. As the studies of mortality salience suggest (Greenberge et al., 1990; Hirschberger & Ein-Dor, 2006; McGregor et al., 1998; Ochsmann & Mathy, 1994; Pyszczynski et al., 2006), when thinking about their mortality, participants may not feel anger, but fear and fear of death. It is interesting, therefore, that both Becker (1973) and Cohen, Solomon, Maxfield, Pyszczynski, and Greenberg (2004) found that increased fear leads individuals to increase their support for candidates who are more resolute and who are engaged in ambitious and risky behaviors. Thus, anger not only increases individuals' aggressive behaviors directly but also indirectly, through its use as a way to cope with intense fear.

A related perspective has been offered by Dasgupta, DeSteno, Williams, and Hunsinger (2009), who proposed the "emotion-specific hypothesis" to investigate whether different emotions have a "spill-over" effect on outgroup judgments, or whether they have the ability to influence the evaluations of specific groups differently according to "the degree to which [they are] applicable to [the] perceiver's expectations of that group (p. 585)." For example, previous research has revealed that anger is the dominant emotion elicited by perceived threats to one's resources and property, and freedoms and rights, from outgroups (Cottrell & Neuberg, 2005; Goodwin & Devos, 2002; Fiske et al., 2002; Mackie & Smith, 2002), and that anti-Arab hate crimes (similar to anti-Islamic hate crimes in the previous section) were predominantly anger-based offenses (De Oliveira & Dambrun, 2007; Johnson, 1992; Oswald, 2005; Skitka, Bauman, Aramovich, & Morgan, 2006). On the other hand, disgust is elicited by threats of physical or moral contamination from outgroups (Dasgupta et al., 2009). These perceived threats are often associated with the stereotype of gays and lesbians engaging in "inappropriate" sexual behavior that violates moral values (Cottrell & Neuberg, 2005; Herek, 1996; Mosher & O'Grady, 1979).

In Dasgupta et al.'s (2009) research testing their "emotion-specific hypothesis," anger was found to increase bias against anger-relevant groups (e.g. Arabs) but not against disgust-relevant groups (e.g. homosexuals). On the other hand, disgust was found to increase bias against disgust-relevant groups but not against anger-relevant groups. These findings suggest that emotion can inflame implicit prejudice toward an outgroup, but only when the emotion-specific threat is applicable to one's existing stereotype of, and expectations for, the group in question.

Potential Personality Predictors: Social Dominance Orientation (SDO) and Right-Wing Authoritarianism (RWA)

A large body of research findings has revealed two personality traits that are associated with prejudice and discrimination (i.e. Levin & Sidanius, 1999; Laythe, Finkelm & Kirkpatrick, 2001), and may be also relevant to hate crimes.

The first of these traits —social dominance orientation (SDO)—refers to the degree of preference for inequality among social groups (Sidanius & Pratto, 1999). Pratto, Sidanius, Stallworth, and Malle (1994) reported that high-SDO individuals tend to seek hierarchy-enhancing roles in society, whereas low-SDO individuals tend to seek hierarchy-attenuating jobs. Levin and Sidanius (1999) found that SDO is linked to negative affect toward members of low status groups. And Pratto et al. (1994) found that high SDO individuals have lower empathy, lower tolerance, and perform fewer helping behaviors than individuals who score lower on this trait.

The second of these traits—right-wing authoritarianism (RWA; Altemeyer, 1981)—was developed from the concept of authoritarian personality (Adorno, Frenkel-Brunswik, Levinson, & Sanford, 1950). This trait has been found to correlate positively with political conservatism (Altemeyer, 1988), beliefs in religious fundamentalism (Altemeyer & Hunsberger, 1992), and negative attitudes toward outgroup members (Laythe, Finkelm & Kirkpatrick, 2001). Lavine, Lodge, Polichak, and Taber (2002) demonstrated that individuals with high RWA scores were more sensitive to threat than individuals with low RWA scores, as assessed by measuring how quickly they recognized and responded to threatening words.

Although SDO and RWA both are related to prejudice and discrimination, there are some important differences between them. Henry, Sidanius, Levin, Pratto, and Nammour (2005) found that Christian students' SDO and RWA scores were both positively associated with their support for anti-terrorist violence, whereas Muslim students' support for terrorism was positively correlated with their RWA scores but negatively correlated with their SDO scores. These findings can be reconciled if we assume that high SDO individuals prefer the current social arrangement when compared to low SDO individuals—an arrangement that gives Christians an implicitly higher status than Muslims (Sidanius & Pratto, 1990).

In other research, interactions between SDO, mortality salience, and RWA have been found. For example, examining U.S residents' SDO and their attitudes toward illegal immigrants, Bassett (2010) found that high SDO was associated with negative attitudes toward illegal immigrants, but only when mortality was salient. In a conceptually similar study, Greenberg et al. (1990) also found that high RWA was related to negative evaluation of dissimilar others when mortality was salient. In general, the research evidence suggests that SDO and RWA are most strongly related to outgroup bias when mortality is salient, which means that a cognitive aspect of mortality salience may moderate the link between personality traits (SDO and RWA) and one's attitude toward outgroups.

In sum, there are several variables that may influence outgroup derogation and therefore help to define the prototypic "perpetrator profiles" for various hate crimes. These include the sociodemographic variables of being an adolescent or young adult male and being a member of one or more hate groups (associated with hate crimes using instrumental aggression). They also include the personality and experiential variables of a heightened awareness of one's own mortality; the outgroup-focused emotions of anger and fear-anxiety; a higher than average level aggressiveness; and higher than average scores on the personality traits of SDO and RWA. Some of these personality and experiential variables have also been found to interact with each other to predict outgroup derogation (i.e., SDO and RWA have been found to interact with mortality salience). Although the available research has, to date, focused mainly on outgroup derogation, the variables that have been identified may also prove to be relevant to the phenomenon of hate crimes.

WHO ARE THE VICTIMS OF HATE CRIMES AND HOW ARE THEY AFFECTED BY THEM?

The analyses reported in this paper reveal that anti-racial hate crimes primarily targeted Blacks; anti-religious hate crimes primarily targeted Jews and Muslims; and anti-sexual orientation hate crimes primarily targeted homosexuals, especiallygay males. Previous research findings have shown that most hate crime victims were strangers (Herek, Cogan, & Gillis, 2002; Keefe, 2006); however, some hate crime offenses, particularly those in the anti-sexual orientation category, are committed by acquaintances, such as neighbors, coworkers, and classmates (Herek et al., 2002). This may be because sex-orientation is not as obvious as race or even religion, and therefore results in strong emotions of anger or disgust when the target's hated status is suddenly discovered.

Crevecoeur (2007) found that hate crimes committed by acquaintances were more severe than those committed by strangers. Crevecoeur also found that anti-sexual orientation hate crimes were more violent compared to racial and religious hate crimes. These results are consistent with those of my previous analyses which showed that anti-sexual orientation hate crimes were more likely to take the form of simple or aggravated assaults rather than intimidation, when compared to anti-racial and anti-religious hate crimes. In general, the amount of injury in anti-sex orientation hate crimes is more severe than in anti-racial and anti-religious hate crimes.

Other data indicate that hate crimes are less likely to be reported by the victims compared with other non-bias crimes, and this is particularly true for anti-sexual orientation hate crimes (Herek, Gillis, & Cogan, 1999). In general, victims tend not to report incidents of crimes if, in their evaluation, reporting these crimes is unlikely to produce satisfactory outcomes (Herek, et al., 2002).[7]

---

[7] For this reason, the relative frequency data reported in the first part of the current paper are believed to be underestimates because of the low report rate of hate crimes. However, it is still valuable to examine hate

Finally, research has also revealed that the victims of hate crimes usually report feelings of helplessness (Root, 1992), anxiety, depression, and restlessness (Wyatt, 1994). There is considerable evidence that hate crimes cause greater physical and psychological damage to victims than non-bias crimes do (Herek et al., 1997; Iganski, 2001; Levein & McDevitt, 1993; McDevitt, Balboni, Garcia, & Gu, 2001). Hate crime victims have been found to suffer from symptoms of posttraumatic stress disorder (PTSD; Kaysen, Lostutter, Goines, 2005). In addition, hate crime victims have also expressed significantly higher level of crime-related fears and beliefs, and a lower sense of mastery, compared with victims of non-bias crimes (Herek et al., 1999).

In summary, most hate crime victims were strangers to the offenders, but hate crimes—particularly those in the anti-sexual orientation category—can also be committed by acquaintances. If the victims and offenders were acquaintances, hate crimes tend to be more severe. Finally, although hate crime incidents are less likely to be reported by the victims, these incidents usually cause greater physical and psychological damage to the victims than non-bias crimes do.

WHY DO HATE CRIMES OCCUR?

When studying the relationship between attitudes and behavior, social psychologists usually note that although attitudes may influence individuals' behavior, attitudes are not always significant predictors of behavior (Fiske & Taylor, 1991; Zanna & Rempel, 2008). For example, Dovidio, Brigham, Johnson, and Gaertner (1996) reported that although the correlation between prejudice and discrimination was moderate ($r = .32$), the correlations between stereotyping and prejudice and between stereotyping and discrimination were relatively small ($r = .25$; $r = .16$, respectively).

Devine (1989) also investigated the relationship between stereotyping and prejudice. She found that both high- and low-prejudiced individuals possessed a knowledge of the cultural stereotype that was automatically activated in the presence of an outgroup member or outgroup symbol. However, low-prejudiced individuals could use a "controlled inhibition" of the stereotype, whereas high-prejudiced individuals could not. Supporting this conclusion, Fiske (1998, 2000) and Macrae and Bodenhausen (2000) also found that stereotype activation exists generally among individuals, but that the low-prejudiced ones can repress the stereotype by means of controlled processes.

Rudman, Ashmore, and Gary (2001) proposed three reasons to explain why prejudice is not highly associated with discrimination. First, individuals may repress their bias because this attitude conflicts with their egalitarian self-image (Gaertner & Dovidio, 1986). Second, individuals may not be willing to express the attitude because of normative pressures and social norms (Dovidio & Fazio, 1992; Fazio et al, 1995; Plant & Devine, 1998). Third, people who possess prejudiced attitudes that are hidden from their conscious awareness may not be able to express them on a self-report measure.

These arguments suggest that hate crime offenders may be unable to use controlled process to inhibit negative stereotypes, and they may not have the kind of egalitarian self-

crime incident reports in the present way in order to understand the general trends, complexities, and nuances of hate crimes.

image that would help them to repress, rather than express, their prejudiced attitudes. On the contrary, hate crime offenders may even believe that their prejudice is consistent with prevailing social norms. For example, Rayburn, Mendoza, and Davison (2003) found that non-prejudiced individuals perceived more guilt on the part of hate crime offenders and assigned less blame to hate crime victims (when compared to non-hate crime offenders and victims). In contrast, prejudiced individuals perceived no difference between hate crime and non-hate crime victims and offenders. This finding suggests that hate crime offenders may have a different perception of the normative pressures and prevailing social norms than other people do.

Why, however, would a person prefer to express a latent hatred than to control its expression? Several possible factors may be involved. Some of these factors have already been noted: the perception of mortality salience; an above-average level of aggressiveness; experiencing the target-focused emotions of anger, fear, and disgust; and having the personality traits of SDO and RWA. However, the social context in which hate crimes occur is also important, and it is sometimes the most crucial element of all. In 2001, the September 11th terrorist attacks occurred, which evoked the hostility of U.S. citizens toward Islamic extremists. When asked to report their feelings upon hearing of the September 11th attacks, 65% of Americans reported anger (Smith, Rasinsski, & Toce, 2001). The hostility in U.S. society toward Islamic extremists appears to have generalized to ordinary Muslims, and the result was a dramatic increase in anti-Islamic hate crimes.

In sum, hate crimes are rooted in prejudiced attitudes, but prejudiced attitudes may not always result in hate crimes. There are several factors that can influence this process. At the macro-level, the national climate of respect versus hostility toward outgroups can influence individuals' perception of the legitimacy of aggression toward outgroups and the tolerance for such behavior. At the micro-level, several individual difference variables such as mortality salience, level of aggressiveness, outgroup-focused emotions of anger or disgust, social dominance orientation (SDO); and right-wing authoritarianism (RWA), may also increase individuals' potential to commit hate crimes within the larger social context.

WHAT CAN REDUCE THE INCIDENCE OF HATE CRIME?

There is evidence that that the 1964 Federal Civil Rights Law has dramatically decreased the overt expression of racism (Schuman, Steeh, Bobo, & Krysan, 1997), and has also increased the normative pressures for the members of U.S. society to abandon (or at least suppress) their prejudice (Dunton & Fazio, 1997; Plant & Devine, 1998). It is clear that laws really do help to prevent crimes. But although hate crime laws help to prevent hate crimes, they cannot eliminate prejudice or the forms of discrimination that do not violate state or federal laws. Laws are better at treating the symptoms of hate crimes than getting at the root of the problem. And, as noted above, the root of hate crimes is an intensely negative prejudice toward one or more outgroups.

Thus, one solution to reducing hate crimes is to reduce prejudice in advance. Prejudice has been found to be reduced by the type of "education" that is based on the contact hypothesis. The contact hypothesis, proposed by Gordon Allport in 1954, asserts that contact can reduce intergroup conflict and facilitate intergroup relations when the four criteria are met. First, the members of the two groups must have equal status; second, they must cooperate with each other to achieve a common goal; third, they must have opportunities to interact face-to-face and get to know each other as persons; and fourth, their cooperation must be sanctioned at a higher level, by an authority, in order to create the desired normative pressure for change.

Extending the third element in Allport's list, Pettigrew (1998) argued that "friendship (quality but not quantity of contact)," which requires repeated contacts, was another important factor of successful intergroup contact because friendship can change the existing group categorizations. An important process involved in this change had been previously described by Brewer and Miller (1984), who proposed that when intergroup members interact with each other at the interpersonal level instead of the intergroup level, a process of *decategorization* occurs. By decategorizing each other, the intergroup members who are interacting with each other can overcome the differences that might impede their future contact.

Other processes are also involved, however. For example, Hewstone and Brown (1986) proposed that individuals would be more willing to have contact with outgroup members if they do not have to weaken or relinquish their own group identifications to do so. They raised the possibility that, in some circumstances at least, the psychological salience of group identifications can help to disprove negative stereotypes and facilitate generalization of positive intergroup contact experiences. Another possibility was suggested by Gaertner and Dovidio (2000), who proposed that ingroup and outgroup members can downplay their intergroup differences and emphasize their similarities at a superordinate level to consensually build a recategorization that enables them to see themselves as "different but at a higher level similar." Viewed collectively, these possibilities suggest that intergroup contacts that meet Allport's four criteria should help reduce to prejudice by means of one or more of the processes of *decategorization, salient categorization*, and *recategorization*.

Although research has not clarified the specific roles of these three hypothesized processes, it has provided solid evidence for Allport's recipe for reducing intergroup prejudice. This evidence is summarized in Pettigrew and Tropp's (2006) meta-analytic study of the effects of intergroup contact. They found that contact significantly reduced prejudice; moreover, this effect was stronger for children than for adults. The relevant research has consistently revealed that children and adolescents showed less prejudiced attitudes toward outgroups if they were in multiracial schools where the ethnic mix was balanced and a positive prejudice in favor of Whites had not been learned (Aboud, 2003; Schofield, 2008; Tropp & Prenovost, 2008; Wright & Tropp, 2005). Therefore, it is reasonable to hypothesize that "education" based on the Allportian contact hypothesis can reduce prejudice.

Another approach to reducing hate crime begins with the recognition that prejudice is based on negative stereotypes of outgroups that are rooted in socialization processes which are not always taught directly but are learned accumulatively from society (Devine, 1989; Fiske, 1998, 2000; Macrae & Bodenhausen, 2000). If these negative stereotypes can be dismissed, or at least called into question, by society, their influence on hate crimes should be reduced. Although this approach may sound a bit naïve and idealistic, its viability is suggested by the recent history of anti-racial hate crimes in the United States. As noted above, anti-racial hate crimes showed a decreasing trend from 1996 through 2008, both in the number of cases reported and in the severity of these crimes (Figure 11). This trend may be attributable in large measure to the hate crime laws that were enacted during this time and to the severe and widely publicized penalties that were attached to them. These laws obviously have more than one effect on society (e.g., fear of punishment as a deterrent from committing hate crimes), but one important effect may be to send a strong message that the society no longer regards the negative stereotyping of outgroup members as a legitimate reason for attacking them.

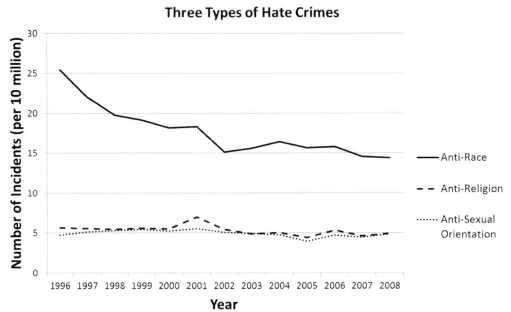

From Cheng, Ickes, & Kenworthy, 2013.

Figure 11. The trend of the adjusted numbers of cases of each type of hate crimes from 1996 to 2008.

Another deterrent of hate crimes may be media attention to high-profile cases that makes the public aware of the severe consequences for committing hate crimes. For example, the most recent case was the "Fort Hood Shooting" that occurred at the Fort Hood military base in Texas on November 5th, 2009. The accused perpetrator was an American-born Muslim of Palestinian descent who murdered 13 people and wounded 32 others (McKinley, 2009). This case quickly received world-wide attention via the media's reports. The media not only reported on the incident itself but also focused on the suspect's possible motivations in regard to his divided loyalties as a Muslim working in the U.S. military. More importantly, the media reported on the dramatic negative consequences experienced by the perpetrator in this case (paralysis resulting from being shot and the prospect of either a death sentence or being sentenced to prison without parole).

In the year of 2008, the first African-American President of the United States, Barack Obama, was elected. Although there were several factors that influenced his election, it is undeniable that the outcome of this election was an important milestone in the quest for racial equality in the United States. This outcome, along with the decrease in anti-racial hate crime incidents in the period from 1996 through 2008, should be viewed as positive signs. Perhaps they can even be seen as indicators that prejudice itself has declined in U.S. society. But we should be under no illusion that prejudice has vanished completely, or that it will not continue to erupt into hate crimes for a long time to come.

CONCLUSION

As noted above, there are several factors that may contribute to hate crimes. In general, the available data suggest that the problem of hate crimes must be addressed at multiple levels. At the macro-level, the local and national climate of respect/disrespect toward outgroups appears to influence individuals' perception of the relevant normative pressures and social norms. At the micro-level, several sociodemographic and personality/experiential variables may affect the likelihood that a particular individual will commit one or more hate crimes. With regard to the socio-demographic variables, the most typical hate crime offenders are adolescent or young adult males who in some cases are members of hate groups (these offenders are more likely to commit proactive/instrumental aggression) but in most other cases are not (these offenders are more likely to commit reactive/symbolic aggression). With regard to the personality/experiential variables, the available evidence is suggestive rather than definitive; however, it appears to implicate such factors as mortality salience, emotion (anger, fear-anxiety, and disgust), individuals' aggression, and the personality traits of SDO and RWA. Some of these variables have also been found to interact with each other to predict outgroup derogation (i.e., SDO and RWA with mortality salience).

When we shift the focus to the victims of hate crimes, the data reveal that the victims are in most case strangers to the offenders, but are sometimes acquaintances. Although hate crime incidents are less likely to be reported by victims than non-bias crimes, they usually cause greater physical and psychological damage to victims than the non-bias crimes do.

There may be two major strategies that can be used to reduce hate crimes. At the macro-level, enforcing anti-hate crime laws may increase the normative pressures for individuals in society to either abandon or suppress their prejudice. At the micro-level, educating citizens to tolerate and respect diversity by implementing the recommendations of contact hypothesis may also decrease hate crimes by reducing prejudice. Combining these two strategies, the media can facilitate the peaceful coexistence of ingroups and outgroups by providing fair and accurate reporting of intergroup conflicts-reporting that not only publicizes the harsh penalties for the commission of hate crimes but also reinforces the message that hate crimes are always wrong and unjust.

It was not until the end of last year (2009) that President Obama signed the Matthew Shepard and James Byrd Hate Crimes Prevention Act, which expands the dimensions of the original hate crime laws. Although the primary intent of hate crime laws is deterrence through the harsh sentences that offenders receive, their secondary effect is to send a strong message to possible victims that society has recognized their problems and will assertively attempt to protect their rights. However, as Judy Shepard, mother of Matthew Shepard, said, "

> The part of the hate-crime bill that I think is most important and I wish was in every hate-crime legislation is education. …. So like driver's school: you get a speeding ticket, you go to driver's school." (Dailey, 2009, ¶ 21).

This comment suggests that the fundamental long-term solution to the problem of hate crimes should be reducing prejudice and negative stereotypes by education rather than threatening people by means of punishment.

Fortunately, many elements of our society, including the government, the media, and some organizations and individuals, have dedicated themselves to reducing hate crimes (especially anti-racial hate crimes) over the course of half a century, and the decline of racial hate crime incidents in the period from 1996 to 2008 is supportive evidence that societal intervention does work. Although this is a long-term process, we should never give up.

REFERENCES

A Byte Out of FBI History: Imperial Kleagle of the Ku Klux Klan in Kustody (March 11, 2004). Retrieved February 20, 2010 from Federal Bureau of Investigation Web site: http://www.fbi.gov/page2/march04/kkk031104.htm

Aboud, F. E. (2003). The formation of in-group favoritism and outgroup prejudice in young children: Are they distinct attitudes? *Developmental Psychology, 39,* 48-60.

Adorno, T. W., Frenkel-Brunswik, E., Levinson, D. J., Sanford, R. N. (1950). The authoritarian personality. New York: Harper & Row.

Allport, G. W. (1954). *The nature of prejudice.* Cambridge, MA: Peruses Books.

Altemeyer, B. (1981). *Right-wing authoritarianism.* Winnipeg: University of Manitoba Press.

Altemeyer, B. (1988). *Enemies of freedom: Understanding right-wing authoritarianism.* San Francisco, CA US: Jossey-Bass.

Altemeyer, B., & Hunsberger, B. (1992). Authoritarianism, religious fundamentalism, quest, and prejudice. *International Journal for the Psychology of Religion, 2*(2), 113-133.

Anti-Defamation League of B'nai B'rith. (1991). *Audit of anti-Semitic incidents, 1990.* New York: Anti-Defamation League.

Bassett, J. (2010). The effects of mortality salience and social dominance orientation on attitudes toward illegal immigrants. *Social Psychology, 41*(1), 52-55.

Becker, E. (1973). *The denial of death.* New York: Free Press.

Brewer, M.B., & Miller, N. (1984). Beyond the contact hypothesis: Theoretical perspectives on segregation. In N. Miller and M. B. Brewer (Eds.). *Groups in contact: The psychology of desegregation* (pp. 281-302). Orlando, FL: Academic Press.

Burge, K. (November 18, 2003). SJC: Gay marriage legal in Mass. *The Boston Globe.* Retrieved February 20, 2010 from http://www.boston.com/news/local/massachusetts/articles/2003/11/18/sjc_gay_marriage_legal_in_mass/

Burns, R. (December 5, 2006). Gates acknowledges U.S. not winning war in Iraq. *Moscow-Pullman Daily News.* Retrieved February 20, 2010 from http://news.google.com/newspapers?nid=2026&dat=20061205&id=OtsyAAAAIBAJ&sjid=NvAFAAAAIBAJ&pg=5765,3461266

Byford, J. (2003) Antisemitism and the Christian Right in post-Milošević' Serbia: From conspiracy theory to hate crime. Internet Journal of Criminology. Retrieved February 20, 2010 from www.flashmousepublishing.com

Cheng, W., Ickes, W., & Kenworthy, J. B. (2013). The phenomenon of hate crimes in the United States. *Journal of Applied Social Psychology, 43*(4), 761-793.

Christie, D. J. (2006). 9/11 Aftershocks: An analysis of conditions ripe for hate crimes. In P. R. Kimmel & C. E. Stout (Eds.), *Collateral damage: The psychological consequences of America's war on terrorism* (pp. 19-44). Westport, CT, US: Praeger Publishers /Greenwood Publishing Group.

Clarke, R. (2004). *Against all enemies: Inside America's war on Terror.* New York: Free Press.

Craig, K. M., & Waldo, C. (1996). 'So, what's a hate crime anyway?' Young adults' perceptions of hate crimes, victims, and perpetrators. *Law and Human Behavior, 20*(2), 113-129.

Craig, K. M. (2002). Examining hate-motivated aggression: A review of the social psychological literature on hate crimes as a distinct form of aggression. *Aggression and Violent Behavior, 7*, 85–101.

Crevecoeur, D. (2007). Provocation, bias and arousal in hate crimes: Cognitive neoassociation re-examined. *Dissertation Abstracts International, 68*(1-B), 668.

Crick, N., & Dodge, K. (1996). Social information-processing mechanisms on reactive and proactive aggression. *Child Development, 67*(3), 993-1002.

Crime Identification Technology Act of 1998, Title I, § 101, 112 Stat. 1871, Public Law 105-251 (1998).

Cohen, F., Solomon, S., Maxfield. M., Greenberg, J., & Pyszczynski, T. (2005). American roulette: The effect of reminders of death on support for George W. Bush in the 2004 presidential election. *Analysis of Social Issues, 5*, 48-62.

Conn, R., Schrader, M., Wann, D., & Mruz, B. (1996). Reduction of anxiety about death: Need for beliefs about immortality. *Psychological Reports, 79*(3, Pt 2), 1315-1318.

Cornell, D. G., Warren, J., Hawk, G., Stafford, E., Oram, G., Pine, D. (1996). Psychopathy in instrumental and reactive violent offenders. *Journal of Consult Clinical Psychology, 64*, 783–790.

Cottrell, C., & Neuberg, S. (2005). Different Emotional Reactions to Different Groups: A Sociofunctional Threat-Based Approach to 'Prejudice'. *Journal of Personality and Social Psychology, 88*(5), 770-789.

Dailey, K. (2009). The Meaning of Matthew: Judy Shepard on Her New Memoir, Her Son's Lasting Legacy, and Moving Forward While Looking Back. *Newsweek.* Retrieved February 20, 2010 from http://blog.newsweek.com/blogs/thehumancondition/archive /2009/09/03/the-meaning-of-matthew-judy-shepard-on-her-new-memoir-matthew-shepard-s-lasting-legacy-and-moving-forward-while-looking-back.aspx

Dasgupta, N., DeSteno, D., Williams, L., & Hunsinger, M. (2009). Fanning the flames of prejudice: The influence of specific incidental emotions on implicit prejudice. *Emotion, 9*(4), 585-591.

De Oliveira, P., & Dambrun, N. (2007). Maintaining the status quo and social inequalities: Is stereotype endorsement related to support for system justification? *Current Research in Social Psychology, 13*, 101–121.

Devine, P. (1989). Stereotypes and prejudice: Their automatic and controlled components. *Journal of Personality and Social Psychology, 56,* 5-18.

Dodge K. A. (1991). The structure and function of reactive and proactive aggression. In Pepler DJ, Rubin KH (eds). *The Development and Treatment of Childhood Aggression* (pp 201–208). Hillsdale, NJ: Erlbaum.

Dovidio, J., Brigham, J. C., Johnson, B. T., & Gaertner, S. L. (1996). Stereotyping, prejudice, and discrimination: Another look. In C. N. Macrae, C. Stangor, & M. Hewstone (Eds.), *Stereotypes and stereotyping* (pp. 276-319). New York: Guilford.

Dunbar, E. (2002). Signs and cultural messages of bias motivated crimes: Analysis of the hate component of intergroup violence. In *Law Enforcement, Communication, and Community*. Giles, Howard (ed.), 201–228.

Dunbar, E. (2003). Symbolic, relational, and ideological signifiers of bias-motivated offenders: Toward a strategy of assessment. *American Journal of Orthopsychiatry, 73*(2), 203-211.

Dunton, B., & Fazio, R. (1997). An individual difference measure of motivation to control prejudiced reactions. *Personality and Social Psychology Bulletin, 23*(3), 316-326.

Ehrlich, H. J. (2009). *Understand Hate Crimes*. The Prejudice Institute. Retrieved February 20, 2010 from http://www.prejudiceinstitute.org/understandinghatecrimes.html

Falomir-Pichastor, J., & Mugny, G. (2009). "I'm not gay...I'm a real man!": Heterosexual men's gender self-esteem and sexual prejudice. *Personality and Social Psychology Bulletin, 35*(9), 1233-1243.

Fazio, R. H., Jackson, J. R., Dunton, B. C, & Williams, C. J, (1995). Variability in automatic activation as an unobtrusive measure of racial attitudes: A bona fide pipeline? *Journal of Personality and Social Psychology, 69*, 1013-1027.

Festinger, L. (1954). A theory of social comparison processes, *Human Relations 7*, 117-40

Federal Bureau of Investigation. (1997). *Hate Crime Statistics, 1996*. Washington D.C. Retrieved February 20, 2010 from http://www.fbi.gov/filelink.html?file=/ucr/hate96.pdf

Federal Bureau of Investigation. (1997). *Crime in the United States, 1996*. Washington D.C. Retrieved February 20, 2010 from http://www.fbi.gov/ucr/96cius.htm

Federal Bureau of Investigation. (1998). *Hate Crime Statistics, 1997*. Washington D.C. Retrieved February 20, 2010 from http://www.fbi.gov/filelink.html?file=/ucr/hc97all.pdf

Federal Bureau of Investigation. (1998). *Crime in the United States, 1997*. Washington D.C. Retrieved February 20, 2010 from http://www.fbi.gov/ucr/97cius.htm

Federal Bureau of Investigation. (1999). *Hate Crime Statistics, 1998*. Washington D.C. Retrieved February 20, 2010 from http://www.fbi.gov/filelink.html?file=/ucr/98hate.pdf

Federal Bureau of Investigation. (1999). *Crime in the United States, 1998*. Washington D.C. Retrieved February 20, 2010 from http://www.fbi.gov/ucr/98cius.htm

Federal Bureau of Investigation. (2000). *Hate Crime Statistics, 1999*. Washington D.C. Retrieved February 20, 2010 from http://www.fbi.gov/filelink.html?file=/ucr/99hate.pdf

Federal Bureau of Investigation. (2000). *Crime in the United States, 1999*. Washington D.C. Retrieved February 20, 2010 from http://www.fbi.gov/ucr/99cius.htm

Federal Bureau of Investigation. (2001). *Hate Crime Statistics, 2000*. Washington D.C. Retrieved February 20, 2010 from http://www.fbi.gov/filelink.html?file=/ ucr/cius_00 /hate00.pdf

Federal Bureau of Investigation. (2001). *Crime in the United States, 2000*. Washington D.C. Retrieved February 20, 2010 from http://www.fbi.gov/ucr/00cius.htm

Federal Bureau of Investigation. (2002). *Hate Crime Statistics, 2001*. Washington D.C. Retrieved February 20, 2010 from http://www.fbi.gov/filelink.html?file=/ucr/01hate.pdf

Federal Bureau of Investigation. (2002). *Crime in the United States, 2001*. Washington D.C. Retrieved February 20, 2010 from http://www.fbi.gov/ucr/01cius.htm

Federal Bureau of Investigation. (2003). *Hate Crime Statistics, 2002*. Washington D.C. Retrieved February 20, 2010 from http://www.fbi.gov/filelink.html?file=/ ucr/hatecrime 2002.pdf

Federal Bureau of Investigation. (2003). *Crime in the United States, 2002*. Washington D.C. Retrieved February 20, 2010 from http://www.fbi.gov/ucr/02cius.htm

Federal Bureau of Investigation. (2004). *Hate Crime Statistics, 2003*. Washington D.C. Retrieved February 20, 2010 from http://www.fbi.gov/filelink.html?file=/ucr/03hc.pdf

Federal Bureau of Investigation. (2004). *Crime in the United States, 2003*. Washington D.C. Retrieved February 20, 2010 from http://www.fbi.gov/ucr/03cius.htm

Federal Bureau of Investigation. (2005). *Hate Crime Statistics, 2004*. Washington D.C. Retrieved February 20, 2010 from http://www.fbi.gov/ucr/hc2004/openpage.htm

Federal Bureau of Investigation. (2005). *Crime in the United States, 2004*. Washington D.C. Retrieved February 20, 2010 from http://www.fbi.gov/ucr/cius_04/

Federal Bureau of Investigation. (2006). *Hate Crime Statistics, 2005*. Washington D.C. Retrieved February 20, 2010 from http://www.fbi.gov/ucr/hc2005/index.html

Federal Bureau of Investigation. (2006). *Crime in the United States, 2005*. Washington D.C. Retrieved February 20, 2010 from http://www.fbi.gov/ucr/05cius/

Federal Bureau of Investigation. (2007). *Hate Crime Statistics, 2006*. Washington D.C. Retrieved February 20, 2010 from http://www.fbi.gov/ucr/hc2006/index.html

Federal Bureau of Investigation. (2007). *Crime in the United States, 2006*. Washington D.C. Retrieved February 20, 2010 from http://www.fbi.gov/ucr/cius2006/index.html

Federal Bureau of Investigation. (2008). *Hate Crime Statistics, 2007*. Washington D.C. Retrieved February 20, 2010 from http://www.fbi.gov/ucr/hc2007/index.html

Federal Bureau of Investigation. (2008). *Crime in the United States, 2007*. Washington D.C. Retrieved February 20, 2010 from http://www.fbi.gov/ucr/cius2007/index.html

Federal Bureau of Investigation. (2009). *Hate Crime Statistics, 2008*. Washington D.C. Retrieved February 20, 2010 from http://www.fbi.gov/ucr/hc2008/index.html

Federal Bureau of Investigation. (2009). *Crime in the United States, 2008*. Washington D.C. Retrieved February 20, 2010 from http://www.fbi.gov/ucr/cius2008/index.html

Ferguson, C., Cruz, A., Martinez, D., Rueda, S., Ferguson, D., & Negy, C. (2008). Personality, parental, and media influences on aggressive personality and violent crime in young adults. *Journal of Aggression, Maltreatment & Trauma, 17*(4), 395-414.

Finn, P., & McNeil, T. (1987, October 7). *The response of the criminal justice system to bias crime: An exploratory review*. Contract Report submitted to the National Institute of Justice, U.S. Department of Justice. (Available from Abt Associates, Inc., 55 Wheeler St., Cambridge, MA 02138-1168)

Fisher, R.A. (1922). On the interpretation of $\chi2$ from contingency tables, and the calculation of P. *Journal of the Royal Statistical Society, 85*(1), 87-94.

Franklin, K. (2000). Antigay behaviors among young adults: Prevalence, patterns, and motivators in a noncriminal population. *Journal of Interpersonal Violence, 15*, 339-362.

Fiske, S. (1998). Stereotyping, prejudice, and discrimination. *The handbook of social psychology, Vols. 1 and 2* (4th ed.) (pp. 357-411). New York, NY US: McGraw-Hill.

Fiske, S. (2000). Interdependence and the reduction of prejudice. *Reducing prejudice and discrimination* (pp. 115-135). Mahwah, NJ US: Lawrence Erlbaum Associates Publishers.

Fiske, S. (2004). *Social beings*. New York: Wiley.

Fiske, S. T. and Taylor, S. E. (1991). *Social cognition* (2nd edn.). New York: McGraw Hill.

Fiske, S. T., Cuddy, A. J. C., & Glick, P. (2002). Emotions up and down: Intergroup emotions result from perceived status and competition. In D. M. Mackie & E. R. Smith (Eds.),

From prejudice to intergroup emotions: Differentiated reactions to social groups (pp. 247–264). New York: Psychology Press.

Gaertner, S., & Dovidio, J. (1986). The aversive form of racism. *Prejudice, discrimination, and racism* (pp. 61-89). San Diego, CA US: Academic Press.

Gaertner, S. L., & Dovidio J. F. (2000). *Reducing intergroup bias: The common ingroup identity model.* Philadelphia: Psychology Press.

Goodwin, S. A., & Devos, T. (2002, October). American identity under siege: National and racial identities in the wake of the September 11th attacks. Paper presented at the Annual Meeting of the Society of Experimental Social Psychology, Ohio State University, Columbus, OH.

Green, D., Strolovitch, D., & Wong, J. (1998). Defended neighborhoods, integration, and racially motivated crime. *American Journal of Sociology, 104*(2), 372-403.

Greenberg, J., Pyszczynski, T., & Solomon, S. (1986). The causes and consequences of a need for self-esteem: a terror management theory. In R. F. Baumeister (Ed.), *Public self and private self* (pp.189-212). New York: Springer-Verlag.

Greenberg, J., Pyszczynski, T., Solomon, S., Rosenblatt, A., Veeder, M., Kirkland, S., et al. (1990). Evidence for terror management theory II: The effects of mortality salience on reactions to those who threaten or bolster the cultural worldview. *Journal of Personality and Social Psychology, 58*(2), 308-318.

Harlow, C. W. (2005). Hate Crimes Reported by Victims and Police. *Special Report.* Washington, DC: U.S. Department of Justice.

Henry, F. J., Sidanius, J., Levin, S., Pratto, F., & Nammour, D. (2005). *Social dominance orientation, authoritarianism, religious identification and support for terrorism in the Middle East.* Working Paper #186. New York: Russell Sage Foundation.

Herek, G. M. (1996). Heterosexism and homophobia. In R. P. Cabaj & T. S. Stein (Eds.), *Textbook of homosexuality and mental health* (pp. 101–113). Washington, DC: American Psychiatric Association.

Herek, G., Capitanio, J., & Widaman, K. (2002). HIV-Related Stigma and Knowledge in the United States: Prevalence and Trends, 1991-1999. *American Journal of Public Health, 92*(3), 371-377.

Herek, G., Cogan, J., & Gillis, J. (2002). Victim experiences in hate crimes based on sexual orientation. *Journal of Social Issues, 58*(2), 319-339.

Herek, G., Gillis, J., & Cogan, J. (1999). Psychological sequelae of hate-crime victimization among lesbian, gay, and bisexual adults. *Journal of Consulting and Clinical Psychology, 67*(6), 945-951.

Herek, G., Gillis, J., Cogan, J., & Glunt, E. (1997). Hate crime victimization among lesbian, gay, and bisexual adults. *Journal of Interpersonal Violence, 12*(2), 195-215.

Hewstone, M., & Brown, R. (1986). Contact is not enough: An intergroup perspective on the "contact hypothesis." In M. Hewstone and R. Brown (Eds.), *Contact and conflict in intergroup encounters.* Oxford: Blackwell.

Hirschberger, G., & Ein-Dor, T. (2006). Defenders of a Lost Cause: Terror Management and Violent Resistance to the Disengagement Plan. *Personality and Social Psychology Bulletin, 32*(6), 761-769.

Hogg, M. A. (2005). Uncertainty, social identity and ideology. In S. R. Thye & E. J. Lawler (Eds.), *Advances in group processes, 22*, 203-230. New York: Elsevier.

Hulse, C. (2009). House Votes to Expand Hate Crimes Definition. The New York Times. Retrieved February 20, 2010 from http://www.nytimes.com/2009/ 10/09/us/politics /09hate.html

Iganski, P. (2001). Hate crimes hurt more. *American Behavioral Scientist, 45*(4), 626-638.

Johnson, S. D. (1992). Anti-Arabic prejudice in "Middletown." *Psychological Reports, 17*, 811–818.

Jost, J. T. & Banaji, M. R. (1994). The role of stereotyping in system-justification and the production of false consciousness. *British Journal of Social Psychology 33*, 1-27.

Jost, J. T., Banaji, M. R., & Nosek, B. A. (2004). A decade of system justification theory: Accumulated evidence of conscious and unconscious bolstering of the status quo. *Political Psychology 25*, 881-919.

Kaysen, D., Lostutter, T., & Goines, M. (2005). Cognitive processing therapy for acute stress disorder resulting from an anti-gay assault. *Cognitive and Behavioral Practice, 12*(3), 278-289.

Keefe, R. (2006). Review of 'Community mental health: Challenges for the 21st century'. *Best Practices in Mental Health: An International Journal, 2*(2), 81-83.

Keiller, S. (2010). Masculine norms as correlates of heterosexual men's attitudes toward gay men and lesbian women. *Psychology of Men and Masculinity, 11*(1), 38-52.

Lavine, H., Lodge, M., Polichak, J., & Taber, C. (2002). Explicating the Black Box Through Experimentation: Studies of Authoritarianism and Treat. *Political Analysis, 10*(4), 343-361.

Laythe, B., Finkel., D., & Kirkpatrick, L. A. (2001). Predicting prejudice from religious fundamentalism and right-wing authoritarianism: A multiple-regression approach. *Journal for the Scientific Study of Religion, 40*, 1-10.

Legal Information Institute. (n.d.). § 994. Duties of the Commission. *U.S. Code.* Retrieved February 20, 2010 from http://www.law.cornell.edu/uscode/28/994.html

Lerner, J., Gonzalez, R., Small, D., & Fischhoff, B. (2003). Effects of fear and anger on perceived risks of terrorism: A national field experiment. *Psychological Science, 14*(2), 144-150.

Levin, J., & McDevitt, J. (1993). *Hate crimes: The rising tide of bigotry and bloodshed.* New York: Plenum.

Levin, S., & Sidanius, J. (1999). Social dominance and social identity in the United States and Israel: Ingroup favoritism or outgroup derogation?. Political Psychology, 20(1), 99-126.

Mackie, D. M., & Smith. E. R. (2002). *From prejudice to intergroup emotions: Differentiated reactions to social groups.* New York: Psychology Press.

Macrae, C., & Bodenhausen, G. (2000). Social cognition: Thinking categorically about others. *Annual Review of Psychology, 51*, 93-120.

Marcus-Newhall, A., Blake, L., & Baumann, J. (2002). Perceptions of hate crime perpetrators and victims as influenced by race, political orientation, and peer group. *American Behavioral Scientist, 46*(1), 108-135.

McCabe, S., Hughes, T., Bostwick, W., West, B., & Boyd, C. (2009). Sexual orientation, substance use behaviors and substance dependence in the United States. *Addiction, 104*(8), 1333-1345.

McDevitt, J., Balboni, J., Garcia, L., & Gu, J. (2001). Consequences for victims: A comparison of bias- and non-bias-motivated assaults. *American Behavioral Scientist, 45*(4), 697-713.

McDevitt, J., Levin, J., & Bennet, S. (2002). Hate crime offenders: An expanded typology. *Journal of Social Issues, 58*(2), 303-317.

McGregor, H., Lieberman, J., Greenberg, J., Solomon, S., Arndt, J., Simon, L., et al. (1998). Terror management and aggression: Evidence that mortality salience motivates aggression against worldview-threatening others. *Journal of Personality and Social Psychology, 74*(3), 590-605.

McKinley, J. (November 12, 2009). Suspect in Fort Hood Attack is charged on 13 murder counts. *The New York Times.* Retrieved February 20, 2010 from http://www.nytimes.com /2009/11/13/us/13inquire.html?_r=1

Mosher, D. L., & O'Grady, K. E. (1979). Homosexual threat, negative attitudes toward masturbation, sex guilt, and males' sexual and affective reactions to explicit sexual films. *Journal of Consulting and Clinical Psychology, 47*, 860–873.

Niesta, D., Fritsche, I., & Jonas, E. (2008). Mortality salience and its effects on peace processes: A review. *Social Psychology, 39*(1), 48-58.

Nouvion, S., Cherek, D., Lane, S., Tcheremissine, O., & Lieving, L. (2007). Human proactive aggression: Association with personality disorders and psychopathy. *Aggressive Behavior, 33*(6), 552-562.

Ochsmann, R., & Mathy, M. (1994). *Depreciating of and distancing from foreigners: Effects of mortality salience.* Unpublished manuscript, universitat Mainz, Mainz, Germany.

Oswald, D. L. (2005). Understanding anti-Arab reactions post-9/11: The role of threats, social categories, and personal ideologies. *Journal of Applied Social Psychology, 35*, 1775–1799.

Quattrone, G. A., & Jones, E. E. (1980). The perception of variability within in-groups and out-groups: Implications for the law of small numbers. *Journal of Personality and Social Psychology, 38*, 141-152.

Pettigrew, T. (1998). Intergroup contact theory. *Annual Review of Psychology, 49*, 65-85.

Pettigrew, T., & Tropp, L. (2006). A meta-analytic test of intergroup contact theory. *Journal of Personality and Social Psychology, 90*(5), 751-783.

Plumm, K. (2007). Hate: Juror perceptions of crime classification, attributions of blame, and impact of extra-legal factors. *Dissertation Abstracts International, 67*(11-B), 6760.

Plant, E. A., & Devine, P. G. (1998). Internal and external motivation to respond without prejudice. *Journal of Personality and Social Psychology, 75*, 811-832.

Pratto, F., Sidanius, J., Stallworth, L., & Malle, B. (1994). Social dominance orientation: A personality variable predicting social and political attitudes. *Journal of Personality and Social Psychology, 67*(4), 741-763.

Pyszczynski, T., Abdollahi, A., Solomon, S., Greenberg, J.,Cohen, F., & Weise, D. (2006). Mortality salience, martyrdom, and military might: The Great Satan versus the Axis of Evil. *Personality and Social Psychology Bulletin, 32*, 525-537.

Rabrenovic, G. (2007). Responding to Hate Violence: New Challenges and Solutions. *American Behavioral Scientist, 51*(2), 143-148.

Rayburn, N., & Davison, G. (2002). Articulated thoughts about antigay hate crimes. *Cognitive Therapy and Research, 26*(4), 431-447.

Rayburn, N., Mendoza, M., & Davison, G. (2003). Bystanders' perceptions of perpetrators and victims of hate crime: An investigation using the person perception paradigm. *Journal of Interpersonal Violence, 18*(9), 1055-1074.

Routledge, C., & Arndt, J. (2008). Self-sacrifice as self-defence: Mortality salience increases efforts to affirm a symbolic immortal self at the expense of the physical self. *European Journal of Social Psychology, 38*(3), 531-541.

Root, M.P.P. (1992). Reconstructing the impact of trauma on personality. InL. Brown&M. Ballou (Eds.), *Personality and psychopathology: Feminist reappraisals* (pp. 229-265). New York: Guilford.

Rudman, L., Ashmore, R., & Gary, M. (2001). 'Unlearning' automatic biases: The malleability of implicit prejudice and stereotypes. *Journal of Personality and Social Psychology, 81*(5), 856-868.

Salfati, C. G. & Canter, D. V. (1999). Differentiating stranger murders: Profiling offender characteristics from behavioral styles. *Journal of Behavioral Sciences and the Law, 1*, 391-406.

Schofield, J. W. (2008). School desegregation research: Outcomes, historical trends, and issues affecting its usefulness in policy and practice. In U. Wagner, L.R. Tropp, G. Finchilescu, & C. Tredoux (Eds.), *Improving intergroup relations: Building on the legacy of Thomas F. Pettigrew* (pp. 262-279). Malden, MA: Blackwell.

Schuman, H., Steeh, C., Bobo, L., & Krysan, M. (1997). *Racial attitudes in America: Trends and interpretations* (rev. ed.). Cambridge, MA US: Harvard University Press.

Shay, J. (1994). *Achilles in Vietnam: Combat trauma and the undoing of character.* New York: Atheneum.

Sidanius, J., & Pratto, F. (1999). *Social dominance: An intergroup theory of social hierarchy and oppression.* New York, NY US: Cambridge University Press.

Skitka, L. J., Bauman, C. W., Aramovich, N. P., & Morgan, G. S. (2006). Confrontational and preventative policy responses to terrorism: Anger wants a fight and fear them "them" to go away. *Basic and Applied Social Psychology, 28*, 375–384.

Smith, C., Haynes, K., Lazarus, R., & Pope, L. (1993). In search of the 'hot' cognitions: Attributions, appraisals, and their relation to emotion. *Journal of Personality and Social Psychology*, 65(5), 916-929.

Stotzer, R. (2007). Comparison of Hate Crime Rates Across Protected and Unprotected Groups. Williams Institute, 2007–06. Retrieved February 20, 2010 from http://www.law.ucla.edu/williamsinstitute/publications/Comparison%20of%20Hate%20Crime%20Formatted.pdf

The New York Times. (September 15, 2005). Massachusetts Rejects Bill to Eliminate Gay Marriage. Retrieved February 20, 2010 from http://www.nytimes.com/2005/ 09/15 /national/15amendment.html?ex=1284436800&en=2fcd2de4099e5435&ei=5090&partner=rssuserland&emc=rss

Tajfel, H. & Turner, J. C. (1979). An Integrative Theory of Intergroup Conflict. In W. G. Austin & S. Worchel (Eds.), *The Social Psychology of Intergroup Relations*. Monterey, CA: Brooks-Cole .

Tajfel, H. and Turner, J. C. (1986). The social identity theory of inter-group behavior. In S. Worchel and L. W. Austin (eds.), *Psychology of Intergroup Relations*. Chigago: Nelson-Hall.

Tropp, L. R., & Prenovost, M. A. (2008). The role of intergroup contact in predicting children's interethnic attitudes. In S. R. Levy & M. Killen (Eds.), *Intergroup attitudes and relations in childhood through adulthood* (pp. 236-248). Oxford: University Press.

USINFO. (January, 2005). The U.S. Relationship to American Indian and Alaska Native Tribes. Retrieved February 8, 2006 from usinfo.state.gov.

United States Department of Justice. (July 25, 2008). Federally protected activates. *Civil Right Division*. Retrieved February 20, 2010 from http://www.justice.gov/ crt/crim /245.php

United States Department of Justice. (December 15, 2009). The Matthew Shepard and James Byrd, Jr., Hate Crime Prevention Act of 2009. *Civil Right Division*. Retrieved February 20, 2010 from http://www.justice.gov/crt/crim/249fin.php

Wright, S. C., & Tropp, L. R. (2005). Language and intergroup contact: Investigating the impact of bilingual instruction on children's intergroup attitudes. *Group Processes and Intergroup Relations, 8,* 309-328.

Wyatt, G. E. (1994, August). *Impact of racism on psychological functioning*. Paper presented at the 102nd Annual Convention of the American Psychological Association, Los Angeles.

Zanna, M., & Rempel, J. (2008). Attitudes: A new look at an old concept. *Attitudes: Their structure, function, and consequences* (pp. 7-15). New York, NY US: Psychology Press.

In: Crime
Editor: Michael Harry Pearson

ISBN: 978-1-62948-657-4
© 2014 Nova Science Publishers, Inc.

Chapter 4

AFTERMATH OF RAPE: STORIES OF RAPE VICTIMS' STRUGGLE AND SURVIVAL

Shahana Nasrin

Institute of Social Welfare and Research, University of Dhaka, Dhaka, Bangladesh

ABSTRACT

Gender based violence features as one of the most pressing human rights, social and public health challenge throughout the world. Rape is one of the attributes and manifestations of such gender based violence. Rape is worldwide epidemic known for dehumanizing victims in multiple ways. This paper explains rape through the lens of victimology. The paper is qualitative in nature and based on empirical data taken from a research project. The purpose of this study is to identify the factors associated with rape and focus on psychological consequences of rape on the victims. The study also explores the victim recovery process and victim assistance programs available in Bangladesh to reintegrate and rehabilitate them. Qualitative approach was followed in doing so. The findings show that gender inequality, power relations, masculinity, propensity of revenge, ill sexual behavior etc. act as influencing factors behind the rape incidents. The study also indicates that psychological effects of being raped are worse than physical injuries. Rape results both short term and long term harm in the life of rape victims. Depression, post traumatic stress disorders, poor self-esteem, destructive behavior, self blame, distrust others are the common effects were found in rape victims. Moreover, victims' personality, life cycle, family and community support, the way they are treated by police, court or hospital services are mentioned by the respondents as important and significant factors affecting rape victims' coping capacities. However, the study concludes that victim recovery process could minimize the trauma of rape victims through crisis intervention along with victim assistance programs. Hence, more government and non-government interventions and community awareness are necessary to address and redress the rape crime and rape victims.

INTRODUCTION

Violence commonly committed against women in Bangladesh, of which rape has been found to be by far the most common, widespread and far-reaching form of gender based violence. The state has generally regarded violence against women as a women's issue and at best crime against an individual (Naripokkho & Bangladesh Mohila Porishad, n.d.). But it is a crime against entire society as it tarnishes not only individual's psyche rather destroys whole social, cultural, ethical norms and standard. Rape is, therefore, crime against human rights and also violation of the victim's most cherished of the fundamental rights mentioned in Article 21 of the Constitution of Bangladesh named the 'right to live' (BNWLA, 2006-2007). There is no age limit of being raped. The girl children to female of different ages (the range is from 03 years to 60 years old) become the victims of rape in Bangladesh. This gruesome crime has been occurring in the life of married, unmarried, divorce, and widow irrespective of their social class, religion, and ethnicity (BNWLA, 1999; ASK, 2013). The men who commit rape come from all walks of life. He may, for example, be a farmer, a rickshaw puller, garments worker, miscreant, police, school teacher, political figure, religious leader, doctor, or advocate (Nari Grontho Probortana, 2003; BNWLA, 2004). Though it is a crime of perpetrator, society construes it to be the victim's crime and the victim undergoes a mortifying and arduous anguish.

Bangladesh government has taken a number of initiatives for the advancement of women and to protect them from any kind of violence including rape. The Constitutional guarantees, Ratification of Convention of Elimination of All forms of Violence against Women (CEDAW), endorsing the Beijing Platform for Action of Fourth World Conference of Women, drafting a National Action Plan, declaring a National Policy on Women in 1997, undertaking five year plans identify violence against women as priority area of concern and government intervention.

Government has also undertaken legislative measures by enacting the Cruelty of Women (Deterrent Punishment) Ordinance 1983, Prevention of Repression of Women and Children Act 2000 (amended 2003) replaced the Repression of Women and Children (Special Enactment) Act 1995, which defines rape and its punishment along with other offences too. Moreover, *Nari Nirjaton Protirodh* Cell (Women Oppression Prevention cell), Women's Investigation Cell has been set up by the government within police headquarters. There are Special Court, established under the Women Children Oppression Act, to try the offences like rape, dowry death, trafficking, kidnapping abducting etc. Special Tribunal courts have been set up under a special status called the Special Powers Act 1974 to try the offences mentioned above.

Furthermore, National Council for Women's Development (NCWD), Inter-Ministerial Advisory Committee, and Committees at the District and Thana level has been established as institutional support services to prevent violence against women. One Stop Crisis Centers, Women Support Centers, *Nari Nirjaton Protikar* Cells (Women Oppression Curative cell) are providing medical examination facilities, care, judicial counseling, shelter homes, vocational training etc. for the victims of violence together with rape. These measures are all indicative of the commitment of Bangladesh government for elimination of discrimination and violence against women. Non-government organizations also extended their support services by providing legal, paralegal, and rehabilitative facilities along with government services. Even after taking so many initiatives by government and non-government agencies for curbing violence against women including rape, the occurrences of rape incidents are on the rise and alarming. Why is this case?

Moreover, the status of women in patriarchal society like Bangladesh is not equal to men who enjoy the privileges and higher status over women. Gender discrimination is widespread in all spheres of life and at all levels as indicated by official statistics on education, health, employment and political participation (Mahtab, 2007). In such gender stratified society, when a girl or woman experience sexual assault like rape, what types of sufferings are faced by her? When a rape victim passes through a condition of anguish, what strategies have been taken by her to cope with that situation? In addition, since rape is a crime that involves the various actors and steps to prove it to get justice. How these actors play the role in her journey through all hideous experience? Whether there are any other influencing factors that could act as impetus to put her humiliating condition or encourage her to reintegrate into society? What kind of recovery assistance programs are provided by the society to promote their recovery process are the key research questions of this study.

PREVALENCE OF RAPE

The statistics gathered by *Ain O Salish Kendra* (ASK), at least 1149 women were raped in 2012 in Bangladesh. Of them, 98 were killed after rape, 14 committed suicides, and only 593 sued case. The number of incidents of rape was 939 in 2011, 626 in 2010 and 446 in 2009 respectively. Of them, 105 in 2011, 79 in 2010 and 62 in 2009 were killed after rape. 28, 07, and 05 were the case of post rape suicide in 2011, 2010 and 2009. However, 652 have been raped from January to June in 2013 (ASK, 2013). The fact is that hardly a day goes by without a number of reports on this dreadful assault on women being published in the national dailies. It is likely that given the nature of the offence, many more such incidents go unnoticed and unreported. The under-reporting of rape is of serious concern and the major reasons for silence in are victim's traumatized situation, the universal acceptance of gender inequality reinforced by social and religious beliefs in favor of male dominance; the deep seated reverence for continuing the existing social values regarding female sexuality within the bounds of marriage and maintaining chastity; and the fear of social censure, stigma, ostracism and loss of face (BNWLA, 1999).

CONCEPTUALIZING VICTIMOLOGY AND RAPE

Victimology

Victimology is the integral part and sub-branch of criminology. Generally, the criminal-victim relationship is called victimology (Devasia and Devasia, 1989). Devasia (1992) refers victimology as the entire body of knowledge regarding victims, victimization and the efforts of society to preserve the rights of the victim. According to Karmen (1990), "victimology refers to the scientific study of victimization, including the relationships between victims and offenders, the interactions between victims and the criminal justice system – the police and courts, and corrections officials – and the connections between victims and other societal groups and institutions, such as the media, businesses, and social movements." [Retrieved from http://faculty.ncwc.edu/mstevens/300/300lecturenote01.htm dated on 04.09.13] Therefore, victimology embraces the antecedents, vulnerabilities, consequences, recoveries and measures taken by community, organizations and cultures to reduce victimization.

This study applies the concept of victimology as to explain the causes of victimization of rape victims through their experiences, to explore its magnitude or pervasiveness through consequences and repercussion of being raped. In addition, coping strategies that have been taken by the rape victims and activities that are applied by society for resumption of their better functionality to be reintegrated have also been discussed under the purview of victomology.

RAPE IN THE VIEW OF LAW

Rape is a prevalent odious and repulsive crime in Bangladesh. It occurs across socio-economic and demographic spectrum. In Bangladesh, the offence of rape has been discussed in the Penal Code of 1860, The Criminal Procedure Code (CrPC) 1898, the Evidence Act 1872, and the Prevention of Oppression against Woman and Children Act of 2000 (Amended 2003) which substitute The Prevention of Repression against Women and Children (Special Act) 1995 (Nari O Shishu Nirjatan Daman Bishesh Ain 1995). The Evidence Act 1872 and the Criminal Procedure Code 1898 explain only the filing and trial procedure of rape. The Penal Code and other acts stipulate the definition and punishments of rape. Under section 375 of the Penal Code "rape" occurs when a man has "sexual intercourse" with a woman under one of the following circumstances:

Firstly, against her will; Secondly, without her consent; Thirdly, with her consent; when her consent has been obtained by putting her in fear of death, or of hurt; Fourthly, with her consent, when the man knows that he is not her husband, and that her consent is given because she believes that he is another man to whom she is or believes herself to be lawfully married; Fifthly, with or without her consent, when she is under fourteen years of age.

An explanation of what qualifies as "rape" is provided at the end of the definition, which states: "penetration is sufficient to constitute the sexual intercourse necessary to the offence of rape."An exception is listed where the sexual intercourse occurs between a husband and his wife. When this occurs, and the wife is not under the age of 13, then the act does not constitute rape.

The maximum punishment for committing the offense of rape, under section 376 of the Penal Code, is life imprisonment. An exception to this punishment exists where the rape is perpetrated by a husband against his wife (who is then under the age of 13). Under such a set of circumstances, the maximum punishment is two years and a fine: [whoever commits rape shall be punished with imprisonment] for life or with imprisonment of either description for a term which may extend to ten years, and shall also be liable to fine, unless the woman raped is his own wife and is not under twelve years of age, in which case he shall be punished with imprisonment of either description for a term which may extend to two years, or with fine, or with both.

The Prevention of Oppression against Women and Children Act of 2000 (Amended 2003) takes the punishment for rape one step further than the Penal Code. The punishment for rape, under this Act, is a maximum of life imprisonment with a fine. But, if the victim later dies, or the rape is committed by more than one man (i.e. gang rape), then the maximum penalty imposed is capital punishment.

According to section 9 of this Act –

i.   Whoever commits rape with a woman or a child shall be punished with rigorous imprisonment for life and with fine.

     Explanation: Whoever has sexual intercourse without lawful marriage with a woman not being under fourteen years of age, against her will or with her consent obtained, by putting her in fear or by fraud, or with a woman not being above fourteen years of age with or without her consent, he shall be said to commit rape.

ii. If in consequence of rape or any act by him after rape, the woman or the child so raped, died later, the man shall be punished with death or with transportation for life and also with fine not exceeding one lac taka.

iii. If more than one man rape a woman or a child and that woman or child dies or is injured in consequences of that rape, each of the gang shall be punished with death or rigorous imprisonment for life and also with fine not exceeding one lac taka.

iv. Whoever attempts on a woman or a child - a) to cause death or hurt after rape, he shall be punished with rigorous imprisonment for life and also with fine.

     b) To commit rape, he shall be punished with imprisonment for either description, which may extend to ten years but not less than five years rigorous imprisonment and also with fine.

v.   If a woman is raped in the police custody, each and every person, under whose custody the rape was committed and they all were directly responsible for safety of that woman, shall be punished for failure to provide safety, unless otherwise proved, with imprisonment for either description which may extend to ten years but not less than five years of rigorous imprisonment and also with fine (Rahman, 2005).

METHODOLOGY

This paper is based on empirical data taken from a research project titled "Psychological Health Effects and Victim Recovery Assistance Program: A Study on Rape Victims." The study is qualitative in nature and follows purposive sampling procedure. Sensitive topics are those that have potential costs or threats to the researcher and participants (Lee and Renzetti, n.d.). In this sense, rape is a sensitive issue to be researched primarily because of emotional and physical threat and speaking about their sexual assault poses threat to rape victim (Lee, 1993). It was not feasible for me to find out the rape victims from any area so I chose to search such organization where the rape victims have asked for assistance. Therefore, Association for Correction and Social Reclamation (ACSR) – an organization which has long-term shelter home named *Nirmol Ashroy Kendro* with accommodation of 100 marginalized, socially or criminally victimized girls aged between 12-21 years, has been selected purposively. The reasons, behind choosing this shelter home, are familiarity with that organization through my University, accessibility of rape victims, availability of research data etc. Furthermore, this organization would be representative in terms of general characteristics of other organizations which are also working for the survivors of violence including rape victims in Bangladesh. The Secretary General as gatekeeper of that organization granted me the permission to do the project with few rules and restriction such as victims would not be exploited or threatened. I got fifteen rape victims from this shelter home and took them as respondents for this study.

Both primary and secondary data have been used in this paper. Primary data were collected through in-depth interview with conscious subjectivity and inter-subjectivity and non-participant observation. The principal method of data collection was face-to-face interview with semi-structured interview schedule consist of open-ended questions. However, formal interview of key informants (KIs) e.g. Secretary General of ACSR, Social Welfare officers, Psychologist were also taken to understand their perception regarding psychological health effects, coping capacities of rape victims, factors influencing coping ability, and nature of recovery assistance programs. Three case studies have been conducted which have also been presented in this paper for in-depth analysis. Data were also collected from secondary sources by consulting research reports, books, journals and internet websites to supplement the data collected through interview. Pseudonyms names have been used for the respondents. Qualitative method of data analysis has been used for analyzing data as a systematic work. Description, explanation of themes and concepts, and verbatim quotations from respondent's oral statements are presented in a narrative way to seek the answers to the research questions. Informed consent, confidentiality, and anonymity have been used as research ethics in this study.

ANALYSIS OF THE FINDINGS

Factors Associated with Rape

Rape is the most outrageous and despicable crime against women. There is no single issue that causes such contemptible offence rather multiple causes are allied with rape incident. Both key informants and respondents reported some of the factors that are linked with rape victimization.

Revenge: Sometimes people use rape as a tool of revenge. It is very common in both urban and rural areas in our country that any young boy proposes for love, marriage, or illegal relationship to an adolescent girl and if it is refused becomes vindictive and could plan for throwing acid or raping the girl. Miscreant use rape as the most appropriate to make women abhorrent and unwelcome to the society. Rina stated her story,

> *"I was a student of class six and I was 13 years old. A young boy aged 20 used to tease me very often on the way of school. I did never give any attention to him. One day he approached me to marry and told me that he would go to my parents too. I denied marrying him and my parents also refused to marry off me with that boy as he was characterless person. He became angry and threatened my family that he took me forcefully from my house.*

And after few months, I was coming from my school alone he took me near the desolate crop field by force and I lost everything."

Fraud/Fake love: In many cases, rape results from false assurance of love or deception acts. Monira said, *"I am from a poor family of a village. I came as domestic worker to work in a family of a town. I fall into love with a hawker who circulates paper at that home. He promised to marry me and I came out of that house without informing anything to anybody. He took me in an isolate house and became the victim of his sexual desire."*

A lack of public safety: Women generally are not protected outside their homes. The country's public places are unsafe for women. Such insecurity is uttered by Rima,

> *"We the garment workers have to work till late night in the factory and sometimes for overtime too. We work for our survival but always suffer from insecurity in work place as well as in the passage to return home. I became the victim of gang rape when I was returning home after finishing my work at 12 midnight. I did not inform it to my sister for shame and fear. But after four months all came to know that I became pregnant. Community people blamed me as I hide the occurrence and did not ask for legal redress. Then we tried to change the address but those people did not stop their disturbance. So for security I took help of ASK."*

Young age: It is evident that in most cases of rape victims are from tender ages. In this study respondents' age limits are found from 12-17 when they were being raped. The authority of this organization informed us, *"The age of the most rape victims whom we get from different source agencies are 10-15. Due to the less understanding of the reality, docile nature of adolescent girl, nice appearance, insecurity, fall in love etc. common reasons for being raped at an early age."*

Gender inequality: Early feminist scholars (e.g., Brownmiller, 1975) argued that rape is not a crime of sex but should be conceptualized as a crime of power. Brownmiller asserted that rape is a tool of a patriarchal system that serves to perpetuate gender inequality and the devaluation of women. According to this theory, fear of rape limits women's freedom and use of power. Men think of women as commodity, sex object and their object of pleasure, in a male-dominated society. Violence against women is the extreme form of chauvinism, adopted by a patriarchal society, where men often go unpunished, even after such deeds. Hence rape considered as social issue rooted in gender inequality and power differentials (Reghr et. al.,1999). Rita's case reflects rape as crime of power. She described, *"I was working as domestic worker in an affluent family. One day khalamma (aunt) went for shopping and nobody was present except Khalu (uncle) and me. I was working in kitchen and suddenly he attacked me. I tried to escape but failed to his strength. After that incident he threatened me not to say anything to her wife and warned to keep quite. But I started to run and shout. The neighbours of that house came after listening my shouting, rescued me and called police."*

Sexual lust: Perverted sexual desire often turns into the cause of rape. This is why, children of three, four, five or six years old befall the victim of rape by the adult person in our country. Rifa's case (described later) could be an example of perverted sexual lust.

Lower rate of convictions: In majority cases, victim or her family do not want to expose the incident to the community due to being stigmatized or shame and thus cases remain unreported. As a result the perpetrators openly roam around the community free from any punishment. On the other hand if any family raises their voice against the offence, often the burden of proof, dealing with police, lawyers, etc. compel them to drop the case or victim does not get the verdict in favor of them. Sometimes they have to compromise with the rapist due to threatening. Either they withdraw the case or proposal comes to marry the rapist. Tulu described,

> *"When I was raped by a depraved young man of our village, my family asked for justice to shalish[1]. But shalish punishes that man only by slapping as he is a kin of one of the shalish member and had political influence. Police, court, trial seem to us as much complicated, embarrassing, and expensive. Moreover, perpetrator was threatening us all the time. At last my family married me off with that rapist under the pressure of influential community people. I could not concur with such repulsive arrangement in one hand and had to face verbal and physical torture from in laws on the other. Hence, after few months I fled from in laws house."*

Such incident proves that the importance of marriage for women's lives get much preference than bringing the rapist to justice. Consequently, perpetrator dauntlessly wander in the society taking a feeling that nothing would be happen if such offence like rape occurs. It is also worth-mentioning that rapist take the shelter of political party to escape from the punishment. The politician also influences the justice process for sake of the rapist by giving some statement that vilifies the rape victims (BNWLA, 2004).

Psychological Implications

The assault is not only an invasion of the victim's physical self but also the intellectual, social and emotional self. The psychological and emotional strain that rape puts on rape victims may lead to short or long term devastating effects for their survival. I categorize the effects into three according to the victim's responses such as psychiatric and psychological health effects, physical and social effects.

Rape Trauma Syndrome (RTS): RTS is first coined by psychiatrist Ann Wolbert Burgess and sociologist Lynda Lytle Holmstrom (1974). They refer to the psychological trauma experienced by a rape victim that includes disruptions to normal physical, emotional, cognitive, and interpersonal behavior. RTS is a cluster of psychological and physical signs, symptoms and reactions common to most rape victims immediately following and for months or years after a rape. Most of the rape victims mention different RTS after the rape. Nitu one of the respondents who has been raped at the age of 12 years old by a stranger spell out the symptoms of acute stages of psychological trauma,

---

[1] Shalish is an age old traditional based system of mediation and dispute resolution in rural Bangladesh, in which disputants, community members and village elders gather locally to mediate a conflict and arrived at a resolution agreeable to all involved parties.

"Immediate after rape I had vomiting, disorganized thought contents, confusion, anxiety. I washed myself several times in a day and always cried. Fear, depression, night terrors, extreme anger as well as a sense of helplessness, nervousness were persisted in my behavior for several months. I sometimes feel headache and tension too. But now I am trying to return into a normal life as I think it was an accident of my life."

Nitu's case reflects that she has renormalization and underground stage of RTS which means the victim is trying to recognize the adjustment stage and has an effort to back to her life before the rape despite her unresolved emotional issues. She does no longer focus on rape as the central focus of her life as she is not responsible for the attack.

Post Traumatic Stress Disorder (PTSD): PTSD is a severe condition that may develop after a person is exposed to one or more traumatic events, such as sexual assault, serious injury or the threat of death and a group of symptoms such as disturbing recurring flashbacks, avoidance or numbing of memories of the event, and hyper-arousal (high levels of anxiety) continue for more than a month after the traumatic events. Women who are particularly at risk for chronic PTSD include those who were injured during the attack, were threatened by the perpetrator (Mezey, 1997; WHO 2007) that they may be hurt or killed, have a history of prior assault, or have experienced negative interactions with family, peers, or law enforcement systems. Rifa, 13 years old adolescent girl was suffering from such disorder as she has been raped by her step father. She described her situation in a sense of defilement (feeling dirty or disgusted) and deeply embarrassed,

"Can you imagine a father can do such a heinous behavior? Though he was not my real father but I honor him as father. I feel dehumanized and humiliation and mortification. I don't want to recall these memories but it comes back to my mind. Everyone can forget her past but it is not possible for me to rethink about my life. I can't sleep and feel severe anxiety. The surrounding environment seems to me hostile and threatening."

This case manifests hyper-vigilance, flashback, and inability to maintain previous close relationship, sleep disturbances or insomnia as symptoms of PTSD which seriously affect Rifa's day-to-day life.

Emotional Numbness: Many rape victims experience periods of emotional numbness which is a shock response. Rina expressed,

"You know, I could not even cry when I could understand that I lost the most important chastity and honor of my life. How do I show my face to everybody? Such thought made me speechless. I was so shocked and felt numb that I was staring at my family members and could not response."

This response is often misinterpreted by others that they are fabricating their experience of the rape and hence calm. However, emotional numbness is interpreted as a victim's 'front line' defense against the overwhelming reality that they have been raped.

Self-blame: *"It is my fault. If I did not believe that man I would never be raped. I ought to be more careful but I was not. Rather I brought shame for my family too"* - Monira expressed. Such response focuses on exaggerated feelings of responsibility for the traumatic event, with guilt and remorse, despite obvious evidence of innocence as well as the feelings that they could have avoided it by acting differently. On the other hand, respondent like Sapna (See Case Study 2) often blame herself for being raped. It is noteworthy that self blame can allow the victim to understand the event but create obstacles to the recovery process (Lobmann et. al. 2003).

Eating Disorder: It is very common psychiatric health effect mentioned by the most of the rape victims. Monira said, *"After being raped I do not find any interest in food. Food becomes distasteful and I do not feel hungry too. I don't think body needs food. I think without having meal I could survive. But I feel tired and weak too."* This response reflects that insufficient food intake is detrimental for their physical and mental health. It is often called as anorexia nervosa means refusal to maintain a healthy body weight and unrealistic perception of body weight.

Sleep Disorder: Sleeping disturbance often occurs following rape. Most of the respondents state that due to stress, anxiety, shame and fear they are unable to fall asleep. Rifa opined, *"It is very difficult to sleep as pain and fear of past memories always irritate me. Many nights I have spent remaining awake. Sometimes I wake up middle of the night and cannot go back to sleep again."* Traumatic life events like rape create such insomnia which results depression, fatigue and irritability among the rape victims.

Depression: Respondents express that they do experience some form of depression after being raped. Nitu said, *"Sometimes I would like to withdraw myself from all kinds of social engagement as I do not find any interest to do any work. Tiredness and lack of energy, unnecessary irritability often hinder me to cope with present situation. I am really hopeless about my life."* Such types of sense of worthlessness and pessimist thought create functional impairment of the rape victim.

Suicidal Thoughts: Suicidal thoughts become apparent through the self destructive behaviors of the rape victims. The case of Rifa can be explained in this regard. She often tries to break the glasses of the window and try to cut her vein. She admitted by saying, *"I tried several times to cut my veins with the piece of window glass. I hate myself. This kind of life is very disgraceful. Relatives, community people abhorred me. So what is the point of such living? It is better to finish my life."*

Flashback: Memories of rape often return without warning. Therefore rape victims feel as if they revisit the place or time where she was experiencing the traumatic event of rape. Such experiences are called flashback. One of the key informant Rafiza, who is working as social welfare officer, informed, *"Generally the rape victim experiences such flashback frequently immediate after being raped. Nightmare is a trauma response of such flashback. Flashback disappears with the course of time through counseling and different therapies make their healing process progressing. Nitu often complained about flashback."*

Denial: Following the initial shock of the rape, or even months later, a victim may deny to others or to themselves that they have been assaulted. They try to suppress the memory of what has happened in an attempt to regain the previous stability of their lives. It is one kind of defense mechanism used by the rape victims. Rashida, the psychologists said, *"As victims faced such trauma at their tender age, they have the coping strategies to adjust their lives. In most cases, if they are asked regarding their past occurrences, they avoid and act in a manner that nothing had happened to them. Actually, they try to suppress those bitter memories as defense mechanism to re-integrate them with present situation. Renu's case is a good instance of denial."*

PHYSICAL HEALTH EFFECTS

Traumatic event like rape is connected with the development of a number of physical health problems. Women who have been raped have been found to be more likely to experience chronic pelvic pain, arthritis, digestive problems, chronic pain, seizures, and more intense premenstrual symptoms. Even some physical symptoms such as difficulties in breathing, muscle tension, nausea, stomach cramps or headaches are manifested from their experience of severe anxiety. Respondents of study agency reported about headache, migration, pain in chest, weakness, bleeding etc as physical problem immediate after rape. Halima stated,

> *"Immediate after rape I had bleeding, weakness and chronic pain in lower abdomen. Now I have only back pain. But all physical sufferings turn into light in comparison with the pain I experienced that night, which was intolerable and unforgettable."* Nitu said, *"Whenever I feel stress high blood pressure, breathing problem and headache is apparent frequently. I have also urinary infection."*

But the social welfare officer mentioned,

> *"Some sort of unhealthy sexual behavior stemming from rape too such as homosexuality or greater attraction towards opposite sex instead of hate them. In our organization, the rape victims except few have the propensity to mix with the male and they try to talk with the unknown people through the window and even they use body languages sometimes. A few of them want to lead an illegitimate life too for meeting their sexual desire."*

Another important finding has been uttered by Rafiza, *"No rape victim has sexually transmitted infections or diseases or any symptom of HIV/AIDS. Rather there are two cases of unsafe abortion and one is about unintended pregnancy as reproductive health problems"*

SOCIAL HEALTH EFFECTS

Stigma: A rape may bring about strong feelings of shame, guilt, anxiety, fear, anger, and sadness. There is a stigma associated with rape which may further increase feelings of shame. Rima conveyed,

"We the raped girls are not accepted in the society. Society hates us. I have a child for being raped who is also brought up in a child home. In our country, such child is not expected person. People scold them and treat them in a bad manner as they are illegitimate. Though I am not responsible for such incident, society imposes shame, blame, and guilt upon me. I feel frustrated whenever I think about myself and my child. Both of us are unexpected and hatred in this world."

Rima is continuing to experience such feelings and some form of distress for years and bearing the burden of unintended pregnancy. Though the Prevention of Women and Children Repression Act 2000 (Amended 2003) has included the state responsibilities for the maintenance of baby born caused by rape, such provision cannot freed them from stigma.

Distrust Others: Rape victims might feel as though they are always in danger or need to always be on guard, and may distrust other people. Runa another rape victim said, *"I feel uneasy in everyday social situation. Whenever I meet any person I do not find any faith to him or her. Both male and female are evil. My neighbor aunt helped a bad man to kidnap me. That person raped me first and tried to sell in a brothel but I was able to escape from him. Who do I believe?"*

Suffer from Isolation: When rape victims become stigmatized and loss their faith on their surroundings, they begin to like the isolation and want to spent more time with her own due to shame. At the same time, negative attitude of natal family, community people, friends and relatives make them excluded from all kinds of relationships. Rina said, *"When my family did not support me and not allow staying with them, community people blame me for such occurrence. I lost my hope to live. I feel alone. Nobody was there to help me."*

Hostility: Rape victim often express their feelings of hostility towards the gender of their offenders. These feelings may be directed against a specific person, such as the offender, or generalized to other men who try to protect the offender or give them any support. Rifa said, *"After such experience, I do not only hate or become destructive to myself but also contain antagonist or aggressive view toward the male group of the world. I felt that it was not possible to trust any men or any relationship anymore."* However, victim's such reactions are quite justified and often these feelings of hostility represent the beginning of a natural, positive emotion rather than a negative one. It indicates that the victim is beginning to view the world and themselves in a different way, consequently placing less trust in what could be abusive relationships.

Loss of Self Confidence: The experience of rape brings vulnerability issues to the fore which can devastate self confidence and destroy assumptions about the world and her place within it. Rita reflected, *"I did never think that I will do something in my life again. After that incident, I lost my hope regarding life and also mental strength to fight against anything."*

Self Esteem: Rape breaks the level of self esteem of a person to establish herself in a society. As a result they feel powerlessness and grow a sense of passivity. The psychologist uttered,

"Most of the raped girl needs the counseling for gearing up their self esteem. They can lead their life by themselves; they have the capacity to participate in work and survive with dignity as well as contribute to society. Such kind of believe we try to create in them. But it is really difficult as they sometimes show more passivity. We had to deal very carefully the case of Halima or Rifa as their experiences ruined their self-esteem deeply."

Secondary Victimization (SV): It is also known as post crime victimization or double victimization. Victims may experience SV by individual or institutions such as medical professional, justice system personnel, or organizational staff through victim blaming language or inappropriate behavior. Renu said, *"We do not have to struggle only with the primary injury of rape rather secondary injuries like bad comments from community people, hatred attitudes of relatives, lack cooperation and support from natal families."* Rina focuses on the role of media and stated, *"In my case, local print media published the incident with all my particulars and I was exposed instantly in my community and they asked me different questions which immediate after rape was really painful."*

Though the Prevention of Women and Children Repression Act 2000 prohibit publishing the identity of victim in newspapers, it is not always abide by them. But the experience of the respondents with the organizations which are providing them counseling, shelter, training is satisfactory. Rina also confirmed, *"We do not have any complaint regarding these organizational professional as they are much cooperative, caring and supportive. They always ensure that the bitter past memories of our life should not be spelt out or recalled by us."*

COPING STRATEGIES AND FACTORS AFFECTING VICTIMS' COPING CAPACITIES

Generally rape victims apply several coping strategies to adjust with the situation what had happened with them and how to overcome such situation. Expressing feelings to other for getting relief, seeking social support for rehabilitation, keeping oneself busy to avoid past thought of rape, suppressing negative thought through positive thinking about life, staying at home to isolate oneself from different relationship or social network are very common and frequently used recovery process or strategies by the rape victims. These strategies or recovery processes are often influenced by several factors which determine how successfully a rape victim may overcome her situation or not. Before probing into the factors affecting coping ability I will present some of the coping responses frequently used by the rape victim.

Avoidance: Rape can be disrupted the normal work capacity of a person for a long time. Victim's avoidance behaviors serve as a psychological defense against severe anxiety. Hence she adopts this technique to avoid certain feelings and situations that remind her abuse she faced. Sapna applied this mechanism for avoiding distress provoking reactions following rape such as agony, emotional numbness, anxiety, stigma etc. This is one kind of social withdrawal by the victim.

Suppression: According to Burgess and Holmstorm (1979), conscious suppression is a defense mechanism used by the victim to be recovered. The function of suppression is to block out the strong emotions and thereby escape the painful feelings for a short time which can be psychologically very exhausting. In such cases, victims try to suppress the trauma experience to escape from anxiety, fear, shame and act proactively through changing their residence. In Rita's, case she does not even eager to mention her past or did not admit that anything happened to her.

Seeking Social Support: Respondents of the study confessed that they sought social support from police, women organization and court for the purpose of safe shelter, legal assistance, and to combat threat by the perpetrator, and rehabilitation. It is very difficult in our country for the people of lower class and especially for women to prove the rape case in court by individual effort. Studies (Ameen, 2005; Nasrin, 2012; Kaushik, 2005, BNWLA, 1999; ASK, 2013) show that lengthy court procedure, backlog of cases, lack of legal knowledge of poor people, intimidation of victim, presentation of false evidence or lack of witness or evidence, corruption of law enforcement agencies, lower socio-economic condition etc. jeopardize the justice process and make it complicated for the victim. In the circumstances, victims and their family face vulnerability and risk. Women organizations like Bangladesh National Women's Lawyers Association (BNWLA), Bangladesh Mohila Parishad (BMP), Ain O Shalish Kendro (ASK), Nari Pokkho etc. are playing important role to provide social and logistic support to these victims.

Isolation: Victim often isolates herself from her surroundings and the outer world. Feelings of guilt, dishonor, indignity, embarrassment, and humiliation generate and produce loneliness in her. She follows this tactic to recover the wound she experienced. Nitu's approach to face rape situation is an example of isolation.

Self-assessment: This mechanism could be both positive and negative. Burgess and Holmstorm (1979) found that positive self assessment is related to adaptive strategy and negative one is linked with poor psychological outcome. When victim could realize that she has to survive and she is not responsible for the occurrence, she starts to assess her situation positively and plan for future life. The case of Tulu is the best example of such coping technique. On the contrary, Halima's case could be considered as negative self-assessment which may create hindrance for her rehabilitation and reintegration to the society.

Ventilation through Disclosure: Researches (Drucker & Stern, 2000; Routbort, 1998) found that victims who were able to speak out regarding their assault experience or victimization to other could recover significantly than other. Similar response has been found in most of the cases of the study organization. In contrast, two respondents Rifa and Rima mentioned that primarily they were not fervent to disclose their experiences to other due to community responses such as victim blaming, stigma, shame, disrespect and so on.

A rape victim could apply several techniques at a time to cope with the situation created aftermath of rape. Coping abilities are shaped or influenced by the following factors:

Victim Related

Victim's personality: Victim's coping approach highly influenced by her nature of personality. Victim with strong mentality and personality can overcome the weariness of shame, fear, and depression but victim with low self esteem often drive by the psychotic, or suicidal behavior. Halima's case replicates her weak personality through suicidal ideation or hostility.

Level of Self Confidence and Esteem: Victim's level of self reliance often expedites her coping capability. The psychologist stated, *"Rape victims who come to our organization, we try to unearth their confidence level. Some victims easily cope with all programs and co-operate us as they are confident to attain their autonomy. But in some cases we have to develop their reliance level through changing their mind set up. Realizing the position and condition in society Monira and Rita tried to their level best to adjust and participate in vocational training."*

Life Cycle and Age of Victim: victim's coping capacity is also affected by the life cycle. Victims explained different meanings of rape at different stages of their life. Rina said, *"It was happened when I was 12 years old and that was a fearful experience for me. I was susceptible to male and incapable to deal with any kind of relationship. But now after three years of that incident I find confidence in myself and could develop optimistic view about my future again."* In contrast, Runa who was raped at her 16 years old explained her position differently,

> *"I was concerned regarding the impression of family or society after losing my dignity and honor. I was scared and perplexed as people treated me differently. But guessing the consequence of such indignity, I determined to change my place. Though I was confused regarding my decision, however I left my home and came at town."*

Assault Related

The Severity of Rape and Physical Injury: The harshness of rape also affects the dealing nature of rape incident by the rape victims. Rashida said, *"Rima who was the victim of a gang rape, took six months to come out from that trauma. She was brutally faced the austerity of rape. She was physically injured as well as disturbed mentally."*

Cultural Perception of Rape: In our society rape is atrocious, immoral and scandalous act. People attach stigma, blame, disgrace and dishonor to both rapist and rape victim. As a result such perception of common people often put the rape victim's recovery process difficult instead of providing social support. All respondent except one mentioned cultural perception of rape often make community distrustful to them. Ranu said,

> *"I was terrified, panic, ashamed and depressed of experiencing such incident without my fault, but the people passing many bad comments to me and to my family. My family also misunderstood me. Though I was the victim of circumstances but they blame me along with*

the rapist. I experienced greater psychological pressure and suffered from mental distress than my physical injury at that time through the community behavior."

Different view expressed only by Sapna,

"I got empathy, support and understanding from my community. They believed me and extend their sympathetic and compassionate concern for me so that I could be reintegrated with the community again. Several times I heard that they charged the degradation of social norms and values and control as responsible factors of such decadent act"

Post Assault Related

Social Network: Another important determinant of coping capability is social network. It could gear up the adjustment ability of the victim as Runa affirmed, *"Though I was thrown in a dark life of indignity and dishonor, I combat the situation through the assistance from the leading women organization of our country. One of the member of that organization was familiar to me and I shared my story with her and sought help about what to do. She arranged to provide all kinds of support such as counseling, medicare, protection etc. I stayed their shelter home for 6 months and then come to this organization and taking training to ascertain my future."*

The Way of Treating by Supportive Organization: For cultural and social stigmatization associated with rape act as significant barriers to women reporting rape. Furthermore, women are more likely not to report rape if there is little support from their families, law enforcement agencies and the health sectors. The case of rape has to be proved to police or court by describing such a manner that rape has been occurred and rapist could be identified. Failure to provide evidence or witness by the rape victims put her in a position of blame and guilt. Even the cross examination of the lawyers often place them in disgraceful situation or prove them characterless or establish that she has the consent for such sexual behavior. Therefore many victims avoid the law enforcement agencies. Renu said,

"In my case, my parents were disinterested to take the shelter of police or court as it will never ensure the justice to us rather our family will be more stigmatized and dishonored in the community. Instead of remaining a law to deter rape, people are not abstained from doing such crime. Rather we find the offender and perpetrator freely moving outside and we the victim face the threatening to withdraw the case."

Halima said, *"Medical test for proving that rape has been happened is another kind of harassment. I heard the process of medical test is embarrassing and also fake report could be made in exchange of money. As a result, culpability and remorse is reinforced for the victim like us."* These reactions mirror or replicate that victims did not take assistance of police or court or hospital as they could jeopardize their self worth and accelerate the feeling of guilt and thus further victimized. But the different scenario is also prevailing in our society. Police played exemplary role in case of Rita.

Social status: Most of my respondents were from lower class. Their social status is very poor from where to struggle with the offenders, face or reintegrate with the community, resist the stigma, achieve legal assistance and guarantees justice, ensure rehabilitation are quite complicated and difficult. Rima said,

> *"Instead of extending the hand of assistance society imposed shame and guilt upon me. I became disheartened and depressed; spending intolerable sufferings and felt powerless. Is this because I am a poor domestic worker?"*

Behavior and Reaction of Family Friends and Relatives: Rape victims need to be supportive. Family, friends, relatives could play a significant role in this regard by allowing them to discuss the assault if she wants to. It will give her an opportunity to ventilate herself as well as provide mental strength to surmount the situation. But the responses of family, friends or relatives in supporting the victims are different in each case. Respondent like Rina said, *"When such occurrence happened to me my family asked me to forget it as they were not to understand the extent of trauma I faced. But they were sympathetic with me in bringing me back to my life."* In another case, Runa informed with distress,

> *"That was the black chapter of my life. I was ashamed, fearful after that night in one hand and my family was not kind to me on the other. Rather they blame me for such incident and refused me to stay with them. Such rejection put me in a vulnerable position and I was unable to decide what to do at that moment. I was stunned and flummoxed. Where natal family was unresponsive what do I say about friends or relatives?"*

Ranu said, *"I had been staying with my brother's family. They burst into anger, misbehaved with me, scolded and denied to keep me with them as they will be stigmatized for me. I became puzzled and flabbergast. I obliged to leave that house after few days of the incident."* These responses reflect the judgmental attitudes of parents or friends which could exacerbate existing conflicts over rape; In contrast, kind attitudes help the victims to deal with the situation positively.

Victim Recovery and Assistance Program

With the aim to normalize the woman's response to the rape, to restore sense of power, dignity and control, to prevent long-term illness and maladaptive coping behaviors, to encourage restoration of healthy psychosocial functioning; to facilitate contact with community groups and family members treatment approach generally applies or follow the crisis intervention, therapeutic intervention, cognitive behavioral therapy and pharmacotherapy (Mezey, 1997)

However, there are now several treatments modalities available throughout the world for victims of rape and sexual assault including: pharmacology; behavioral therapeutic techniques such as flooding, systematic desensitization, eye movement desensitization and retraining (EMDR); cognitive behavioral therapy; cognitive therapy; relaxation; rational-emotive therapy; group therapy; hypnosis; family/couple therapy; existential therapy; humanistic approaches; and psychodynamic therapy. In Bangladesh, therapeutic interventions or assistance programs for recovery of rape victims are not well build up (Khan et al., 2008). Despite limitation of various kinds, government and nongovernment agencies are providing victim assistance programs.

Legal Assistance Program

There are some government agencies and NGOs in our country who provide the legal aid services to the rape victims. But it is evident that few women choose to disclose their victimization experiences to legal systems. Thus, many rape cases remain unreported in one hand and many reported cases unable to proceed through the system of prosecution for several reasons on the other. Poverty, threatening by the perpetrator, mediation by the local *shalish*, political pressure, negative attitudes towards the law enforcement agency due to dishonesty and corruption of police, weak FIR and charge sheet, lack of cogent evidence, legal complexities, hide the evidence for saving perpetrator etc. create a victim unfriendly legal or judicial atmosphere (BNWLA, 2008). Therefore distrust and skepticism remains to obtain justice through the legal system.

In Tulu's case, perpetrator has only been slapped by the community leader as he is the kin of them and also he has the affiliation with the political party in power. Pressure of local elites thus sometimes compel victim like Tulu asking for legal assistance from ASK. She was threatened and left her village and got shelter in ACSR through the help of ASK. Such example creates additional psychological pressure for the victim and other victims lost their faith on law enforcement agencies and refrain themselves from reporting.

Rupa and her family were denied by the local police station when they went to file the case. Non co-operation of law enforcement agents obliged Rupa taking the legal help from BNWLA. The social welfare officer expressed,

> *"Sometimes police are not sensitive to the rape victim. They are not concerned regarding the victims needs of safety, control or healing process due to lack of training. As a result the recovering process has often been disrupted or hindered. Even submission of weak charge sheet in court makes the justice questionable, delayed and perpetrator may be freed and the threat of re-victimization of the rape victim occurred. Rupa is such a case of our agency."*

Moreover the lengthy procedure of judicial procedure, backlog of cases, lack of evidence, attacking questions towards the victims by the lawyers, lack of intimidation etc. undermine the credibility of judicial system and commitment to protect the victim. Another social welfare officer of the agency informed,

> *"Most of the rape victims have been staying in this agency for 4 or 5 years. Their cases are still in court. Only one case has been dissolved after 6 years among the 15 cases. Poor investigation by the police, loopholes in legal systems, prolonged justice delivery system and problem during the medical examination were the major challenges for a rape victim to get justice. Furthermore, provide the proof of being raped that she did not have consent, giving answers of embarrassing questions of lawyers of perpetrators, failing to deduce her statement to police under section 164 of Criminal Procedure Code or provide evidence or witnesses, etc. also slow the judicial procedure."* These findings conform to the findings of a study of BNWLA (1999).

The study organization directly does not provide any legal assistance, support, or counseling to the rape victim but the referral organization offers the logistic support in this regard. The rights groups have long been campaigning for revision of the law, legal reform and the activists demand came as Bangladesh in recent years has witnessed growing complaints of rape or sexual assaults.

Medical Assistance Program

By law, a woman filing a charge of rape must undergo a full examination by a hospital Resident Medical Officer (RMO). Medical test is an important tool used in court to prove the rape experienced by the victim so that the rapist get punished. Until now, though, many victims balked at the exam because they did not want to disrobe nor have their private parts examined by a male doctor. As a result, the rape charges are dropped and thus the rapists got off scot free. After a long time of advocacy by the women organizations of our country for appointing female forensic expert in case of sexual violence against women especially in cases of rape, last 6 May 2013 High Court division of Supreme Court of Bangladesh handed down a landmark decision to ensure that female victims of sexual violence are examined by female doctors, rather than male. The ruling is being seen as a major step forward in combating rape, as it will encourage more victims to follow through with the physical examination needed in order to press charges. Ranu like all respondents described briefly, *"We need privacy as well as sensitivity, empathy and compassion during medical test but it was embarrassing to examine myself by a male physician."*

The social welfare officer of the agency informed, *"All the rape victims must be checked after arrival to our agency by the female doctors of Delta Medical Hospital or Child Hospital of our country. We mainly emphasize on pregnancy test as no pregnant victim is allowed to stay in our agency. Besides, serologic tests for syphilis, hepatitis B, and HIV, M. T. test also are conducted before admission to identify the infectious or sexual diseases. In few cases, tranquilizer has been provided according to the advice of doctor for reducing sleep disturbances of the rape victim."*

Mental Health Assistance Program: Therapy may be necessary to help the victim work through the traumatic experience. It is important that the woman is not made to feel guilt or responsibility after a sexual assault (which harms instead of helps) and to help her understand the real reasons for rape. The General Secretary of the agency emphasized,

> *"After experiencing the traumatic event like rape, the victims comes to organization with fear, distrust, guilt, self blame, avoidance nature, suicidal ideation; We try to wither away the tendency of scaring and self destructive behavior, heighten their self esteem stronger, and making optimistic about their future life through counseling. A psychologist, from Ain O Shalish Kendro - a renowned national NGO, comes to our agency for counseling these residents including rape victims. Two social welfare officers also counsel the victims."*

The psychologist informed, *"Rape victims who are damaged psychologically and socially need treatment. Cognitive behavior therapy, reality therapy, feminist therapies, relational therapies, psycho-education are the common techniques applied by the psychologists in our country for addressing the psychological needs and for the treatment of the rape victims.*"

Cognitive Behavior Therapy: Systematic desensitization, flooding, prolonged exposure treatment, psycho-education, and stress inoculation training are various application of Cognitive Behavior Therapy (CBT). All these are aimed at systematically managing the memory of the trauma and cognitively reinterpreting it to reduce anxiety. Agency employs mainly SIT, psycho-education, and desensitization for improving victim's functioning and to lessen the anxiety and depression.

Psychologist informed, "*As the victims get the CBT approaches immediate after arrival and 10 to 15 days later of their rape experience, their progress in the areas of fear, anxiety and depression is notable. Skill building for relaxation, education, and behavior rehearsal are the components of SIT. Counseling is also provided along with these components to relieve the victims from the PTSD symptoms.*"

Social welfare officer also reported, "*Systematic desensitization is helpful to reduce the anxiety, fear, phobia and symptoms of PTSD that are attached to rape incident. We mainly use muscle and imagery relaxation, deep breathing, anxiety hierarchy and counterpoising through imagery the anxiety evoking stimuli from the hierarchy and relaxation.*"

Feminist Therapy: Feminist therapeutic approaches are frequently used along with the CBT to address both immediate distress as well as longer-term symptoms of guilt, shame, and self blame. This approach emphasizes the view of sexual victimization as a crime against the self and integrates the social causes of rape into the client's world-view (WHO, 2007). A key goal of feminist therapy is helping survivors understand that the problem of rape is a societal problem, not merely an individual problem. Many feminist therapists prefer group therapy as treatment choice in a group setting that can break down post-rape isolation, promote sharing of experiences, and develop supportive relationships (Koss &Harvey, 1991). Social welfare officer said,

> "*We stress on feminist therapy to shatter the individual thinking of guilt and shame in a group setting which encourage the victims to develop an understanding that such occurrences have not only happened to single one and many societal factors are actually contribute to these incidents. Thus healing process of victims accelerated and they can come out of their self blaming nature.*"

Relational therapy: Social support from family, friends or relatives has been documented as essential and significant component for victim's recovery. Hence relational therapy amalgamates the victim's social network into her treatment. Incorporating relational therapy along with individual therapy diminish the symptom of PTSD, RTS, depression. Secretary General of the agency informed,

> "*Our agency tries to find and contact with the family members of victims and maintain the communication for reintegrating them to their community again. Sometimes, they come to our agency or they call to the victim. Even our agency allows the victim with social welfare officer to go to her own home so that she could be re-socialized after the occurrence. We found this approach fruitful to bring back them into their social functioning. It is noteworthy*

that sometimes we provide family counseling to their parents through home visit. It is also supportive for attitudinal change to the victim and as a whole perception towards rape too."

Reality Therapy: The focus of this therapy is on present and future as past cannot be changed; it emphasized on behavior rather than feelings and seeks to help rape victims to achieve realistic goals. Psychologist said, *"We exercise this therapy for concentrating on the victim's responsibilities and attempts to train them to have appropriate social functioning."*

Crisis Intervention: The experience of rape represents a crisis, which precipitates the individual into a state of disequilibrium. For rape victims, immediate intervention may be helpful in correcting distorted perceptions of what happened, reducing guilt and self-blame, mobilizing effective coping skills and facilitating the victims' use of their wider social network and family members for continuing support. Crisis intervention has been promoted as a rapid, brief, focused intervention, designed to stabilize the individual and help them to master the situation (Mezey, 1997). Crisis intervention (CI) postulates that in a crisis situation current levels of functioning may be disrupted and previously manageable internal psychological difficulties stirred up. CI views the emotional disturbances presented by people facing crises as being the result of: 1. the stressful situation which a person faces; and 2. underlying emotional dispositions which only come to the surface in crisis situation (Zastrow, 1989). Different treatment techniques used in crisis intervention are role-playing, confrontation, rational self-analysis, counseling with active listening. Social welfare officer informed,

"Crisis intervention generally should be taken for a rape victim through immediate medical attention and counseling on victim's feelings and thoughts about the assault and on legal implications. Hospital settings, mental health clinics, half-way houses; one-stop crisis centers provide the crisis intervention services in our country. But this facility often interrupted in hospital settings or in police station due to lack of knowledge and training regarding CI. Presumptions regarding victim's bad character, interference of influential person, legal complexities as rape is criminal case also hinder the process of crisis intervention. When we receive a case, we counsel the victim and try to eradicate the disabling thoughts through ventilation, understand the dynamics of her problem and check out her perception then determine the remedial measures for restoring the equilibrium and ensure she will work on agreed upon goals."

Rehabilitation Program

Shelters: Shelters are typically designed to address the need for protection of individuals experiencing physical or sexual abuse or both (WHO, 2007). Shelters generally provide residential programs with the facilities of education, training, recreations etc. support groups, individual, group and family counseling etc. The aim of this shelter program is to help women develop safety future plan and to gain access to the services they needed. Social welfare officer of the study agency said,

"Our shelter can serve hundred victims of different types. It is considered as long term shelter as aim of our agency is to reintegrate the victims into society or family or new

community. When rape victims become calm and start to cooperate with us confidently for future planning, we provide moral and non formal education as well as training on garment block printing, designing, cutting and sewing to rehabilitate them. Moreover, indoor and outdoor recreational activities, gardening, painting are being provided by the agency for their refreshment and reenergizing them."

Nitu, one of the respondent said, *"Facilities of food, lodge, clothes, education, training, family visit, recreation, games, medical assistance, and counseling are offered by this shelter."*

Training and Economic Opportunities: Economic opportunity is critical in any successful rehabilitation. Victims need the skills to earn an adequate income for surviving as the shelter will not provide those lifelong facilities. Skills development training programs should be created to match the needs of the local job market. The Secretary General of the agency informed,

"Victims are now taking trade/occupational skill training on embroidery, garments, block printing, designing, cutting and sewing under guidance and instruction of Sub-committee. We have a plan to train them as beautician so that they will work in beauty parlors. Rape victims themselves express their interest for such kind of training too. Here it should be mentioned that after successful completion of education and training victims appear in examination and evaluated by the examination committee."

Referral Network: This network generally addresses the needs of rape victims through coordinated community services. Secretary General informed,

"Our organization gets the victims from different referral organization like Victim Support Centre, Bangladesh National Women Lawyer's Association (BNWLA), Ain O Shalish Kendro (ASK), Families for Children, Government Shelter Centre, Bangladesh Mohila Porishad (BMP). These organizations facilitate our victims through providing legal assistance for filing and prosecuting cases, sending psychologist for counseling, etc. Even they advocate for raising community responses, creating awareness, drawing attention of law makers, policy planners to initiate victim responsive services."

Ripa said, *"I came to this organization from Ain O Shalish Kendro. That organization has a short term shelter where I stay for five days and got immediate medical and counseling service. They also contact police for filing and investigate my case and now my case is in court. They assist me in prosecuting my case also."*

Thus referral organizations try to deliver the coordinated community supports for the rape victims in our country.

Reintegration: The reintegration of rape victims often is a difficult, complex, and long-term process. It is different for each victim, and it involves not only the victim but also the environment, community and culture within which the reintegration is going to take place. The organization providing support may need to make a long-term commitment to the victim to help in this process (USAID, 2005). Sathi said,

"After finishing training and qualified in the examination, I was selected for reintegration with community. Agency provided me a sewing machine, money for maintenance of one month. They also hire a flat for me and paid the rent of that flat for one month. Now I am surviving by myself and got confidence to struggle. I have been under follow up of social welfare officer of the organization till now."

On the other hand the residents who could not have been integrated in the society for want of family antecedents were engaged as apprentice in the design cum production centre of the study organization. Social welfare officer said, *"During the year six skilled victims are engaged in the centre on payment of wages. The materials produced by them have been kept on display at the Display cum Sales centre at the ground floor for casual marketing. Money earned from such products and outside work orders are used for the welfare activities of the victims only."*

CASE STUDIES

Case-1: Halima

Halima is from a poor family. Her father died when she was on two years old. Elder brother and sister worked in a biscuit factory. She also started to work there when she was a student of class four. She left school due to poverty and want of money. Negligence of family and misbehavior of mother obliged to leave village and she came to Dhaka in searching job and she joined in a garment factory. Sometimes she came late night from garment factory after finishing the overtime work. Some of the young boys teased her on the way of returning home from her working place. But Halima did never response to them. One night she was alone to return home at 11o'clock, four men forcefully brought her in a lonely place and raped her. It was happened when she was only 16. She became faint and when she got sense, she informed the incident to house owner. That person called Rapid Action Battalion (RAB) police. Perpetrators tried to minimize the case by giving money of one lac BDT. But Halima was not agreed to this proposal. Halima was physically weak, had chronic headache, and bleeding. She also passing through the Rape Trauma Syndrome, flashback, stress, sleep disorder, frustration, depression and always felt threatened. Considering her safety RAB sent her to victim Support Centre (VSC) and VSC sent her to ASK. She stayed there for six months and get psychological counseling, medical treatment and legal aid to prosecute the case in court. Then ASK sent her to ACSR for her rehabilitation. She has been staying in ACSR for 2 years and 8 months. Now she has been taking skill development training, education from ACSR and planning for future. But she still needs counseling for frustration, distrusting other and keeping quite. Her case has been dissolved successfully and the perpetrators got punished. Though she was a victim of gang rape, her effort and thought for future life encourage her to be rehabilitated again.

Case -2: Sapna

Sapna is an orphan girl. She has been staying in an organization named Families for Children from 7 years old. She could not remember her parents. She was a student of class five. She became involved with bad association of young boys and started to mix with them illegally. In the mean time, FFC arranged a job in a garment factory and kept her under supervision of a woman. But she did not listen to anybody and returned home late night. When that woman asked her to change the behavior, she quarreled with that lady and left her house. She changed her job and started to stay with some of her female colleagues in another place. Then she fall in love with a man of that area and left this address with that man. But that man consecutively raped her for three days and left her. She was then 14 years old. Then she could understand her mistake and got back to FFC again. She apologized to the authority but she became mentally upset. She blamed herself always and thought her powerless. Shame, feelings of guilt, depression, loss of self esteem sleep disorder were common symptom in her case. Therefore FFC sent her ACSR for her rehabilitation. After medical treatment, hope therapy, reality therapy and cognitive behavior therapy has been applied for her. These helped her to overcome mental distress, destructive behavior, to correct her behavior pattern and to dream about her life again. She is taking education and training for reintegrating herself to the community again.

Case-3: Renu

Renu is also from a lower poor class family. She was living with her family in a slum of Dhaka. She did not continue her study after class three due to economic inability. She helped her mother in domestic chore. One day her mother sent her to bazaar (market) to buy some grocery with her younger brother. But one young boy named Raju who was their neighbor brought her brother with him. Renu's mother sent her to bring back younger brother. When she went their house, Raju and his friend Rubel locked the door and tied up her mouth with a cloth. Then they raped her. Getting the sound of their scuffle, a women passerby near that room shouted and made a crowd. Those people rescued Renu and her parents called for a shalish and filed a case in police station. But Raju threatened Renu and her family to withdraw the case in one hand and slum dwellers created pressure to married off Renu with Raju on the other. Instead of giving punishment to that rapist as he was the nephew of a political leader, they offered me to marry him. Her family agreed to this proposal as they want to save the family from stigma and criticism as well as save ourselves from political rage. Hence they married off Renu with Raju. But Renu was tortured by Raju and her in laws verbally and physically. So she left Raju's house after three months. Raju threatened to kill her. Then Renu's parents came to know about Ain O Shalish Kendro and sent her for safety and legal assistance. ASK sent Renu for long time shelter and rehabilitation in ACSR. Renu is a self confident girl and positively taking education and training to start her life in a new dimension.

COMMUNITY RESOURCES FOR RAPE VICTIMS

Rape victim needs protection, support, safe accommodation, counseling and legal assistance. Comprehensive assistance requires not only medical personnel, but also counselors, social workers, legal aid providers and the police. It emphasizes the need to establish a sustainable counseling, medicare and legal aid for women victims. Several government, non-government and women's organizations such as One Stop Crisis Centre (OCC), Nari Nirjaton Protirodh Cell (NNPC), The Bangladesh Mohila Parishad (BMP), Bangladesh National Women Lawyer's Association (BNWLA), Ain O Shalish Kendro (ASK), The Bangladesh Legal Aids Trust (BLAST), Marie Stopes Clinic Society (MSCS), Naripokkho, Centre for Women and Children's Studies (CWCS), Bangladesh Unnoyon Parishad (BUP) and many other are working for the victims of violence against women including rape victims through different interventions.

BMP, BNWLA provide legal support, legal education, legal advocacy, legal counseling, legal awareness training to government and non-government personnel, lawyers, police, and work together with legal, judicial and medical personnel to support rape victims, lobbying with government for law reform. ASK has a collaboration of legal aid clinic with BRAC called Legal Aid outreach clinic through which clients get to know the progress of their cases, causes behind delay due to legal procedures or court procedures. ASK also expedite the slow legal process though it's Raid Response & Mediation Unit (RRMU). This mediation unit is also effective means for women to negotiate the settlements. Litigation is the third means of settling dispute by ASK through its litigation unit (ASK, 2005).

Rokeya Sadhan by BMP, Proshanti by BNWLA, half-way house by ASK and shelter homes run by government were built in the response to the need for referral centre for temporary period (one month to maximum 6 months) before victims are reintegrated into the mainstream society. These shelter homes basically provide shelter, medi-care, psychological care, legal aid, nutrition, education, skill development training, capacity building and job opportunities, recreational facilities, regular follow up etc. These shelter homes actually act as referrals and send victims to other shelter home where they could stay for long period and improve their situation like *Nirmal Asroy Kendro, Shishu Polli Plus*.

Psycho-education, psychological counseling, family counseling, group counseling, counseling in community, are offered by these organizations for emotional rehabilitation. Even they refer the victims to Mental Health Institute, hospital and clinics. Naripokkho has the collaboration with department of Clinical Psychology of Dhaka University for counseling program.

Moreover, mobilizing women and communities through creating awareness, utilizing campaigns and advocacy, publishes books, leaflets, and reports, newsletters, on women's legal rights, specific laws, and incidents of violence. They also lobbies and advocates for legal reform, form public opinion through dissemination of information and holding dialogues with policy makers. Furthermore, forensic laboratory services with DNA profile, support services are overseen by The Ministry of Women and Children's Affair's (MOWCA) Project Implementation Unit. The *Nari Nirjaton Protirodh* Cell located within the Police headquarters is a means of monitoring violence against women at the national level by the Department of Women and Children's Affairs under the MOWCA. It also offers legal aid to victim and assists Deputy Commissioner for taking legal action against perpetrator by reporting of violence. In addition, health professionals, lawyers, magistrates, judges, civil society organizations, media professionals, people representatives, health and public sector administrators, development partners participation, Women Friendly Hospital Initiative (WFHI) developed by Government and UNICEF as violence against women is considered as public health issue in project implementation plan of Health and Population control program.

DISCUSSION AND CONCLUSION

The main thrust of this paper was to analyze the factors associated with rape and health consequences faced by the victims. It also attempts to focus on coping strategies taken by the victims and identify the factors influencing these coping capabilities. Finally, this paper explores and expounds the community based resources that are working as victim recovery assistance programs in our society. Thus this paper elucidates and explicates the process of victimization, its aftermath and action taken by the society in response to the victimization.

Rape is a menacing and insidious violence in Bangladesh. Its prevalence is becoming higher in throughout the Bangladesh day by day despite of different legal and social measures undertaken by government, civil society, non-government agencies. Revenge, fake love, tender age, and lower rate of convictions have been found as the factors associated with rape. Traditional gender norms that dictate man's superiority over women legitimate and promote the patriarchal ideology are also unearthed as important factor associated with rape. It is also evident that women's mobility in public places apparent as harmful aspect as well as insecurity to experience of being raped or gang raped on the way of house to working place or market or crop field.

The prevalent nature of rape in Bangladesh confirming it is as major social and public health issue. Recurrent and profound health sequelae of rape are widespread and grave. The health consequences of rape are not only physical but also psychological and social. PTSD, RTS, suffering from depression, flashback, anxiety, suicidal thought and attempt, chronic pain, bleeding, stigma, and self-blame are the post-rape responses of the victim. Immediate after the incident of assault, expression of such emotions are tended to be very high. Health effects vary from victim to victim and duration of sufferings also depends on several factors such as mental strength, age structure, support of families, severity of incident, prior sexual abuse, etc. It has also been noted that psychological harm and distress is stated more cavernous and ruthless than physical injuries.

The study finds that successful recovery depends on the use of adaptive coping strategies such as positive self-assessment by the victim. On the contrary avoidance and social withdrawal make recovery process longer. Victims also applies some defense mechanism for instances denial, suppression and minimization are common among rape victims as coping strategies. Unfortunately, societal attitudes towards rape, victim blaming generate and increase the risk of secondary victimization that gears up the psychological distress and delayed recovery. It is not unusual that the victim blames herself for the rape, and the public's attitude may increase this feeling. Blame and doubt by the public most likely stem from their own psychological defense system rather than from an uncaring attitude. Loss of social support and assistance may lead someone to develop the sense of helplessness and push someone to attempt suicide. But support from community, formal and informal network cannot be ignored at all. Indeed, disclosure of experience to such network and community people has been documented as significant means to assist the rape victim to take emotional, legal and social support and protection from different organizations.

However, maximum penalty of life imprisonment and even death penalty for committing rape remain unable to curtail the alarming rate of rape incidents that manifests the inadequate enforcement of the laws. Furthermore, it is noticed that lengthy procedure, expensive nature, lack of evidence, backlog of cases, complex prosecution of judicial system along with intimidation by perpetrator, influence of powerful people make justice far reaching and in many cases denied to women. As a result, the accessibility of legal services to poor victim is limited and expensive that may pose insurmountable hurdle for many victims and their families. In addition, lower socio-economic condition, powerlessness, stigmatization, limit their justice seeking behavior and compel them to compromise with the perpetrator even in some cases *shalish* has given decision to marry the rapist. It is also worth mentioning that litigations do not always guarantee that the verdict will be received. Thus laws have limited impact on reducing crime like rape. Moreover, incidents of rape that are reported, not all proceed for prosecution as few women choose to disclose their victimization experiences to legal system.

Roles of law enforcement agencies are most significant in investigating the incident, filing FIR, collect the evidence, submit the charge sheet, take initiative against the perpetrator etc. But, their role often becomes questionable regarding rape allegation which characterized by the tendency of focusing on victim's bad character, provocation, temptation, influenced by the powerful people of the community, political pressure. Thus masculine ethos of police organization is exacerbated. Even by hiding the evidence, threatening the victim and her family, restraining from arresting the perpetrator, submitting of weak charge sheet, they act on behalf of assailants rather than alleged them.

Rape itself exhibits shame, dishonor, lost of chastity. Additional burden of proving the assault put victim again in embarrassment and disgrace. Though very recently a praiseworthy decision regarding recruitment of female doctors for medical examination of raped has been passed yet to be implemented due to lack of training and knowledge, lack posting in rural settings etc. Women organizations still advocates for banning the 'Two-finger' test as it further humiliate the victim and no legal implication.

No doubt victims need mental health services following rape. Hence therapy approaches are useful for their recovery. But crisis interventions and therapeutic interventions yet to well developed in our country to assist victim to be recovered. Some facilities have been provided by the GOs and NGOs, hospitals and clinics or trauma centers those are also located urban based in a limited sphere. Moreover, scarcity of number of psychologists and therapists, lack of proper training, disinterest to work in rural setting, recruiting non-psychologists, non-existence of therapeutic treatment hinders the victim recovery assistance programs for getting psychological support in our country.

Shelter homes are documented as significant component of community based victim recovery assistance programs used by victim for safe accommodation, rehabilitation and reintegration into society. Such support is provided by both government and nongovernment agencies but services are limited to meet the needs of the society. It is noteworthy that these shelter homes have scarcity of facilities, dearth of fund, less opportunity to rehabilitate the victim caused by the negative perception and societal attitude toward raped and rape as taboo in one hand and lack of awareness of the community people also impede to take facilities of such shelter homes on the other.

The following recommendations are identified that might be helpful to curb the rape incidents and ensure the effective services for the rape victims in the context of Bangladesh. Awareness building campaign regarding women's right, nature of violence against women and its devastating consequences need to be administered and provision of women empowerment should be strengthened. The judicial procedure should be more people friendly and non-complicated; legal reform in the definition of rape; a community approach could be undertaken to create a gender sensitive attitudes for fostering a healthy and women friendly environment in the society; society should be informed regarding the available prevailing victim recovery assistance programs which encourage them to take shelter of such programs; referral service and community based network should be more strengthened; violence against women including rape as a topic to learn to be incorporated in syllabus curricula from school level to tertiary level; medical intervention for rape victim ought to be simpler and uncomplicated and ensure the crisis intervention in hospital settings; training program should be arranged for all professional who will provide services for rape victims; Media can play an important role for portraying women's image positively, disseminating information through announcement and advertisement of different community based recovery services, legal punishment for rape as preventive approach etc. More research should be conducted on reasons behind occurring rape and health effects of rape, victims' as well as community perception regarding rape, needs of victims, intervention approaches, prevention practices in community etc.

REFERENCES

Ameen, N. (2005). *Wife Abuse in Bangladesh: An Unrecognized Offence*. Dhaka: The University Press Limited.

Ain O Shalish Kendro (2013). *Dhorshon-Poroborty aini Lorai* (Legal fight of post Rape). Dhaka. ASK

Annual Report (2013). Association for Correction and Social Reclamation. Dhaka.

BNWLA (1999). *A Research on Rape and Burden of Proof*. Dhaka. BNWLA.

BNWLA (2005). *Violence Against women in Bangladesh 2004*. Dhaka. BNWLA.

BNWLA (2008). *Violence Against women in Bangladesh 2006-2007*. Dhaka. BNWLA.

Burgess, A. W. & Holmstrom L. L. (1974). Rape Trauma Syndrome. In *American Journal of Psychiatry*, *131*, 981-986.

Burgess, A. W. & Holmstrom L. L. (1979). Adaptive Strategies and Recovery from Rape. In *American Journal of Psychiatry*, *136*, 1278-1282.

Bangladesh Legal Aid & Services Trust (2013). National Conference: Medical Evidence in Rape: Policies, Practices and Procedures. Concept Note. Dhaka. BLAST.

Baseline Report on Violence Against Women, (n.d.) Prepared by Naripokkho and Bangladesh Mahila Parishad, Coordinated by International Women's Right Watch Asia Pacific (IWRAW Asia Pacific).

Brownmiller, S. (1975). *Against our will: Men, women, and rape.*, Bantam Books. New York.

Chowdhuri, Sabiha (n.d.) Violence Against Women in Bangladesh: Situational Analysis/Existing Interventions, Monograph Series:*4*, Dhaka. BRAC University

Devasia, V. V. & Devasia, Leelamma (1992). *Criminology Victimology and Corrections.* Delhi. Ashis Publishing House.

Drucker C. B. & Stern, P. N. (2000). Women's Responses to Sexual Violence by Male Intimates. *Western Journal of Nursing Research, 22,* 385-406.

Kaushik, T. S. (2003). The Essential Nexus Between Transformative Law and Culture: The Ineffectiveness of Dowry Prohibition Laws of India. *Santa Clara Journal of International Law. 1,* 74-117.

Khan. M.E. Bhattacharya, A. Bhuiya, I. & Aeron, A. (2008) A Situation Analysis of Care and Support for Rape Survivors at First Point of Contact in India and Bangladesh. The United States. USAID.

Koss, M. P. & Harvey, M. R. (1991). *The rape victim: Clinical and community interventions.* Newbury Park: Sage Publications.

Lee, R. & Renzetti, C. (EDs) (1993). Researching Sensitive Topics. California. Sage Publication.

Lobmann R. et al., (2003). Violence Against women: Conditions, Consequences and Coping. In *Psychology, Crime and Law, 9,* 309-331.

Mahtab, Nazmunnessa (2007). *Women in Bangladesh.* Dhaka. AHD Development Publishing House.

Mezey, Guillan C. (1997). Treatment of Rape Victims. In *Advances in Psychiatric Treatment.* Vol-*3.* 197-203.

Nasrin, S. (2010). Impediments to Enforce Dowry Prohibition Act 1980 in preventing Dowry Practice in Rural Bangladesh. *The Journal of Social Development.* Vol.*22.* No. 1. Institute of Socia welfare and Research. University of Dhaka. 63-80.

Nari Grantho Probortana (2003). Dharshon Sambad (Rape News), Dhaka. Naro Grontho Probortona.

Ostermann, Jannet E. e. al. (2001). Emergency Psychiatry: Emergency Interventions for Rape Victims. In *Psychiatric Services.* Vol. *52.* No. 6.

Rahman, Mahbubur Muhammad. (2005). *Nari O Shishu Nirjation Daman Ain, Act No viii of 2000.* Dhaka. New Warsi Book Corporation.

Reghr, C. Cadell, S. & Jansen, k. (1999). Perceptions of Control and Long Term Recovery from Rape. *Journal of the American Orthopsychiatry, 69,* 110-116.

Routbort, C. (1998). What happens when You Tell: Disclosure Attributions and Recovery From Sexual Assault. *Dissertation Abstracts International, 58,* B-5655B.

USAID (2007). The Rehabilitation of Victims of Trafficking in Group Residential Facilities in Foreign Countries, A Study conductedPursuant to the Trafficking Victim Protection Reauthorization Act 2005. United States. USAID

Wahed, Tania & Bhuiya, Abbas (2007). Batters Bodies and Shattered Minds: Violence Against women in Bangladesh. *In Indian Journal of Medicine Research, 126,* 341-354.

WHO (2007). Rape: How Women, the Community and the Health Sector Respond. Geneva. World Health Organization.

Zastrow, Charles. (1989). The Practice of Social Work (3rd Ed). Chicago. The Dorsey Press.

In: Crime
Editor: Michael Harry Pearson

ISBN: 978-1-62948-657-4
© 2014 Nova Science Publishers, Inc.

Chapter 5

YOUTH SEXUAL AGGRESSION AND VICTIMIZATION: A EUROPEAN AGENDA?

Christian Diesen[1]*, Katrin Lainpelto[1] and Ine Vanwesenbeeck[2]
[1]Stockholm University, Stockholm, Sweden
[2]Utrecht University, Utrecht, Neverlands

ABSTRACT

During the period 2010–2013 an EU research project – "Youth Sexual Aggression and Victimization" (Y-SAV) – has investigated the problem of sexual aggression towards young people (12–25 years). The first aim of the project was to create a knowledge base of studies on the prevalence, incidence and risk factors of sexual aggression as well as legal and public health responses, covering all 27 EU states. The collection of these data shows that there seems to be a great variety between different regions and cultures in Europe. The awareness of the problem, the reporting of rape, the legal, research and policy standards vary. In general it can be stated that the attention to the problem is proportional to the incidence, i.e. that the countries that have most rape reports per capita also have most research and policies on the issue. The relation between attention to the problem and the amount of police reports also works in the opposite direction; with more awareness more victims turn to the legal system (and other institutions) for assistance.

The prevalence research on national levels indicates that the risk for a young person of being sexually abused seems to be relatively high in all European countries. A problem in making comparisons between countries has been the use of different methods and criteria. Therefore, another aim of the project was to create a standard set of indicators and standards for prevalence studies that will, in the future, make it possible to compare the extent of youth sexual aggression in different countries. A third aim of the Y-SAV project was to establish an international interdisciplinary network for exchange on best practices, state responses and legal rules to prevent youth sexual victimization. This article concentrates on the governmental issues and concludes that legal harmonization would be difficult to obtain, but that some legal standards, e.g. a rape law based on non-consent, would improve the teenagers´ situation. A discussion within the European

---

* Corresponding author: Christian.diesen@juridicum.su.se.

community about the age of consent, which varies from 13 to 18 years, could be a way to get the sexual victimization of teenagers on the agenda.

1. THE PROJECT

In 2010, project Y-SAV (Youth Sexual Aggression and Victimization) was launched. Y-SAV is a three-year project that received funding from the European Union in the framework of the Health Programme to address the issue of sexual aggression and victimization among young people. The project aimed to build a multidisciplinary network of European experts in all member states, to gather the available knowledge on youth sexual aggression and victimization in a state-of-the-art database, to develop a standard way of measuring these issues, and to provide recommendation for addressing the problem under different circumstances in different EU member states.[1] The knowledge base gathered in the project presents information regarding youth sexual aggression and victimization for each EU member state: policies, legislation, organizations, prevalence, risk factors, and evidence-based interventions in the area of youth sexual life. The collected data is based on information gathered through searches in various scientific databases, the Internet and the EU Youth Portal, and from national experts in all EU countries (except Luxemburg). Other important sources are the EU-surveys "Different systems, similar outcomes?" (Lovett & Kelly, 2009) and "Feasibility Study on Harmonization of National Legislation on Gender Violence and Violence Against Children" (Hagemann-White et al., 2010).

The project data reveal that in many countries there is a shortage of studies concerning prevalence, risk, and resilience in the young age group.[2] Some studies in domestic languages may have been missed in the search for data in the non-English speaking countries in the EU, but these eventual deficiencies do probably not affect the general picture of the research and policy situation. The conclusion regarding the situation is that more research is needed and that research has to be more uniform to enable comparison.

2. TEENAGE RAPE – A PUBLIC HEALTH ISSUE?

There is ample evidence that youth sexual violence is highly prevalent in many European countries, and that young people's sexual health is strongly endangered by it. In a number of EU countries more than half of reported sexual assault cases are of young people, primarily young women (Regan & Kelly, 2003), in some countries (e.g. England, Sweden, Ireland)

---

[1] More information regarding the project can be found at http://ysav.rutgerswpf.org. Most of the facts without other references (e.g. on prevalance studies, statistics, domestic law) can be found in the knowledge base of the project. The project was lead by Rutgers WPF in The Netherlands with participation of partner organisations in Sweden, Germany and Greece and network members from all 27 EU member states.

[2] The Y-SAV project has used the age range 12–25 years as the definition of "young people". From a legal point of view this definition creates some problems: Nowhere within the EU is there a specific sex crime legislation for that age category – in most jurisdictions special consideration for the vulnerability of the young ends much earlier than at the age of 25. The general view of what constitutes young age finishes at the age of 18, as the UN Child convention definition of a "child" is no longer applicable. But in many legal matters the age limit is set at a lower age, in spite of the convention. Nor is the age of 12 a universal starting point for division between child sexual abuse (where consent is irrelevant) and rape of adults.

between two-thirds and three-quarters (Lovett & Kelly, 2009). In many countries, the number of reported teenage rapes is low – as reported rapes are generally fewer. The differences between police reports of rape per capita in different EU countries are striking. In Sweden there are 6,000 reported rapes (all ages) per year, representing 58 per 100,000 inhabitants; in Bulgaria, Hungary, Greece and Portugal approximately 300 rapes are reported, representing 2–4 cases per 100,000 inhabitants. The corresponding figures for the UK, Germany and France are 23, 10 and 16 respectively.[3] In Sweden the reporting rates have increased year on year, but in Eastern Europe the number of cases has remained at the same level for many years (or has decreased).[4] The figures of reported rape make it seem as if the risk of a (young) woman being raped is very high in northern Europe and much lower in eastern and southern Europe. But the figures of police reports might be misleading. Differences in definitions and registrations may be factors of some relevance,[5] but more important certainly are the differences in willingness of the victims to report the crime to the police. The expected treatment by others (police, family, friends) and the social stigma on the rape victim are likely reasons for the reluctance to report, but probably even more important is rape myth acceptance (RMA – Burt & Albin, 1981; Davies et al., 2012; Grubb & Turner, 2012; Kahn et al., 2003; Krahé, 1988; Lonsway & Fitzgerald, 1994 Bauger et al 2010, Heath et al 2011).[6] One of the aspects of RMA is that only forced sexual penetrations with physical coercion, resistance and injuries are regarded as "real" rapes. If such a myth is widely spread, other rapes (within relations, date rapes, party rapes, et cetera) are much less likely to be reported. This narrow interpretation of rape prevents many victims from turning to the legal system for rehabilitation and compensation.

A better way (than police reports) to compare the situation in different EU countries may be to collect domestic studies and surveys of sexual habits and risks among young people. In most of the EU countries there are studies on the prevalence of youth sexual victimization or at least on lifetime prevalence of rape. The problem is comparing different studies, both nationally and internationally. Researchers use different definitions of sexual aggression (some are limited to rape and sexual assault, others include all forms of sexual harassment) and different age ranges (some measure prevalence at a certain age, e.g. from 16–18 years, others measure lifetime prevalence). Also the methods of collecting data differ greatly (some use online surveys, others interviews etc.) and so does the size of the study populations.[7] Some surveys are 10 years old; others are recent. In other words: The methodology of the surveys varies a lot and the lack of uniformity prevents reliable comparisons. Another factor

---

[3] According to the study there were, for instance, 46 rapes reported per 100,000 of the population in Sweden in 2006, 23 in England, 15 in France, 12 in Belgium, 11 in Finland, 10 in Denmark and Germany, 8 in Italy and 2–4 in Hungary, Portugal, Greece and Czech Republic (Lovett & Kelly, 2009). In 2011 the reports in Sweden reached 58 per 100,000 inhabitants.

[4] Between 1997 and 2006 the change was e.g. -71% in Hungary, -19% in Hungary and Romania, while it was +186% in Belgium, +154% in Italy, +143% in Sweden and +89% in England (Lovett & Kelly, 2009).

[5] Not only different definitions of "rape", according to the domestic law, may have been used, but it also differs what is meant by a "report".

[6] Recently, some controversy on the importance of RMA has arisen. For example, Reece (2013) questions its importance, a standpoint that will in its turn surely be met with criticism in the nearby future.

[7] How the questions are asked – whether the description of abuse is more general or specified to certain acts – will also affect the rates of prevalence; the more specified questions are likely to result in higher rates.

worth considering when evaluating the level of youth sexual victimization is that many prevalence studies include child sex abuse (i.e. experiences before the age of consent).[8]

However, some conclusions can be drawn, at least as hypotheses until some all-European studies are produced. Significant differences between some countries in the northwest (e.g. Scandinavia, UK, Germany, Belgium and The Netherlands) and some eastern or southern countries (e.g. Hungary, Bulgaria, Romania, Portugal and Greece) have been noted in terms of reporting rates. When comparing the incidence from reported sexual victimization statistics, there is a certain correspondence between low police reporting mainly in the eastern and southern countries (of rape, all ages) and low survey prevalence figures (of youth sexual victimization). There is also some correspondence between high police reporting in the north-western countries and high figures of reported prevalence.[9] This can be an *indication* that the risk of being subjected to sexual victimization may be lower in EU countries with low prevalence rates, implying that the incidence data available in fact reflect real differences between different regions in Europe. On the other hand the differences in reporting are much bigger than the differences in prevalence – if we disregard the lower end, most countries are relatively close in prevalence figures: the range is then from 7 to 20%.[10]

But, once again, all comparisons are problematic. If only rape with penetration is registered in one country, and the definition of rape is much wider in another country, or if a survey only considers rape and sexual assault while another includes other forms of sexual victimization, it is impossible to draw conclusions on differences in incidence. To give an estimation of the risk for a young European girl of being raped during her lifetime is too difficult a task today, but it seems that *the problem in all European countries is big enough to be declared a public health issue.* In some of the countries sexual aggression against young girls seems to be at a lower level than in others, according to the available studies,[11] but as a general conclusion it can be stated that youth sexual aggression and victimization is a common problem in Europe.[12]

3. STATE RESPONSIBILITIES

Sexual violence is not only a suffering for the victims, it is also accompanied by high costs in terms of expenditures on health, social work, police and courts, as well as losses in terms of productivity, and it is a noted impediment towards gender equity.[13] There are many reasons for governments to act against youth sexual aggression and victimization – and there are obligations to do so. These obligations do not follow directly from EU law, except when the problem is transnational. In case there is a risk of a viral epidemic (e.g. HIV) or

---

[8] Krahé and others will describe these difficulties –and the need for uniformity – in more depth in an article from the Y-SAV project. See also http://ysav.rutgerswpf.org/content/research-instrument.

[9] It should be noted that Sweden, which has the highest reporting rate, shows a moderate prevalence; 13,5% (Priebe, 2009).

[10] For details, see Y-SAV home page http://ysav.rutgerswpf.org/content/country-reports.

[11] Hungary, Cyprus, Bulgaria, Romania and Poland have figures between 2 and 5%.

[12] According to the WHO report, 2013, 25,4% of the women in Europe will experience physical and/or sexual violence by a partner or sexual violence by a non-partner. Note that these figures do not refer to youth specifically.

[13] See WHO Health & Violence Report, 2013.

international organized crime (e.g. trafficking in humans), the EU can take measures to fight the problem. And if a criminal issue concerns the protection of children, the EU also has the power to take action (according to Articles 165 and 166 in the Treaty of the Functioning of the European Union). However, if youth sexual aggression is regarded as just a criminal act, the Lisbon Treaty provides neither regulations on criminal and procedural law (considered as national matters), nor laws against sexual exploitation. The state obligations to fight these crimes are merely founded on other legal and political grounds. As sexual integrity is a matter of human rights, the responsibility of the EU member states (and other nations in Europe) to cope with the problem is closely linked to the Council of Europe (CoE), the European human rights organization where not only the EU member states, but also 20 more countries in the region (e.g. Russia and Ukraine) are united. The European Convention on Human Rights and its practice in the European Court of Human Rights are the principal instruments for efficient and harmonized efforts to stop youth sexual aggression and victimization.

In general three obligations (relevant to this field) are derived from international human rights standards, commonly referred to as "the 3 Ps":

1. To *prosecute* with due diligence – to criminalize violent acts and to perform adequate investigations and fair trials;
2. To *protect* and assist victims – to assure the right to privacy, the right to be heard and the right to effective remedy, economic and social assistance;
3. To *prevent* violence by addressing the underlying causes – to initiate activities to raise awareness, research on perpetration, rehabilitation of offenders, equality policies.[14]

More concrete recommendations on how the obligations should be fulfilled are found in two conventions: a) *The Lanzarote Convention 2010* (Council of Europe Convention on Protection of Children against Sexual Exploitation and Sexual Abuse) and b) *The Istanbul Convention 2013* (Council of Europe Convention on Preventing and Combating Violence against Women and Domestic Violence).[15] Both these conventions comprise recommendations on legislative measures. The fact that these conventions are needed, demonstrates that European countries today respond differently to the issue of sexual aggression and victimization against women and children and that standards differ. The awareness of the problem – especially when it concerns young victims – seems to vary greatly, at least if law, legal discussions, government policies, research, and activities by NGOs are used as measures of a country's response to youth sexual victimization. The differences in law and law practice will be discussed below, but the Y-SAV database on national activities demonstrates other imbalances as well.

In some countries teenage sexual victimization is not an issue at all, in others it constitutes a problem that is explicitly discussed at a political level and considered an issue that has to be dealt with. An observation from the database is that the more the focus is set on youth affairs in general (in government organizations and general policies), the less the focus seems to be set on sexual matters. In most countries, general *policies and plans to promote youth interests* have been formulated in relation to health, education, work, culture, and

---

[14] "Feasibility study", supra note p.16.
[15] Signed by 26 member states of the CoE, ratified by 14 in June 2013.

participation in society. Some countries even have a Youth Department (e.g. Estonia, Italy, Romania, and Slovakia) and many more have a Youth Unit within some other department (Cyprus, Finland, France, Greece, Hungary, Ireland, Latvia, Malta, Slovenia, and Spain). However, the work and plans of these governmental institutions seldom have a special branch or explicit policy directed towards youth sexual life. Only a third of the member states pay special attention to the problem of youth sexual victimization in government action plans. In most EU countries, campaigns on a related issue are launched from time to time, such as information campaigns about HIV or strategies against trafficking, but sexual aggression against teenagers has not often been the focus of such campaigns. It seems that the issue of teenage sexual victimization has not yet reached the political agenda in the majority of the EU states, that sexual abuse amongst and against teenagers is not considered such a problem that it has to be dealt with by the government. In contrast, some EU countries have specifically addressed the issue of sexual aggression and victimization in the age range 12–25 years.[16] These exceptions are found in Finland, France, The Netherlands, Sweden and the UK, where explicit strategies against sexual exploitation of young people can be found in government action plans (2000–2010). In some of these countries (France, The Netherlands and the UK) there have also been some campaigns against teenage rape.

Another indication of the level of awareness of the problem (other than governmental institutions and plans for youth) is the activities amongst the *NGOs in the field of sexual violence*. In most EU countries there seems to be a tendency from the governments to leave issues of relational violence to the NGOs (but to support them financially). The question is if the existing organisations have the ability to fulfil the task of fighting youth sexual aggression and victimization. In some countries there are no specialized NGOs at all in this area and very few others that take youth sexual victimization under their umbrella (e.g. Cyprus, Czech Republic, Greece, Malta, Romania, Slovenia, and Spain). In other countries there are many NGOs dealing with the problem within a larger framework (like women's organizations and child protection groups) as well as NGOs that are specialized in the matter (e.g. Bulgaria, Denmark, Germany, Ireland, The Netherlands, Sweden, and UK). Yet another group of countries within the EU provides a more disparate picture: there are some NGOs at national level and/or some regional/local initiatives against youth sexual aggression, but the general impression from the Y-SAV data base is that the efforts are not covering the needs on a national basis (e.g. Belgium, Estonia, Finland, France, Hungary, Italy, Latvia, Lithuania, Poland, Portugal, Romania, and Slovakia). Today most EU countries have a Children´s Ombudsman (or equivalent), helplines for abused children and abused women, and women's shelters for victims of relational violence. But most countries lack certain institutions (GOs and NGOs) to deal with the problem of sexual victimization specifically among young people who are not children anymore. The consequence is that *teenagers fall between two stools*: in the existing structure they are either treated as children or as adults. The special needs of youth are thereby neglected.[17]

This is mirrored even better (than the number of NGOs) through the existence of *research* in the field in each nation. Knowledge on gender-based violence is presently starting

---

[16] Less explicit or more limited plans (e.g. on youth at risk or on sex education) can be found in e.g. Greece, Malta, Portugal and Slovenia.

[17] Also meaning that the obligations of the Lanzarote Convention are not fulfilled.

to be built up in several databases[18], but specific visibility of young people is notably limited in these datasets. Whereas child sexual abuse is often explicitly addressed, and rightly so, sexual violence against adolescents remains mostly invisible. Data on adolescence, specifically, is often absent or hidden in general datasets or local studies. Youth sexual violence has also been marginalized in research and responses to gender-based violence more generally. In one nation (Slovakia) there are no scientific studies at all about youth sexual victimization and aggression. In other nations some single studies can be found on this matter, but most research made on relational violence is about family violence (e.g. in Bulgaria, Czech Republic, Cyprus, Hungary, Latvia, Lithuania, Malta, Portugal, Romania, and Slovenia). Some studies may also be found on the subject of incest, but our impression is that *youth sexual victimization is a blind spot on the national research map in most EU countries.*[19] Still there are some countries where a lot of research can be found in this specific area: In the UK, Sweden, Germany, The Netherlands, and Spain there are many studies in sociology, criminology, psychology, sexology, political and legal science, et cetera, dealing with this issue. The Y-SAV database covers the years 2000–2011 and during that period more than a dozen studies on prevalence were found in Germany, the Netherlands, and Spain, and many studies on youth sexual attitudes and risk in Sweden and in the UK. This seems to be an adequate illustration of the interest in the issue of youth sexual victimization when you compare the different EU nations. It also seems that research on specific youth sexual issues often is a fruition of research on gender-based violence and child abuse. When discussion about family violence has been taken on in a country, it leads to the creation of women's shelters, to the forming of NGOs for women and GOs for child protection and, sooner or later, to national research about these matters. Then studies on teenage sex and abuse may follow as a result of the findings about adult women or child sexual abuse, at least if the problem is considered to have some magnitude in the society.

A reasonable conclusion could be that most countries within the EU need more research on youth sexual victimization in order to measure the size of the problem. When performing these studies it is also important to use the same standards, definitions, and methods in all EU states to make it possible to make comparisons between them (and that is, as said above, one of the aims of the Y-SAV project).

Summing up, it seems that *the awareness of the problem* of youth sexual victimization varies between regions and that Eastern and Southern Europe are lagging behind in addressing the problem.[20] This is mutually related to a low number of reports to the police. If very few cases of teenage sexual victimization get reported to the police, the interest of governments to tackle the problem will probably be less. When analysing the data of the Y-SAV project, it is evident that there is a correlation between the reporting rate of rape and the interest in the issue of youth sexual victimization: A *high reporting* rate will thus be related to an on-going public and political discussion on sexual abuse, many NGOs working in the area, and a lot of research about sexual abuse (child sexual abuse, and rape). On the other hand, a *low reporting* rate will be mutually related to an absence of debate on youth sexual

---

[18] E.g. the European Policy Action Centre on Violence Against Women (EPACVAW), The Violence Against Women Monitor of The Advocates for Human Rights, the UN Secretary General's database on violence against women, the OECD Social Institutions and Gender Index, SIGI.

[19] In bigger countries like Italy, France, and Poland there is a number of studies in the field, but not in proportion to the population and often by the same research group. (The latter remark is valid also for Germany.)

[20] Regarding the number of scientific studies in the field, Spain seems to be an exception.

victimization, few NGOs working in the field, no or little research on sex crimes and only single prevalence studies.

Whatever way one likes to look at the relation between reporting rates and national awareness of and attention to youth sexual aggression and victimization across European member states, what is common to all European nations is that most rapes are never reported to the police. A common estimation is that at least 80% of these crimes remain unreported (Wolitzski-Taylor et al., 2011).[21] If the assumption is accepted, that youth sexual victimization is a problem everywhere in Europe, a governmental obligation must be to acknowledge that fact and to make efforts to fight the abuse. One of the practical obligations is then to prosecute, but in order to do that it must be possible and reasonable for the victim to report the abuse to the police. As *the reporting rate seems to be strongly related to awareness, support and research* in the field, *one way* of raising awareness and action is to increase the willingness to report youth sexual abuse.

5. PSYCHOLOGICAL AND LEGAL OBSTACLES TO REPORTING RAPE

If youth sexual abuse is under-reported the problem may not get public attention and less efforts will be made to prevent abusive behaviour. Certainly there are other ways to raise the awareness and the efforts, e.g. through media and NGOs, but an important issue in this respect is why these crimes are not reported while most other crimes of the same severity are.

As shown above there is an immense difference between countries in reporting rape, e.g. there are 30 times more rapes reported in Sweden than in Greece (two countries with about the same number of inhabitants). The explanation behind that difference cannot rationally be a reflection of factual occurrence – the main reason must be a difference in reporting. It might be a fact that many more teenage girls get raped in Sweden than in Greece, but it is enough to check the contents of the police reports in both countries to realize that the main difference probably is the willingness to report: In Greece you find cases of "real rape", with good evidence (e.g. injuries) and the possibility to charge a suspect. In Sweden many reports are weak, with no evidence other than the victim's story and no real possibility to prosecute (unless the perpetrator admits the abuse) (Diesen & Diesen, 2013). In spite of these poor prospects many Swedish victims choose to make a report. Reasons why a complaint could be made are to establish a harmful experience as a criminal act, to get rid of self-blame and to show "everybody" that the behaviour of the perpetrator cannot be accepted. And in this situation, the victim does not expect to be mistrusted and/or treated only as a victim, not as a person, by the environment. The reporting victim expects to be regarded as a violated person in need of support – and that it is a duty for her/him to report the incident to prevent others from being victims of the same kind of abuse (Diesen & Diesen 2013).[22]

The first and most important obstacle to reporting rape is probably the concept "real rape" and the corresponding Rape Myth Acceptance (Bauger et al., 2010, DuMont et al., 2003; Estrich, 1987; Grubb & Turner, 2012; Heath et al., 2011, Lonsway & Fitzgerald, 1994;

---

[21] This is an estimation for countries with high reporting, like the USA and the UK. See also Y-SAV Country reports at Y-SAV home page; supra note 1, and Women´s Lobby, Rape Barometer 2013.

[22] This attitude (expressed by reporting Swedish rape victims) – not expecting mistrust - can in reality be somewhat optimistic.

Nagel et al., 2005; Stewart et al., 1996; Suarez & Gadalla, 2010; Temkin & Krahé, 2008;). When "rape" is conceptualised as an act of violence, mostly performed by a stranger, overcoming the resistance of the woman and the act results in evidence of that resistance, everybody will recognize it as "real rape". In Europe, this recognition is finally also given to marital rape,[23] provided there is evidence of violence. But if the rape is committed without evidence of violence, e.g. on a drunk victim who has "taken risks" and the act is not immediately reported to the police, it is, according to the majority of the population – and perhaps according even to the legislator and to the victim herself[24] – outside the general concept of rape. Then, the act of rape – as a main rule – will not be reported. Not only is the concept of "real rape" an obstacle to reporting, but it also promotes the self-blame of the victim and the expected social stigma of being a rape victim. And even if the non-violent attack on sexual integrity is reported to the police, the evidential problems and the prejudices of the police and the trial jury may prevent investigation, prosecution and/or conviction (Fisher et al., 2003; Grubb & Turner, 2012; Kelly, 2002, Kelly et al. 2005, Nagel et al., 2005; Skinner & Taylor, 2009; Spohn & Tellis, 2011, Temkin & Krahé, 2008; Ward, 1995).[25]

It could be argued that differences in criminal legislation must be a factor to consider when evaluating the differences between regions and nations in reporting, but the rape law in itself seems to have no or little bearing on the reporting rate or the attrition process (Lovett & Kelly, 2009). A rape law based on lack of consent (as in the UK, Ireland, and Belgium) is wider and should lead to more reports – and more convictions – than the traditional rape law based on coercion. But whether it really works that way is doubtful. It may be so that the English experience of the modern rape law (introduced in 1976) shows that the reporting rate goes up and the conviction rate goes down with such a law (Temkin & Krahé, 2008), but corresponding developments in other countries have occurred without changing the rape law. More important than the change in the law itself seems to be the general concept of "real rape", as understood by the public, and the response by the environment to a rape victim. The *conviction rate* varies greatly, from 6 to 80% within the different jurisdictions of the EU.[26] Countries with a low reporting rate have a high conviction rate and countries with a high reporting rate have a low conviction rate. The main explanation of this is that in all jurisdictions it is primarily "real rape" cases that lead to convictions. Cases outside that concept – whether they are many or few – will most often be closed (or lead to an acquittal).[27] In spite of that fact, the formulation of the rape law probably has importance in the long term – if it is combined with information and education on respect and responsibility (Temkin & Krahe, 2008).

A rape victim is vulnerable, not only psychologically but also legally, especially if the perpetrator is not a complete stranger. The accusation will in most cases be challenged and

---

[23] Such legislation is still missing in Lithuania. In Greece, Latvia, Bulgaria and Malta it seems that this amendment has not yet been used.

[24] In an American study 42% of the women who made a report to the police were uncertain if it was a "rape" they reported (Kahn et al., 2003).

[25] The jury system is demonstrated to have a negative impact on convictions; the majority of jury trials in England, Ireland and Norway lead to acquittals (Lovett & Kelly, 2009; Nygard 2012). It should be discussed if specialist courts in sex crime cases could substitute jury trials.

[26] Lovett & Kelly, 2009. The lowest rate (2006) in the UK (6%), the highest in Hungary (80%), followed by Lithuania (44%).

[27] A factor that may restrain an integrity-based case evaluation according to the non-consent law might be the harsh punishments: rape is a crime that in England (in theory) can lead to a lifetime imprisonment.

the victim will be under extreme pressure over a long period of time. In some European countries, the outcome of the reporting can be even worse. For instance in Bulgaria, Czech Republic, and Hungary there is a major risk that the victim will be sued for defamation of the suspect if the case is closed or the suspect is acquitted. It is also important to know that in these countries (but also in Finland, Malta, Poland, Portugal, and Spain) *the complaint of the victim* is needed for prosecution; if the victim withdraws her/his complaint, the prosecutor cannot take the case to trial.[28] This situation is another obstacle to reporting, as (especially if the rape has been performed within a relationship) and makes the victim a target for threats and negotiations (as the victim holds the key to the legal process). The nature of rape crime in these countries, as a semi-public offence that can only be taken to trial if the victim agrees, makes the victim more vulnerable and therefore is an obstacle to reporting. When it comes to young, not legally competent victims, the needed involvement of custodians (parents) is an additional barrier to report.[29]

To have the strength to report and stand trial the victim needs help, not least the young victim (Skinner & Taylor, 2009). An important trend within the EU is the growing awareness of the need for *victim support* in sex offence cases. Most European countries today give the victim not only social and psychological support, but also legal aid (free of charge). In some countries (Austria, Finland, Germany, and Sweden) the victim has the status of a party (beside the prosecutor) in the proceedings in these cases, a position that provides the possibility – through a victim's counsel – to be involved in the presentation of evidence. In other countries the victim holds a weaker procedural position, but still has the right to be accompanied by counsel (for support and for the compensation claim). Only in a few countries (e.g. Estonia, Latvia, and Slovakia) is such a reform – recommended by several European institutions[30] – still not implemented. Certainly it is of the utmost importance that victims of sexual offences get this legal support, and also the psychological support to deal with the stress of the process and the trauma of the victimization. Especially for young victims these services are essential to help them cope with the consequences of the crime.

6. LEGAL HARMONIZATION?

As demonstrated above (part 5) *the formulation of the rape law* in itself seems to have no direct bearing on the reporting rate or the attrition process. In line with this, the EU "Feasibility study" in 2010 also concluded that a European harmonization of criminal laws on sexual offences would probably not drastically effect the situation in different countries. In addition, there would be legal difficulties (due to the Lisbon Treaty) in creating a uniform EU-law only in the field of sexual offences. However, that conclusion does not mean that a discussion about sex crime law has no influence on the situation, nor does it mean that harmonization is not an option.

---

[28] In Slovenia a complaint is needed for marital rape. In Greece the prosecutor can close the case on the request of the victim. Other exceptions can also be found. In Finland a complaint is needed for prosecution of sexual assault (not for rape). In Italy a sort of plea bargain (including the participation of the victim) can occur, thereby reducing the sentence to a suspended prison verdict.

[29] In some countries, e.g. Italy, exceptions are made for young victims.

[30] See The Council of Europe Framework Decision on the standing of victims in criminal proceedings, 2001/220/HA, 15 March 2001).

The process of making sex crime laws more uniform within Europe will not be by means of EU-legislation. For the foreseeable future the harmonization will, instead, follow the recommendations and conventions of the European Council and the verdicts in the European Court of Human Rights. So far these rulings and recommendations have been used to include marital rape and "helpless state" in the definition of "rape" and will continue as new cases reach the court. The on-going discussion will also show that some EU countries have lessons to learn from the legislation in other countries, not least on the protection of teenagers. But accordingly it must be said that no country in Europe has a legislation that is comprehensively sufficient enough to legally cope with all the problems of youth sexual victimization.

The European discussion about rape law is very important for the domestic court practice – and for the public understanding of the nature of the crime. Only three states in the EU today have a rape law based on non-consent (the UK, Ireland, and Belgium), the rest keeps the old concept of coercion as a requisite of rape. But as a result of the MC / Bulgaria case in the European Court of Human Rights[31] many of the countries in the second category have added the situation of when the victim is in a "helpless condition" as an alternative to coercion in defining rape (e.g. Germany and Sweden). Some countries, e.g. The Netherlands, Portugal, and Spain, even recognize non-consent as the basis for criminalization but without abandoning the basic element of coercion. The main difference between the old and the modern rape law is that a coercion-based law presumes that a woman is available for sex unless she resists (a crime of physical assault), while the non-consent law presumes that a person is willing to have sex when consenting (a violation is a crime against integrity). In theory the modern law abandons the "real rape" concept, but in legal practice the effects have been minor so far. It seems difficult to have a wider definition of sexual abuse accepted and one part of the resistance is the unwillingness (by laymen and lawyers) to look upon other forms of sexual abuse than assaults as "rape". The risk is that other acts of abuse (even when involving penetration) will remain unpunished.

A solution of the "legal threshold problem" – that "rape" is associated with physical assault, resistance, injuries, and many years in prison in the case of a conviction – is used in Finland and France,[32] where a minor crime of "sex abuse" can be used in cases of rape without violence but with lack of consent.[33] An alternative, used in Italy, is to use the expression "sexual abuse" as the principal sex crime and to differentiate by severity, not by terminology ("rape" or not).

The challenge for the legislator in Europe (and elsewhere) is to overcome the common concept of "real rape" and the workings of Rape Myth Acceptance. In the longer term it can be expected that the members of the EC will follow the recommendation by the EC Ministerial Committee 2002, which explicitly says that the member states should penalize any sexual act committed against non-consenting persons even if they do not show signs of

---

[31] ECHR 2003-XII (2003).

[32] The same technique is used in Norway (not an EU member) and has been proposed in Sweden (but rejected). The Italian solution is different from the others as sexual crimes are sorted under the same headline of "sexual abuse" and graded in severity by interpretation. The expression "rape" is not used in law.

[33] In both countries this secondary crime is commonly used as a charge in cases of rape within relationships and this practice is a matter of criticism as it underestimates the trauma of being raped by someone you trust. As a paradox, rape within marriage is an aggravating factor in French rape law.

resistance.[34] The same, or at least similar, recommendation is found in the CoE Istanbul Convention 2013. Chapter V, article 36 on "sexual violence, including rape", states that

1. Parties shall take the necessary legislative or other measures to ensure that the following intentional conducts are criminalized:
   a) Engaging in non-consensual vaginal, anal or oral penetration of a sexual nature of the body of another person with any bodily part or object;
   b) Engaging in other non-consensual acts of a sexual nature with a person;
   c) Causing another person to engage in non-consensual acts of a sexual nature with a third person.
2. Consent must be given voluntarily as the result of the person's free will assessed in the context of the surrounding circumstances.

Changing the rape law definition from a crime of violence to a crime against integrity, basing it on non-consent and not on coercion, could, step by step, change the view of the crime. A rape law based on coercion creates a situation of (legal) mistrust when a report is made if there are no injuries to prove the crime (Diesen & Diesen, 2010). *A rape law based on non-consent is a way to support the vulnerable and to change attitudes.* Such a law probably would not change the legal practice drastically, at least not on the short term, but in the long run it may be expected to affect the sexual attitudes and habits of young people. To be certain that he is not performing a criminal act, the boy must be sure that he has clear consent from the girl – if not (e.g. if she is too drunk to have that capacity) he is taking the risk of committing a crime.

To prevent youth sexual aggression and victimization, *parts of the sex crime legislation other* than rape and sexual assault can be of some or equal importance. Chapter V in the Istanbul Convention not only deals with rape and sexual violence, but also with victim compensation, forced marriages, stalking, female genital mutilation, forced abortion, sexual harassment, and unacceptable justification of crimes, including honour-related crimes. All EU countries have laws against trafficking, procuration, sexual molestation, and sexual harassment, but many countries are completely lacking legislation that covers all the other behaviours, which should be criminalized according to the convention. A few countries also have laws against grooming – seeking sexual contact with children under 18 through the Internet – and in some countries with a broader legislation, there are legal provisions against forced marriages and honour-based violence, and also debate about giving LGTB persons a special protection. The UK, The Netherlands, and Sweden seem to be the countries closest to full coverage.

In our opinion, it should be on the agenda in all EU states to implement legislation that covers all kinds of sexual abuse and discrimination effectively. The specific strategy in this legislation may differ – either choosing a broader concept (e.g. Italy) which makes way for new interpretations, or a more specified "catalogue" (e.g. the UK) to cover new types of sexual offences. It is also obvious that some EU countries have lessons to learn from the legislation in other countries, not least on the protection of teenagers. It is obvious that legislation in some countries today does not reach the minimum standards of the Istanbul Convention, as the existing laws do not cover all situations that should be prevented and

---

[34] CoE Minister Committee 2002, art 35.

sanctioned. In addition, the recommendations of the Lanzarote Convention must be taken into consideration when dealing with the risk of youth sexual victimization. In particular, the protection of the age category between the age of consent and adulthood is often neglected in legislation.

It will probably take some time before these two conventions are ratified by all states and implemented in national legislation and practice. At the same time it is quite obvious that the legal practice (by police, prosecutors, and courts) is a bigger problem than the law itself. As shown above there are extreme differences between countries in reporting rape and also some regional differences in prevalence, but when you compare convictions these differences are much smaller. The official criminal statistics are hard to compare, but a valid general statement is that *the convicted rape rate per capita seems to be about the same everywhere in the EU*. Only "real rape" cases are – as a main rule – brought to conviction and what differs between the EU states is the number of police reports. As an example, Denmark can be compared to Sweden: in Denmark there are approximately 400 rapes reported each year of which 150 lead to conviction; in Sweden 6,000 rapes are reported and 250 perpetrators convicted.[35] Apparently, the difference between EU states is more a matter of the amount of closed cases than of efficiency in dealing with rape crimes – in a country with few reports there are almost as many convictions as in a country of the same size with many reports. A simple explanation could be that with a large number of reports one gets many cases with evidential problems; a more drastic conclusion is that the legal system is not yet prepared to expand the rape concept to situations where the victim has "taken risks" (Lovett & Kelly, 2009; Temkin & Krahé, 2008). In short, *only "real rape" is punishable in Europe today*. That practice needs to change. But the principal question is not if it, one way or another, will be possible to achieve more convictions – the principal question is how to avoid the sexual abuse of teenagers, especially the girls.[36] Or in other words: the crime and its determinants are bigger problems than deficiencies in the sex crime law and investigations.

In summary, to prevent young people from being sexually abused, the legal framework has its importance. But even more important are attitudes and processes related to (young) people's respect of sexual integrity and self-determination. A rape law based on non-consent, not on coercion, may have an impact on these attitudes and processes, gradually making the need for clear consent a natural condition for sexual acts. *Countries that still have the traditional basis for rape should, not least in the interest of young people, make a reform and change the law*.[37] Another change that might be necessary is to fill the gap between "rape" and "sexual molestation". As there is a reluctance to label sexual abuses with penetration but without resistance/injuries as "rape", a more lenient crime perhaps is necessary to criminalize the non-consensual sexual acts which teenagers are often subjected to. The Italian legislation, where all these crimes are kept within the same label of "sexual abuse" may be an example to

---

[35] When comparing official criminal statistics it should be noted again that the figures might not be compatible; some countries register "crimes", others "cases", and still others "charged persons".

[36] Little has been said in this article about *young boys*. In proportion to the girls the problem of victimization is less, but that does not mean that the masculine side of the problem is of perpetration only. Many young boys suffer from child and youth sexual abuse, performed not only by older males and same-sex peers and partners, but also by girls and women. In some countries, where prevalence studies have been conducted (Belgium, Germany, Italy, The Netherlands and Sweden), 3–5% of the boys report sexual coercion before the age of 18.

[37] This is also a recommendation of the "Feasibility study" p.181.

follow.[38] Improved legislation constitutes more clear norms and thereby a hope for less abuse, and more reports raise the awareness of these norms, but in order to create better prevention tools against youth sexual victimization the crucial point seems to be the understanding of the nature of the crime: the violation of integrity.

8. AGE OF CONSENT

As the interpretation of "rape" is often rigid – as much in the practice of the legal system as by the public – legal measures other than the legal description of different sexual crimes may also be promising. One of these measures might be an all-European debate about the adequate age of consent. This threshold – when a young person can consent to sex – probably is common knowledge in all countries and affects the life of young people everywhere. Raising or lowering the age of consent in a certain country would have direct impact on the sexual habits of teenagers there. But is there a *rationale* to set the age of consent at a certain level – at 7, 15 or 16 years? And is there a reason to have a uniform age of consent all over Europe?

There is a great variety between the EU countries in determining the age of consent. In Spain the age of consent is 13, in Portugal and Italy 14, in Belgium, Finland, Latvia, Lithuania, Luxemburg, Netherlands, and the UK 16, in Ireland and Cyprus 17, and in Malta 18 years, while the remaining countries have 15 years as the age where young people are supposed to be able to give consent to sex. This signifies a lack of uniformity that is hard to explain.

The reasons for the differences are historical and in most European countries originally linked to the acceptable age of marriage. The first definition of the age of consent was given as early as in the 13th century (in the UK), but in many countries the age limit was not decided until the 19th century. In the beginning, the age limit was low, at the age of 12 or 13, but in the beginning of the 20th century it was often raised to a somewhat higher level (Graupner, 2002). Another common pattern in the development of the law in EU member states is that the age for allowing marriage has been separated from the age of consent (by a rise of the former) and that until recently most countries had a higher age level for same-sex relationships.[39] Another similarity (with some exceptions, e.g. Germany, Spain, Ireland, and England[40]) is the lack of discussion around the age of consent today. A general view seems to be the acceptance of the existing age of consent as a national tradition. Only a few countries have made decisions on the age of consent during the last few decades. Exceptions are found in some of the nations within the former Yugoslavian federation, which had the age of 14 as the limit, and lately have raised it to 15 years. The same has been the case in Slovakia (former part of

---

[38] The argument against a "two-level" rape crime is that rape within relationships (and other rapes within the second category) will be considered less severe, but the fact is that the loss of trust through such an abuse often leads to, or can be a trauma of the same or even higher gravity as a stranger rape.

[39] In 1997 the European Commission of Human Rights declared that a higher age for homosexual conduct should be regarded as discrimination, but some countries within the EU, e.g. Ireland, Portugal, Bulgaria, Cyprus, Estonia, Finland and Lithuania, still have a higher age of consent for same-sex relations.

[40] In Spain 2013 the government has made a proposal to raise the age from 13, which created a discussion about the appropriate age, and in England there was a less serious debate in May 2013 after a female lawyer had suggested that the age should be lowered from 16 to 13, with the argument that the present rule means that "old men are persecuted for relatively minor offences".

Czechoslovakia). In Spain, which has had the lowest age in Europe for a long period of time and where it has been raised from 12 to 13 years in 1998, the government has now proposed another raise to 15 or 16.

As the age of consent is regarded as a tradition, seldom challenged, it is hard to find any reasonable and elaborated motives for setting the age at a certain level. Not even when there has been a recent change has there been a proper discussion about what should be considered as a reasonable age. What has been discussed a lot all over Europe over the past decades is the age of consent in same-sex relationships (Graupner, 2002), but it seems that a serious debate on the age of consent in all its aspects is lacking in most countries. Pleas for a raise are heard now and then, but the motives are mostly of a moral kind. It seems that the sexual liberty of adolescents is a very delicate matter from a legal point of view, and discussion about it best avoided.[41]

The proposal of a raise has been historically motivated with the prevention of child prostitution, e.g. in England in 1885 (when the age of consent was raised there from 13 to 16), or with child protection in general, often using the simple argument that a person under a certain level "is still a child".[42] This means that a person above the decided age is no longer considered a child (in this respect) in one national jurisdiction, while other countries draw the same conclusion at another level. It is strange that the European countries have come to such diverging conclusions about the maturity of young people. If the gap was 1–2 years it could be understandable, but at present the age of consent in Europe ranges from 13 to 18. This lack of uniformity is hard to explain. Certainly there are differences in cultures, but the differences in maturity are probably much bigger on an individual level than between nations.

This should be a matter to consider. A general discussion about the *legal age of consent* serves several purposes. First of all, it is a matter of child protection deciding at what age a young person should be protected from sexual abuse – when is a person mature enough to decide about having sex or not? Discussions should focus on whether the legal age of consent is important as a tool for controlling unwanted teenage sexual habits or whether it would be possible today to make a more individual evaluation of the involved persons' maturity. Secondly, a discussion about the legal age of consent will draw attention to the importance of consent, not only in situations where consent is considered irrelevant (because of defined childhood), but also in situations where non-consent is an issue (in relation to the issue of coercion). That discussion also provides an adequate opening to the problem of sexual victimization among teenagers. Thirdly, the consideration of a universal legal age within the union – or a national debate on changing the existing age – will draw attention to the problem where the boy and the girl in a sexual relationship are close in age. This situation seems to be handled differently in the national jurisdictions; in some countries (e.g. Sweden and England) there will be no prosecution e.g. when the girl is one year under the legal age and the boy is less than two years above it, in other countries practice is more rigid in following the age rule, and in still others prosecution is a more discretionary matter, where it is possible to screen out cases where no punishment seems required. Some jurisdictions (e.g. Germany and The Netherlands) also have multistage age levels for this discretionary assessment, e.g. for seduction or relationships of authority; in Germany the minimum age of consent is 14 years, but 16 in cases of seduction and 18 in cases of dependence (Graupner, 2002). The way in

---

[41] It is significant that the Istanbul Convention declares (in Art. 18:2) that the age of consent is a national issue.

[42] E.g. Slovenia, when the age was raised to 15 in 2008.

which the rule of age of consent is handled – in a rigid or liberal way – probably influences the sexual habits of young people.

In summary, it may be suggested that a common discussion in Europe about a uniform legal age within the EU could be a way to highlight the problem of youth sexual victimization. The legal age of consent is also an interesting rule in itself; it draws an important line between childhood and adolescence. A child should always be protected from abuse, but at a certain age the personal responsibility of the young person begins and the lack of agency that is supposed in childhood ends. If this starting point occurs before the age of 18 (the age to which one is a child according to the UN Convention on the Rights of the Child), legal protection is limited. This leads to a risk that the vulnerable age group between the legal age of consent and 18 years will not have enough legal protection.

CONCLUSION

The first conclusion that can be drawn from the knowledge base of the Y-SAV project is that *more research is needed*. The awareness of the problem depends on reliable and comparative statistics. In some countries the available prevalence and incidence studies may demonstrate youth sexual victimization as a minor problem compared to the situation in other countries, but the prevalence figures are high enough in the EU to make this an issue of public health. Adequate legal responses as well as preventive measures are required everywhere. Perhaps different countries or regions have to tackle the problem in different ways, but EU cooperation – in research and strategies – on this matter is bound to improve public health across the union.

The knowledge about youth sexual abuse patterns must not only be shared with researchers in other countries, but of course also with the young generation itself to fight stereotypical gender prejudices and misinterpretations of what constitutes a rape or sexual assault. *Sex education* in schools and other meeting places for young people – not only on contraceptives and on sexual diseases, but also on the right to sexual integrity – must be used as a tool to prevent further sexual oppression, especially of teenage girls.

It has been discussed here whether harmonization of sex *crime legislation* within the EU can be another tool to stop the development of increasing sexual offending. The Lisbon Treaty prevents direct interference in national crime legislation, but certainly single governments can learn from more experienced legislators in other EU countries. For instance, domestic sex crime legislation may be improved and cover more aspects of abusive behaviour (such as grooming and stalking). New laws may have important signal functions, but the main problem in the legal area seems to be the present legal practice. The (social, emotional, and judicial) pressure on the rape victim during the criminal process (from report to trial) is still so strong that it oftentimes prevents reporting of the crime. To make it possible to overcome these obstacles, all efforts must be made to lighten the burden of the victim, first of all by eliminating the stigmatization. As more reports seem to be key to more public and governmental attention, awareness, debate, research, support, and protection, it is important to lower the barriers that prevent reporting.

One such barrier is a rape law historically based on coercion. A change to a non-consent rape law may be a way to change attitudes, prevent prejudices and promote self-determination. There is a general reluctance to punish rape other than "real rape" and the abuses that teenagers often experience (acquaintance rape, date rape, partner rape etc.) remain unpunished. In practice, the prosecutors and the courts are unwilling to accept these experiences as "rape", which means that there is *a gap between "real rape" and sexual molestation* that the legislators have to deal with to give protection to a vulnerable group. Of course, evidential problems often exist and it is hard indeed to prove an abuse without witnesses or injuries beyond reasonable doubt. But *the main problem seems to be the unwillingness to punish a man for an abuse if the woman/the girl has taken risks.*

There are measures other than the law itself connected to fighting deficiencies in legal practice. The official crime statistics are of diverging quality and incompatible. There are also inadequacies in investigation and prosecution, leading to high rates of attrition in most countries, especially in member states with high reporting rates. There is a lack of specialization in police, prosecutors and courts, and an absence in most countries of guidelines and protocols for the investigation of sexual crimes. The support of crime victims has improved in most EU countries during the last years, but the access to this support differs greatly, both between countries and within countries. A tendency seems to be that while growing attention is given to partner violence (and also to child sexual abuse), *special provisions for teenagers are lacking*. Another trend is, especially in countries where family violence and sexual victimization more recently have been put on the agenda, that NGOs are expected to have a prominent role in tackling these "relational issues". This "solution" demonstrates that the government in question does not consider legislation and police investigation as the primary tools to cope with the problem of sexual victimization. There is also a continued ambivalence about interfering in private life, stronger in some regions than in others.[43]

EU harmonization can be a way of preventing more teenage sexual abuse. The prime way to make the protection of the vulnerable more uniform seems to be through the Council of Europe and the implementation of the Istanbul Convention. In combination with the Lanzarote Convention (and a discussion about the age of consent), the prospects of a change and a widened protection of the young are positive. But legal reforms and improved legal practices can only be a part of the solution and, no matter how the sex crime legislation is formulated, it can be assumed that the majority of sex crimes will remain unreported. Therefore the law must be seen as one tool amongst many others, among which changing attitudes towards youth sexual aggression and victimization and fighting Rape Myths are of the utmost importance.

REFERENCES

Bauger, N., Bauger, J., Monroe, J. R. & Grey, M. J. (2010). Rape myth acceptance, sexual trauma history and posttraumatic stress disorder. *Journal of Interpersonal Violence, 25,* 2036–2053.

Burt, M. R. & Albin, R. S. (1981). Rape myths, rape definitions, and probability of conviction. *Journal of Applied Social Psychology, 11,* 212–230.

---

[43] Most conclusions about the practice are the same as in the "Feasibility study", p.14–16.

Davies, M., Gilston, J. & Rogers, P. (2012). Examining the relation between male rape myth acceptance, female rape myth acceptance, victim blame, homophobia, gender roles and ambivalent sexism. *Journal of Interpersonal Violence*, *20*, 1–17.

Diesen, C. & Diesen, E . F. (2010). Sex crime legislation – proactive and anti-therapeutic effects. *International Journal of Law and Psychiatry*, *33*, 329–335.

Diesen, C. & Diesen, E . F. (2013). *Övergrepp mot kvinnor och barn – den rättsliga hanteringen*. Stockholm, Sweden: Norstedts Juridik.

DuMont, J., Miller, K. & Myhr, T. (2003). The role of "real rape" and "real victim" stereotypes in the police reporting practices of sexually assaulted women. *Violence Against Women*, *9*, 466–486.

Estrich, S., (1987). *Real rape: How the legal system victimizes women who say no.* Cambridge, Mass: Harvard University Press.

European Women's Lobby (2013). Rape Barometer: Creative Commons 2013.

Fisher, B. S., Daigle, L. E., Cullen, F. T. & Turner, M. G. (2003). Reporting sexual victimization to the police and others: Results from a national-level study of college women. *Criminal Justice and Behaviour*, *30*, 6–38.

Graupner, H. (2002). *Sexual consent; The criminal law in Europe and Overseas.* Keynote lecture at the 7th International Conference of the International Association for Treatment of Sexual Offenders, September 2002.

Grubb, A. & Turner, E. (2012). Attribution of blame in rape cases: A review of the impact of rape myth acceptance, gender role conformity and substance use on victim blaming. *Aggression and Violent Behaviouor*, *17*, 443–452.

Hagemann-White, C., Kelly, L. & Römkens, R. (2010). *Feasibility study to assess the possibilities, opportunities and needs to standardise national legislation on violence against women, violence against children and sexual orientation violence.* Daphne II: Publications of the European Union.

Heath, N. M., Lynch, S. M., Fritch, A. M., McArthur, L. & Smith, S. L. (2011). Silent survivors: Rape myth acceptance in incarcerated women's narratives of disclosure and reporting of rape. *Psychology of Woman Quarterly*, *35*, 596–610.

Kahn, A. S., Jackson, J., Kully, C., Badger, K. & Halvorsen, J. (2003). Calling it rape: Differences in experiences of women who do or do not label their sexual assault as rape. *Pschology of Women Quarterly*, *27*, 233–242.

Kelly, L. (2002). *A research review on the reporting, investigation and prosecution in rape cases.* London: Her Majesty's Crown Prosecution Service Incorporate.

Kelly, L., Lovett, J. & Regan, L. (2005). *A gap or a chasm? Attrition in reported rape cases.* London: Home Office.

Krahé, B. (1988). Victim and observer characteristics as determinants of responsibility attributions to victims of rape. *Journal of Applied Social Psychology*, *18*, 50–58.

Lonsway, K. & Fitzgerald, L. (1994). Rape myths. *Psychology of Woman Quarterly*, *18*, 133–164.

Lonsway, K. & Archambault, J. (2012). The justice gap for sexual assault cases: Future directions for research and reform. *Violence Against Women*, *18*, 145–156.

Lovett, J. & Kelly, L. (2009). *Different systems, similar outcomes? Tracking attrition in reported rape cases across Europe.* London: CWASU, London Metropolitan University.

Nagel, B., Matsuo, H., McIntyre, K. & Morrison, N. (2005). Attitudes toward victims of rape: Effects of gender, race, religion and social class. *Journal of Interpersonal Violence, 20*, 725–737.

Nygard, L-J. (2012). *Lekdommere i strafferetspleien*, (Doctoral diss.). Oslo, Norway: Oslo University.

Priebe, G. (2009). Adolescents' experiences of sexual abuse, (Doctoral diss.), Lund, Sweden: Lund University.

Reece, H. (2013). Rape myths: Is elite opinion right and public opinion wrong? *Oxford Journal of Legal Studies, March 25*, 1–29.

Regan, L. & Kelly, L. (2003). *Rape: Still a forgotten issue*. London: CWASU, London Metropolitan University.

Skinner, T. & Taylor, H. (2009). "Being shut out in the dark": Young survivors' experiences of reporting a sexual offence. *Feminist Criminology, 4*, 130–150.

Spohn, C. & Tellis, K. (2012). The criminal system's response to sexual violence. *Violence Against Women, 18*, 169–192.

Stewart, M. W., Dobbin, S . A. & Gatowski, S. I. (1996). "Real rapes" and "real victims": The shared reliance on common cultural definitions of rape. *Feminst Legal Studies, 4*, 159–177.

Suarez, E. & Gadalla, T. M. (2010). Stop blaming the victim: A meta-analysis on rape myths. *Journal of Interpersonal Violence, 25*, 2010–2035.

Temkin, J. & Krahé, B. (2008). *Sexual assault and the justice gap: A question of attitude*. Oxford, England: Hart Publishing.

Ward, C. A. (1995). *Attitudes toward rape. Feminist and social psychology perspectives*. London: Sage Publications.

WHO. (2013). *Responding to intimate partner violence and sexual violation against women*, WHO Health Report (2013). Geneva.

Wolitzky-Taylor, K. B. Resnick, H. S. McCauley, J. L., Amstadter, A. B., Kilpatrick, D. J. & Ruggiero, K. J. (2011). Is reporting rape on the rise? A comparison of women with reported versus unreported rape experiences in the women's study replication. *Journal of Interpersonal Violence, 26*, 807–832.

In: Crime
Editor: Michael Harry Pearson

ISBN: 978-1-62948-657-4
© 2014 Nova Science Publishers, Inc.

Chapter 6

ANOTHER PUSH FOR RESTORATIVE JUSTICE: POSITIVE PSYCHOLOGY AND OFFENDER REHABILITATION

Theo Gavrielides[1] and Piers Worth**

[1] Founder and Director of Independent Academic Research Studies (IARS),
Co-Director of the Restorative Justice for All (RJ4All) Institute,
Adjunct Professor at the Centre for Restorative Justice of Simon Fraser University
and Visiting Professor at Buckinghamshire New University, Buckinghamshire, UK
[2] Head of Academic Department, Psychology, Faculty of Society and Health,
Buckinghamshire New University, Buckinghamshire, UK

ABSTRACT

Traditionally, criminologists have used psychology to understand and reduce violence by focusing on the negative traits that lead people to crime. This approach is encapsulated in the Risk Need Responsivity (RNR) model of rehabilitation, which is now being challenged at practical, policy, political and financial levels internationally. The Good Lives Model (GLM) was recently developed as an alternative approach focusing on nurturing the offender's personal strengths and goals. This paper takes the next step in deepening the relationship between rehabilitation theory and restorative justice. We use the perspectives and tools of positive psychology and the GLM to provide a fresh critical analysis of restorative practices, which have recently received much attention by policy makers and politicians. What can restorative justice learn from positive psychology? Is there anything to be gained from this relationship for rehabilitation theories? How can the victim and the community be brought into the rehabilitation debate?

Keywords: restorative justice, positive psychology, risk-need-responsivity (RNR), Good Lives Model (GLM), offender rehabilitation

---

* Email: T.Gavrielides@iars.org.uk | Website: www.iars.org.uk and www.rj4all.info | @TGavrielides
* Email: piers.Worth@bucks.ac.uk

1. PROBLEM STATEMENT

In an increasingly specialist age where expertise is valued and innovation is questioned, it is rare to see a lawyer collaborating with a psychologist to mutually influence each other's work. This paper encapsulates our attempt to bring a fresh perspective to the re-born social justice movement of restorative justice by combining our disciplines and minds. We feel that offender rehabilitation could benefit from a more integrative approach to desistance, while the barriers of restorative justice could be pushed further by stop downplaying rehabilitation theory.

Offender rehabilitation has traditionally focused on all that is wrong with the offender (psychologically, socially, biologically etc.) by trying to minimise risk through treatment programmes (Bonta and Andrews, 2007). This is also called the Risk Need Responsivity (RNR) model of rehabilitation (Andrews and Bonta, 1994; 2008). Its focus is on reducing and managing risk as well as on studying the process of relapse. Pathology-focused research and intervention have consequently been developed as tools for RNR based approaches to rehabilitation. Despite of being criticised by clinicians and researchers, RNR is generally accepted as the benchmark against which rehabilitation programmes should be measured and tested (Mapham and Hefferon, 2012).

As a result, policies, laws and practices have focused on setting up and managing a criminal justice system that aims to deal with offenders' negative traits. Desistance is seen as a result of being 'tough on crime' and criminals (Gavrielides, 2012a). According to Andrews and Bonta (1998), Hollin (1999), McGuire, 2002) and others, RNR has resulted in effective therapy for many offenders and has led to lowered recidivism rates. The fact that the model emphasises empirically supported therapies makes its scientific approach appealing.

However, Ellerby et al (2000), Maruna (2006), Ward and Steward (2003), Gavrielides (2012b; 2012c) and others have argued that concentrating on criminogenic needs to reduce risk factors may be necessary, but not a sufficient condition for effective correctional intervention. Furthermore, McAdams (1994; 2006) argues that integration and relatedness are crucial in encouraging desistance. His research suggests that self-narratives and the recognition of offenders' personal strivings have the most potential for change over the course of a life. Ward and Langlands (2009), Laws and Ward (2011), Ward and Maruna (2007) all agree with this conclusion. The expanded RNR model by Andrews, Bonta and Wormith (2011) tried to address some of this criticism, but the truth of the matter is that it continues to underplay the contextual nature of human behaviour. Maruna's (2006) Liverpool Desistance Study is revealing. His qualitative investigation (1996-1998) of desistance that involved long-term field observations and numerous in-depth interviews with British ex-convicts concludes that to desist from crime, ex-offenders irrespective of age "need to develop a coherent, pro-social identity for themselves" (2006: 7).

Politicians and the public now seem to agree with the extant literature that our RNR-based criminal justice system is failing. For instance, in June 2010, the UK Justice Secretary said that prison often turns out to be "a costly and ineffectual approach that fails to turn criminals into law-abiding citizens" (Travis 2010: 1). We also know that the reoffending rate post-custody is high compared with other disposals. While the overall reoffending rate across all disposals is 40%, the reoffending rate post-custody is almost 50%, meaning that approximately half of all offenders sentenced to prison will go on to commit a further offence

(Ministry of Justice, 2010). "Banging up more and more people for longer is actually making some criminals worse without protecting the public" the justice secretary said in his speech at the Centre for Crime and Justice Studies in June 2010.

This disappointment is also reflected in the spiralling incarceration rates. For example, in October 2010, in England and Wales, the prison population stood at 85,494. This accounted for 2,150 places above the usable operational capacity of the prison estate, and it is forecast to rise to 94,000 before the next general election (Berman, 2010: 1). There are now 139 prisons including high security prisons, local prisons, closed and open training prisons, young offender institutions and remand centres. The statistics on young prisoners are not encouraging either. In September 2010, there were 1,637 young people (15-17 years) in prison, 273 children (12-15) in privately run secure training centres (STCs) and 160 in local authority secure children homes (SCHs). In addition, there were 10,114 young adults (18-21) in prison (Berman 2010: 7). Compared to the rest of the world, England and Wales comes 10th with the US at the top.

Financially, the RNR has not proved viable either. Again, looking at the UK as an example, keeping each prisoner costs £41,000 annually (or £112.32 a day). This means that if there are 85,076 prisoners at the moment, prisons cost as much as £3.49bn annually. If we add the cost of courts then according to Home Office statistics, this goes up to £146,000 annually (quote in Prison Reform Trust, 2010). Putting one young offender in prison costs as much as £140,000 per year (£100,000 in direct costs and £40,000 in indirect costs once they are released) (Knuutila, 2010). Two thirds of the Youth Justice Board budget, or about £300 million a year, is spent on prisons, while the money it uses for prevention is roughly one-tenth (Youth Justice Board, 2009). More worryingly, as a result of inflation and the rising costs of utilities and food, the costs of custody will keep rising even if prisoners' numbers stay the same.

According to a 2010 report by the New Economics Foundation, "a person that is offending at 17 after being released from prison will commit on average about 145 crimes (Knuutila, 2010). Out of these crimes about 1.7 are serious crimes (homicides, sexual crimes or serious violent offences). Given that a prison sentence is estimated to increase the likelihood of continuing to offend by 3.9 per cent, this translates into an average of about 5.5 crimes caused, out of which about 0.06 are serious" (Knuutila, 2010: 40).

This disappointment provided an opportunity for restorative justice, which is based on the foundation of promoting human goods in the pursuit of restoration of harm and the correction of deviant behaviour (i.e. approach goals as well as avoidance goals). Restorative justice practices, such as mediation, circles and conferencing bring to the fore states of affairs, activities and experiences that are strongly associated with well-being and higher level of personal satisfaction and social functioning. They aim to create empathy and remorse and through constructive and honest dialogue create sense of responsibility in the offender and a feeling of empowerment and justice in the victim. Restorative justice is also a community born and community led ethos (Gavrielides, 2012a) and as such its practices are informed or led by or found within a community context. They might also involve the community directly by allowing community representatives to be part of the dialogue and the restorative process.

In the UK, EU and internationally, restorative justice is receiving increasing attention. For example, in December 2010, the UK coalition government published the Green Paper "Breaking the Cycle", announcing its intentions for key reforms to the adult and youth justice sentencing philosophy and practice. This consultation set out the resulting proposals, which aim to break the destructive cycle of crime and protect the public, through more effective methods of punishing and rehabilitating offenders and by reforming the sentencing framework. In October 2012, the government published a national restorative justice strategy (Gavrielides, 2013a), while legislation has been passed to provide restorative justice to all offenders independently of the crime they committed and their age. Training is being rolled out in all prisons in England and Wales while the Ministry of Justice is introducing restorative justice targets in all their contracts with probation trusts and prisons.

In the eyes of a criminologist, or indeed any thinking citizen, the growing interest of governments in restorative justice should come as no surprise. In a financial climate where public services are being reduced, legislative reforms are expected. The truth is that independently of the motives behind the review of our sentencing philosophy and practice, it provides a unique opportunity for also renewing our social contract for law and order in modern society.

Restorative justice has received much evaluation and scrutiny in a number of areas. However, certain aspects of its practice remain uncovered and untested particularly some of the psychological implications involved (Gavrielides 2007: Sherman and Strang 2007; Gavrielides and Artinopoulou, 2013). The relationship between restorative justice and positive psychology is yet to be examined in detail (Ward and Langlands, 2009; Tweed et al, 2011; Mapham and Hefferon, 2012), while there is still confusion about the contribution that restorative practices can make to rehabilitation theories (Zernova, 2009).

This paper will use the perspectives and tools of positive psychology to deepen the relationship between restorative justice and rehabilitation theory. It will also explore the role of victims and offenders in the normative and practical development of rehabilitation theories and practices. The paper is developed as part of a larger project supported by Buckinghamshire New University aiming to test the contribution of positive psychology for the theoretical development of restorative justice as well as the design, evaluation and delivery of its practices. By bringing positive psychology into the restorative justice debate, the larger project may be able to generate a much needed normative and practical direction for improved implementation of restorative justice including minimising the risks associated with its delivery as well as increasing the positive effects that we now know it can have on victims, offenders and the community.

The paper is divided into three sections. The first will aim to establish a common point of understanding for some key concepts such as restorative justice, positive psychology, rehabilitation and desistance. It will also provide a descriptive account of the RNR and GLM models of offender rehabilitation. We are aware of the tensions between the two models and the developing literature supporting both sides of the argument. This debate is beyond the scope of our paper.

The second section will focus on the relationship between restorative justice and offender rehabilitation theory. The literature on the potential of this relationship is thin and this paper will start from Gavrielides' 2007 definition of restorative justice, which accepts "certain rehabilitative goals" (p. 139). To this end, the GLM and positive psychology will be used. Does positive psychology helps us understand better the techniques, strength-based approach and ethos of restorative justice? Is there anything to be gained from positive psychology for restorative justice?

The third section will move beyond rehabilitation theory to understand how restorative justice engages the victim and the community in the pursuit of its goals, and whether these are supportive of desistance. Is justice within the community and victim empowerment and restoration possible alongside offender rehabilitation? Furthermore, what is the role of forgiveness and how can the victim and the community be engaged in offender rehabilitation; how relevant is forgiveness to restorative justice outcomes and offender rehabilitation?

It should not be expected that this think piece will provide 'handbook solutions'. Here, we only aim to lay the conceptual framework within which positive psychology can strengthen its contribution to restorative justice both normatively and empirically. Following this paper, pilots and fieldwork with qualitative methodologies will be carried out.

We also acknowledge three key limitations. First, the paper develops some critical thinking using secondary analysis of data. Up to date there hasn't been a research project with an exclusive focus the collection of primary data on positive psychology and restorative justice. The arguments and issues raised here are triangulated through relevant studies that looked at specific issues where positive psychology was touched upon as a side matter in the investigation of restorative justice.

Second, the extant studies that were used to provide a check for our arguments are scarce. Third, it must be acknowledged that psychology can only provide a certain, limited perspective, which must be combined with the social, economic, cultural, political and policy environments of its time. As Maruna points out, the narratives that are generated through offenders' self-reporting although psychologically analysed cannot be understood "outside of their social, historical and structural context. Self-narratives are developed through social interaction (2006: 8). Foucault (1988) reminds us that our stories, as offenders, victims or community members are "proposed, suggested and imposed on [us] by [our] culture, [our] society and social group" (p. 11).

2. SOME DEFINITIONAL AGREEMENTS

Restorative Justice

The definition of 'restorative justice' has occupied the attention of the bulk of the restorative justice literature and hence we do not intend here to add to this traffic. Here, we only attempt to lay some basic foundations that will allow us a shared understanding to pursue our paper's objectives.

A number of international and national documents attempted to identify the key principles underlying the restorative practice. Some examples include the UN Basic Principles on the use of Restorative Justice Programmes in criminal Matters 2002, the Canadian Department of Justice Restorative Justice Values 2010 and the New Zealand Principles and Values for Restorative Justice 2004. Gavrielides concluded in his 2007 fieldwork:

> "Restorative justice is an ethos with practical goals, among which is to restore harm by including affected parties in a (direct or indirect) encounter and a process of understanding through voluntary and honest dialogue" (p. 139).

For Braithwaite (2002) and McCold (2000), the principles underlying the restorative justice 'ethos' are: victim reparation, offender responsibility and communities of care.

McCold argues that if attention is not paid to all these three concerns, then the result will only be partially restorative. Gavrielides understands this ethos in a broad way: "Restorative justice, in nature, is not just a practice or just a theory. It is both (Gavrielides, 2007). It is an ethos; it is a way of living. It is a new approach to life, interpersonal relationships and a way of prioritising what is important in the process of learning how to coexist" (2007: 139). In a similar vein, Daly (2000) said that restorative justice places "...an emphasis on the role and experience of victims in the criminal process" (p.7), and that it involves all relevant parties in a discussion about the offence, its impact and what should be done to repair it. The decision making, Daly said, has to be carried out by both lay and legal actors (see also Zehr 1990).

Similarly, in *Fundamental Concepts of Restorative Justice*, Zehr and Mika provided a list of principles to clarify what constitutes restorative justice (1998). Their list was composed of three major headings: (a) Crime is fundamentally a violation of people and interpersonal relationships. (b) Violations create obligations and liabilities. (c) Restorative justice seeks to heal and put right the wrongs. Under each of these headings, a number of secondary and tertiary points specified and elaborated on the general themes providing elements, which, according to their opinion, can address the critical components of one vision of restorative justice practice. In *Restorative Justice: Variation on a theme*, McCold recorded four principles, which he attempted to put to test. He said restorative justice is:

a) moralizing
b) healing
c) empowering
d) transforming.

According to Gavrielides (139), "Restorative justice adopts a fresh approach to conflicts and their control, retaining at the same time certain rehabilitative goals".

Rehabilitation

The literature on rehabilitation theories is rich and is often combined with theories of punishment, penology and criminal law. According to Gavrielides (2005; 2013b) there are four main arguments for explaining punishment in modern society:

- **Deterrence:** Either specific for the given offender or 'general' for the society that watches the offender being punished.
- **Incapacitation:** Removing the offender from society making it physically impossible to harm others, even for a certain period of time.
- **Retribution or 'just deserts':** encapsulating the Old Testament saying "an eye for an eye".
- **Rehabilitation:** "Rehabilitation is the idea of curing an offender of his or her criminal tendencies. It consists, more precisely, of changing an offender's personality, outlook, habits, or opportunities so as to make him or her less inclined to commit crimes" (Von Hirsch, 1998: 1). Von Hirsch continues: "Often, rehabilitation is said to involve helping the offender, but a benefit to the offender is not necessarily

presupposed: those who benefit are other persons, ourselves, who become less likely to be victimised by the offender (1998: 1).

If we shift our focus from criminal law to psychology, the definitions for rehabilitation change. For instance, according to Ward and Mann rehabilitation "refers to the overall aims, values, principles, and etiological assumptions that should be used to guide the treatment of offenders, and translates how these principles should be to guide therapy" (2007: 89). They see rehabilitation theory as the broader framework within which therapy and treatment should be placed. The latter two terms, they argue, are narrower in scope and refer to the process of applying psychological principles and strategies to change the behaviour of offenders in a clinical setting.

Positive Psychology

The origins of positive psychology exist in the work of psychologists such as Abraham Maslow (e.g. 1970) and Carl Rogers (e.g. 2004). The proposal and development of positive psychology as a focused discipline came through the Presidential address of Professor Martin Seligman to the American Psychological Association in 1998. Seligman and Csikszentmihalyi (2000: 5) suggest:

> "...positive psychology at the subjective level is about valued subjective experiences: well-being, contentment, and satisfaction (in the past); hope and optimism (for the future); and flow and happiness (in the present). At the individual level, positive psychology is about positive individual traits: the capacity for love and vocation, courage, interpersonal skill, aesthetic sensibility, perseverance, forgiveness, originality, future mindedness, spirituality, high talent and wisdom. At the group level, it is about civic virtues and the institutions that move individuals toward better citizenship: responsibility, nurturance, altruism, civility, moderation, tolerance and work ethic."

Writing deliberately at the turn of the millennium these visionaries used defining words that also link positive psychology to the questions and challenges of restorative justice, desistance and rehabilitation being explored here. The important practical question is 'how'.

Positive psychology has over a decade of progress in theorising and research in such areas as psychological well-being (Ryff and Singer, 1998), the development of human strengths (Peterson and Seligman, 2004), the nature and contribution of positive emotions (Fredrickson, 1998; 2001), hope (Snyder, 2002) and forgiveness (Enright and Fitzgibbons, 2000). How some of these ideas have been brought together in the GLM will be summarised below. Yet, drawing on the definition above, it also leaves us with the possibility and question of how experiences such as 'hope', 'love', 'vocation', 'courage', 'interpersonal skill', 'perseverance', 'future-mindedness' and more may be found in or brought to restorative justice, rehabilitation and desistance through positive psychology research and method. The need to do so is highlighted when one considers the psychological focus of RNR.

The Risk Need Responsivity (RNR) Model of Rehabilitation

Developed in the 1980s and first formalized in 1990 by Andrews, Bonta and Hope (1990), RNR uses three basic principles to guide the assessment and treatment of offenders with the purpose of advancing rehabilitative goals such as recidivism. These are:

- **Risk** i.e. matching the level of risk to be caused by the offender and the amount of treatment that they are to receive
- **Need** i.e. targeting treatment with offending and criminogenic needs that can be altered
- **Responsivity** i.e. the treatment programme must be able to reach and indeed make sense to those for which it was designed (Andrews and Bonta, 1994)

It is generally accepted that RNR is the dominant model of offender rehabilitation at least in the Western world. Its pursuit of psychometrically sound assessments for effective prevention and treatment resonates with the evidence based policies of many governments. Even Ward and Maruna (2007) who are considered to be adversaries of RNR have commented that RNR has "an impressive research record to back up its claims (p. 74).

In 2008, Andrews expanded RNR to include a total of 18 principles. These are grouped into overarching principles (respect of the person, theory, human service and crime prevention), RNR principles (risk, need, responsivity: general and specific), structured assessment principles (assess RNR, strengths, breath, professional discretion), programme delivery principles (dosage), staff practices principles (relationship skills, structuring skills) and organisational principles (community-based, continuity of service, agency management and community linkages).

According to Andrews, Bonta and Wormith (2011), "RNR-based prevention can be promoted as an honourable, positive, strength-based, and legitimate objective of human service" (p. 751). However, does RNR still overlook some key aspects of the path to rehabilitation, recovery and desistance? Psychology faced comparable questioning in the need for and development of 'positive psychology'. Mainstream psychology grew out of the need to solve problems, and remove or cure 'illness'. Professional training and the focus of activity were based largely on attention to the negative. As our attention narrows to focus on the 'deficient', abnormal and unhealthy, we run the risk that we will overlook and misunderstand the nature of health and positive adjustment (Joseph and Linley, 2008: 5). Further, this focus emphasises the role of the individual perhaps at the expense of understanding the interactions with or contribution of the social context.

Whether it is 'illness' in psychology, or 'wrong-doing' in the discipline of criminology, the 'problem' (such as wrong-doing) becomes a distinct entity from this perspective and the scope to understand systemic influences, particularly the opportunities for growth and change, reduces or is blocked (Ibid: 6). The GLM offers an illustration of how the two perspectives may be linked and developed.

The Good Lives Models (GLM)

The contrast in names is stark between RNR and GLM in considering the rehabilitation of offenders. This difference in emphasis is explored and articulated in academic literature, e.g. Andrews, Bonta and Wormith (2011) and Ward, Yates and Willis (2012).

The Good Lives Model (GLM), (now referred to as Good Lives – Comprehensive) assumes that we are goal-influenced and all seek certain 'goods' in our lives, not 'material', but qualitative, all likely to increase or improve our psychological well-being. The model sees us as driven in search of at least ten primary human goods: healthy living and functioning, the experience of mastery, autonomy and self-directedness, freedom from emotional turmoil and stress, friendship, happiness and creativity (Ward, Mann and Gannon 2007: 90). The majority of these areas have a base of research within the discipline of positive psychology.

Offending behaviour is seen as an inappropriate or unskilled means of achieving primary 'human goods', particularly where it lacks internal or external conditions to work towards a positive or good life plan (Scottish Prison Service 2011: 37). The GLM operates in both a holistic and constructive manner in considering how offenders might identify and work towards a way of living that is likely to involve the goods we seek in life, as well as a positive way of living that does not involve or need crime (ibid: 36). In this process the argument is that the model works towards a positive, growth-oriented change in life where an offender works on the development of the values, skills and resources towards life based on human goods that is a necessary counter-balance of managing risk alone (Ward, Mann and Gannon 2007: 92), i.e. risk is managed as well as seeking to develop positive life alternatives. To illustrate the importance of this balance, Emmons (1999 and 2003) has made an articulate and moving case for why positive personal goals and the skill to attain them are central to psychological well-being and conversely how avoidance-based extrinsic goals may lead to lower levels of functioning.

While Ward and colleagues describe this positive psychology model as 'strengths-based' we believe this is an understatement of evaluation because its component parts go beyond strengths to a more comprehensive and profound attempt to influence well-being and positive development over time.

Desistance

When attempting to define notions such as restorative justice and desistance, we must be careful not to assert that they can ever fully capture the normative and practical elements of their lived manifestations. Gavrielides has argued that definitions for restorative justice are temporary constructs that very quickly become out of date and in some cases misleading and counterproductive (Gavrielides, 2008).

This is also true for desistance, which has traditionally being associated with a 'termination event'. Maruna argues, "The criminal career literature traditionally imagines desistance as an event – an abrupt cessation of criminal behaviour" (2006: 22). The field of criminology has come a long way from trying to understand deviant behaviour as a single dimensional phenomenon, whether this is due to biological, psychological, social, financial or other factors. However, we agree with Maruna that despite progress and an acceptance that a multi-disciplinary approach must be adopted in understanding deviance "the notion of intractable criminality is still very much alive in criminology and popular thought" (2006: 19). In other words, although common logic tells us that people are not born criminals, subconsciously and through our overt bias for those who deviate we may believe that there was something inevitable. Characteristically, Glaser said "Despite this shift from hereditary to environmental interpretations of crime, there is still a tendency to think of the person who experiences make him [or her] criminal as distinctly different fro the non-criminal" (1964: 466). Shover for instance, defined desistance as "the voluntary termination of serious criminal participation (1996: 121). Farrall and Bowling (1999) defined it as the "moment that a criminal career ends" suggesting that one quits crime in much the same way as one resigns from a legitimate occupation.

Indeed, there is a plethora of theories and definitions on desistance. Social bond theory, labelling theory, ontogenic and sociogenic paradigms are some of the approaches that have been adopted over the years. We do not wish to engage with this dialogue. What is important to note here is that if we are to engage with the arguments of this paper we must acknowledge a much broader understanding of desistance that focuses not on that 'moment of clarity' that takes people away from being deviant, but on their journey to change. Maruna argues that desistance "might more productively be defined as the log-term abstinence from crime among individuals who had previously engaged in persistent patterns of criminal offending" (1996: 26). Here we look at the factors that trigger and then maintain a crime-free behaviour in the face of life's obstacles. Looking at Foote and Frank's definition of 'resistance', then desistance is "no end state where one can be; rather than it is a perpetual process of arrival" (1999: 179).

3. REHABILITATION THEORY AND RESTORATIVE JUSTICE: FRIENDS OR FOES?

Paradoxically, the literature on the relationship between restorative justice and rehabilitation theory is rather thin. Ward and Langlands argue that the "comparative neglect of offender rehabilitation theory and principles within the restorative justice literature is problematic because evidence-based rehabilitation programmes have been shown to be effective in reducing recidivism" (2009: 206). We argue that restorative justice and rehabilitation theory are not foes as we accept that "restorative justice adopts a fresh approach to conflicts and their control, retaining at the same time certain rehabilitative goals" (Gavrielides, 2007: 139). Our aim here is to advance the restorative justice field, its tools, practices and evaluation techniques by bringing rehabilitation theory into its current debate and vice versa. Rehabilitation has also much to gain from a needs-based approach to antisocial behaviour such as restorative justice, and positive psychology can show us the way in how to achieve this.

We agree with Ward and Langlands that "by failing to adequately address offender rehabilitation, restorative justice does not live up to its promise as a needs-based justice system" (2009: 206). We also agree that the restorative justice movement has downplayed the value of rehabilitation for far too long in its attempt to highlight the role of victims and communities. We disagree with Zernova (2009) that rehabilitation approaches and restorative justice practices cannot co-exist. It is in fact because we believe that the two are complimentary and necessary for achieving better results through a needs-based, positive approach to anti-social behaviour. The restorative justice concept is now well supported by theory and philosophy (Braithwaite and Strang, 2001; Gavrielides and Artinopoulou, 2013) for its proponents to fear a compromise of its conceptual integrity.

We believe that this reluctance reaches deep into the very foundations and history of restorative justice. When its notion was first coined in the 1970s, its early advocates such as Cantor (1976), Christie (1978), Barnet (1977) and Zehr (1990) portrayed the relationship between the then emerging restorative justice and the existing criminal justice system as being 'polar opposites' in almost every aspect. Cantor (1976) for instance, argued in favour of a total substitution of civil law for criminal law processes with a view to 'civilising' the treatment of offenders.

Barnett (1977) spoke of a "paradigm shift", defining 'paradigm' as "an achievement in a particular discipline which defines the legitimate problems and methods of research within that discipline" (1977: 280). Barnet (ibid: 280) claimed that we are living a "crisis of an old paradigm" and that "this crisis can be restored by the adoption of a new paradigm of criminal justice-restitution". Christie (1978: 5) claimed that the details of what society does or does not permit are often difficult to decode, and that "the degree of blameworthiness is often not expressed in the law at all". Christie (ibid: 5) argued that the state has 'stolen the conflict' between citizens, and that this has deprived society of the "opportunities for norm-classification".

By introducing restorative justice as a radical concept, its proponents were hoping to make the then new concept of restorative justice appealing and interesting enough for writers and politicians who knew nothing about it. However, once the excitement was over, and while restorative justice was leaving the phase of 'innovation' to enter the one of 'implementation', its advocates (e.g. Braithwaite, 1999) started to talk about the need to combine its values and practices with existing traditions of criminal practice and philosophy including rehabilitation.

However, restorative justice purists continue to believe that restorative justice should sit outside the current criminal justice system. Some hold the view that if integrated into current traditions of punitive philosophy, some restorative practices will be co-opted, while others will be marginalised and gradually withdrawn. For example, Zernova believes that " Merging the two models may serve to individualise problems with social-structural roots and disable search for ethical responses which are not centred on values of healing crime's harm and offender rehabilitation" (2009: 73). Zernova is not alone in this as her view is shared by Walgrave (1995), Bazemore (1996) and McCold (2000).

Undoubtedly, there is still strong debate both inside and outside the restorative justice movement about the compatibility of restorative justice and punishment theories and practices including those of rehabilitation. For the sake of brevity, I will attempt to divide the many views from the extant literature into two broad categories. The first denies that restorative justice measures can, in any way, be punitive (e.g. see Wright 1996). The second argues that restorative justice is not "alternative to punishment," but "alternative punishment" (Duff, 1992) yet in the act of being so involves what we conceive of as links or 'doorways' to the possibility of desistance and its development. The argument of the first group is that restorative measures' primary purpose is to be constructive. Therefore, they are not inflicted "for their own sake" rather than for a higher purpose. The second group, however, has argued, "this purported distinction is misleading because it relies for its effect on the confusion of two distinct elements in the concept of intention. One element relates to the motives for doing something; the other refers to the fact that the act in question is being performed deliberately or wilfully" (Dignan, 2003: 179).

We argue that this approach has led to division that is not constructive while it serves very little the field of implementation. We also argue to gain all society seeks from restorative justice, we have to conceive of the two as linked. If we take a step back we realise that this division is merely a construct of historical events and the current political priorities and populist agenda. For example, Gavrielides (2011) argues that today's dominant understanding of punishment as retribution and rehabilitation is the outcome of historical events and the demands of modern society. In Europe, what is really believed to have caused this change was the increasing power of kingships as trans-local and trans-tribal institutions. This is mainly because they united the tribes and large areas, changing in this way the structure of societies from communitarian/tribal to hierarchical/feudal. Sharpe (1980) and Rossner (1989) explain that in Europe contemporary punishment was constructed after the Norman Conquest when crime was seen as a violation of the law of the King. The understanding of what is crime and harm was key in defining society's response.

In the pursuit of increasing the success of the criminal justice system as constructed within the aforementioned understanding, crime control was formalised in communities. Cohen (1985) describes how justice and social control were reconstructed from being informal local and regional control systems to becoming a centralised machinery of processing justice. The formalisation and professionalization process of the criminal justice system was also a key consequence of trade development and economics (Marx, 1954). Barnett (1977) also reminds us the role of religious institutions and the significance of the ecclesiastic law of that time. This claim is also supported by Tallack (1900) who noted that the greedy ecclesiastical powers of the time aimed to exact a double vengeance upon the offenders by taking their property and by applying corporal punishment or imprisonment.

In consequence, as the rights of the state gradually overshadowed those of the victim, the concept of punishment took a more punitive meaning. What also emerged from this development was the division of law between public and private. Crime was mostly dealt with as an act against the state and the public interest, while offences against individuals' rights were pursued separately as torts. The terms offender and victim started to be used.

In 2005, Gavrielides introduced a different type of punishment. He argued that in practice there are only two kinds of ποινή (poene/ punishment/ pain); "The first is what we *experience today*, as the outcome of a criminal process, and is based on the understanding of the punitive paradigm. The second is what we *normatively experience* in a restorative process, and has little to do with what retribution and other punishment theories deal with" (Gavrielides 2005: 91). Gavrielides names this type "Restorative Punishment" (ibid: 91). He argues that irrespective of whether we decide to go with the first group of critics who deny that restorative measures are punitive, or with the second who claim that they are alternative punishments, we still have to accept that RJ is surely neither punishment nor is it interested in it, at least in the form that it has taken under the punitive paradigm of our criminal justice systems. Gavrielides (ibid: 93) moves on to conclude that Restorative Punishment aims to restore the harm done. Deterrence (general or specific), just deserts and rehabilitation are all welcomed side effects of restorative justice. However, it must be pointed out that they are not among the primary goals of restorative measures.

In his follow up 2013 work, Gavrielides further developed the notion of Restorative Punishment. He explains that "restorative justice does entail pain, but of a different kind; Not pain that is triggered by state and top- down punishment, as we understand it through the current paradigm. Restorative justice triggers pain that is personal and specific to each participant and is the consequence of his or her own actions, behaviour, self-observation and self-reflection. This pain is a gift and is not always present. It cannot be imposed but it can be nurtured" (Gavrielides, 2013: 321).

This is where the tools of positive psychology and the GLM can assist us in further developing the undervalued relationship between restorative justice and rehabilitation theory. If we explore Maruna's (2001) milestone work on desistance as an illustration it suggests to us that certain experiences will be found in desisting ex-offenders. The individual will gain a sense of a 'true self' that may have existed pre-offending and contrasts with that of being a criminal and offender (ibid: 88 and 95). The catalyst for change will commonly come from outside events initially, which in turn can create the insight into the damage done by their offending, and the wish and the actuality of 'giving something back' in order to seek change and redemption (ibid: 96/7). Gaining a deeper understanding of the story of their actions and bad events may prompt shifts in self-perception that in turn creates the possibility of a new personal 'narrative' (ibid: 98, 102 and 105). The ability and the opportunity to give something back to another person becomes a form of influence and self-efficacy. The act of 'giving back' also becomes a form of restitution, a paying of a debt, and a means of coming to terms with shame, guilt and past mistakes (ibid: 118 – 121).

While this is a simple summary of some longer term and complex experiences involved in desistance, it is intended to illustrate that aspects of these will also be seen in short-term restorative justice encounters and longer-term wider restorative practices. Gavrielides' 'restorative pain' (2005; 2013) and Braithwaite's 'reintegrative shaming' (1989) are two theoretical models that may explain the connection. Here, we suggest that restorative justice is a natural doorway into longer term desistance and that facilitators should be alert to behaviours that indicate further change may follow. Maruna (2001: 114) observed that as a desisting ex-offender started to change they might find social support absent. Where the possibility of longer-term change is apparent, this should be further built-upon by separate support within the social context.

4. BEYOND REHABILITATION

We will now turn our attention away from offenders alone. Although they constitute important players in the pursuit of justice, restorative justice reminds us that there are two other critical parties that must also be considered. These are the victim and the community. Bearing in mind that even the victims' movement (particularly those relating to violence against women) have traditionally being sceptical about the role that restorative justice gives to victims (Gavrielides and Artinopoulou, 2012), we will ask how they can be brought into the rehabilitation-restorative justice debate through the use of positive psychology. A possible reason why RNR-based interventions have only a 17%-35% desistance rate (Bonta and Andrews, 2007) maybe because programmes that focus on offender risk management in effect bar themselves from incorporating the victim and the community in the intervention. It is therefore important, when looking at the GLM through the eyes of restorative justice to expand it beyond the field of offender rehabilitation.

Van Ness and Strong argued that reintegration must be seen as "re-entry into community life as whole, contributing productive persons" (1997: 103). If we start from this premise, then it is not difficult to see how the inclusive and strength based approach of restorative justice can contribute to rehabilitation theory through the involvement of the victim and the parties' communities. We have accepted that desistance is a journey to transformation and that rehabilitation is about making that journey worthwhile. The more specific and communicative the intervention, the more success it will have to produce a life story of change. We have also accepted that restorative justice is not punishment as this is understood by the criminal justice system. It is a form of constructive pain that can lead to catharsis. As in any Greek tragedy, before catharsis is achieved the key players must be identified and watched as they generate a series of emotions and pain (Gavrielides, 2013b). Victims and communities are as important as offenders in this play. Because without them there is no dialogue, no pain and no catharsis. And they engage in this dialogue not by patronising the offender or by being afraid of his [or her] criminogenic needs. They enter the dialogue because they aim for that constructive pain that will lead to catharsis. They are not afraid of it; they welcome it; they seek it. And once the dialogue has taken place and an agreement must be reached, the follow up actions tab into the strengths of the person that needs to restore and heal. They are not meant to control their passions, desires and habits but to encourage their strengths and nurture them by using them as tools for the much sought healing that needs to take place for all involved.

Achilles has argued that rehabilitation facilitates restoration as evidence has shown that a large number of victims who participate in restorative justice do so in order to help prevent future offending (2004). The best way for offenders to repair the harm caused by crime may be to become a "productive citizen" (Achilles, 2004: 70). The involvement of the victim and the community in the restoration of harm gives offenders "new optimism and relief of being reconnected with their communities (Mapham, A. and Hefferon, 2012: 402). Schoeman brings this back to the African concept of Ubuntu. She explains, "The African ethic and humanistic philosophy of Ubuntu encompasses issues of human dignity and respect within the understanding that an individual's humanity is interconnected with the dignity and humanity of others" (Schoeman, 2013: 292). In other words, it is not possible to better oneself without the inclusion of the other.

Furthermore, by paying attention to offenders' experiences of victimisation or needs, the community may be better mobilised to support them in their reintegration and desistance from crime (see Towes and Katounas 2004). Robinson and Shapland's advise that "Instead of thinking about restorative justice as a new-style intervention – something that is done to offenders – we might better advised to re-reframe it as an opportunity to facilitate a desire, or consolidate a decision to desist" (2008: 352). Indeed, restorative encounters should be seen as stepping-stones in the provision of the necessary scaffolding for offenders.

Bazemore and O'Brien spoke of a model of 'relational rehabilitation' grounded in restorative principles of informal social support and control, inclusiveness, the repair or relationships and the development of community (2002). Up to date this is the only theoretical attempt to reconcile rehabilitation theory with restorative justice. Bazemore and O'Brien believe that repairing and restoring relationships is the first step towards building the skills and social capital that is necessary to desist from crime. Therefore, offender rehabilitation is conceptualised as a cyclical process with restorative justice its starting point. Gavrielides' (2007) fieldwork with a representative sample of restorative practitioners from around the world agrees with Bazemore and O'Brien only it points out that the goal of restorative justice is to repair broken relationships not offenders. The latter is a bi-product of the restorative justice approach.

Positive psychology helps us understand the triggers that restorative justice engages to achieve this objective, and the GLM is a good illustration of how this takes place. Mapham and Hefferon's evaluation of the Khulisa restorative justice project reminds us of Gavrielides' understanding of restorative punishment as being contingent of an painful interplay of emotions triggered through interactions with offenders, victims and their communities. They note"

> "Participants were seen to develop emotional intelligence as they became sensitive to the experiencing, feelings, thoughts and attitudes of others. They felt the pain of the others in the group when they listened to their secrets and when they heard the stories that lay behind the masks that their fellow group members had created" (2012: 402).

Positive psychology suggests that strengths and virtues such as empathy, forgiveness, humility, sense of meaning and civic values "may be incompatible with violence or at least produce behaviour that can displace violent behaviour" (Tweed et al, 2011: 8). Focusing on youth violence, they claim "Population interventions that create even small increases in relevant character strengths could potentially reduce incidences of violence" (ibid, 8). This is not possible to achieve without involving the victim. For example, in relation to empathy, Mapham and Hefferon note that their "participants recounted developing compassion for their victims and for their family's pain by their criminal activity" (2012: 402).

Turning our focus on forgiveness, despite of attracting the literature's attention only recently, the narrative around its advantages as well as the psychological stages that must be undertaken is rich (e.g. see Peterson and Seligman, 2004). Here we do not wish to engage with the wider debate on forgiveness but to provide a focused analysis of its mechanisms in engaging the victim and the community in the transformation of the offender. To this end, we must look at the communicative requirement of forgiveness and not so much on its impact on the forgiver. Much has been said about the healing benefits of those who forgive, in this case the victim and the community. Not so much has been said, however, about the significance of the process of forgiving for the offender. We contest that if theory, research and practice are further developed in this area, the "addition of forgiveness into the legal process might change how we think about and serve justice. Perhaps forgiveness may be one avenue of humanising the quest for justice"(Enright and Kittle, 1999: 1631).

Depending on whether we are viewing forgiveness from a certain spiritual, philosophical, psychological or other scientific perspective, its definition and priorities may change. One understanding that may encapsulate most of spiritual and philosophical writings is that developed by North:

> People, upon rationally determining that they have been unfairly treated, forgive when they wilfully abandon resentment and related responses, and endeavour to respond to the wrongdoer based on the moral principle of beneficence, which may include compassion, unconditional worth, generosity, and moral love (to which the wrongdoer, by nature of the hurtful act has not right)" (1987: 499).

The latest scientific research on forgiveness suggests that those who receive it are encouraged to enter into a path of transformation. Enright and Kittle's research into forgiveness and deviance identifies four stages in the forgiving process. Although these relate to the forgiver and the challenges that he [or she] has to overcome to taste the fruits of forgiveness, most units identified within each stage are not esoteric related challenges, but communicative strategies for reaching forgiveness. The process of forgiveness, independently of whether forgiveness is reached, is often followed by apology and ultimately reconciliation.

However, a few words of caution from positive psychology for restorative justice. Forgiveness is a moral concept and not a technique that can be learned to reduce crime and rehabilitate the offender. We agree with Enright and Kittle who see it as a "merciful act of giving a gift to someone who does not necessarily deserve it" (1999: 1630). Braithwaite, one of the leading advocates of restorative justice, agrees with this (2002). In particular, Braithwaite spoke about three groups of restorative justice standards: constraining, maximising and emergent. Constraining standards specify precise rights and limits, maximising standards pursue restoration and justify the constraining standards and emergent standards are gifts that are given in the process of restorative justice and may include, forgiveness, apology and remorse.

Therefore, in any training, delivery or preparation for restorative justice, facilitators must understand that a careful assessment of the readiness of a victim to forgive and the intent of the forgiver is critical. In fact, due to the powerful nature of the process of forgiveness for both the receiving and giving objects, if not managed carefully it may lead to negative effects including re-victimisation of victims, or trauma for the offenders; a sensitive rather than forced pace is essential. Gavrielides' (2011b) research of restorative justice in prisons has pointed out examples where restorative justice triggered fears and anxieties among young offenders who due to lack of proper support were traumatised and left damaged by the well-intended process that were implemented. This is not to suggest that all in-prison restorative justice projects are inappropriate. On the contrary, the research supports that when properly applied, restorative justice can indeed provide a unique experience for incarcerated offenders who search for an opportunity to reintegrate and restore (Gavrielides, 2011b). The mapping exercise that is included in the same study bears evidence to this claim and includes projects such as the Forgiveness Project and Khulisa UK. Similarly, Gavrielides and Coker (2005) and Gavrielides (2012c) work on clergy child sexual abuse and restorative justice warns that the process of forgiveness for this particular type of offence encompasses high risks for survivors since their world is shaken as they are awaken from the trauma that they often bury for years.

This is indeed one area where positive psychology can help restorative justice to develop further its tools and methodologies while guiding facilitators to minimise risk. For example, how much information should be given about forgiveness? Does the victim forgive because the facilitator or the information he [or she] received created false expectations or because they feel pressurised? What can be done if the victim or the offender are not ready to enter all stages of the forgiveness process but may be willing to do so at a later stage?

The willingness to be open to and include the possibility of forgiveness having an accepted place in restorative justice also involves the possibility of what is termed 'post-traumatic growth' (e.g. Tedeschi and Calhoun 1995). Joseph and Linley (2008: 9) describe how post-traumatic reactions are based on an individual's psycho-social interpretation of their experiences; with the support to process, more deeply understand and learn from their interpretations, such as occurs in restorative justice, the potential is created for growth, a growth that may in turn lead to the capacity to forgive in a victim. Yet in a challenging development of thinking, we are also seeing interpretations and reports of an offender's experiences as potentially being a form of trauma that they, in turn, must process more constructively and move beyond (E.G.Mapham and Heffron, 2012).

The need to increase awareness of these possibilities also exists beyond the field of practice. Politicians, decision makers and funders often impose unrealistic timescales and expectations that take away the very foundations of the restorative justice practice. As Enright and Kittle note: "Genuine forgiveness is never forced. It can take time and is the choice of the one offended" (1999: 1630). It must also be acknowledged that forgiving, receiving forgiveness and reconciliation may not occur. If an encounter fails, another meeting may be possible. Forgiveness should not be seen as a substitute for justice either. Forgiving does not mean that the harm has been restored. Unlike the adversarial process of criminal justice, in order to enter the restorative justice dialogue, first there must be acceptance of the harm that was caused and even if apology is achieved in order to complete the process there must be a mutual agreement that will lead to restoration.

CONCLUSION

This paper has reviewed why the 'good' in a person and in a life needs to be given place in the treatment and rehabilitation of an offender in order to achieve the potential for a healthier outcome. This is reflected in the GLM, but also has its seeds and possibilities in other positive psychology practices. The use of positive psychology perspectives is not a soft option, it is a balanced one. The same applies for restorative justice and the constructive and often deep pain that it entails.

We may choose to consider restorative justice as separate from other parts of the justice system. However, when we can see that the psychological reactions within its practise are also triggers and doorways to potential longer term desistance, there is a skill-based, training, financial and practical case to act on this, incorporate this in future training and create links to other forms of support to develop this in the offender or ex-offender. Further, where the age curve of desistance generally argues that it occurs with increased maturity, why would we or could we ignore an opportunity to support and develop doorways to desistance appearing for younger offenders.

As the restorative justice social justice movement expands internationally and matures, its relationship with other fields such as psychology, positive psychology and rehabilitation theory must deepen. We have attempted such a step here by adopting a multi-disciplinary approach that is compatible with the nature of restorative justice a field that has been cross-fertilised and infused by ideas taken from social and political sciences, religion, philosophy, art and cultures, our own worldviews and biases.

ACKNOWLEDGMENTS

The research was supported by Buckinghamshire New University Research Challenge. We are grateful for this. Many thanks also go to Dr. Matthew Smith and Daniel O'Donoghue for their involvement in the research. We are also grateful to Prof. Artinopoulou (Panteion University, Greece) and Simon Fulford (Khulisa UK) for their feedback and advice.

REFERENCES

Achilles, M. (2004). 'Can restorative justice live up to its promise to victims?' in Zehr, H. and B. Toews (Eds)., *Critical issues in restorative justice*, Cullompton, UK: Willan, 65-73.

Andrews, D. (2008). 'Extensions of the Risk Need Responsivity model of assessment and correctional treatment', in G. Bourgon et al (Eds), *Proceedings of the North American Correctional and Criminal Justice Psychology conference*, Ottawa, Ontario: Correctional Services Canada, 7-11.

Andrews, D. and Bonta, J. (1994), *The psychology of criminal conduct*, Cincinnati, 1st Edition, OH: Anderson.

Andrews, D. and Bonta, J. (1998) *The psychology of criminal conduct*, Cincinnati, 1st Edition, OH: Anderson.

Andrews, D., Bonta, J. and Hoge, R. (1990) 'Classification for effective rehabilitation: Rediscovering psychology'. *Criminal Justice and Behaviour*, 17, 19-52.

Andrews, D. A., Bonta, J., & Wormith, J. S. (2011). The risk-need-responsivity (RNR) model: Does adding the good lives model contribute to effective crime prevention? *Criminal Justice and Behavior*, 38, 735–755.

Barnett, R. (1977) 'Restitution: A New Paradigm of Criminal Justice', *87(4) Ethics: An International Journal of Social, Political, and Legal Philosophy*, 279-301.

Bazemore, G. (1999). 'Three paradigms for juvenile justice' in Galaway, B. and J. Hudson (Eds), *Restorative justice: International perspectives*, Monsey, NY: Criminal Justice Press, 37-67.

Bazemore, G. and O'Brien, S. (2002). 'The quest for a restorative model of rehabilitation: Theory for practice and practice for theory', in Walgrave, L. (Ed), *Restorative justice and the law*, Cullompton, UK: Willan, 31-67.

Berman, G. (2010). "Prison population statistics" in *House of Commons Library*.

Bonta, J.and Andrews, D. (2007), *Risk-need responsivity model for offender assessment and rehabilitation*, (User Report No 2007-06). Ottawa: Public Safety Canada.

Braithwaite, J. (1989) Crime, shame and reintegration. Cambridge, UK: Cambridge University Press.

Braithwaite, J. (1999). "Restorative Justice: Assessing Optimistic and Pessimistic Accounts", *Crime and Justice, 25, 1-127*.

Braithwaite, J. (2002). "Setting Standards for Restorative Justice", *42 British Journal of Criminology*, 563-577.

Braithwaite, J. and Strang, H. (2000) *Restorative Justice: Philosophy to Practice*. Aldershot: Ashgate.

Cantor, G. (1976). "An End to Crime and Punishment", *39(4) The Shingle (Philadelphia Bar Association)*, 99-114.

Christie, N. (1977). "Conflicts as Property", *17(1) British Journal of Criminology*, 1-15.

Cohen, S. (1985). *Visions of Social Control: Crime, Punishment and Classification*, Cambridge: CUP.

Daly, K. (2000) "Revisiting the Relationship between Retributive and Restorative Justice" in *Restorative Justice: Philosophy to Practice*, edited by J. Braithwaite and H. Strang. Aldershot: Ashgate, 33-54.

Dignan, J. (2003) "Towards a systemic model of Restorative Justice" in *Restorative Justice and Criminal Justice: Competing or Reconcilable Paradigms?*, edited by A. Von Hirsch et al. Oxford: Hart Publishing.

Duff, A. (1992) "Alternatives to Punishment-or Alternative Punishments?" in *Retributivism and its Critics*, edited by W. Cragg, Stuttgart: Franz Steiner, 44-68.

Ellerby, L., Bedard, J., & Chartrand, S. (2000). 'Holism, wellness and spirituality'. In D. R. Laws, S. M. Hudson, & T.Ward (Eds.), *Remaking relapse prevention with sex offenders Newbury Park*, CA: Sage. 427−452.

Emmons, R.A. (1999) The Psychology of Ultimate Concerns. London, The Guildford Press.

Emmons, R.A. (2003) Personal Goals, Life Meaning, and Virtue: Wellsprings of a Positive Life. In: Keyes, C.L.M. and Haidt, J. (Eds) (2003)Flourishing: Positive Psychology and the Well-Lived Life. Washington: American Psychological Association.

Enright, R. and Kittle, B. (1999). 'Forgiveness in psychology and law: The meeting of moral development and restorative justice', *Fordham Urban Law Journal*, 27:5, 1622-1631.

Enright, R.D. and Fitzgibbons, R.P. (2000) Helping Clients Forgive: An Empirical Guide for Resolving Anger and Restoring Hope. Washington, American Psychological Association.

Farrall, S. and Bowling, B. (1999). 'Structuration, human development and desistance from crime'. *British Journal of Criminology, 39*, 253-268.

Farrall, S. and Bowling, B. (1999). 'Structuration, human development and desistance from crime'. *British Journal of Criminology, 39*, 253-268.

Foucault, M. (1988). 'The ethic of care for the self as a practice of freedom'. In J. Bermauer and D. Rasmussen (Eds)., *The final Foucault*, Cambridge, MA: MIT Press, 16-49.

Foote, J. and Frank, A. (1999). *Foucault and therapy*, In Chambon, A. et al (Eds). *Reading Foucault for social work*, New York: Columbia University Press, 157-187.

Fredrickson, B. (1998) What Good Are Positive Emotions? Review of General Psychology. Vol. 2 (3) p300-319

Fredrickson, B. (2001) The Role of Positive Emotions in Positive Psychology. American Psychologist. Vol. 56 (3) p218-226.

Gavrielides, T. (2013a). "Where is Restorative Justice Heading?" *Probation Junior, Vol IV: 2, pp. 79 -95.*

Gavrielides, T. (2013b), 'Restorative pain: A New vision of punishment", in Gavrielides, T. and V. Artinopoulous (Eds) *Reconstructing the Restorative Justice Philosophy*, Furnham, UK: Ashgate Publishing, , 311-337.

Gavrielides, T. (2012a) *Rights and Restoration within Youth Justice*, Witby, ON: de Sitter Publications.

Gavrielides, T. (2012b) "Clergy sexual abuse: the restorative justice option" in (Ed) K.V Wormer & L. Walker *Restorative Justice Today: Applications of Restorative Interventions*, Sage: California.

Gavrielides, T. (2012c). "Clergy Child Sexual Abuse & the Restorative Justice Dialogue", *Journal of Church and State*. doi: 10.1093/jcs/css041.

Gavrielides, T. (2011a). "Restorative Practices: From the Early Societies to the 1970s". Internet Journal of Criminology ISSN 2045-6743.

Gavrielides, T. (2011b). *Restorative Justice and the Secure Estate: Alternatives for Young People in Custody*, London, UK: IARS Publications.

Gavrielides, T. (2007). *Restorative Justice Theory and Practice: Addressing the Discrepancy*, Helsinki: HEUNI.

Gavrielides, T. (2005) "Some Meta-theoretical Questions for Restorative Justice", *18:1 Ratio Juris*, 84-106.

Gavrielides, T. and V. Artinopoulou (2013). *Reconstructing Restorative Justice Philosophy*, Furnham, UK: Ashgate Publishing.

Gavrielides, T. and V. Artinopoulou (2012). "Violence against women and restorative justice" 8:1, *Asian Journal of Criminology*, 25-40.

Gavrielides T. and D. Coker (2005) "Restoring Faith: Resolving the Catholic Church's Sexual Scandals through Restorative Justice", 8:4 Contemporary Justice Review, 345-365.

Glaser, D. (1964). *Effectiveness of a prison and parole system*. Indianapolis, IN: Bobbs-Merrill.

Hollin, C. (1999) 'Treatment programmes for offenders: Meta-analysis, what works and beyond', *International Journal of Law and Psychiatry*, 22, 361-372.

Joseph, S. and Linley, P.A. (2008) Positive Psychology Perspectives on Posttraumatic Stress: An Integrative Psychosocial Framework. In: Joseph, S. and Linley, P.A. (Eds) (2008) Trauma, Recovery and Growth: Positive Psychology Perspectives on Posttraumatic Stress. London, John Wiley & Sons Inc.

Knuutila, A. (2010). *Punishing costs: How locking up children is making Britain less safe.* London: New Economics Foundation

Laws, D. R., & Ward, T. (2011). *Desistance from sex offending: Alternatives to throwing away the keys*. New York, NY: The Guilford Press.

Mapham, A. and Hefferon, K. (2012). 'I used to be an offender – Now I' m a defender: Positive psychology approaches in the facilitation of posttraumatic growth in offenders', *Journal of Offender Rehabilitation*, 51, 389-413.

Maruna, S. (2006). *Making Good*, Washington, DC: American Psychology Association.

Maslow, A.H. (1954 / 1970) Motivation and Personality (3rd Edition). London: Harper Collins.

Marx, K. (1954) *Capital*, London: Lawrence and Wishart.

McAdams, D. P. (1994). Can personality change? Levels of stability and growth in personality across the life span. In T. F. Heatherton and J. L. Weinberger (Eds.), Can personality change? Washington, DC: American Psychological Association. 299–313.

McAdams, D. P. (2006). *The redemptive self: Stories Americans live by*. New York, NY: Oxford University Press.

McCold, P. (2000). 'Toward a holistic vision of restorative juvenile justice: A reply to the maximalist model', *Contemporary Justice Review, 3*, 357-414.

McGuire, J. (2002). "Criminal sanctions versus psychologically based interventions with offenders: A comparative empirical analysis, *Psychology, Crime and Law*, 8, 183-208.

Ministry of Justice (2010). *'Reoffending of adults: results from the 2008 cohort, England and Wales'*.

North, J. (1987). 'Wrongdoing and Forgiveness', *Philosophy*, 62, 499-508.

Peterson, C. and Seligman, M. (2004). *Character strengths and virtues*, Toronto, ON: Oxford University Press.

Robinson, G. and Shapland, J. (2008). 'Reducing recidivism: A task for restorative justice?', *British Journal of Criminology*, 48, 337-358.

Prison Reform Trust (2010). *Punishing Disadvantage: a profile of young people in custody*, London: Prison Reform Trust.

Rogers, C. (1967 / 2004) On Becoming A Person. London, Constable and Company Ltd.

Rossner, D. (1989) "Wiedergutmachen statt Ubelvergelten", in *Tater-Opfer-Ausgleich: Vom zwischenmenschlichen Weg zur Wiederstellung des Rechtsfriedens* edited by E. Marks and D. Rossner, Bonn: Unverdnderte Auflage.

Ryff, C.D. and Singer, B. (1998) The Contours of Positive Human Health. Psychological Inquiry, Vol. 9, Num. 1, 1 – 28.

Scottish Prison Service (2011) The Good Lives (SO) Programme Theory Manual Version 1. Sourced from the internet / Google.

Sharpe, J. (1980) "Enforcing the Law in the Seventeenth Century English Village", in *Crime and the Law* edited by V. Gatrell, London: Europa.

Sherman, L.W., & Strang, H. (2007). *Restorative justice: The evidence*. London: The Smith Institute.

Schoeman, M. (2013). 'The African Concept of Ubuntu and Restorative Justice', in Gavrielides, T. and V. Artinopoulous (Eds) *Reconstructing the Restorative Justice Philosophy*, Furnham, UK: Ashgate Publishing, 291-311.

Shover, N. (1996). *Great pretenders: Pursuits and careers of persistent thieves*. Boulder, CO: Westview Press.

Snyder, C.R. (2002) Hope Theory: Rainbows in the Mind. *Psychological Inquiry*, Vol. 13, No. 4, p249 – 275.

Tallack, W. (1900) *Reparation to the Injured and the Rights of Victims of Crime Compensation*, London: Wertheimer.

Tedeschi, R.G. and Calhoun, L.G. (1995) Trauma and Transformation: Growing in the Aftermath of Suffering. London, Sage Publications.

Travis, A. (30 June 2010). "Ken Clarke to attach bank' em up prison sentencing" *Guardian* accessed on 7/1/2011 http://www.guardian.co.uk/uk/2010/jun/30/clarke-prison-sentencing-justice-jail

Tweed, R. G., Bhatt, G., Dooley, S., Spindler, A., Douglas, K. S., & Viljoen, J. (2011). 'Youth violence and positive psychology: Research potential through integration'. *Canadian Psychology, 52*, 111-121.

Towes, B. and Katounas, J. (2004). 'Have offender needs and perspectives been adequately incorporated into restorative justice?' in in Zehr, H. and B. Toews (Eds)., *Critical issues in restorative justice*, Cullompton, UK: Willan, 107-118.

Van Ness, D. and Strong K. H. (1997) (2010). *Restoring Justice*, Cincinnati, OH: Anderson Publishing Company.

Von Hirsch, A. (1999), "Punishment, Penance and the State", in M. Matravers (Eds) *Punishment and Political Theory*, Oxford: Hart Publishing, 69-82.

Walgrave, L. (1995). 'Restorative justice for juveniles: Just a technique or a fully fledged alternative?', *The Howard Journal*, 34, 228-249.

Ward, T. and Maruna, S. (2007) *Rehabilitation: Beyond the risk paradigm*, New York: Routledge.

Ward, T. and Langlands, R. (2009). 'Repairing the rupture: Restorative justice and the rehabilitation of offenders', *Aggression and Violent Behaviour*, 14, 205-214.

Ward, T., & Stewart, C. (2003). 'Criminogenic needs and human needs: A theoretical model'. *Psychology, Crime & Law*, 9, 125−143.

Ward, T., Yates, P.M. and Willis, G.M. (2012) The Good Lives Model and the Risk, Need Responsivity Model: A Critical Response to Andrews, Bonta and Wormith (2011). *Criminal Justice and Behaviour*, 39: 94.

Wright, M. (1996) *Justice for Victims and Offenders: A Restorative Response to Crime*, Winchester: Waterside Press.

Youth Justice Board (2009). *Annual Report and Accounts 2008–09,* London: Youth Justice Board.

Zehr, H. (1990) *Changing Lenses: A New Focus for Crime and Justice*. Scottdale: Herald Press.

Zehr, H. and Mika, H. (1998). "Fundamental Concepts of Restorative Justice", *1 Contemporary Justice Review*, 47-55.

Zernova, M. (2009). 'Integrating the restorative and rehabilitative models: Lessons from one family group conferencing project', *Contemporary Justice Review,* 12:1, 59-75.

In: Crime   ISBN: 978-1-62948-657-4
Editor: Michael Harry Pearson   © 2014 Nova Science Publishers, Inc.

Chapter 7

THE EFFECTS OF CRIME ON MARRIAGES, DIVORCES, AND BIRTHS TO SINGLE MOTHERS IN BORDERING STATES OF MEXICO

Mingming Pan, Benjamin Widner‡ and Carl E. Enomoto#*

Department of Economics, Applied Statistics, and International Business,
New Mexico State University, Las Cruces, NM

ABSTRACT

Crime and drug-related violence in Mexico have resulted in job losses, decreases in incomes, business closures, a drop in tourism, and the migration of thousands of individuals trying to escape the violence. The purpose of this chapter is to determine the effects of this crime on marriages, divorces, births to single mothers, and the percent of births to teen mothers in Mexico. Using a spatial model and a panel dataset, it was found that the effects of crime transcend state borders. In particular, states with higher birth rates to single mothers and higher percents of births to teen mothers were found bordering those states with high crime rates. Furthermore, states with high birth rates to single mothers tended to have bordering states with low birth rates to single mothers. Given these additional spatial effects of crime, the true social costs of crime to Mexico may far exceed initial estimates, justifying the use of more resources in the fight against crime and drug-related violence.

Keywords: crime, marriage, divorce, births, single mothers, Mexico

---

* E-mail: mpan@nmsu.edu; 575-646-2597.
‡ bwidner@nmsu.edu; 575-646-5989
# cenomoto@nmsu.edu; 575-646-1992

INTRODUCTION

Mexico has faced significant challenges and obstacles with the crime and drug-related violence it has experienced. The drug cartel wars that erupted after 2006 resulted in thousands of business closures and homicides and thousands of people in Mexico left cities where the violence was particularly unbearable. Tourism, investment, and growth were adversely affected. Rios (2007) has estimated annual losses of $4.3 billion in Mexico due to the illegal drug trade. According to the BBC (British Broadcasting Corporation) News (2008), "Mexico's finance minister has said that crime and violence have had a significant impact on the country's economy, cutting growth by 1%."

The purpose of this research is to determine the effects of crime and drug-related violence in Mexico on marriages, divorces, births to single mothers, and percent of births to teen mothers. If crime and drug-related violence are leading to more divorces and births to single mothers as well as a higher percent of births to teen mothers, then the social cost to Mexico from crime and drug-related violence may far exceed the initial cost estimates. If this is indeed the case, more resources used in fighting crime in Mexico can be justified, and perhaps a multinational solution is called for with resources coming from abroad. Furthermore, the adverse effects of crime and drug-related violence are not bound by state borders. Crime and violence in the state of Chihuahua for example, affects businesses, incomes, decisions of where to live and work, marriages, divorces, and births to teen mothers, in the border states of Sonora, Sinaloa, Durango, and Coahuila. While there has been much concern in the U.S., especially in southern Arizona and parts of Texas, over spillover effects of crime from northern Mexican states that border the U.S., this paper will examine cross-border state effects throughout Mexico. A spatial model will be estimated to account for these cross-border effects of crime.

Steps have recently been taken to address the high divorce rate in Mexico City. In 2011, a bill was introduced there to allow for two-year marriage contracts (Romo, 2011). Couples would sign the contract which would specify how assets would be divided up after two years and there would be the opportunity to renew the contract. The bill was introduced as a response to the high divorce rate in Mexico City which was close to fifty percent. Others disagreed with the temporary marriage bill, stating that marriage should be for life.

The country with the highest number of divorces per 100 marriages is Belgium with 59.8 divorces (nationmaster.com—most recent data). Mexico was in the 20th spot from the top with 7.4 divorces per 100 marriages. Economists and sociologists have long debated the factors affecting marriage, divorce, and births to unmarried mothers. Economists have stressed economic factors such as differences in male and female wages and the principle of comparative advantage where two individuals can gain by specializing in what they do relatively better than the other and then trading for services of the other, to explain the benefits of marriage. Economies of scale have also been used to justify marriage in which case the married couple only has to buy one washer/dryer set instead of two separate sets or one refrigerator instead of two. Sociologists and even some economists have argued that these oversimplified models fail to consider strategy and tactics involved by the partners and the differences in tastes and preferences of married couples. Marriage and divorce may be more affected by those emotional and subjective forces not captured in general economic models. Furthermore, divorce has social repercussions that go beyond the immediate family involved.

Children from a divorce can suffer from depression, poverty, low levels of educational attainment, and lack of self esteem. The costs of divorce may well be borne by much of society. There also exists the situation of an increase in the number of births to single women which can also lead to children with similar characteristics as those who come from a broken family. While many researchers have looked at factors affecting these family and social issues, little or no work has been done concerning the effects of crime in bordering states on these issues.

The outline of this paper is as follows. In the next section, a review of the literature on marriages, divorces, and births to single mothers will be presented. The current crime situation in Mexico will then be discussed, followed by the spatial model to be estimated. The final section will contain the empirical results with conclusions and a summary.

LITERATURE REVIEW

Becker (1973) was among the first group of economists to develop a formal model of marriage. In his model, an increase in property (nonwage) income would lead to an increase in the number of marriages. An increase in female wages would reduce the gains from marriage if female wages were less than male wages and divorce was less likely the longer the couple had been married and if the couple had children. Freiden (1974) found that income was negatively related to the proportion of females married. He used the median monthly gross rent for SMSAs and the median value of owner-occupied housing for his income variables. In Freiden's model, the greater the difference between male and female wages, the greater would be the gain from marriage. One spouse would specialize in market activities (working at a job away from home) while the other spouse would specialize in home activities (working at home). This result, however, was not confirmed for younger adults under age 25. He hypothesized that the gains from marriage may be different to younger adults and in particular, gains from specialization could be irrelevant to them. McKenzie and Tullock (1978) discussed the costs and benefits of marriage. The costs included loss of freedom and costs of joint-decision making. The benefits included the production of goods that could not be easily produced outside of marriage including children, prestige, and family relationships. The longer a marriage was expected to last and hence the greater the benefits associated with marriage, the higher would be the costs individuals will be willing to take on to search for a mate.

Barham, Devlin, and Yang (2009) stated that the early literature on marriage has been criticized because it explained differences in the roles of spouses as a comparative advantage problem, when in fact, strategic considerations and decisions were important. Using a theoretical/mathematical model of marriage, they concluded that if the husband's earnings increased, the wife gained if she stayed in the marriage but she also stood to get more in support payments if she got a divorce. Furthermore, the increase in the husband's wage could also cause him to spend more time in market activities (working at a job) and less time on housework which could lead to divorce.

A sizeable portion of the literature has also analyzed the effects of welfare payments on marriage and divorce. Blau, Kahn, and Waldfogel (2000) for example, found that welfare benefits reduced marriage rates. Bitler, Gelbach, Hoynes, and Zavodny (2002) stated that welfare reform that affected work incentives had an ambiguous effect on marriage and divorce rates. However, they found that TANF (Temporary Assistance for Needy Families) reduced marriage and divorce rates.

Some researchers have taken a different approach to the study of marriage and divorce. Ressler and Waters (2000) used a simultaneous equations model to analyze divorce rates and Tzeng (1992) analyzed the effects of age and educational gaps of spouses on marriage stability. Huber and Spitze (1980) found that the age when married, the duration of the marriage, and declining fertility rates, had an effect on divorces. They also pointed out that from a sociological perspective there were many more complicating factors that had to be taken into account when looking at marriage and divorce. For example, while increases in the wife's income may give her more opportunities outside of the marriage, it may make her more attractive to the husband who is willing to invest more in the marriage. Thus an increase in the incomes of wives would not necessarily lead to more divorces.

Stevenson and Wolfers (2007) stated that the early literature on marriage and fertility that looked at production complementarities and specialization in the household may no longer be as relevant today, since many individuals are now getting married later in life without the intention of having children and women are now actively participating in the labor force with both spouses working outside the home. They also stated that in some cases, children may be better off after a divorce compared to the case of staying in a bad marriage. Further, it could be the attributes of the parents that lead to depressed children who engage in delinquent behavior, rather than the divorce itself. Siebel (2004) discussed reasons for divorce. Some factors that led to more divorces included the changing of laws that made it easier to get a divorce, changing views and attitudes towards divorce that made it more socially acceptable, changing opportunities for women in the workforce that allowed women to no longer depend on the earnings of a husband, coming from a divorced family, and having traits and characteristics very different from the spouse including differences in religion, income, and education.

Many studies have shown that children of divorced parents were more likely to suffer from depression, more likely to engage in delinquent behavior, and more likely to end up in bad relationships. Eagan (2004) analyzed the effects and consequences of divorce. She stated that the divorce can create stress not only in the children of the broken marriage, but in the adults as well. Children who come from divorced families can display delinquent behavior, may perform poorly in school, may have low self-esteem, and may be less trusting of those they get involved with in future relationships. Divorce could also lead to poverty for the spouse and children who are left without any means of supporting themselves.

Much has also been written on births to single mothers. Gonzalez (2005) found that increased levels of public support for single mothers led to higher levels of divorced mothers and mothers never married. Higher child support payments also led to higher levels of divorced mothers. Musick (1999) analyzed the determinants of births to unmarried women. She found that cohabitation and time spent in a single-parent family were positively related to number of children to unmarried women.

According to Child Trends Data Bank (2007), the percent of births to unmarried women has increased in the U.S. from 5.3% in 1960 to 36.8% in 2005. The report stated that unmarried mothers tended to have lower levels of education and income compared to their married counterparts. Children of unmarried mothers tended to live in poverty, experience emotional problems, and ended up with less education and lower income levels when they grew up. Sheffield (2010, p. 1) stated "Data clearly show that children raised by single mothers are more than five times more likely to be poor than are children raised by married mothers with the same education level." Korn (2012) discussed many of the problems and challenges unmarried mothers and their children face. He cited Coontz (an Evergreen State College professor of history and family studies) as saying that "…studies show that a woman's education level and the emphasis she places on education for her children have a greater predictive effect on her child than whether she marries or not." Other researchers have stated that a stable home environment for children where the unmarried mother is not moving in and out of relationships continuously is what is important for how the children turn out.

Jayson (2009) reported work by Ventura of the National Center for Health Statistics showing that there were many reasons for the increase in births to unmarried mothers in the U.S. Some of these reasons included less of a stigma attached to single motherhood, larger incomes earned by females, and a decline in marriages. Conners (2012) reported that there were large racial differences in births outside of marriage. He stated, "73 percent of black children are born outside marriage, compared with 53 percent of Latinos and 29 percent of whites.

The Heritage Foundation (2012) stated, "One of the greatest drivers of poverty in the United States is the breakdown of marriage. Eighty percent of all long-term poverty occurs in single-parent homes, over 70 percent of poor families are headed by a single parent, and children in single-parent families are approximately five times more likely to be poor than their peers from married-parent homes."

An area of research that has not been explored in the literature is how crime affects marriages, divorces, births to single mothers, and percent of birth to teen mothers. In the next section, the current situation in Mexico will be described, outlining the surge in drug-related violence and the possible connections it may have with marriages, divorces, births to single mothers, and percent of births to teen mothers.

The Situation in Mexico

Marriages, divorces, and births to single mothers per 100,000 inhabitants in Mexico, are shown in figures 1, 2, and 3, for 2004 to 2008. In Figure 1, marriages per 100,000 inhabitants have been decreasing over most of the period, 2004-2008. Divorces and births to single mothers per 100,000 inhabitants have been increasing over the same period, with noticeable spikes in 2006. In December 2006, President Felipe Calderon declared a war on drugs and dispatched troops throughout Mexico to fight the drug cartels. The effort upset the former balance of power between the cartels and resulted in more drug-related violence as fragmented and weakened cartels fought each other over the profitable drug corridors into the U.S. According to Rios and Shirk (2011, p. 8), drug-related homicides surged to 34,550 from 2007 to 2010, during the first four years of the Calderon administration. This was more than four times the number of drug-related homicides of the previous administration of President Vicente Fox which stood at 8,901 from 2000 to 2006. The violence and homicides have been especially high in the northern border states of Mexico such as Chihuahua, Baja California, Tamaulipas, and Nuevo Leon, and they have spread to other parts of Mexico including the states of Guerrero, Sinaloa, Durango, Morelos, Jalisco, Nayarit, and the state of Mexico (Beittel, 2011, p. 20).

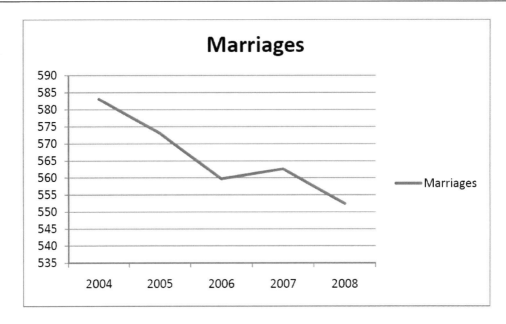

Figure 1. Marriages per 100,000 inhabitants in Mexico.

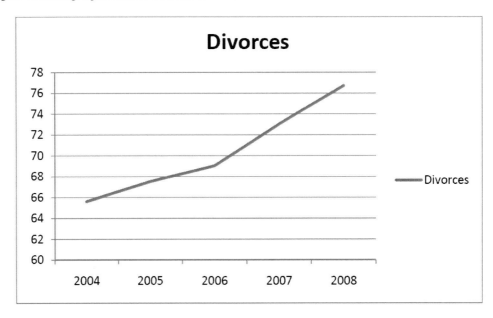

Figure 2. Divorces per 100,000 inhabitants in Mexico.

One of Mexico's major problems was addressed by Shirk (2011, p. 2). He stated, "According to official estimates, illegal drug production and trafficking provides employment opportunities for an estimated 450,000 people, and perhaps 3-4 percent of Mexico's more than $1 trillion GDP. Today, the illicit drug sector involves large numbers of young men aged 18-35 who have neither educational nor employment opportunities, known commonly in Mexico as —ni-ni's (*ni estudian, ni trabajan*). Where other options have failed them, these young men have found substantial economic opportunities in the illicit global economy for drugs."

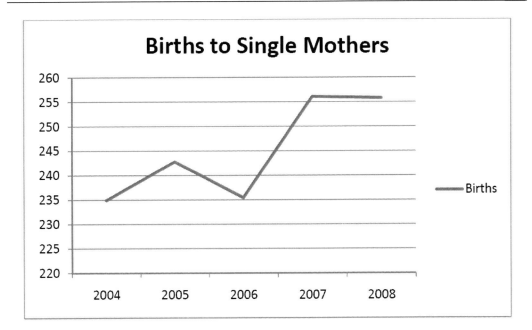

Figure 3. Births to Single Mothers per 100,000 inhabitants in Mexico.

The illicit drug trade in Mexico has also led to increases in kidnappings for ransom, extortion, and human smuggling, as the cartels have engaged in activities to help pay for the drugs they purchase and to pay for their enforcement gangs. This increased level of criminal activity has placed even more demands on a police force with few resources which has further decreased the probability of criminal arrests. The impunity rate in Mexico is close to 93% (Azaola and Bergman, 2007, p. 96), which has created an environment where criminal activity can thrive.

With the increased crime and drug-related violence, tourism has suffered in Acapulco, Cancun, Mazatlan, Taxco, and Cuernavaca (Beittel, 2011, p. 21). Thousands of businesses have closed and the Internal Displacement Monitoring Center has estimated that 230,000 Mexicans have moved away from violent regions (Rios, 2011, p. 17). This rising tide of crime and violence in Mexico has resulted in lower incomes, which seems to have taken a toll on marriage rates, divorce rates, and births to single mothers. Faced with declining incomes and job opportunities, couples may delay marriage and wait for better times. Declining incomes may lead to fewer divorces if the couple feels that they must stay in the marriage until more job opportunities become available. However, declining incomes can also lead to more stress for a married couple and be a motivating factor for a divorce. A decrease in incomes and job opportunities may also be a contributing factor to the higher incidence of births to single mothers with males avoiding the financial responsibility of raising a family.

In Figure 1, the marriage rate was declining before 2006 with a noticeable change after 2006. In Figure 2, the increased drug-related violence starting in 2006 may have contributed to the increase in the divorce rate. The shift towards more violence may also have led to the jump in births to single mothers in 2006 which is illustrated in Figure 3.

In the next section, a model will be developed to account for the effects of crime and violence on marriages, divorces, births to single mothers, and percent of births to teen mothers in bordering states of Mexico.

A Model of the Effects of Crime on Marriages, Divorces, Births to Single Mothers, and Percent of Births to Teen Mothers

When an individual is trying to decide if he or she should get married, a comparison of the perceived benefits of marriage to the perceived costs must be made. If the perceived benefits of marriage exceed the perceived costs then the individual will get married provided his/her potential spouse reaches a similar decision.

The benefits of marriage to an individual include:

- children
- being in a loving relationship with a trusted partner who offers their support
- admiration and high regard of friends and others for those who are married
- safety and security offered by marriage
- economies of scale where two individuals living together can live more cheaply than two alone
- access to additional earnings from a spouse

The costs of marriage to an individual include:

- loss of freedom
- costs associated with joint-decision making which occur when two individuals must either agree on a plan of action or compromise (McKenzie and Tullock, 1978)
- costs of raising children including expenditures on food, clothing, and education
- psychic or emotional costs when either a spouse or children are put in harm's way

An increase in crime and violence can affect both the perceived benefits and costs of marriage to an individual. If the individual perceives that crime poses a potential threat to his/her potential spouse and children they may eventually have, the perceived cost of marriage increases and the individual is less likely to get married. Marriage, however, can also offer safety and security to a spouse living in an environment filled with crime. Even if only one partner in the marriage feels safer, the other may benefit since the one feeling safer may take more steps to ensure the perpetuation of the marriage. Thus crime can increase the perceived benefit of marriage to an individual which increases the likelihood of him/her getting married.

An increase in income also affects the perceived benefits and costs of marriage to an individual. With additional income, a person can afford goods such as a larger house, a second car, vacations, and medical care that can increase the perceived benefits from marriage. Furthermore, an increase in income can allow the individual to expand his/her search for a marriage partner which could possibly result in a better choice of a spouse leading to higher perceived benefits from marriage. However, individuals with higher incomes also face additional perceived costs of marriage. These individuals may be more concerned about their career and work longer hours in their profession, placing their marriage or potential marriage in jeopardy. These individuals may simply view the perceived cost of marriage (due to taking time away from their career) too high and avoid it.

Government grants or subsidies that lower the cost of education and the cost of child care can also affect the decision to get married. These grants lower the cost of raising children and should lower the perceived cost of marriage.

The characteristics of the potential spouse also affect one's decision to get married. The spouse's personality, appearance, education, religion, cultural background, and whether he/she has children from a previous marriage, can influence a person's decision to get married. Many of these characteristics are difficult to quantify but still enter one's decision when comparing perceived benefits and costs of marriage.

While crime, personal income, government grants, and characteristics of the potential spouse, affect one's decision to get married, they also affect one's decision to get divorced, the number of births to single mothers and the percent of births to teen mothers. As an example, an increase in crime may increase the perceived benefits of divorce to an individual if he/she believes that the psychic or emotional cost of having and raising children in such an environment is too high. On the other hand, an increase in crime may increase the perceived benefit of being in a marriage for the safety and security it provides which would lead to a decrease in the number of divorces.

An increase in one's income can also lead to more or fewer divorces. As previously discussed, additional income allows the purchase of goods that can potentially increase the benefits from marriage and increase the cost of a divorce. However, additional income provides an individual the wherewithal to get divorced and live alone.

These effects of crime and income on marriage and divorce can also affect the number of births to single mothers and the percent of births to teen mothers. If young women are getting married earlier for the safety and security of marriage when crime is present, the percent of births to teen mothers would increase. If, however, teenagers are concerned that the emotional cost of raising children in a crime-ridden environment is too high, they may not get married or delay getting married which decreases the percent of births to teen mothers.

There are also spatial effects of crime on marriage, divorce, and births to single mothers that have been largely ignored.

Figures 4, 5, 6, 7, and 8, show that spatial effects might exist. In figure 4, marriages per 100,000 inhabitants are relatively low (lighter shaded states) in the states of Baja California, Chihuahua, Coahuila, Queretaro, Jalisco, San Luis Potosi, and Oaxaca.

These states have bordering states with high levels of crime per 100,000 inhabitants (darker shaded states) as illustrated in figure 8. Crime and violence in one state may be partly responsible for low marriage rates in bordering states.

In figure 5, the states of Coahuila and Jalisco (lighter shaded states) have relatively low divorce rates. They border states with relatively high crime rates. Crime in one Mexican state may be leading to lower divorce rates in bordering states.

In figure 6, states with relatively high births per 100,000 inhabitants to single mothers (darker shaded states) include Baja California Sur, Sonora, Coahuila, Sinaloa, Durango, Oaxaca, Nayarit, and San Luis Potosi. They border states with relatively high crime rates. A similar story emerges for percent of births to teenage mothers in figure 7 and total crime rates in figure 8.

To test for and capture these spatial (border) effects of crime on marriage rates, divorce rates, births to single mothers, and percent of births to teenage mothers, the following spatially auto-regressive model with spatially auto-regressive errors was estimated (Anselin, L., 1988; LeSage, J.P. and Pace, R.K., 2009; Lee, L.F. and Yu, J., 2010).

$$y = \beta_1 + \beta_2 \cdot rgdp + \beta_3 \cdot grants + \beta_4 \cdot crime + \beta_5 \cdot W \cdot crime + \rho \cdot W \cdot y + \varepsilon \quad (1)$$

where $\varepsilon = \lambda \cdot W \cdot \epsilon + u$. The dependent variable y is the marriage rate (or divorce rate, or births to single mothers, or percent of births to teenagers) in a given Mexican state. $Rgdp$ is real GDP for a given state per 100,000 inhabitants to account for the effects of income and job opportunities on marriage. $Grants$ is total federal grants to states per 100,000 inhabitants for education, public security, and social infrastructure. $Crime$ is total number of crimes in a given state per 100,000 inhabitants including theft, homicide, assault, rape, damage to property, and fraud. $W \cdot crime$ is the spatially-weighted average of total number of crimes per 100,000 inhabitants in bordering states. $W \cdot y$ is the spatially-weighted average of marriage rates in bordering states and u is the stochastic disturbance term. State fixed effects were also included in the model to allow for variations in other state variables that affect marriage rates (and divorce rates, births to single mothers, and percent of births to teens) across states such as appearance, cultural values, education, religion, personality, and other characteristics of the potential spouse.

W is the spatial weight matrix. For a panel dataset with N cross sections and T time periods, W is a block-diagonal NT $\times$NT matrix, as follows: (note: NT=N*T)

$$W = I_T \otimes W_t$$

where I_T is a T$\times$T identity matrix and

$$W_t = \begin{pmatrix} 0 & w_{12} & \cdots & w_{1N} \\ w_{21} & 0 & \cdots & w_{2N} \\ \vdots & \vdots & \ddots & \vdots \\ w_{N1} & w_{N2} & \cdots & 0 \end{pmatrix}$$

t denotes discrete time periods from 1 to T.

In this study, W_t is a binary contiguity weight matrix. If two states have a common border, the element in W_t is set equal to 1, otherwise equal to 0. Here, W_t does not vary over time, and thus it is the same across observation time periods. Following the common practice, the weight matrix W is standardized so that each row sums to unity. The variable $W \cdot crime$ is thus the spatially weighted average of crime rates in bordering states. If β_5 is positive, then a particular state's marriage rate increases (decreases) when crime rates in bordering states increases (decreases). If β_5 is negative then a particular state's marriage rate decreases (increases) when crime in bordering states increases (decreases).

Similar interpretations apply to the variable $W \cdot y$, which is the spatially weighted average of marriage rates in bordering states. A positive ρ means that a particular state's marriage rate will increase (decrease) when marriage rates in bordering states are increasing (declining). A negative ρ means that a particular state's marriage rate will decrease (increase) when marriage rates in bordering states are increasing (declining).

The variables rgdp, grants, and crime were all lagged one year. The reason for lagging these variables is to avoid the problem of simultaneity. Real GDP, grants, and crime affect a state's marriage rate but marriage rates may also affect real GDP, federal grants received by a state, and state crime. By using lagged values of crime in a state, crimes in 2007 are allowed to affect state marriage rates in 2008 and not the other way around. A summary of the variables, their means and standard deviations, is presented in Table 1.

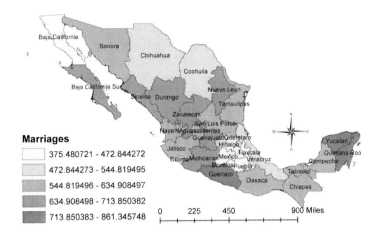

Figure 4. Marriages per 100,000 Inhabitants by State, 2008.

Table 1. Sample Statistics

Variable	Description	Mean	Std. Dev.
rgdp	real GDP by state at 2003 prices in billions of pesos per 100,000 inhabitants	8.27	7.14
grants	real federal grants by state per 100,000 inhabitants for education, public security, and social infrastructure	293.46	65.98
crime	total number of crimes by state per 100,000 inhabitants including theft, homicide, assault, fraud, damage to property, and rape	197.29	96.37
marriage	number of marriages by state per 100,000 inhabitants	596.64	113.53
divorce	number of divorces by state per 100,000 inhabitants	81.09	36.78
birthsngl	births per 100,000 inhabitants to single mothers	244.57	87.73
teenbirths	percent of births to teen mothers (under age 20	18.06	1.71

Source: Anuario de Estadisticas por Entidad Federative: INEGI.

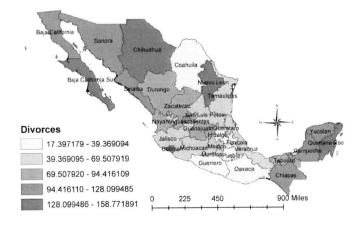

Figure 5. Divorces per 100,000 Inhabitants by State, 2008.

Total federal grants, total number of crimes, marriages, divorces, births to single mothers, and percent of births to teen mothers by state and by year from 2005 to 2008, were taken from various issues of *Anuario de Estadisticas por Entidad Federative* (Yearbook of Statistics by State), published by INEGI—Instituto Nacional De Estadistica Y Geografia (National Institute of Statistics and Geography). Real GDP and the implicit GDP deflators for 2005 to 2008 were collected from INEGI's web site and state population estimates were collected from CONAPO's web site (Consejo Nacional de Poblacion—National Population Council). As of February 2013, the latest figures reported in *Anuario de Estadisticas por Entidad Federative* for marriages, divorces, births to single mothers, and percent of births to teen mothers by state, were for the year 2008.

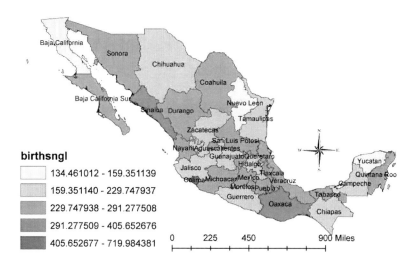

Figure 6. Births to Single Mothers per 100,000 Inhabitants by State, 2008.

Table 2. Diagnostic Tests for Spatial Autocorrelation in a Fixed-Effects Panel Data Model

	Marriage (Model 1)		Divorce (Model 2)		Birthsngl (Model 3)		Teenbirths (Model 4)	
Hypothesis	LR value	LM value	LR value	LM value	LR value	LM value	LR value	LM value
$H_0: \rho = \lambda = 0$	0.970	3.177	23.006***	0.128	11.087***	6.709**	56.710***	51.483***
$H_0: \rho = 0$	0.180	0.117	0.026	0.024	5.412**	6.701***	45.707***	40.476***
$H_0: \lambda = 0$	0.002	0.001	0.054	0.061	5.011**	6.547***	53.108***	51.403***
$H_0: \lambda = 0$, with ρ possibly $\neq 0$	0.790	0.589	22.980***	0.354	5.675**	41.298***	11.002***	148.207***
$H_0: \rho = 0$, with λ possibly $\neq 0$	0.969	0.164	22.952***	0.014	6.076***	0.025	3.602*	1.190

Notes: The spatial diagnostic tests follow the LR and LM tests developed in Debarsy and Ertur (2010).
* suggests that H_0 is rejected at 10% level; ** H_0 is rejected at 5% level; *** H_0 is rejected at 1% level.

The quasi-maximum likelihood method (Lee and Yu, 2010) was used to estimate equation (1) and Likelihood Ratio (LR) and Lagrange Multiplier (LM) tests (Debarsy and Ertur, 2010) were used to test for spatial dependence. The tests indicated the presence of spatial dependence for the models where births to single mothers and percent of births to teen mothers were used as the dependent variable. Spatial dependence was not found when the marriage rate or the divorce rate was the dependent variable. Therefore rho and lambda in equation (1) were dropped from the marriage and divorce models and both models were estimated using least squares. These tests and test statistics for spatial dependence for all four models are presented in Table 2.

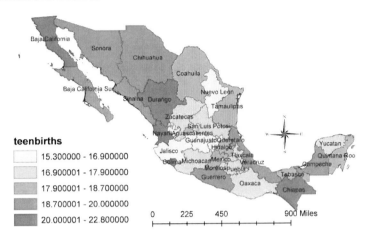

Figure 7. Percent of Births to Teen Mothers by State, 2008.

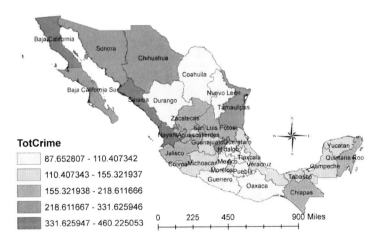

Figure 8. Total Crimes per 100,000 Inhabitants by State, 2008

In the next section, the empirical results will be presented and discussed, followed by conclusions and a summary.

FINDINGS

The spatial model in equation (1) was estimated using a panel dataset which included variables for Mexico's thirty-two state entities (31 states plus the Federal District) for the years 2005 to 2008. The total number of observations in the panel dataset was 128 (32x4). Four versions of equation (1) were estimated with different dependent variables: marriage (number of marriages by state per 100,000 inhabitants), divorce (number of divorces by state per 100,000 inhabitants), birthsngl (births per 100,000 inhabitants to single mothers), and teenbirths (percent of births to teenage mothers). The results are presented in Table 3.

Table 3. Estimation Results of the Spatially Auto-Regressive Models with Spatially Auto-Regressive Errors and State Fixed Effects

	Marriage† (model 1)	Divorce (model 2)	Birthsngl (model 3)	Teenbirths (model 4)
Variables†	Coefficient	Coefficient	Coefficient	Coefficient
rgdp	-4.675 (-0.805)‡	3.385 (1.522)	4.411 (0.907)	0.161** (2.289)
grants	-0.289 (-1.511)	0.146** (1.998)	0.067 (0.235)	0.002 (1.176)
crime	-0.022 (-0.175)	-0.114** (-2.360)	0.284* (1.897)	-0.003* (-1.846)
W*crime	-0.131 (-0.776)	0.028 (0.441)	0.530** (2.115)	0.004** (2.125)
rho			-0.711*** (-4.481)	0.786*** (11.098)
lambda			0.754*** (8.923)	-0.448** (-2.343)

†Intercepts are not reported.
‡t-statistics are in parentheses.
*Indicates significance at the 10% level.
**Indicates significance at the 5% level.
***Indicates significance at the 1% level.

In model 1, federal grants to states were negatively related to marriage rates. However, the effect was not significant. Similarly, crime in the state and crime in bordering states were negatively related to marriage rates (as given by the coefficients of *crime* and *W*crime*, respectively) although their effects were not significant.

In model 2, a decrease in a state's divorce rate was associated with an increase in crime within the state. Crime in Mexico has resulted in thousands of business closures, losses in jobs, and decreases in income. Under these circumstances, couples might not be able to afford to get divorced and have had to delay getting a divorce given the lack of job opportunities and the costs associated with living alone. Furthermore, an increase in crime within the state increases the cost of divorce since marriage partners lose the safety and security of being married with a divorce. The result is fewer divorces. Federal grants to states for education, public security, and social infrastructure, have had an opposite effect on divorces. These federal grants and the resources they have provided have enabled individuals to leave a marriage.

In model 3, an increase in the state's crime rate increased the number of births to single mothers per 100,000 inhabitants. Furthermore, an increase in crime rates in bordering states reinforced this effect. High levels of crime are not only lowering incomes and destroying jobs in Mexico but they are imposing an additional social cost with young men avoiding the financial responsibility of raising a family. Several studies have shown that children of unmarried mothers tend to grow up in poverty, have more emotional problems, and also end up with lower levels of education.

The estimate of rho in model 3 was negative, indicating that an increase in a state's birth rate to single mothers (as measured by number of births to single mothers per 100,000 inhabitants) was associated with a decrease in birth rates to single mothers in bordering states. Many single mothers may take their children and leave states where their children were born, in search of a new life and better opportunities for their children. Such migration lowers the birth rate to single mothers in a state that borders states with higher birth rates to single mothers.

In model 4, an increase in real GDP per 100,000 inhabitants led to a larger percent of teen births. Younger parents may be more optimistic about future incomes and jobs than their older counterparts when incomes are rising. They may also be first time entrants into the labor market when incomes are rising and faced with the sudden increase in earnings, be more willing to start a family or increase the existing size of their family.

A higher crime rate within a state of Mexico lowered the percent of births to teen mothers in model 4. If crime results in a disproportionate number of younger adults unable to find jobs there may be a drop in teen births. Younger adults may be the ones who delay starting a family in an environment with crime and drug-related violence. A larger percent of births to teen mothers in a state, however, was associated with more crime and violence in bordering states. Younger adults may find it easier to pick up and move from high crime states to lower-crime states before starting a family. In this case, states with a high percent of teen births would be surrounded by high crime states.

The estimate of rho in the model of teen births was found to be positive. A state with a high percent of teen births had bordering states with similar problems. This result may reflect general demographic trends within Mexico. Rising (falling) proportions of younger adults are leading to rising (falling) percents of teen births across the nation.

Conclusion

Crime and violence have taken their toll on Mexico's economy. Businesses have closed, tourism has dropped, thousands have migrated away from the violence, and foreign investment has moved to safer locations. How have marriages, divorces, births to single mothers, and percent of births to teen mothers in Mexico, been affected by this? Several studies have shown that decreases in marriages, rising divorce rates, increases in births to single mothers, and a larger percent of teen births, can have serious consequences not only for the individuals involved but for society in general. In particular, unmarried mothers and their children tend to live in poverty. Many of these children are also beset by emotional problems, depression, low levels of education, and lack of job opportunities when adults.

The following results were found in this study. (1) A state in Mexico experienced an increase in its birth rate to single mothers and an increase in percent of births to teen mothers with an increase in crime in bordering states. (2) Crime within a given state increased births to single mothers and reduced the percent of teen births in the given state. It also led to a decrease in the divorce rate within the state. (3) Increases in real GDP increased the percent of teen births. (4) A high birth rate to single mothers in a state was associated with low birth rates to single mothers in bordering states. (5) A high percent of births to teen mothers in a state was associated with a high percent of teen births in bordering states.

This study has shown that the effects of crime transcend state borders and the lives of individuals in entire regions are affected by crime. Births to single mothers and percent of births to teen mothers in Sonora, Durango, and Nayarit for example, are affected by crime and drug-related violence in Sinaloa as illustrated in figures 6, 7, and 8. Furthermore, births to single mothers per 100,000 inhabitants are low in Yucatan but high in neighboring Quintana Roo (see figure 6).

There are several important implications that can be drawn from these results. Even though crime has reduced the divorce rate in a given state, these reductions may only be temporary. When the crime and violence subside and job opportunities and incomes rise, divorce rates may very well increase in the affected regions. Furthermore, the overall divorce rate in Mexico has been increasing (see figure 2) which presents a challenge to Mexico given that divorce leads to broken homes and single spouses with children who will face future hardships.

Crime in bordering Mexican states has also increased births to single mothers in a given state as younger males who cannot find a job and have no means of raising a family, avoid the financial responsibilities of raising a family. This will impose even higher costs on Mexico as single mothers with children seek financial aid from the state. Crime in bordering states has also increased the percent of births to teen mothers in a given state as young families migrate to less crime-ridden states. As the percent of births to teen mothers rises, Mexico will face even more challenges ahead as it must provide aid for these mothers and their children. These children will also face many challenges in the future if they are not able to get an education and escape a potential life of poverty.

The results of this study have shown that the true costs of crime to Mexico, including the costs of more births to single mothers and a larger percent of births to teen mothers, far outweigh the costs that are traditionally calculated. This suggests an even greater urgency to end the drug-related violence and crime it has perpetuated. Several suggestions have been made regarding the restructuring of Mexico's legal system and continued war on the cartels waged by the Mexican army. However, with Mexico's prisons filled to capacity, corruption throughout the legal system, and resources stretched to their limits, international efforts and resources to resolve Mexico's drug wars between cartels may also be needed.

The results of this study also strengthen the case for the importance of regional/state policies regarding crime, divorce, births to single mothers, and percent of births to teen mothers, rather than a federal "one-size-fits-all" policy. States with high crime rates are next to states with high birth rates to single mothers and a high percent of births to teen mothers. Thus regional policies designed to fight crime and provide aid to unmarried and teen mothers and their children, may be better suited for specific clusters of states.

REFERENCES

Albuquerque, P.H., & Vemala, P.R. (2008). A Statistical Evaluation of Femicide Rates in Mexican Cities Along the U.S.-Mexico border. Manuscript.

Alvarado, R., Martinez, J., & Chavez, N. (2011). Mexodus—Unrelenting Violence and Lawlessness Forces Thousands of Middle-Class Mexicans to Relocate Seeking Safety inthe U.S. and in More Peaceful Regions in Mexico. *Borderzine*, Aug. 4.

Anselin, L. (1988). *Spatial Econometrics: Methods and Models*. Dordecht: Kluwer Academic Publishers.

Azaola, E., & Bergman, M. (2007). The Mexican Prison System. In W.A. Cornelius and D.A. Shirk (Eds.), *Reforming the Administration of Justice in Mexico*, 91-114. Indiana: University of Notre Dame Press.

Barham, V., Devlin, R.A., & Yang, J. (2009). A Theory of Rational Marriage and Divorce. *European Economic Review* 53: 93-106.

BBC News. (2008). Crime Damages Mexico Economy. Available at: http://news.bbc.co.uk/2/hi/7597138.stm

BBC News. (2012). Latin America & Caribbean. Q&A: Mexico's Drug-Related Violence. Available at: http://www.bbc.co.uk/news/world-latin-america-10681249.

Becker, G. (1968). Crime and Punishment: An Economic Approach. *Journal of Political Economy* 76(2): 169-217.

Becker, G. (1973). A Theory of Marriage: Part I. *Journal of Political Economy* 81(4): 813-846.

Becker, G. (1974). A Theory of Marriage: Part II. *Journal of Political Economy* 82: S11-S26.

Beittel, J.S. (2011). Mexico's Drug Trafficking Organizations: Source and Scope of the Rising Violence. *Congressional Research Service Report for Congress*. September 7.

Bitler, M.P., Gelbach, J.B., Hoynes, H.W., & Zavodny, M. (2002). The Impact of Welfare Reform on Marriage and Divorce. Working Paper 2002-9. Federal Reserve Bank of Atlanta.

Blanco, L., & Villa, S.M. (2008). Sources of Crime in the State of Veracruz: The Role of Female Labor Force Participation and Wage Inequality. *Feminist Economics* 14(3): 52-75.

Blau, F.D., Kahn, L.M., & Waldfogel, J. (2000). Understanding Young Women's Marriage Decisions: The Role of Labor and Marriage Market Conditions. Working Paper 7510. NBER Working Paper Series.

Books LLC. *Illegal Drug Trade in Mexico*. http://www.booksllc.net.

Borderland Beat. (2010). Sinaloa Cartel Takes Ciudad Juarez. April 10.

Borderland Beat. (2011). Tijuana Violence Slows as One Cartel Takes Control. September 6.

Caldwell, A.A., & Stevenson, M. (2010). Sinaloa Drug Cartel Wins Turf War in Juarez. http://www.azcentral.com/news/articles/2010/04/09/20100409cartel-wins-turf-war-juarez-mexico09-ON.html/.

Child Trends DataBank. (2007). Percentage of Births to Unmarried Women. Available at: http://www.childtrendsdatabank.org/pdf/75_PDF.pdf

Connors, M. (2012). NYT Reports That Majority of Births to Single Mothers Under the Age of 30. Available at http://blog.timesunion.com/conners/nyt-reports-that-majority-of-births-to single-mothers-under-the-age-of-30.

Control-Risks. (2011). Mexico: The Battle for the North East. http:// www.control-risks.com.

Control-Risks. (2011). Mexican Northern Border Situation Report. http://www.control-risks.com.

Cornelius, W.A., & Shirk, D.A. (eds.) (2007). *Reforming the Administration of Justice in Mexico.* University of Notre Dame Press and Center for U.S.-Mexican Studies, University of California, San Diego.

Debarsy, N., & Ertur, C. (2010). Testing for Spatial Autocorrelation in a Fixed Effects Panel Data Model. *Regional Science and Urban Economics* 40: 453-470.

Detotto, C., & Otranto, E. (2010). Does Crime Affect Economic Growth? *Kyklos* 64(3): 330-345.

Eagan, C.E. (2004). Attachment Theory or Socio-Psychological Theories? More Research Needed. Available at: http://www.personalityresearch.org/papers/eagan.html.

Fleming, G. (2008). *Drug Wars: Narco Warfare in the 21st Century.* A Producers Journal.

Freiden, A. (1974). The U.S. Marriage Market. In T.W. Schultz (Ed.), *Economics of the Family*, 352-371. Chicago and London: The University of Chicago Press.

Gamez, A., & Angeles, M. (2010). Borders Within. Tourism Growth, Migration and Regional Polarization in Baja California Sur (Mexico). *Journal of Borderlands Studies* 25(1): 1-18.

Garza,C. (2009). The New Refugees: Mexican Business Moving to Laredo. Manuscript. Texas A&M International University.

Gonzalez, L. (2005). The Determinants of the Prevalence of Single Mothers: A Cross-Country Analysis. Economics Working Papers 876, Department of Economics and Business, Universitat Popeu Fabra.

Heritage Foundation. (2012). Married Parents Have More Money than Single Moms. Available at: http://www.opposingviews.com/i/politics/national-marriage-week-marriage%E2%80%99s.

Huber, J., & Spitze, G. (1980). Considering Divorce: An Expansion of Becker's Theory of Marital Instability. *American Journal of Sociology* 86(1): 75-89.

INEGI. Anuario de Estadisticas por Entidad Federative (Yearbook of Statistics by State), published by (INEGI)—Instituto Nacional De Estadistica Y Geografia (National Institute of Statistics and Geography). Various years.

Jayson, S. (2009). Out-of-Wedlock Births on the Rise Worldwide. *USA Today*. Available at:http://www.usatoday.com/news/health/2009-05-13-unmarriedbirths_N.htm.

Korn, P. (2012). Women Choose Different Paths as Single Mothers. *The Portland Tribune,* March 15, 2012.

Kouri, J. (2011). Grenade Attack on Mexican Casino May be Part of a 'Fast and Furious Scandal.' http://www.newswithviews.com/NWV-News/news274.htm.

Latin American Herald Tribune. (2011). Banco de Mexico: Violence Has Affected Investment, Growth, November 22.

Latin America News Dispatch. (2010). Fleeing Violence, Immigrants and Restaurants Move from Tijuana, Mexico to San Diego. http://latindispatch.com/2010/01/20/fleeing-violence-immigrants-and-restaurants-move-from-tijuana-mexico-to-san-diego/.

Lecuona, G.Z. (2007). Criminal Investigation and the Subversion of the Principles of the Justice System in Mexico. In W.A. Cornelius and D.A. Shirk (Eds.), *Reforming the Administration of Justice in Mexico,* 133-152. Indiana: University of Notre Dame Press.

Lee, L.F., & Yu, J. (2010). Estimation of Spatial Autoregressive Panel Data Models with Fixed Effects. *Journal of Econometrics* 154: 165-185.

LeSage, J.P., & Pace, R.K. (2009). *Introduction to Spatial Econometrics*. CRC Press.

Lin, V.L., & Loeb, P.D. (1980). An Economic Analysis of Criminal Activities in Mexico. *Journal of Behavior Economics* 9(2): 25-39.

Marin, J.R. (2011). Crime Costly for Mexico's Businesses and Economy. *Latin American Herald Tribune,* Nov. 11.

McKenzie, R.B., & Tullock, G. (1978). Marriage, Divorce, and the Family. In *The New World of economics,* 117-131. Illinois: Richard D. Irwin, Inc.

Moloeznik, M.P. (2007). Public Security, Criminal Justice, and Human Rights: A Critique of PAN Governance in Jalisco, 1995-2006. In W.A. Cornelius and D.A. Shirk (Eds.), *Reforming the Administration of Justice in Mexico*, 463-487. Indiana: University of Notre Dame Press.

Musick, K.A. (1999). Determinants of Planned and Unplanned Childbearing Among Unmarried Women in the United States. CDE Working Paper No. 99-09. Center for Demography and Ecology, University of Wisconsin-Madison.

Nationmaster.com. (2012). Available at: http://www.nationmaster.com/graph/peo_div_per _100_mar-people-divorces-per-100-married.

O'Leary, A.O., & Sanchez, A. (2011). Anti-Immigrant Arizona: Ripple Effects and Mixed Immigration Status Households Under "Policies of Attrition" Considered. *Journal of Borderlands Studies* 26(1): 115-133.

Payan, T. (2006). *The Three U.S.-Mexico Border Wars: Drugs, Immigration, and Homeland Security*. Connecticut: Praeger Security International.

Reams, B.N. (2007). A Profile of Police Forces in Mexico. In W.A. Cornelius and D.A. Shirk (Eds.), *Reforming the Administration of Justice in Mexico*, 463-487. Indiana: University of Notre Dame Press.

Ressler, R.W., & Waters, M.S. (2000). Female Earnings and the Divorce Rate: A Simultaneous Equations Model. *Applied Economics* 32(14): 1889-1898.

Riley, M.A. (2011). The Drug War in Mexico, Now on the Blogosphere. *Bloomberg Businessweek*, Nov. 14-20, 45-47.

Rios, V. (2007). Evaluating the Economic Impact of Drug Traffic in Mexico. Manuscript.

Rios, V. (2011). Security Issues and Immigration Flows: Drug-Violence Refugees, the New Mexican Immigrants. Manuscript.

Rios, V. & Shirk, D.A. (2011). *Drug Violence in Mexico: Data and Analysis Through 2010*. Trans-Border Institute: Joan B. Kroc School of Peace Studies, University of San Diego.

Romo, R. (2011). Mexican legislator proposes 2-year marriage dissolution option. CNN.U.S. Available at: http://articles.cnn.com/2011-10-03/americas/world_americas_mexico-2-year-marriages_1_...3/21/2012.

Seelke, C.R., & Finklea, K.M. (2011). U.S.-Mexican Security Cooperation: The Merida initiative and beyond. *Congressional Research Service*, 7-5700. http://www.crs.gov

Segura, J. (2009). Crime and Fraud in Mexico. *Risk Management*, April, p. 90.

Sheffield, R. (2010). Fewer Teen Moms But More Babies Born to Single Moms Than Ever. Available at http://blog.heritage.org/2010/12/22/fewer-teen-moms-but-more-babies-born-to-single-moms.

Shirk, D.A. (2010). Drug Violence in Mexico: Data and Analysis From 2001-2009. *Trends in Organized Crime* 13: 167-174.

Shirk, D.A. (2011). Transnational Crime, U.S. Border Security, and the War on Drugs in Mexico. Speech delivered to the House of Representatives Sub-Committee on Oversight, Investigations, and Management.

Siebel, J.E. (2004). The Decision to Divorce: A Socio-Psychological View of Reasons Other Than Attachment Separation. Available at http://www.personalityresearch.org/papers /Eagan.html

Stevenson, B., & Wolfers, J. (2007). Marriage and Divorce: Changes and Their Driving Forces. *Journal of Economic Perspectives* 21(2): 27-52.

Torres, M. (2011). Businesses Flee Juarez as Customers Stop Knocking. *Mexodus,* June 31.

Tzeng, M. (1992). The Effects of Socioeconomic Heterogamy and Changes on Marital Dissolution for First Marriages. *Journal of Marriage and Family* 54(3): 609-619.

Widner, B., Reyes-Loya, M.L., & Enomoto, C.E. (2011). Crimes and Violence in Mexico: Evidence from Panel Data. *The Social Science Journal* 48(4): 604-611.

Reviewed by:

Dr. Soumendra N. Ghosh

Professor and Department Head: Economics and Finance

College of Business

Tennessee State University

In: Crime   ISBN: 978-1-62948-657-4
Editor: Michael Harry Pearson   © 2014 Nova Science Publishers, Inc.

Chapter 8

COMPARISON OF GEOSPATIAL DATA CONCERNING CRIME IN CHINA AND IN THE USA

Xinyue Ye[1], and Mark Leipnik[2]*
[1]Computational Social Science Lab, Department of Geography,
Kent State University, Kent, OH, US
[2]Department of Geography and Geology, Sam Houston State University,
Huntsville, TX, US

ABSTRACT

The use of geographic information systems (GIS) based crime mapping to analyze disseminate information about crime rates, locations and characteristics has been a growing trend and has recently become widespread enough that a comparison between major countries on several continents is possible. While comparisons between nations that are advanced users of GIS like the USA, United Kingdom, Canada and Germany is easy crime data is just starting to become available in a geocoded format in China. A comparison of crime data between China and the USA is therefore feasible. Increasingly web-based data portals are the means for researchers, law enforcement professionals and the general public to understand the pattern and occurrence of crime in their communities and nations and can be used for international comparisons as well. The rapid evolution of regional and local crime data in China and USAwill also be discussed. In particular geospatial data related to crime incident locations, patterns and characteristics will be discussed. One important focus will be the precision and accuracy of the available geospatial data.

1. INTRODUCTION

This paper focuses on the current status and future prospects for the development and dissemination of crime data in China and USA. The motivation for this is to identify opportunities for researchers and technology professionals to participate in the application of

---

* Email: xye5@kent.edu

a burgeoning GIStechnology in these two populous nations. Due to its spatial extent, massive population and rapid and transformational economic growth and expansion and the early stage of geospatial technology (GST) adoption in crime analysis, China offers more challenges and opportunities for the application of GST than arguably any other nation with the possible exception of India which is undergoing similar transformative changes but lacks as centralized, powerful and well-coordinated law enforcement system as China. When this is coupled with the complex role of the Chinese government in the process of technology adoption (Calantone, et al 2006), the importance of understanding both the character of the technology, instructive examples of exemplary applications and possible barriers to success are underscored. The term Geo-Spatial Technologies (GST) generally refers to a variety of combinations of Geographic Information Systems (GIS) and related technologies such as digital remotely sensed imagery, aerial photography, global positioning systems (GPS), and vehicle navigation and tracking systems. These technologies depend on geo-referenced data often structured into a series of co-registered layers portraying such features as topography, hydrography, jurisdictional boundaries and locations of man-made features such as streets, buildings or other "points of interest" (POI's). Chinese geospatial data is rapidly developing and is mostly related to infrastructure, cadastral and natural resources themes. Geocoded crime data is a rarity and in this regard the development of geospatial data in China is similar to the situation in the U.K. and USA in the 1980's however means such as GPS and high resolution imagery are available now to China so the process of development of advanced multi-layer GIS in China will be accelerated relative to North America and Western Europe, one can anticipate that instead of taking several decades for use of GIS in law enforcement to become widespread as was the case for early adopters that before the end of the decade China will have embraced the technology to deal with one of its most rapidly growing socio-economic challenges: the growth and spread of violent and property crime. Fraud is also quite widespread but GIS has less applicability to "white collar" type crime, although one can imagine that dissemination of imagery and details of the property ownership of certain individuals would make bribery less feasible. Of course the recent case of Bo Xilai indicates that property obtained by Chinese officials in an illegal manner might be on the French Rivera and thus hard to track down in a regional cadaster no matter how transparent and easy to navigate an on-line property ownership GIS might be (New York Times, September 27, 2013). Putting property data on-line has led to the exposure of corrupt officials such as US Congressman Randy Cunninghamof California who was living in a luxury yacht that a web search showed to be the property of a defense contractor in his district (Washington Post, August 1 2006).

   U.S. law enforcement jurisdictional issues are complex. But in most cases informal arrangements, mutual cooperation, goodwill and sharing of information between various agencies is the norm. There is also an inadvertent upside to the complex jumble and vast number of jurisdictions in the USA. In most other developed nations there is a top down hierarchical quasi-militaristic law enforcement structure, generally under a national police agency answerable to a Minister of the Interior. In contrast, in the USA there is a decentralized and in a way libertarian structure. Given the fear of tyrannical heavy-handed government by the founding fathers and going back to English history (the Sheriff of Nottingham being an exception) this inadvertent might have an upside. If so the outgrowth of the desire for small and limited government power might have an added benefit of easy access of citizens to smaller and more localized law enforcement agencies. That abuses can still occur in such a decentralized system is demonstrated by situations like that prevailing in the past in San Jacinto County. But perhaps even the overlap of multiple authorities has benefits in reducing the potential to substitute a "police state" for the sort of dynamic multifaceted but chaotic pattern of jurisdictional boundaries and authorities that has evolved in so many different ways in U.S. law enforcement.

2. CHINA CASE

Crime has increasingly become a key issue for Chinese urban areas.Analyzing and comprehending patterns of crime in urban areas has long been an important focus for criminologists, sociologists and law enforcement professionals alike in the U.S. and U.K. and Germany for example (Shaw and McKay, 1969).Although China has a much longer history of centralized jurisprudence than any "Western" nation Chinese magistrates were court officials and not as interested in comprehending crime patterns as in punishing malefactors. Historically torture was used both to extract confessions and punish crimes in a system from which the magistrate was both judge, jury and executioner as well as investigator (Van Gulik, 1957). In more recent times in China crime has declined to relatively low levels due to stringent authoritarian controls. In particular, the quasi-military organization of urban residents into "blocks' overseen by designated "block captains" responsible for observing and reporting on the activities of all residents and visitors deterred criminal acts in China. Of course the excesses of the 1950's campaign against landlords and the brutality of the *Red Guards* during the chaos of the Cultural Revolution, as well as the large number of arrests for political crimes are not included in this halcyon view of revolutionary China's crime situation (Moise, 1983, Esherick, et. al. 2006). Growing economic inequality and the influx of peasant migrants from rural areashave recently been particularly consequential for changing the nature and number of urban crimes.

By way of contrast according to the Federal Bureau of Investigation in 2008 there were 3,225 property and 424 violent crimes per 100,000 population respectively in the United States as a whole (FBI, 2008). Crime rate in 2008 in China is at 728 crimes per 100,000 population, which is about one third as high as for the USA as a whole in 2008. However, these rates are roughly 60 times and 120 times those experienced in the 1950s and 1960s. Consumption related motivations are an important driving force for the changing crime patterns during the market transition in China. In the days of the "iron rice bowl" stealing someone else's rice bowl had few attractions, but with cars, home appliances and personal jewelry becoming commonplace items in the urban landscape temptations have multiplied.

China remains safe by Western standards, but crime is more common and data are scarce. In this partial information vacuum, fear can grow in the absence of official reports and statistics and with other outlets including print, broadcast and to some extent social media subject to government censorship. Last June, hours after her students went home, Sunny Shi, the principal at a kindergarten in Shanghai's Pudong district, was bludgeoned to death in her office. The suspect was another school employee. Officially, it was as if the murder never happened. Not a word was reported publicly by Shanghai police or local media. As talk circulated among parents, the school's administrators offered trauma counseling but requested their silence. "Now the case is under police investigation," the chief administrator said by email, and "we regret that we cannot provide any details." The treatment of this case was not unusual. All across China, authorities are thought to hush up episodes like Ms. Shi's killing, which explains in large part why no one knows how much crime occurs in the world's most populous nation. But few doubt that crime is increasing as economic growth divides rich from poor and China permits more personal mobility.

"In the era of Mao, China was known as a virtually crime-free society," says Steven F. Messner, a University of Albany sociology professor who studies criminality. "To get rich is glorious" is the philosophy today, he added, "but there would be a darker side in terms of crime."China's national crime statistics show a sharp escalation in cases over the past decade, led in particular by non-violent larceny, like motor scooter and bicycle theft and purse snatching. But, as in the U.S., the official numbers also point to steep declines in violent crime, with the murder rate dropping by half between 2000 and 2009 (although the murder rate is still higher than in 1981).

Experts consider China's crime statistics both problematic and politicized. They also generally agree that the country remains safe by Western standards. Dark streets don't imply danger in China.Evidence abounds, however, that the Communist Party leadership's ideal of a "harmonious society" remains a target, not the reality. In China's growing cities, aluminum bars over windows and doors make most apartments resemble jails. Homeowners are snapping up security devices like video surveillance cameras and alarms. Anxious about kidnapping, China's newly wealthy often drive bullet-proof Land Rovers and hire martial arts experts as body guards.Television contributes to public fears with real-crime shows modeled on "America's Most Wanted" and "Cops" becoming popular. China Central Television says its law-and-order channel grabs more viewers than its sports offerings. Every day, CCTV's one-hour documentary "Legal Report" follows detectives as they crack sensational abduction, extortion and robbery cases. Its coverage of a spate of apparently random attacks on seven women this year in Hebei province, for instance, featured the nighttime capture of 23-year-old Zhang Yunshuai. His foldable knife decorated with a butterfly was shown as evidence. He was led to a subsequent interview wearing a reflective orange prison vest and cuffed at the wrists and ankles, during which he tilted his shaved head and muttered, "It's all because a women broke my heart…"

Shorter installments draw on security cameras that captured a thief shielding his pilfering hand beneath a menu in a crowded Beijing restaurant and thugs casing hotel lobbies for handbags.On these true-life crime shows, "the man" consistently finds and arrests his "perp". A popular notion holds that the censors permit these shows about China's petty unorganized criminals because they allow the leadership to demonstrate how the pervasive surveillance of the government equates to swift justice. Notably shows about more organized crimes such as narcotics smuggling, real estate fraud and environmental crimes do not exist. However there have been highly publicized trials of local officials for corruption and adulterated food cases that received nationwide publicity.

Canadian Debra O'Brien got an up-close look at China's criminal justice system after her 22-year-old daughter Diana was stabbed to death three years ago in Shanghai, bombshell case just weeks before the start of the 2008 Olympics. Authorities quickly won a confession from Chen Jun, a penniless 18-year-old migrant from rural Anhui province. Mr. Chen admitted he struggled with the aspiring model during his bungled attempt to burgle her apartment, located steps from a tea shop that recently fired him.Ms. O'Brien left impressed. She received extensive briefings by senior police and personal copies of forensic photos. The judge even sought her opinion about a death sentence for Mr. Chen. She had a face-to-face meeting with the apologetic killer. "It was all shocking and horrific, but everything was done really respectfully and transparently," Ms. O'Brien said by telephone. "You don't feel there is a lot of ego going on. People are doing their jobs."But the public wasn't offered many details. Ms. O'Brien herself admits she isn't sure of what happened to Mr. Chen but believes he became eligible for release two months ago. Mr. Chen's lawyer says he is serving life.

Pi Yijun, a professor of criminal justice at China University of Political Science and Law in Beijing, says that he sees crime rising and getting more violent, which he attributes to anger and frustration among society's have-nots. "The accepted mindset seems to think, 'fists are more powerful than reason,'" he said.But in a rare 2004 survey of crime victimization, centered on the northern city Tianjin, the University of Albany's Mr. Messner found that few people were touched personally by crimes worse than a stolen bicycle. He credits traditional features of Chinese society. "You still have a much more communitarian orientation than the extreme individualism you see in the U.S.," he said. However that survey was conducted in a less cosmopolitan urban area than Shanghai, Chungking, or Beijing and almost a decade ago during a time in China during which change has been unabated.

There are a series of factors that account for the adoption, development, spread and refinement of geospatial crime mapping technologies in the PRC. Examples of indigenous geospatial development efforts in China include development of a government wide geospatial initiative involving the adoption of GIS by numerous Chinese Government Ministries. This initiative was featured in the keynote address at the 30th annual ESRI GIs conference in July 2010 in San Diego, California. This meeting was the largest such conference in the history of the world with over 15,000 in attendance. Another example is the Chinese Government funded effort to launch high resolution remote sensing satellite systems starting in 2006 with 9 satellites lunched by 2010 in the series. These remote sensing satellites are providing digital optical and synthetic aperture radar imagery to the PRC for a wide variety of applications of GST. The prospect of a Chinese global navigation satellite system (GNSS) which is scheduled to begin launch in 2015, is an even more ambitious example of GST in China since it would be among only 4 such systems in existence and would involve launch of a minimum of 20 and possibly 30 satellites with a need to maintain that number with periodic replacements (Jacobson, 2008).

In the case of the PRC, a special issue is posed by the existence of Hong Kong and Macau which as special autonomous areas have a different development history and economic and political status. In Hong Kong in particular GIS was well developed by the territorial government by the time of reunification in 1999. These areas serve as an inspiration for the rest of China for economic development and that also applies in the GST area with respect to Hong Kong. Hong Kong serves a model for other wealthy regions in China as to how GIS and related technologies can be used in urban planning and infrastructure management (Hong Kong GIS Association, 2009). Taiwan also has a role in the PRC's adoption of geospatial technologies, but it is more equivocal. Taiwan has a very well developed GIS and remote sensing capability developed by the Council of Agriculture and Ministry of Defense with the assistance largely of the U.S. Defense Department over several decades starting in the 1970's. GIS expertise is also centered at Taiwan National University in their Planning and Building Department. The adoption of GST by Taiwan poses more of a challenge to the PRC than it serves as a model for the PRC. However, challenges often spur adoption of advanced technologies especially in the case of dual use technologies. However, in the event of closer ties, Taiwan's greater expertise in many application areas such as large scale mapping, and vehicle navigation systems, hazard reduction and precision agriculture using GST would be an asset. In any case the adoption of these technologies by Taiwan serves as a spur for "Mainland" Chinese efforts at matching the "Republic of China on Taiwan". Taiwan has its own outreach programs through the Pacific Nation Consortium in this area, but is not cooperating with the PRC currently.

3. U. S. CASE

In the United State of America, law enforcement agencies have traditionally had spatially limited jurisdictional authorities. They may also have authorities limited in other ways, for example local municipal police agencies generally do not enforce state fish and game regulations nor federal immigration and customs regulations, this later limitation is the source of on-going controversy in several states notably Arizona. The history of spatially limited jurisdiction predates the Republic. Historically, police power was vested in county government or in city police departments. State governments have authority however for overseeing training and registration requirements. In point of law, a sworn peace officer may exercise his authority anywhere within the boundaries of a state. But by tradition that authority is prescribed by the boundaries of the jurisdiction that employs him or her. County sheriffs have primacy in the absence of a viable local authority, and anytime a local authority feels they are incapable to handling a particular matter, the county sheriff can be called (in fact must provide that support). State (as in the 50 States of the Union) imposed police power generally did not exist, or if it did it was more in the nature of paramilitary force such as a State Militia (Parfaniuc, 2011). Even with more very limited number of law enforcement agencies inter-jurisdictional conflicts did exist in the 19th century, notable example being the violence in Colorado and Pennsylvania mining towns between local sheriff's supporting (or ignoring) striking miners and state militias working at the behest of mine owners and in league with Pinkerton agents and private "Coal and Iron" police (Broehl, 1983). Another legendary conflict between a local police chief (Wyatt Earp of Tombstone, Arizona) and the County Sheriff (Johnny Behan of Cochise County) had as its denouncement at the famous shoot out at the OK Corral.

A jurisdictional boundary that artificially divides an urban area can pose significant issues in US. Thus crimes occurring near the boundary of Kansas City, Kansas and Kansas City, Missouri impacts two separate states as well as two cities. Accompanying Maps of the Kansas City area show the complexity of the boundaries in this area. In addition to a state boundary that runs clear through the urban core of the area, each of the major cities spans multiple counties. Each of the major cities borders other cities (such as Overland park, Kansas). More problematic is that each city has several cities that are enclaves inside it. In one case the enclave inside Kansas City Missouri also has another small city inside of it. One of the enclaves also has a county boundary passing through it. Many times areas near the boundary of a city may be in a high crime area that is also neglected by law enforcement since the full impact of crime in the area is divided among several jurisdictions which may not cooperate effectively. In the case of such enclaves and extensions, provision of law enforcement services may be delayed, especially if the agency with primacy has to pass through multiple jurisdictions such as other cities and into other counties into which a projection of the city has penetrated.

That some law enforcement agencies have jurisdictions or authority that overlaps can further complicate inter-jurisdictional cooperation. Thus a port or airport police may cross a city to reach their jurisdiction, but crime in that area will be their primary responsibility, not that of the municipal police department in the jurisdiction in which that port or airport is located. The same is true of university police departments, school district police and many other specialized agencies. Constables in Texas have limited authority to investigate crime, but can make traffic stops inside other jurisdictions. Many communities, home owners associations and small incorporated municipalities have opted to contract with outside law enforcement agencies or private security companies further muddying which agencies have jurisdiction in any given location. The result is the not infrequent phenomena of multiple jurisdictions responding to an emergency. However, when it comes to a complex and costly investigation, many local or contract agencies prefer shifting responsibility and avoiding involvement. Conversely, some tiny law enforcement agencies assert primacy, not just in collecting traffic fines which sustain their budgets but in handling major cases. Thus the 8 person police department in Tiki Village, Texas (population 968 in 2010) took the lead on a homicide investigation as have the Weimar, Texas (also an 8 person department) and Hughes Springs, Texas (a 4 person department) Police. While local attention may be more focused and responsive, tiny departments lack specialists like homicide investigators or even detectives. Many small departments call on assistance from county and/or state agencies but have no legal obligation to do so. In the worst case clarifying responsibility can delay response, as in the Columbine High School shooting incident where over 20 jurisdictions responded ineffectively, or as in the Los Angeles area where undercover officers from one jurisdiction have been fired upon by police from another jurisdiction.

Complex jurisdictional boundaries can make determination of responsibility for investigation of crimes difficult. Another related issue is that many city governments own facilities that are not actually inside the city limits. Responsibility for criminal investigation in cases of bodies dumped in a city owned reservoir outside the city limits, in an assault on a municipal golf course outside the city limits are both examples of this issue. Many cities now exist in several counties including large ones like Chicago and Houston, Oklahoma City (located in 4 counties), Kansas City, Missouri (also in 4 counties and bordering a city in another state), Corpus Christi, Texas (located in 4 counties) but also Frannie, Wyoming (Pop. 209), Idanha, Oregon (Pop. 218) or Minerva, Ohio (Pop. 3,934). Minerva is located in three counties and joins seventy other Ohio towns located in multiple of the 88 counties in Ohio. An aspect of cities spanning county boundaries is that small "orphan" areas of county sheriff's jurisdiction often get created near the edge of these cities. These areas often receive poor service due to longer response times as well as confusion as to which jurisdiction has primary responsibility. Complex jurisdictional boundaries most of which have been created by the fiscally driven desire to annex areas with tax revenue generating potential, all tend to make provision of law enforcement services more problematic.

State police range from departments that provide a full gamut of law enforcement services in most unincorporated localities and where there are no county law enforcement agencies. This is the case in Alaska (the "boroughs" of Alaska except for the North Slope Borough lack law enforcement). In Delaware there is only one county (out of 3) that has a

Sheriff's Department (there are 39 municipal police agencies). This creates an odd situation where if one calls 911 one reaches a county sheriff's dispatcher, but if one chooses to dial the State Police troop number, a State Police officer may be dispatched to respond to an incident. This might include responsibility for high profile investigations, as well as public corruption investigations. Thus if an inmate dies in a city or county jail that is automatically investigated by the State Department of Public Safety in Texas rather than by perhaps biased local authorities. Finally, in some states like Iowa and California, the Highway Patrol is limited to only patrolling state highways and Interstates. In California there was until recently a separate State Police, but they only safeguarded State of California buildings and functions. Last and least is the Hawaiian State Police which only patrol State property like the grounds of the State Capital (it is ironic that popular television shows of the past featured two of the least empowered State Police Agencies, those of Hawaii (Hawaii 5-0 and California (CHIPS) in heroic roles that were imaginary particularly for the Hawaiian State Police).

It might seem like conflicts between law enforcement agencies over jurisdiction and incidentally power and money are ancient history. But in point of fact, a variety of factors are making jurisdiction conflicts and confusion an increasing issue today. These orphan areas are often small wedges ("groins") of unincorporated territory wedged between a large city and a county line, they are separated by a large area of municipal police jurisdiction from other areas of county sheriff jurisdiction.

Another complicating factor is the growth of numerous suburban bedroom communities and special purpose entities (like ports, airports, industrial parks, universities, school districts, malls) that form their own "police forces" or contract with existing agencies or hire off-duty peace officers or private security guards. All of these trends challenge an existing paradigm for jurisdiction. This paradigm that evolved in the middle years of the 20th century is based on a concept of a well defined urban area (typically a county seat) which has a municipal police department. The remaining areas within a county are the jurisdiction of a county sheriff and his or her deputies, the growth of intercity (and later Interstate) highways challenged this structure as the success of criminals like Dillinger and Bonnie Parker and Clyde Barrow using with high speed cars that could easily be in another county before a "posse" could be organized attests. Parenthetically, Clyde Barrow sent a testimonial letter to Henry Ford praising his Model a V8 roadster for its value in eluding local law men by passing out of their jurisdictions. Thus the State Police, Highway Patrol and State Troopers were organized, but their jurisdictions were quite limited in point of fact.

State police jurisdiction varies from only having authority on state property to exercising primary law enforcement responsibilities in the majority of the state majority of the area of the state. In fact in most states, the default law enforcement agency is the county Sheriff's Department. Likewise in many smaller incorporated towns, the county sheriff is likely to be the sole source of law enforcement services. In Texas there are more than 20 (of 254) counties without a municipal police department, including the bizarre case of Loving county which has a 3 person Sheriff's Department for its less than 100 residents (57 in the 2010 census). In New Hampshire, in towns with fewer than 3,000 population, incorporated or not, the State Police have primary jurisdiction. But in most states, county sheriffs have primary jurisdiction to this day. Large municipal police departments are often more numerous, with higher paid and better trained officers than the county Sheriff's Departments they share over lapping jurisdictions with. This tends to obscure the fact that in spatial terms, county sheriff's departments have real functional primacy in more of the United States than any other type of law enforcement agency.

An indication of the chaotic character of law enforcement in the USA is that it is impossible to pin down the actual number of law enforcement agencies. Partly this is a definitional problem: do mall cops count as a separate entity? Perhaps not, but consider the Mall of America (with over 100 officers) or Disney World (with several hundred uniformed and undercover officers) both have larger "security forces" and make more arrests that most municipal police departments (Joh, 2004). What about the situation facing police at a Community College? The Jared Lougner case at Pima County Community College shows the autonomous character of even these small special purpose police departments (Carr, 2011). But if one only considers police agencies with sworn and certified law enforcement personnel, one is still looking at something like 18,000 agencies. It is important to note that while states do not take the lead in providing law enforcement (except perhaps in Alaska) they do take responsibility for certification of peace officers. All states have an agency that tests and certifies peace officers, in Texas it is the Texas Commission on Law Enforcement Officer Standards and Education (TCLEOSE) in Ohio it is the Ohio Police Officer Training Commission. The Bureau of Justice Statistics in 2004 tackled the issue of total number of jurisdictions and came up with a count of 17,876 State and local law enforcement agencies with the equivalent of at least 1 full-time officer that were operating in the U.S.

While the Bellaire Police and Harris County Sheriffs' Department have adequate resources to handle any manner of investigation, the same is not true for the smaller Police Departments of West University Place and South Side Place. These departments have an agreement with the Houston Police Department those major crimes specifically homicides will be investigated by homicide detectives and crime scene officers from the Houston Police Department. This fact figured importantly in a major serial homicide case. The case is worth discussion since it brings to light another facet of the fragmented and often limited capability of local law enforcement agencies in the USA. The case involves the 1998 murder of a West University Place physician Dr. Claudia Benton who was murdered and raped (in that order) in her home. West University Place has a 25 member department and along with smaller neighboring enclave of Southside Place has relied on an informal arrangement with the Houston Police Department to provide support services in homicides including crime scene officers who gathered forensic evidence in the case and homicide investigators that had the ability to link the case via DNA evidence to the subsequent murder of a minister and his murder and rape of his (dead) wife in the small town of Weimar, Texas population 1,981 (a town with eight police officers) , Then a earlier murder of 87 year old Leafie Mason in Hughes Springs, Texas (Population 1,856, a town with a Police Chief, a sergeant and 3 patrol officers) was linked to him. Once it was clear that a serial killer was responsible for a series of other crimes. Ultimately, 14-15 murders were linked to Angel Resendez (also known by a dozen other aliases). It is notable that this intelligent (though psychotic) killer took advantage of the fragmented nature of local law enforcement to carry out at least 16 serious crimes in 6 states. Most the victims were in small towns or unincorporated areas (Lexington, Kentucky was an exception) located near rail road tracks. Part of his *modus operandi* was to ride the rails up from his home in the town of Rodeo in Durango, Northern Mexico and jump off at a likely spot using found objects like a hoe, a flat iron a trophy or a pick ax kill the inhabitant of an isolated residence and pile stolen goods into their car and drive the car toward or into Mexico.

Perhaps the killer did not care that West University Place was a small town with a small police department, but the fact that it, unlike the other rural areas where he committed crimes, had forensic and investigative resources available to it via its relationship with the Houston Police Department is important. How can a town like Hughes Springs, or Weimar, Texas or a Carl, Georgia (population 205, where another man was arrested for a murder that Resendez later confessed to) handle a complex homicide investigation that might appear to be a random local act of violence? Another interesting aspect of the case Resendez case which also illustrates the poor cooperation between law enforcement entities is that based on a Justice Department Inspector General Special Report (which calls him RafealResendezRamarez) he was deported 11 times from the USA starting first in 1976 and ending after he was listed on the FBI's 10 most wanted in June 1999. Although he was apprehended by the Border Patrol and photographed and fingerprinted in Santa Teresa New Mexico he was released later the same day back into Mexico, only subsequently did the Border Patrol check and find they had just released a man who had been sought for multiple murders by a FBI task force. Resendez was also arrested 17 other times by Police in 9 states and was once sentenced to 20 years in prison in Florida a sentence of which he served only a short portion before yet another deportation. It is doubtful that most of the many law enforcement agencies that dealt with him realized they were dealing with the same serial offender since he generally used a different aliases on each arrest.

The jurisdictional aspects of the case do not end there, since he was apprehended ultimately not by the FBI or Border patrol (or Mexican *federales*) but by Texas Rangers Drew Carter who traveled to New Mexico to contact his relatives who in turn prevailed on other relatives in Mexico both to share in a reward and to avoid the risk of Mexican bounty hunters taking family members hostage or using torture or extortion to obtain his return. The whole proceeding being rather odd (it also involved a faith healer in Mexico) although it resulted in Resendez voluntarily walking across a border bridge in El Paso where he was seized inside the USA but short of the border patrol checkpoint. The whole legally blurry nature of the case from beginning to end underscores the complex characterertics of jurisdictional boundaries. In any case, Resendez was executed in 2006 in Huntsville, Texas and was not extradited to any other states to stand trial for his many crimes (Roh&Leipnik, 2005).

The way that jurisdictional boundaries are defined can have a dramatic impact on reported crime rates. Looking at the regional picture of crime, many people including research and law enforcement professionals take uniform crime reports at face value without thinking critically about the numbers. Thus one might see reported that in Las Vegas the violent and property crime rate was lower than Saint Louis. Specifically, in 2010 according to FBI uniform Crime Report statistics the number of violent crimes in Saint Louis, Missouri was 6,205 for a rate of 1,747 per 100,000 population and there were 27,324 property crimes for a rate of 7,695 per 100,000 population. Conversely, in Las Vegas, Nevada in 2010 there were 12,648 violent crimes for a violent crime rate of 893 per 100,000 population and there were 43,219 property crimes for a rate of 3,051 per 100,000 population. Both Las Vegas, Nevada and Saint Louis Missouri are perceived as being large cities. But Las Vegas is served by a metropolitan police department that serves an area with a 2010 population of 1,416,401 while Saint Louis is a landlocked jurisdiction surrounded to the north south and west by other incorporated jurisdictions in Missouri and squeezed against the Mississippi River to the East which is a state and jurisdictional boundary. The City of Saint Louis cannot grow spatially and it like some older urban areas such as Detroit is actually being hallowed out as flight of population to the suburbs occurs. The population of Saint Louis was only 355,151 in 2010. Thus while Las Vegas has more crime, the crime rates for Las Vegas are lower since the population of the (in many cases unincorporated) areas served by the Metropolitan police force is much larger.

Therefore the violent crime rate in Saint Louis in 2010 was 1.95 times higher than the violent crime rate in Las Vegas and the property crime rate was 2.5 times higher in Saint Louis than in Las Vegas. Compared to national rates both of these areas had high crime rates but the rate in Saint Louis for violent crimes in 2010 was 4.3 times the national rate which indicates the basis for the perception that Saint Louis is a very violent city. A similar situation exists between the Miami, Florida area which is served by the Miami Dade metropolitan Police and the Dallas, Texas area. The jurisdiction of the Dallas police is circumscribed by a ring of incorporated cities and the swampy fold plain of the Trinity River. But to really appreciate what this means one would need to understand that Both Miami and Las Vegas have metropolitan police departments while Saint Louis and Dallas not only have municipal police departments but their cities are unlike, for example Houston, Texas or Tucson, Arizona landlocked. The term landlocked here does not imply they have no outlet to the sea, but that they cannot grow in aerial extent since they are effectively hemmed in by incorporated cities and or physical features that are not going to yield to expansion easily (in the case of Saint Louis, the Mississippi River).

So far the discussion has focused on jurisdictional authority, but one aspect of criminal justice is the location of crimes and rate of crime. The way jurisdictional boundaries are drawn may influence where a crime is ascribed as occurring. A common misconception in the minds of many is that population of census subdivisions is roughly equal. While the U.S. Census Bureau has sought to create and maintain census tracts have a population of between 2,000 and 8,000 residents for a variety of reasons this is often not the case. To understand the character of census enumeration areas one needs to comprehend the structure of Census geography starting at the block level with blocks built up into block groups, then tracts and then counties and states. There are many counties with less than the ideal number of residents for a tract (such as Loving County, Texas with only 57 residents). Other factors that complicate the situation are a tract with only 5 residents occupied by a shopping mall. It might have had more residents once but land use changes may have reduced the population. If crime rates are calculated based on population for an area like a tract that has law population but a higher level of human activity the result can be a higher crime rate.

One persistent issue with low population areas is that they generally have the highest murder rates in the USA in any given year. The reason is a result of the probably of rare events. When a rare event such as a homicide that occurs at an overall rate of perhaps 5 in 100,000 population in the USA is analyzed county by county for the approximately 3,200 counties in the USA, it will happen that some small pollution county with far fewer than 100,000 resident that is the average population of a county will have a homicide. One year it will be Kennedy County, Texas (population 388 in 2010), or Motley County, Texas (population 1,210 in 2010) or in another year it will be Catron County, New Mexico (population 3,275 in 2010) or Sublette County, Wyoming or some other less than 10,000 population county. All of these counties have experienced homicides in recent years. When put on the standard basis of murders per 100,000 population the rates are automatically above 10 per 100,000 for any county with less than 10,000 population. This means that any murder in a sub 10,000 population county yields a murder rate more than double the current national rate which was 4.8 per 100,000 population in 2010 and has been trending downward for over a decade. For example the homicide rate in Kennedy County, Texas was 255 per 100,000 population about 50 times the national average in the one year in the last decade it had a murder. To put that number in perspective the homicide rate in East Saint Louis, Missouri has ranged from 70 per 100, 000 up to 125 per 100,000. The more than 60 murders per year in this city in the early 1990's and the consistent number of homicides above 20 per year truly mark this city as a dangerous area in contrast to Kennedy County which may never see another homicide (Illinois Criminal Justice Information Authority, 1996) These homicide rates in small population counties are easily the highest rates in each state and likely not only to be higher than any other large or average population county, but exceed the most dangerous of cities such as East Saint Louis, Baltimore, Detroit, Oakland, California, etc. Of course if a murder occurred in Kennedy County every year then indeed it would be a very crime ridden place. In fact, each of the named counties had a homicide and ranked at the top for county level homicide rates in their respective states in that year, but the homicides were not repeated. In such rural areas crime rates are generally in reality lower, although local factors such as an oil and gas boom in Wyoming or the requirement in Catron county New Mexico that "every resident keep and bear arms" perhaps contributed to a rise in violent crimes in these rural counties (Vanderbilt University, 1994). While the National Atlas web site is not typically used by either geospatial or law enforcement professionals it is one of the more widely accesses sources for comparative county level crime interactive maps.

Although most of the situations discussed above are ones where the multiplicity of law enforcement jurisdictions results in problematic issues, it is far from the case that cooperation is generally lacking among law enforcement agencies. Informal cooperation is the norm among police departments and sheriff's offices. There are many examples of formal mutual aid and multi-agency task force agreements. "Hot pursuit" statutes in many states, allow law enforcement agencies to cooperate pretty well in general. Where the without question jurisdictions do cooperate is in terms of capture of fugitives where there is broad cooperation and where the Federal Marshall's Service has a broad range of authority (U.S. Marshall's Service, 2011). Were law enforcement jurisdictions do not cooperate very effectively is with respect to traffic enforcement since competition for traffic fine monies may be at stake. IN some cases officers from one jurisdiction have arrested officers from other jurisdictions for traffic offenses. The advent of YOUTUBE and similar on-line sites for viewing videos has made the dash board camera videos of such arrests popular fare. For example the gun point the arrest of a Miami Dade Police Officer driving a patrol car outside his jurisdiction after a 120 mile per hour extended chase by a Florida Highway patrol officer or the arrest of an Ohio County Sheriff by an Ohio State Trooper (CNN, 2011)

The reason that arrest of fugitives is a source of cooperation is that fleeing felons pose a threat in a community to which they have fled and generally are an easy source for a positive outcome (an arrest and extradition) although often the jurisdiction from which the felon has fled has to send an officer to the jurisdiction in which the arrest was made to return with the fugitive. With respect to traffic enforcement the issue is the potential to make money from traffic fines. This is being made worse by tight budgets. A frequent complaint is about small cities or private gated communities or shopping malls etc. that outsource patrol (including the potential to earn money form traffic stops) but do not have investigative capabilities.

REFERENCES

Bellair, P. E., & Browning, C. R. (2010). Contemporary disorganization research: An assessment and further test of the systemic model of neighborhood crime. *Journal of Research in Crime and Delinquency, 47*(4), 496-521.

Buckingham, Alan, (2006) "Speedtraps or Lifesavers" Center for Independent Studies.

Cahill, M., & Mulligan, G. (2007). Using geographically weighted regression to explore local crime patterns. *Social Science Computer Review, 25*(2), 174-193.

Carr, Forest (2011) "Loughner Case: Pima Community College Police did not Follow Their Own Guidelines" KGUN News, Tucson AZ. March 5, 2011.

Chainey, S., Tompson, L., & Uhlig, S. (2008). The utility of hotspot mapping for predicting spatial patterns of crime. *Security Journal, 21*(1), 4–28.

Charlton, M., & Fotheringham, A. S. (2009). Geographically weighted regression: A tutorial on using GWR in ArcGIS 9.3. Maynooth, County Kildare, Ireland: National Centre for Geocomputation, National University of Ireland Maynooth.

CNN (2012) "Miami Cop Accused of Driving 120 mph to Off Duty Job" http://articles. cnn.com/2011-10-29/us/us_florida-cop-reckless-driving_1_miami-officer-police-car-squad-car?_s=PM:US.

Cooper, Anderson (2009) "Highway Robbery by Law Enforcement" CNN report http://ac360.blogs.cnn.com/2009/05/05/highway-robbery-by-law-enforcement/FBI (2008). Crime in the United States, 2008 http://www2.fbi.gov/ucr/cius2008 /index .htmlFBI (2010) Uniform Crime Reports for City Agencies.FBI, (2010) "What is the Basis of FBI Authority" http://www.fbi.gov/about-us/faqs.

Hebenton, B., & Jou, S. (2010). Criminology in and of China: Discipline and power. *Journal of Contemporary Criminal Justice, 26*(1), 7-19.

Kingston, B., Huizinga, D., & Elliott, D. S. (2009). A test of social disorganization theory in high-risk urban neighborhoods. *Youth & Society, 41*(1), 53-79.

Korosec, Thomas (2007). "Small Town in Texas Relies on Lead Footed to Pay its Bills". Houston Chronicle, October 17, 2007.

Landry, Alysha, (2011) " Navajo Town Waits 3 Hours on Average for Cops" March 26, 2011 Fammington New Mexico Daily Times.

Larsen, Christina (2013) "China's New Migrant Workers Want More" *Bloomberg Business Week*. July 30, 2013.

Leipnik, Mark. (2003) Inter-jurisdictional Law Enforcement data Sharing With GIS. ESRI International GIS Conference Proceedings. San Diego Ca.

Liu, J. (2005). Crime patterns during the market transition in China. *British Journal of Criminology, 45*(5), 613-633.

Los Angeles County 2010. "Cities in LA County" http://ceo.lacounty.gov/forms/09-10%20cities%20alpha.pdf.

Matthews, S. A., Yang, T. C., Hayslett, K. L., & Ruback, R. B. (2010). Built environment and property crime in Seattle,1998-2000: A Bayesian analysis. *Environment and Planning A, 42*(6), 1403-1420.

McKinley, James. (2010) "Texas Officer Acquitted in Shooting" New York Times. April 6, 2010.

MoïseE. (1983) Land Reform in China and North Vietnam:Consolidating the Revolution at the Village Level. Chapel Hill: University of North Carolina Press, 1983. xiv, 305 pp.

New York Times, September, 27, 2013. "Bo Xilai Scandal"http://topics.nytimes.com /top/reference/timestopics/people/b/bo_xilai/index.html.

Parfaniuc, Natasha (2011) "Historical Development of Police Agencies and their Jurisdiction". http://www.scribd.com/nparfaniuc.

Roh, S. & Leipnik, M.R. (2005). Geographic Profiling and Spatial Analysis of Serial Homicides, Paper 8 in Geographic Information Systems and Crime Analysis. Edited by Fahui Wang. Published by Idea Group, Inc. Hershey, PA.

Shapiro, Rich (2009) "Sergeant Kimberley Munley Took Down Fort Hood Shooter". New York Daily News. November 6, 2009.

Shaw, C. R., & McKay, H. D. (1942). Juvenile delinquency and urban areas: A study of rates of delinquents in relation to differential characteristics of local communities in American cities. Chicago, IL: The University of Chicago Press.

Speedtrapped (2011) http://www.speedtrapped.com/ Texas Rangers Association (2009) http://www.texasrangers.org/history.asp Time Magazine (2012) "Cracking Down on Super Bowl Prostitution".http://www.time.com/time/nation/article/0,8599,2046568,00. html, U.S. Marshalls Service (2011) "Broad Range of Authority (to Arrest Fugitives) http://www.usmarshals.gov/history/broad_range.htm.

Van Gulik, R.H. (2007) Crime and Punishment in Ancient China 212 pp. Orchid Press Bangkok Thailand (Originally published in 1957.

Washington Post June 4 2006 "DOD to scrap site connected to Cunningham Scandal". http://www.washingtonpost.com/wp-dyn/content/article/2006/07/31/AR20060 73101051.html.

Weisburd, D., Morris, N., & Groff, E. (2009). Hot spots of juvenile crime: A longitudinal study of arrest incidents at street segments in Seattle, Washington. *Journal of Quantitative Criminology,* 25(4), 443-467.

Wong, K. C. (2008). The study of criminology in China, Part II. *China Report,* 44(4), 323-346.

Zhang, L., Messner, S. F., & Lu, J. (2007). Criminological research in contemporary China. *International Journal of Offender Therapy and Comparative Criminology,* 51(1), 110-121.

In: Crime
Editor: Michael Harry Pearson

ISBN: 978-1-62948-657-4
© 2014 Nova Science Publishers, Inc.

Chapter 9

PROSECUTION OF WHITE-COLLAR CRIMINALS: THEORETICAL PERSPECTIVES ON DEFENSE LAWYERS

Petter Gottschalk[*]

BI Norwegian Business School, Nydalsveien, Oslo, Norway

ABSTRACT

Defense lawyers in white-collar crime cases tend to take charge over information management at an early stage. It is difficult to overstate the importance of theory to understand white-collar crime lawyers and attorney-client relationships. Important theories include agency theory with principal and agent, transaction cost theory of cooperation, neutralization theory about guilt, attribution theory for explanations, conspiracy theory of external causes, resource-based theory for knowledge access, and stages of growth theory for relationship.

Keywords: Agency theory, transaction cost theory, neutralization theory, attribution theory, conspiracy theory, resource-based theory, stages of growth theory

INTRODUCTION

It is difficult to overstate the importance of theory to understand white-collar crime lawyers and attorney-client relationships. Theory allows analysts to understand and predict outcomes on a basis of probability (Colquitt and Zapata-Phelan, 2007). Theory also allows analysts to describe and explain a process or sequence of events. Theory prevents analysts from being bewildered by the complexity of the real world by providing a linguistic tool for organizing a coherent understanding of the real world.

[*] Petter Gottschalk, BI Norwegian Business School, Nydalsveien 37, 0484 Oslo, Norway. E-mail: petter.gottschalk@bi.no. Tel: +47 46 41 07 16.

Accordingly, theory acts as an educational device that creates insights into criminal phenomena (Colquitt and Zapata-Phelan, 2007):

> A theory might be a prediction or explanation, a set of interrelated constructs, definitions, and propositions that presents a systematic view of phenomena by specifying relations among variables, with the purpose of explaining natural phenomena. The systematic view might be an argument, a discussion, or a rationale, and it helps to explain or predict phenomena that occur in the world. Some define theory in terms of relationships between independent and dependent variables, where theory is a collection of assertions, both verbal and symbolic, that identifies what variables are important and for what reasons, and that specifies how they are interrelated and why. It identifies the conditions under which variables should be related or not related. Other scholars have defined theory in terms of narratives and accounts.

Sutton and Staw (1995: 378) define theory in the following way:

> Theory is about the connections among phenomena, a story about why acts, events, structure, and thoughts occur. Theory emphasizes the nature of causal relationships, identifying what comes first as well as the timing of such events. Strong theory, in our view, probes underlying processes so as to understand the systematic reasons for a particular occurrence or nonoccurrence. It often burrows deeply into microprocesses, laterally into neighboring concepts, or in an upward direction, tying itself to broader social phenomena. It usually is laced with a set of convincing and logically interconnected arguments. It can have implications that we have not seen with our naked (or theoretically unassisted) eye. It may have implications that run counter to our common sense.

A theory is often a statement predicting which actions will lead to what results and why. Every action that defense lawyers take, and every plan they formulate, is based on some theory in the back of their minds that makes them expect the actions they contemplate will lead to the results they envision (Christensen and Raynor, 2003).

According to Christensen and Raynor (2003), the construction of a solid theory proceeds in three stages. It begins with a description of some phenomenon we wish to understand. We wish to understand what are the roles and behaviors of white-collar attorneys. It follows with classifying aspects of the phenomenon into categories. Aspects for white-collar attorneys include themselves, their clients, attorney-client relationship, as well as situations. Finally, stage three is to formulate a hypothesis of what causes the phenomenon to happen and why.

Also Weber (2003) uses the term phenomenon, when trying to explain what is meant by theory. A phenomenon is an observable occurrence. It is the state of a thing or events that occur to a thing. A thing may change its state because of events. We try to explain or predict a phenomenon in an account. That is theory.

In this chapter, a number of management and behavioral theories are applied to white-collar lawyers. Agency theory suggests that success is dependent on the principal-agent relationship, transaction cost theory argues that costs should be kept to a minimum, neutralization theory implies that both lawyer and client may consider the crime without guilt, attribution theory argues that external reasons are often preferred, resource theory suggests that strategic resources increases the likelihood of a mild sentence, and stages of growth theory implies that individuals and organizations move through stages over time in their unethical and criminal behavior.

AGENCY THEORY WITH PRINCIPAL AND AGENT

While the client can be defined as the principal who needs a lawyer's knowledge work, the lawyer can be defined as the agent carrying out knowledge work on behalf of the client. In this perspective, the relationship between client and lawyer can be studied in terms of agency theory with principal and agent. Agency theory has broadened the risk-sharing literature to include the agency problem that occurs when cooperating parties have different goals and division of labor. The cooperating parties are engaged in an agency relationship defined as a contract under which one or more persons [the principal(s) engage another person (agent) to perform some service on their behalf]delegate some decision making authority to the agent (Jensen and Meckling, 1976). Agency theory describes the relationship between the two parties using the concept of a contract.

According to Eisenhardt (1985), agency theory is concerned with resolving two problems that can occur in agency relationships. The first is the agency problem that arises when the desires or goals of the principal and agent conflict and it is difficult or expensive for the principal to verify what the agent is actually doing. The second is the problem of risk sharing that arises when the principal and agent have different risk preferences. The first agency problem occurs when the two parties do not share productivity gains. The risk-sharing problem might be the result of different attitudes towards the use of new technologies, for example. Because the unit of analysis is the contract governing the relationship between the two parties, the focus of the theory is on determining the most efficient contract governing the principal-agent relationship given assumptions about people [e.g., self-interest, bounded rationality, risk aversion)], organizations (e.g., goal conflict of members), and information (e.g., information is a commodity that can be purchased). Conflict of interest in a principal-agent relationship can lead to unintentional or intentional corrupt behavior. Conflict of interest can distort decision making on both sides.

Garoupa (2007) applied agency theory to criminal organizations. He models the criminal firm as a family business with one principal and several agents. He has an illegal monopoly in mind where it is difficult to detect and punish the principal unless an agent is detected. Furthermore, it is assumed that agents work rather independently so that the likelihood of detection of one agent is fairly independent from that of another. An example of such agents is drug dealers in the street with the principal being the local distributor. Another example would be agents as extortionists or blackmailers distributed across a city with the principal being the coordinator of their activities providing them with information or criminal know-how.

Gross (1978: 65) discusses criminals as agents for a criminal organization in the following way:

> Although organizations are here held to be criminogenic and although courts no longer exhibit much hesitation in charging the organization itself with crime, organizations of course cannot themselves act - they must have agents who act for them. Who will the persons be who will act for organizations in their criminal behavior?

In general, agency models view corruption and other kinds of financial crime as a consequence of the principal's inability to effectively prevent the agents from abusing their power for personal gain. The main reasons for this inability are the principal's lack of information about the agents' work, lack of effective checks and balances, and ineffective enforcement and punishment for criminal executives (Li and Ouyang, 2007).

TRANSACTION COST THEORY OF COOPERATION

Attorney and client need to cooperate before, under and after the trial. Transaction costs include both costs associated with conflicts and costs associated with misunderstandings (Wright, 2006: 58):

> Transaction costs apply both to legitimate business and to illicit enterprises. They include the costs of conflicts and misunderstandings that lead to delays, to breakdowns and to other malfunctions. They can include such things as the costs of incentives, of ensuring co-ordination and the enforcement of regulations, rules or customs. In the case of a criminal organization, controlling transaction costs is necessary to keep it protected from betrayal and from prosecution. This includes the need to protect the organization from informers and from others (such as law enforcement agencies) who threaten its profits and stability. For such organizations, the use of violence and coercion is often the most effective way of reducing transaction costs.

Knowledge sharing between attorney and client can be a problem according to transaction cost theory. Transaction cost theory argues that if the costs of obtaining knowledge from others is too high, then it is more relevant to apply the knowledge one already has. Costs are measured in terms of time, effort, problems, communication and other elements that make knowledge transfer difficult or even impossible (Walker, 2010).

There are several reasons why attorney-client knowledge sharing might be associated with high transaction costs. First, individuality in the legal profession implies that each professional is rather independent of colleagues as well as clients in his or her work. By nature, law firms tend to foster a culture of individual practices. The individuality of lawyers complicates knowledge sharing. Lawyers and their departments within a law firm generally consider themselves - or want to consider themselves - as self-employed. This is reflected on the client relationship, where the client is considered a source of information, and not as a resource to find an optimal solution. Another reason why knowledge sharing might be associated with high transaction costs is the relative power of a defense counsel, which may diminish if he or she lets the client learn the same kind of skills and gain the same kind of insights. Amongst professionals, power is part of their skills as knowledge and skills offer the lawyer power. If too much knowledge is shared, then transaction costs may emerge in the form of criticism from the client. There are many more reasons why knowledge sharing is associated with high transaction costs. As a result of the individualistic nature of the legal profession, there is a lack of sufficient trust and loyalty between attorney and client in order to accommodate effective knowledge transfer. Often, knowledge workers need to know each other to trust each other.

NEUTRALIZATION THEORY ABOUT GUILT

Even if the defense lawyer thinks his client is guilty, it can make sense to help the client into a state of mind of not feeling guilt. Guilt is a feeling that can be reduced or eliminated by applying neutralization techniques. A prosecuted white-collar criminal will behave more professional in court if he or she does not feel too much guilt. The defense lawyer may try to convince the client of less guilt than previously perceived.

Criminals apply techniques to make them feel they have done nothing wrong. These techniques are called neutralization techniques, where the feeling of guilt is neutralized. Neutralization theory is the umbrella for all these techniques. In their original formulation of neutralization theory, Sykes and Matza (1957) proposed five techniques of neutralization: denial of responsibility, denial of injury, denial of the victim, condemnation of the condemners, and appeal to higher loyalties. Later, other researchers added the metaphor of the ledger and a technique named the defense of necessity (Siponen and Vance, 2010).

The following neutralization techniques are included in neutralization theory (Bock and Kenhove, 2011; Heath, 2008; Siponen and Vance, 2010):

1. *Denial of responsibility.* The offender here claims that one or more of the conditions of responsible agency were not met. The person committing a deviant act defines himself as lacking responsibility for his actions. In this technique, the person rationalizes that the action in question is beyond his/her control. The offender views himself as a billiard ball, helplessly propelled through different situations.

2. *Denial of injury.* The offender seeks to minimize or deny the harm done. Denial of injury involves justifying an action by minimizing the harm it causes. The misbehavior is not really serious because no party suffers directly as a result of it.

3. *Denial of victim.* The offender acknowledges the injury, but claims that the victim is unworthy of concern. Any blame for illegal actions are not justified because the violated party deserves whatever injury they receive.

4. *Condemnation of the condemners.* The offender tries to accuse his critics of questionable motives for criticizing him. According to this technique, one neutralizes his or her actions by blaming those who are the target of the action. The offender deflects moral condemnation to those ridiculing corporations by pointing out that they engage in similar disapproved behavior.

5. *Appeal to higher loyalties.* The offender denies the act was motivated by self-interest, claiming that it was instead done out of obedience to some moral obligation. This technique is employed by those who feel they are in a dilemma that must be resolved at the cost of violating a law or policy. In an organization context, an employee may appeal to organizational values or hierarchies. For example, an employee could argue that he/she must violate a policy in order to get his/her work done.

6. *Normality of action.* The offender argues that everyone else is doing it, thus he has done nothing wrong.

7. *Claim to entitlement.* The offender claims he was in his right to do what he did, maybe because of a very stressful situation or because of some misdeed perpetrated by the victim. This is defense of necessity, which is based on the justification that if

the rule-breaking is viewed as necessary, one should not feel guilty when committing the action.

8. *Legal mistake.* The offender argues the law is wrong, and what he did should indeed not be illegal. One may break the law because the law is unreasonable.

9. *Acceptable mistake.* The offender argues that what he did is acceptable given the situation and given his position. The person feels he has been doing so much good for the organization, that he should be excused for more wrongdoings than other people. He feels that he has done so much good, that his crime is a minor matter that should be ignored. This is in line with the metaphor of the ledger, which uses the idea of compensating bad acts with good acts. That is, an individual believes that he/she has previously performed a number of good acts and has gained a surplus of good will, and as a result of this, can afford to do some bad actions. Executives in corporate environments neutralize their actions through the metaphor of the ledger by rationalizing that their overall past good behavior justifies occasional rule-breaking.

10. *Dilemma tradeoff.* The offender argues there was a dilemma for him where he made a reasonable tradeoff before committing the act. Tradeoff between many interests resulted in the offence. Dilemma represents a state of mind where it is not obvious what is right and what is wrong to do. For example, the offence might be carried out to prevent a more serious offence to happen.

Justifications are socially constructed accounts that individuals who engage in criminal acts adopt to legitimate their behavior. Justifications are beliefs that counteract negative interpretations by articulating why the acts are justifiable or excusable exceptions to the norms (Aguilera and Vadera, 2008).

ATTRIBUTION THEORY FOR EXPLANATIONS

In addition to establishing the facts and identifying relevant laws for white-collar crime, behavioral explanations in terms of motives are of importance in the court. Motives are reasons for actions. If the motive is personal greed, it is not so good. If the motive is environmental pressure or even necessity, then it is better. Motives in terms of causal relationships between cause and effect may be subject to interpretation by lawyer and client. Attribution theory can help us understand what is going on here.

Attribution theory is concerned with how one chooses explanatory factors for a phenomenon. Usually a distinction is made between internal and external explanatory factors. If a criminal act occurs, then the act can be explained by internal factors that are attributed to the criminal, or by external factors that are attributed to the environment and the situation.

Attribution theory is about identifying causality based on internal and external circumstances (Eberly et al., 2011: 731):

> Identifying the locus of causality has been at the core of attribution theory since its inception and has generated an extensive research stream in the field of organizational behavior. But the question emerges whether the "internal" and "external" categories capture the entire conceptual space of this phenomenon.

Based on this argument, Eberly et al. (2011) suggest there is a third category in addition to internal explanation and external explanation, which is labeled relational explanation. These three categories of attributes can be explored to find causal explanations regarding how persons react in criminal situations.

Attribution theory is a part of social psychology that studies how humans spontaneously place reasons, guilt and responsibility in situations that occur. The fundamental attribution error is a term used on overemphasis on person factors rather than situational factors to explain behavior (Ho et al., 2010).

CONSPIRACY THEORY OF EXTERNAL CAUSES

One of the most widely held theories of organized crime today in the United States are known as the *alien conspiracy theory*. This theory blames outsiders and outside influences for the prevalence of organized crime in society. Over the years, unsavory images, such as well-dressed men of foreign descent standing in shadows with machine guns and living by codes of silence, have become associated with this theory. The alien conspiracy theory posits that organized crime (the Mafia) gained prominence during the 1860s in Sicily and that Sicilian immigrants are responsible for the foundations of U.S. organized crime, which is made up of twenty-five or so Italian-dominated crime families (Lyman and Potter, 2007).

In line with this thinking, a lawyer and/or a client may introduce a conspiracy thinking about the police, the prosecution, the court, the prison and all other organizations involved in criminal handling. It can be argued that prestige has entered into the heads of crime investigators, that the court wants to set an example, and that everyone is out to get the white-collar suspect, including the press and other media. Both the defense lawyer and the client might be convinced – or at least express – that there is a larger conspiracy surrounding and driving the white-collar crime case.

Lyman and Potter (2007: 60) discuss this theory in the following way:

> Although some skeptics insist that the alien conspiracy theory was born out of hysteria incited by the media, it has received considerable support over the years from federal law enforcement organizations, public officials, and some researchers. It has been argued, however, that federal law enforcement organizations have self-serving reasons to promulgate this theory: It explains their inability to eliminate organized crime, it disguises the role of political and business corruption in organized crime, and it provides fertile ground for new resources, powers, and bureaucratic expansion.

Lombardo (2002) has challenged the alien conspiracy theory as an explanation of the origin of organized crime in America, as he reviewed the history of Black Hand (organized crime group) activity in Chicago in the early 20th century, arguing that the development of Black Hand extortion was not related to the emergence of the Sicilian Mafia, but rather to the social structure of American society.

RESOURCE-BASED THEORY FOR KNOWLEDGE ACCESS

White-collar criminals tend to have access to more resources than street criminals. Resources enable a more favorable process and verdict. Resources include knowledge, money, network and alliances. The defense lawyer is an important resource to the defendant. According to the resource-based theory, performance differences in court cases can be attributed to the variance in the defendant's resources and capabilities. Knowledge that is valuable, unique, difficult to imitate, combinable, difficult to substitute and exploitable can provide the basis for attorney's competitive advantages. The essence of the resource-based theory of the defense lies in its emphasis on the internal resources - here knowledge - available to the defense, rather than on the external opportunities and threats dictated by the prosecution and the court.

The resource-based view posits that competitiveness comes from unique bundles of tangible and intangible assets that are valuable, rare, imperfectly imitable, non-substitutable, combinable and sustainable.

STAGES OF GROWTH THEORY FOR RELATIONSHIP

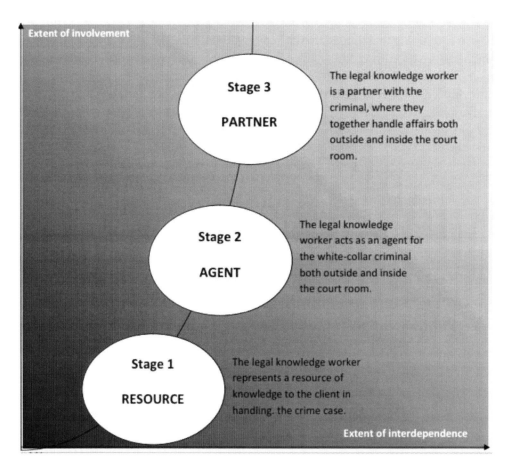

Figure 1. Stages of lawyer involvement in client affairs.

The powerful concept of stages of growth is extremely important in management research. To capture this concept, we introduce stages of growth modeling and present elements of a growth stage theory exemplified with the case of lawyer-client relationships. We propose that a relationship may change over time as caused interactions and challenges. The changes occur in terms of discrete stages with their own unique characteristics.

Researchers have struggled for decades to develop stages of growth models that are both theoretically founded and empirically validated (e.g., Nolan, 1979; King and Teo, 1997). However, stages of growth models have the potential of creating new knowledge and insights into organizational phenomena. Such models represent theory-building tools that conceptualize evolution over time in a variety of areas. For researchers, a stage model represents a theory to be explored and empirically validated. For practitioners, a stage model represents a picture of evolution, where the current stage can be understood in terms of history and future.

A model of client-lawyer relationships is presented below in terms of three stages. The stages are resource stage, agent stage, and partner stage, respectively.

COMPARISON OF THEORETICAL PERSPECTIVES

Theories presented above can be summarized in the table below. For each theory, a few statements typically indicating theory core are listed in the second column. The table can be applied to evaluate one specific white-collar lawyer at a time. Evaluation is carried out by answering yes or no to each statement, and then arguing the case for yes or no in the column for explanation.

Table 1. Theories to provide insights into the role of a white-collar crime lawyer

Theory	Characteristics	Yes/No	Explanation
Agency Theory Principal= Criminal Agent= Lawyer Opportunistic behavior?	The principal is unable to know what the agent is doing. The agent is unable to know what the principal is doing. Principal and agent are in a state of goal conflict. Principal and agent have different degrees of risk willingness.		
Transaction Cost Theory Huge costs of cooperation?	Client crime case is quite unusual and rare. Client has a hard time communicating with lawyer. Lawyer has a hard time communicating with client.		
Neutralization Theory Defendant feels not guilty?	Lawyer thinks client is not guilty because there is no injury, no victim, no responsibility etc.		

Table 1. (Continued)

Theory	Characteristics	Yes/No	Explanation
Attribution Theory External explanatory factors?	Lawyer argues external factors – for which the client is not responsible – are reasons for the crime.		
Conspiracy Theory External conspiracy against client?	Lawyer argues that the police and prosecutor have decided to win and defeat the white-collar defender at all costs. Lawyer argues there is substantial prestige invested in the case on the prosecution side.		
Resource Theory Better access to a fair trial?	Lawyer pre-presents the case in the media. Lawyer is extra paid by client. Lawyer knowledge is unique, non-substitutable, non-imitable exploitable, valuable, non-transferrable, and combinable.		
Growth Theory At what stage is the relationship?	Lawyer is a resource to the client. Lawyer is an agent for the client. Lawyer is a partner with the client.		

ABOUT THE AUTHOR

Petter Gottschalk is professor of information systems and knowledge management in the Department of Leadership and Organizational Management at BI Norwegian Business School. Dr. Gottschalk has published a number of books and research articles on crime and policing. He has been managing director of several corporations, including ABB Data Cables and Norwegian Computing Center.

REFERENCES

Aguilera, R. V. and Vadera, A. K. (2008). The Dark Side of Authority: Antecedents, Mechanisms, and Outcomes of Organizational Corruption, *Journal of Business Ethics*, 77, 431-449.

Bock, T. D. and Kenhove, P. V. (2011). Double Standards: The Role of Techniques of Neutralization, *Journal of Business Ethics*, 99, 283-296.

Christensen, W. and Crank J. P. (2001), Police work and culture in a nonurban setting: An ethnographical analysis, *Police Quarterly*, 4 (1), 69-98.

Colquitt, J. A. and Zapata-Phelan, C. P. (2007). Trends in theory building and theory testing: A five-decade study of the Academy of Management Journal, *Academy of Management Journal*, 50 (6), 1281-1303.

Eberly, M. B., Holley, E. C., Johnson, M. D. and Mitchell, T. R. (2011). Beyond internal and external: A dyadic theory of relational attributions, *Academy of Management Review*, 36 (4), 731-753.

Garoupa, N. (2007). Optimal law enforcement and criminal organization. *Journal of Economic Behavior & Organization*, 63 (3), 461-474.

Gross, E. (1978). Organizational crime: A theoretical perspective, *Studies in Symbolic Interaction*, 1, 55-85.

Eisenhardt, K. M. (1989). Agency Theory: An Assessment and Review. *The Academy of Management Review, 14*(1), 57-74.

Ho, V. T., Ang, S. and Straub, D. (2003). When Subordinates Become IT Contractors: Persistent Managerial Expectations in IT Outsourcing. *Information Systems Research, 14*(1), 66-86.

Jensen, M. C. and Meckling, W. H. (1976). Theory of the firm: Managerial behavior, agency costs and ownership structures. *Journal of Financial Economics, 3*(4), 305-360.

Lyman, M. D. and Potter, G. W. (2007). *Organized crime*, 4th edition, Pearson Prentice Hall, Uppler Saddle River, New Jersey.

Li, S. and Ouyang, M. (2007). A Dynamic Model to Explain the Bribery Behavior of Firms, *International Journal of Management*, 24 (3), 605-618.

Lombardo, R. M. (2002). Black hand: Terror by letter in Chicago. *Journal of Contemporary Criminal Justice*, 18 (4), 394-409.

King, W. R. and Teo, T. S. H. (1997). Integration Between Business Planning and Information Systems Planning: Validating a Stage Hypothesis. *Decision Science, 28*(2), 279-308.

Nolan, R. L. (1979). Managing the crisis in data processing. *Harvard Business Review, 57*(2), 115-126.

Siponen, M. and Vance, A. (2010). Neutralization: New Insights into the Problem of Employee Information Systems Security Policy Violations, *MIS Quarterly*, 34 (3), 487-502.

Sutton, R.I. and Staw, B. M. (1995). What theory is not, *Administrative Science Quarterly*, 40, 371-384.

Sykes, G. and Matza, D. (1957). Techniques of Neutralization: A Theory of Delinquency, *American Sociological Review*, 22 (6), 664.670.

Walker, K. (2010). A Systematic Review of the Corporate Reputation Literature: Definition, Measurement, and Theory, *Corporate Reputation Review*, 12 (4), 357-387.

Weber, M. (1922). Wirtschaft und Gesellschaft. In G. Albrecht (Ed.), *Grundriss der Sozialökonomik*. Tübingen, Germany: J. C. B. Mohr.

Wright, A. (2006). *Organised Crime*. Devon, UK: Willan Publishing.

In: Crime
Editor: Michael Harry Pearson

ISBN: 978-1-62948-657-4
© 2014 Nova Science Publishers, Inc.

Chapter 10

ARE MINORITIES OVER-REPRESENTED IN CRIME? TWENTY YEARS OF DATA IN ISÈRE (FRANCE)

Mirta B. Gordon[1,*], *Sebastian Roché*[2] *and Marie-Aude Depuiset*[1,2]
[1]Univ. Grenoble Alpes, CNRS-LIG/AMA,
Domaine Universitaire, Grenoble Cedex, France
[2]CNRS, Institut d'Etudes Politiques, PACTE,
Domaine Universitaire, Grenoble Cedex, France

Abstract

We address the question of whether minorities are over-represented in delinquency in France, based on an exhaustive database of all the juveniles below 19 years old convicted for serious crimes (liable to imprisonment according to the French Law) in the period 1985-2005 in Isère (about 1 million inhabitants), one of the French Departments. Serious crimes have a higher clearance rate than petty crimes and are thus less biased by police differential selection because authors are actively searched.

Since neither religion nor ethnic traits are available in French legal documents, it is not possible to trace back the offenders' geographic, religious or ethnic origin accurately. Following the practice of the INSEE (the French National Institute of Statistics and Economic Studies) we use the birthplace of the parents as a proxy to differentiate between juveniles that belong to stigmatized minorities – which in France are mostly African and Turkish immigrants and their offspring – from those of European origin. Our bare data are consistent with the widespread opinion that stigmatized minorities are over-represented in crime: they represent about 50% of the convicted juveniles in our database, while in the same period their proportion in Isère slowly declined from 25% to less than 20% of the juvenile population.

We explore whether this apparent over-representation remains upon restricting comparisons to populations with similar socioeconomic status. According to our estimations based on the parents' status, the overwhelming majority of offenders (all origins taken together) live in urban areas, below the poverty threshold. Based on detailed census data of the same period in Isère we estimate that among the poor urban juveniles, minorities represent roughly half of the population. Thus, within the juvenile sub-populations of similar socioeconomic status, there is no evidence of minority over-representation among those convicted of serious crimes.

*E-mail address: mirta.gordon@imag.fr (Corresponding Author)

Keywords: Poverty, sentencing, disparity, race/ethnic bias, juvenile court

Introduction

In almost every Western country some minority groups are disproportionately likely to be arrested and convicted [1]. Blacks and Latinos are about 7 times more likely to be incarcerated in the US than Whites. In England and Wales the minorities are Blacks and Asians; Arabs, South Americans and East-Europeans in Sweden; etc. Are minorities victims of segregation by the penal system due to racial profiling [2], or are there other reasons (cultural [3], economic [4], genetic [5], etc.) for this overrepresentation? These questions are often raised in public debates (see for example [6]). In contrast, partly due to the lack of data about the origin and socio-economic characteristics of the incriminated populations, French academic research addresses this issue very cautiously. Since it is very difficult to obtain information about the racial, ethnic, religious or geographic origin of individuals in Europe, sometimes the assertions are based on unclear criteria like the family names or visual perception by the police (like in a recent study [7] concerning England and Wales).

There is an ongoing debate in France – as well as in other developed countries – in which some politicians, journalists and scholars claim that minorities issued from recent immigration currents are over-represented in prisons. Such affirmations underpin the idea that minorities have more pronounced criminal inclinations that the native population. These claims would need clear-cut definitions of what is meant by "native" population, specially in France, where a large proportion of the inhabitants are issued of quite recent immigration currents of the XIXth and XXth centuries. According to a recent publication [8] 10% of the French population in 2008 are direct descendants (born in France) of immigrants (born abroad); the latter represent 8% of the population.

Impartiality of the criminal justice system (CJS) has been challenged. It has been argued [9] that differential deployment of police and other criminal justice officials against Black and Latinos is the primary factor underlying their overrepresentation in US prisons. Recent studies [10, 11] show that the representation of minority youth along the justice system process – arrest, intake, detention, adjudication and disposition – increases at each stage of the CJS process.

Poverty and educational level are highly correlated with delinquency. In a recent paper, Johnson and Betsinger [12] point out that Asian Americans, who have a higher mean level of education and lower rates of poverty and unemployment than other minority groups, are underrepresented in official crime statistics. Notice that poverty seems to have a high correlation with imprisonment, but in the mentioned work there are no direct measures of socioeconomic status. This is a common trait of criminological studies. Quoting Zatz [13]: *"Class is one of the paramount sociological variables, yet our measures of it in criminal justice data are abysmal"*.

In most studies that include poverty as an explicative variable, the individuals' actual incomes are not precisely known. The offenders are given the average poverty level of the neighborhood where they live (see for example [14, 15, 16, 17, 18, 19, 20, 21, 22] and papers cited therein). This is a reasonable practice for normally distributed variables, and within small, homogeneous enough, neighborhoods. At more aggregated spatial levels, since inequality distributions have heavy tails [23, 24], the mean is *not* a good estimate of individuals' characteristics because there are more cases far from the average than in gaussian distributions. Using the mean of the income distribution to characterize the population's poverty level may lead to incorrect conclusions since it overestimates the living standard of the poorest. Also, delinquents are not necessarily typical individuals of their neighborhoods, so that average descriptors of non-homogeneous areas may not be well correlated with the characteristics of the offenders.

The correlation between poverty and offending behavior has been investigated using other indicators. For example, using data generated by a randomized housing-mobility experiment in Baltimore, Ludwig et al [20] present evidence that relocating families from high- to low-poverty neighborhoods reduces juvenile arrests for violent offenses by 30 to 50 percent of the arrest rate of controls. Another indirect evidence of the incidence of poverty on crime is the fact that in big cities (where crime rates are larger) one third to one half of the urban effect on crime (with respect to rural crime rates) can be explained by the presence of more female-headed households in cities [25]. These are generally poorer than households where the two parents are present.

Another interesting strand of research focus on the fact that white and black communities are highly segregated [26, 27, 28, 29, 30, 31, 32, 33]. Their poverty levels are so different that they do not overlap in the majority of US cities. Analyzing homicide data, Krivo and Peterson [34] argue that usual regressions may not capture the main determinants of crime. They find that "... *racial differences in disadvantage are so great that it is impossible to assess what the effects for whites would be if they were as disadvantaged as the average African American in most urban areas*".

There are very few studies of the influence of race or ethnicity in the CJS of European countries. Since it is very difficult to obtain information about the racial, ethnic, religious or geographic origin of individuals in Europe, most studies are based on unclear criteria like family names. For example, members of racial minorities in England and Wales, particularly Blacks (according to visual perception by the police), are stopped and searched by the Police far more frequently than the corresponding disparity in offending [7]. In a panel data analysis of violent crime including 45 different countries in homicide regressions and 34 in robbery regressions, over 24 years, Fajnzylber et al. [35] find that increases in income inequality raise crime rates, that crime tends to be counter-cyclical (stagnant economic activity induces heightened crime rates), and it is self-perpetuating (high past crime rates are correlated with actual crime rates, i.e. criminal inertia is significant). Similar conclusions are presented in [17] and [36]: violent crime is found to be poverty-driven while some forms of property crimes are found to be largely opportunity-driven.

In the present paper we examine the relationship between criminality, poverty and minorities in France. Our results are based on empirical data that include *individual* characteristics and sentencing outcomes of juveniles convicted of serious crimes in Isère (one of the 96 Metropolitan French Departments) in the 20-years period ranging from 1985 to 2005. Juveniles are among the most active offenders for street crimes according to the national statistics of most countries. Serious crimes (liable to imprisonment) have a higher clearance rate than petty crimes, and are thus probably less biased by police differential selection, because authors are actively searched (while petty crimes authors are often found due to denunciation). This assumption is supported by a recent study [37] of juvenile arrests based on the FBI's National Incident-Based Reporting System that revealed indeed no direct evidence of racial bias in juvenile arrests for violent crimes.

This is the first time, to our knowledge, that such a study is carried out in France. In contrast with North American studies, where discriminated minorities are mainly Blacks and Latinos, in France they are mainly Muslims [38] of first and second generation, descendants of African – mostly from Maghreb – and Turkish immigrants. Since there are neither ethnic nor racial indications in French official documents, we classify the convicted juveniles as belonging to the majority or the stigmatized minority populations according to the parents' birthplaces – i.e. their geographic origin – a practice introduced by the French National Institute of Statistics and Economic Studies (INSEE). In this paper we label AT the African and Turkish stigmatized populations, hereafter also referred to as minority population, and group together under the label EU the population of European origin (including springoff of French nationals), referred to as the majority population in the following.

Our bare data are consistent with the widespread opinion that minorities are overrepresented among the convicted population, *with respect to their share in the overall population*. But, according to our estimations presented below, our data correspond to *juveniles* belonging to the *poorest population* living in *urban* areas. One should compare populations with similar sociological characteristics. This is why we address the following question: is the proportion of AT juvenile delinquents larger than the proportion of AT urban juveniles with similar poverty levels?

The poverty levels of youngsters according to their origin is an information unavailable in France. The statistics published by the INSEE give the poverty distribution among immigrants and non-immigrants, aggregating together, in the latter category, households that belong to the stigmatized minorities and households of European immigrants. We circumvent these lacks by combining census information of the juvenile population in Isère with recently published poverty levels of households according to their geographic origins. Our estimations allow us to define a juvenile reference population whose socioeconomic status is similar to that of the delinquents. We compare the offenders' majority and minority sub-populations against this reference population.

The article is organized as follows: in section 1 we describe the database and the pertinent characteristics of the offenders. In section 2 we detail how we estimate the offenders' poverty level using the available information about their parents and siblings. In section 3 we determine the composition of the reference population. The main result of our paper is presented with a graphic in section 4. Our conclusions are discussed and summarized in section 5. Some technical data and results are left to the Appendices.

1.   The Sentences Database (Isère, France: 1985-2005)

Our database[1] contains information about all the sentences (1 868) passed on juveniles (below 19 years old) tried for serious crimes during the 20 years period 1985-2005 in the three judicial jurisdictions of the French Department Isère – population according to the

---

[1] A report with descriptive statistics of the data set has been published in French [39].

1990 census published by the INSEE: $1,016$ million inhabitants; 8% foreigners[2]; $283\,413$ juveniles less than 20 years old, among which $149\,684$ children 10-19 years old (15% of the population) –.

Detailed information has been encoded through 217 numerical descriptors and additional textual fields. The considered offenders are charged with one of the 8 more frequent crime types that are punishable with prison according to the French Law (see Table 1). These offenses belong to two categories: *serious offenses* which may entail up to 7 years imprisonment, and *crimes*, for which prison sentences may be even longer. We will call them both indifferently either *crimes* or *offenses* in the following.

Since we are interested in the criminal population, we only include data of actually convicted juveniles, declared guilty by the Courts; we excluded:

- 264 records of convicted juveniles for which we could not trace back their origin, as explained in section 1.1,

- 8 records where prosecution has been barred under the statute of limitations[3],

- 12 records of offenders not yet tried,

- 90 acquittals,

leaving thus $1\,494$ records for our analysis.

1.1. Offenders' Origins: Minority (AT) and Majority (EU)

Different minority populations have existed historically in France. In the recent decades, South Italian, Spanish and Portuguese immigrants, nowadays quite well integrated, have suffered from discrimination until the sixties. According to reference [38], since the independence of Algeria in 1962 the main stigmatized populations are mainly muslims, immigrated from Africa and Turkey and their offsprings.

Most of the sentences in our database (precisely 84.5%) concern juveniles that are French, either because their parents or themselves are French-born or because they have adopted the French nationality. Since neither religion nor ethnic traits are available in French documents, it is not possible to trace back the offenders' geographic, religious or ethnic origin accurately. In this paper we apply the same criteria as the INSEE (the French National Institute of Statistics and Economic Studies) to characterize the origin of the juveniles: we use the birthplace of the parents as a proxy to label whether an individual belongs or not to the discriminated minority. More precisely, we label AT individuals having at least one parent born either in **A**frica (Maghreb —Algeria, Morocco, Tunisia— or other African countries) and/or in **T**urkey. In contrast, we assume that individuals whose parents are **Eu**ropean, born either in France or in another European country, belong to the majority

---

[2]Foreigners and immigrants cover two different concepts: a foreigner is a French resident that does not have the French nationality; an immigrant is born abroad and entered France with a foreign nationality. Thus, not naturalized immigrants are counted both as immigrants and as foreigners while French naturalized ones are only counted as immigrants. Conversely, a foreigner born in France – i.e. with foreign parents – who adopted the French nationality is neither counted as foreigner nor as immigrant.

[3]In French: prescription de l'action publique

group (hereafter denoted EU). In the next section we discuss the pertinence of this classification. Notice that the AT population is thus composed of immigrants and immigrant offsprings. The EU population is composed of native French offsprings and of European immigrants and their offsprings. We are unable to trace back the origins beyond one generation because we do not have any information about the grandparents of the juveniles. Those with French born parents are thus considered French. This means that we are unable to track back possible discrimination against individuals of the third generation of immigrant descendants. This is not a strong drawback for our study. The main AT immigration current dates back to the sixties, and was mainly composed of males. The women entered France mostly after 1976, when family reunification was again authorized, after complete suspension of immigration in 1974. Thus, given the covered period (1985-2005) we expect that there are very few, if any, grandchildren with African or Turkish ancestors in our database.

Following the criteria used by the INSEE in some of their statistics, criteria also used in [40] and in a recent large survey [41] called TeO ("Trajectoires et Origines") covering 22 000 persons living in Metropolitan France in 2008, we adopted the following criteria to attribute an origin to each individual:

- if both parents are born in Europe, the origin is EU,

- if one of the parents is born in Europe and the other abroad, the offender is attributed the origin of the latter,

- if only one parent's birthplace is known, it determines the offender's origin,

- if both parents birthplaces are unknown, and the offender is not French, we assume that the origin is given by the offender's nationality,

- if both parents' birthplaces are unknown, and the offender is French, we exclude the record from our study because nationality in our database is a poor indicator of the origin.

Besides the offenders with unknown geographic origin we also excluded from the present analysis those with Asian origin. They constitute a too small subset of our database (16 cases) to give significant results. Also, according to [42] – based on the already mentioned TeO survey –, the burden of being Asiatic in France is slighter than that of being AT[4]
.

After data streamlining, our study is based on 1 478 sentencing dispositions concerning juveniles in Isère in the period 1985-2005[5] which, according to the above criteria, are classified into 677 sentences concerning EU, 801 concerning AT, juveniles.

Among the 1 478 records, 986 correspond to lone offenders (476 EU, 510 AT) and 203 to group offenses (two or more offenders). The latter have given raise to 492 individual sentences (i.e. there are in average 2.42 juvenile offenders per group. Adults also participate in some of these groups, but we do not have any information about the corresponding

---

[4]This burden is measured by the proportion of persons that answered "often" or "sometimes" to the question (translated from reference [42]): "Have you suffered from discriminative treatments during the last five years?"

[5]We do not have complete information for all the 1 478 cases. Some of the results are thus based on subsets of these data. For example, 105 records do not have any information indicating whether the offender is or not recidivist.

sentences. Thus, we do not know precisely the actual size of the groups, only the number of juveniles that participate in them.).

Interestingly, 1 249 sentences correspond to offenders that are French nationals: 645 EU (95.3% of the EU) and 604 AT (75.4% of the AT). Clearly, nationality is a poor proxy for the juvenile offenders' origins.

Our classification suffers from two pitfalls. We are blind to skin color, which has been identified as one of the strongest reasons of discrimination in France [42]. We consider EU the Black native French population, mostly descendant of African slaves in the French Antilles. This should not affect qualitatively our results because the overall population issued from the French Territories and Departments living in the Metropolitan (European) French Area in 1999 is smaller than 0.6%. In Isère they are less than 0.4%. Another miscounting arises from the offsprings of the French settlers in the former French colonies. They belong to the EU majority, but those whose parents were born in the colonies – generally in Maghreb– are considered AT. This introduces some distortion in our counting (both the number of AT delinquents and the AT reference population are overestimated) which in turn influences our estimations of poverty[6]. These counting errors – unavoidable with French data – should not have a big incidence in our results because the sub-populations that belong to the above mentioned categories are small fractions of the overall population. Consistently, the same criteria are used in our determination of the reference population in section 3

1.2. Considered Offenses

Table 1. Considered types of crime and sentences distribution

crime type	total		EU	AT
description	N	%	%	%
homicides	18	1.2	1.5	1.0
AGBH with WD > 8 days	407	27.5	26.0	28.8
AR	191	12.9	10.9	14.6
robbery with GBH	50	3.4	2.5	4.1
rape	68	4.6	4.6	4.6
sexual assault	265	17,9	25.6	11.5
AW without WD	190	12.9	12.1	13.5
AW with WD < 8 days	289	19.6	16.8	21.8
total	1478	100.0	100.0	100.0

AGBH: Assault causing Grievous Bodily Harm; WD: Work Disruption;

AR: Armed Robbery; AW: Assault with a Weapon

Our data base corresponds to sentences passed on juveniles that committed one of the crimes punishable by prison according to the French Law. The types of crimes as well as the corresponding number of sentences passed on offenders of each origin are detailed on Table 1. Homicides, robbery with grievous bodily harm (GBH) and rape represent altogether less

---

[6]According to reference [43], in 1990, 7.5% of the less than 18 years old in Isère belong to repatriated families.

than 10% of the sentences (more precisely, 9.2%) while armed robbery with bodily harm (AGBH) with > 8 days of work disruption (WD) is the most frequent type of offense, with 27.5% of the sentences. The sentence harshness is determined to a large extent by the legal category of the crime, assessed by the courts. However, there is no agreement on any scale of offense seriousness: the legal categories used by judges are not specific enough and allow for large variations inside categories [44]. In particular, this latitude may leave place to ethnic bias in sentencing. We further investigate this question using the same database in [45].

Table 2 details the share of EU and AT convictions corresponding to each type of crime. EU offenders are more represented than AT in sexual assaults, while AT are relatively more numerous in all the other types of crimes. Globally, 54% of the sentences are passed on AT offenders, clearly a much larger proportion than the share of the AT juvenile population in Isère, which is of the order of $\approx 10\%$ [43] according to the censuses of 1982, 1990 and 1999 (source: database SAPHIR [46]).

Table 2. Share of EU and AT convictions for each type of crime

crime type description	EU		AT	
	N	%	N	%
homicides	10	55.6	8	44.4
AGBH with WD > 8 days	176	43.2	231	56.8
AR	74	38.7	117	61.3
robbery with GBH	17	34.0	33	66.0
rape	31	45.6	37	54.4
sexual assault	173	65.3	92	34.7
AW without WD	82	43.2	108	56.8
AW with WD < 8 days	114	39.4	175	60.6
total	677	45.8	801	54.2

AGBH: **A**ssault causing **G**rievous **B**odily **H**arm; WD: **W**ork **D**isruption;

AR: **A**rmed **R**obbery; AW: **A**ssault with a **W**eapon

Notice however that figures both in Table 1 and Table 2 correspond to *sentences* and not to offenders. Among the latter there are recidivists that have been sentenced several times in the considered period. We further discuss this point in the next section.

1.3. Yearly Sentences: First Offenders and Recidivism

Criminality in France has increased along the 20 years covered by our survey; consistently, the number of sentences in our database is a noisy increasing function of the year of crime perpetration, as shown on figure 1. There is a drop at the end of the period because some crimes perpetrated after 2003 have not yet been sentenced in 2005. Also, the database includes some sentences of crimes committed before 1985. In the regressions presented in this section we only take into account crimes committed in the period 1984-2003, to minimize the bias due to delays in police elucidation or court sentencing.

Figures 2 present the number of sentences as a function of the offense perpetration year. EU convictions increase at a rate slightly larger than 1 per year while the increase

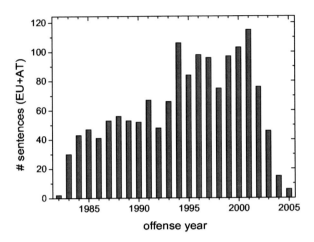

Figure 1. Number of sentences as a function of the year of crime perpetration, all the minors together.

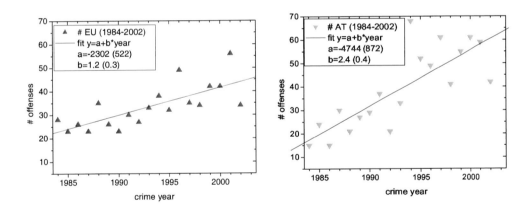

Figure 2. Number of sentences as a function of the crime perpetration year. Left: EU offenders. Right: AT offenders. In parenthesis, standard errors.

for AT offenders is about twice as large. Thus, even if in the eighties (at the beginning of the considered period) there were more EU than AT sentenced offenders, at the end of the nineties the latter are much more numerous. This might explain the perception that the AT population is more prone to criminality than the EU one. Notice that the increase of the Courts' activity after 1993 seems concentrated on AT offenders, soaring dramatically in 1994. This striking increase in the number of sentences between 1993 and 1997 may be due to the fact that the Police was asked to bring more systematically before the Courts the cases involving minors [47].

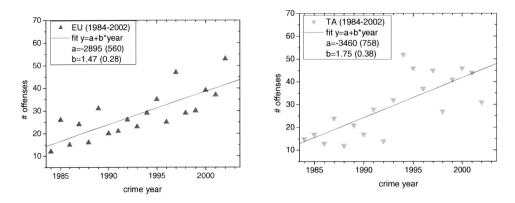

Figure 3. Number of sentenced first offenders as a function of crime perpetration year.

In fact, the number of offenders in our database is 1 216, 598 EU, 618 AT. Among these there are 100 recidivists, 75 AT and 25 EU, who committed 262 offenses, 199 and 63 respectively, thus totalizing the 1 478 records. Given our precision, the average number of offenses per recidivist is of the order of 2.6, roughly the same for EU and AT. In contrast, there are slightly more EU first offenders (convicted only once in the period) than AT (573 and 543 respectively). Taking into account the large dispersion of the data, we observe that on average EU and AT offenders commit their first crime at the same age, ≈ 15.4 years old.

In order to count offenders instead of offenses, on Figures 3 we plot the numbers of offenders versus the perpetration year of their first conviction. Clearly, AT and EU juveniles enter the CJS for their first serious crime roughly at the same rate. Thus, the larger sentencing rate of AT juveniles in Figure 2 is mainly due to punished reoffending, which is less frequent among EU offenders.

It remains that the proportion of AT young offenders seems abnormally large, given that the proportion of youngsters of foreign origin (including offsprings of AT and of non-French European immigrants) in Isère in the period 1982-1999 has dropped from $\sim 25\%$ to $\sim 20\%$ [43]. The rest of the paper is devoted to explore whether poverty may explain this apparent overrepresentation of the stigmatized minority population in juvenile crime.

2.   Estimation of the Offenders' Living Standard

The poverty of a household is measured by its *living standard*, which is equal to the income of the household divided by the number of consumption units. The latter takes into account that living expenditures are a decreasing function of the family size: the householder represents one consumption unit, 0.5 units are added for each of the other members of the household older than 14 years old, 0.3 units for children below 14 years old. By definition all the components of the household have the same living standard. Thus, the parents' profession, the type of family and the number of siblings are strong indicators of poverty levels.

Most offenders' fathers are workers (52% of EU and 70% of AT), followed by employees (20% and 15% respectively). Less than 2% have higher socio-professional situations. Among the mothers, 32% of EU (68% of AT) do not have any profession; 44% of EU and 24% of AT are employees. With respect to the working status, 83% of the EU but only 63% of the AT fathers have a job; 15% of AT fathers are retired and 17% unemployed, against 3% and 8% respectively for EU fathers. The fathers of the remaining households are either invalid or have other status. Summarizing, AT fathers have on average less well-remunerated professions, and are more numerous to be unemployed. Also, the AT mothers are less numerous to contribute to the household incomes: 53% of EU, but only 25% of AT have a job.

Since we do not know the families' incomes, we use the parents' professions and working status to estimate them. We adopt as monetary unit the inflation indexed minimal wage (named "SMIC"). Introducing this unit allows us to get rid of variations in the living standards due to inflation and other monetary drifts along the 20 years period under consideration. All the monetary quantities (like the median income, etc.) are calculated through percentages of the minimal wage.

We attribute a professional level and a working status to each parent. The professional level is a binary variable that depends on his/her profession: managers, artisans, farmers, shopkeepers and individuals having a qualified professional education are considered high-level. Less qualified workers are considered low-level. We assume that when employed, workers of high socio-professional level earn 1.7 times the unit wage, which corresponds to the relation between the median and the first decile of the immigrants' income distribution in 2007[7]. Notice that for non-immigrants this relation is 1.8. Our estimations are not sensitive to such small differences. The working status depends on the occupational level. The household income is the sum of the parents' (or the single parent) estimated incomes. Whenever there is some latitude to attribute incomes, we have assumed maximal values, not to underestimate the living standard. We have used the following criteria to attribute incomes based on the status:

employed or unknown : employed workers earn the wages that correspond to their professional level. When we do not know the status, we assume it to be "employed";

unemployed or retired : in France the Social Security provides help to unemployed, usually a fraction of the last wage, fraction that decreases with the time spent as unemployed. We assume that, irrespective of the time unemployed, the unemployment benefit is 75% (the legal upper bound) of the income when employed. Similarly, we assume that retired earn 75% of the salary corresponding to the professional level, which is a seldom reached upper bound;

other status : this covers mainly invalidity. We assume that the income is 50% of the corresponding professional wage when employed;

no profession : a small proportion of persons do not have any profession; we assume that

---

[7]The relations between incomes of different socio-professional levels are based on the analysis [48] of a large survey called TeO ("Trajectoires et Origines") covering 22 000 persons living in Metropolitan France, realized in 2007. We verified, whenever data were available, that these percentages did not vary significantly, at least during the preceding ten years.

these, as well as the house-women, do not have any income. We discuss below the effect of including possible welfare income.

In order to determine the offenders' living standards we need the number of consumption units of their households. As expected for minors, most of the offenders in our database are school children or apprentices living either with their two parents, with one parent and a stepparent or with a single parent; a small fraction lives in other, mostly social, structures. In particular the majority of AT (65.5%), but only 47.8% of EU, live with their two parents. We also have to consider the number of siblings of each offender. In contrast with the national census statistics, the average number of children in the offenders' families is extremely large: 4.69 ± 2.58 (offender included; 98 EU and 92 AT missing values). Offenders with AT origin have on average larger families than those with EU origin (average number of siblings: AT: 4.9 ± 2.6; EU: 4.4 ± 2.5). We do not know the ages of the offenders' siblings; we estimate the number of consumption units assuming that one half of the siblings are older, and the other half younger, than 14. The offender is counted according to his age. In the cases where we do not know the number of siblings we assume that the offender is the only child in the household. Thus, if there were more children, our assumption leads, like with the income, to an overestimation of the living standard.

We have the necessary information for only 1 130 records (522 EU, 608 AT). Figures 4 present our results with the abscissas in SMIC monetary units. In 1999 the minimal wage or SMIC was slightly higher than 1 000 euro (precisely 1049 euro) per month; an order of magnitude of the living standard (in euro of the year 1999) of the children in our database may thus be obtained by just multiplying the x axis values by 1 000.

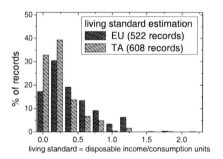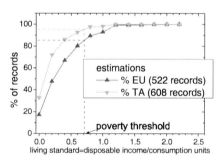

Figure 4. Left: Offenders' families estimated living standard distribution (see text). Right: Cumulative living standard distribution; the poverty threshold of $0.709 \times \mathrm{SMIC}$ is indicated.

The left hand side of figure 4 presents the histograms of AT and EU offenders' living standards. Each bin represents the percentage of offenders with the corresponding living standard (in our SMIC units). The maximum at 0.25 means that most delinquents' households live with $1/4$ of the minimal wage. Notice that there are more AT than EU households with a living standard below 0.25.

In European countries families are considered to live below the *poverty threshold* if their living standard is below 60% of the median income. The *poverty rate* is the percentage of the population living below this poverty threshold.

In the absence of official information about poverty levels of different subpopulations in France, we estimate the delinquents' poverty rates with information grasped from other sources. A recent INSEE publication by Lombardo and Pujol [48] gives very detailed informations about poverty in France in 2007. In particular, the poverty threshold corresponds to a living standard of 908 euro per month. Since the minimal wage before tax deduction in 2007 was 1 280 euro per month, the poverty threshold of the French population corresponds to $\approx 70.9\%$ of the minimal wage. Since poverty is persistent, we assume that the poverty threshold in SMIC units has not significantly changed in the period under consideration. We use thus the percentage of 70.9% of the SMIC to estimate the offenders' poverty rates. Figure 4 (right) presents the living standard cumulative distributions. The abscissas represent the living standards (in our SMIC units), the ordinates represent the percentage of offenders living below the corresponding living standard. It is clear that both EU and AT offenders are very poor, the latter being poorer than the former: 85% of the EU, 96% of the AT, live below the poverty threshold of 0.709 SMICs.

In our income estimations we did not include possible welfare payments, that depend on the number of children, on the family's situation, etc. Had we include them, our living standard estimation would be on average $\approx 9\%$ larger. Correspondingly, the cumulative distribution would be shifted $\approx 9\%$ to the right, and the corresponding percentages of EU (resp. AT) living below the poverty threshold would be slightly lower: 81% (resp. 93%).

Given the imprecision of our information, we may conclude that a large majority of the offenders in our database – if not all – live below the poverty threshold, TAs being poorer on average than EUs. Notice also that we probably underestimate the poverty rate because in our calculations we have systematically overestimated the household living standards (whenever we lacked information we assumed upper values for incomes and lower values for the number of siblings).

3. Reference Population

In the period spanned by our study Isère's population, according to the censuses, has increased from 936 728 in 1982 to 1 094 768 in 1999, i.e. roughly 17%. There are 429 047 households in 1999; a majority (299 792) correspond to families; among these 34 644 are single-parent families. The average number of children is slightly smaller than 2. The total number of children younger than 18 years old living in households with an adult householder (usually, but not necessarily, a parent) are quite stable along time: 246 904 in 1982, 245 704 in 1990, 248 148 in 1999, fluctuations being of the order of 1% or smaller.

The INSEE database SAPHIR, collected by INSEE Alsace [46], details the number of minors of different origins in urban and rural areas according to the censuses of 1968, 1975, 1982, 1990 and 1999. Part of these data have been published in a detailed report in 2007 [43][8]. In order to estimate the composition of the Isère juvenile population with socio-economic profile similar to that of the offenders we keep the information of the census years 1982, 1990 and 1999, which cover roughly the period under consideration. Since we have

---

[8]In the mentioned database are called urban those areas under supervision of the "Police", non-urban those areas under the supervision of the "Gendarmerie". The latter correspond to the less densely populated regions, mostly rural.

excluded from our study the records of Asiatic and American offenders (that represented 1.1% of the sentences), we consistently exclude them from our reference population (these are 3 704 in 1982, 4 904 in 1990, 5 657 in 1999, representing respectively 1.5%, 2.0% and 2.3% of the juveniles). Thus, whenever we present percentages of EU and AT in the following, they add up to 100% because the juveniles corresponding to other origins have been excluded. Comparisons between the reference demographic data and our crime data are thus straightforward.

Table 3. Percentage of children of EU and AT origin in Isère (global) and the composition of urban and non-urban areas. Other origins are excluded in the calculation of the percentages, as explained in the text

population type	origin	year		
		1982	1990	1999
global	AT (%)	19	19	16
	EU (%)	81	81	84
urban	AT (%)	26	29	27
	EU (%)	74	71	73
non-urban	AT (%)	15	15	12
	EU (%)	85	85	88

Globally, the percentage[9] of EU youngsters less than 18 years old has varied smoothly in the period of interest (first line of Table 3) around $\sim 82\%$ (ATs are close to $\sim 18\%$) with deviations smaller than $\pm 2\%$. However they are very unevenly distributed in the Department's territory: the AT youngsters are relatively more numerous in urban areas and less numerous in rural areas (lines 2 and 3 of Table 3).

Thus, without taking the socio-economic status into consideration, we would expect the same proportion of EU and TA among juvenile criminals as in the SAPHIR database, i.e. roughly ≈ 1 AT for 4 EU. This is far from being the case: as detailed in section 1.3 above, there is a ratio AT:EU of $\sim 1:1$.

3.1. Juvenile Poverty Rates in Isère

Poverty of children is not well documented in any country of the European Union. According to the 2010 report for the European Community [49] "... *statistics are not well suited to issues such as the situation facing the children of migrants or of minority ethnic groups*". Obviously, the same remark applies to French statistical data.

According to the 1999 national French census, there are 16 096 782 households in France; there is a single adult in 12.3% of the cases, 87.7% are couples; 45.3% of the households do not have children, 22.9% have one child, 20.6% and 8,1% have respectively two and 3 children; only 3.1% have 4 children or more. The most frequent number of children is 2.

The poverty rate in France has not changed significantly since 1984: in the period 1990-2002 it has slowly decreased from 14.7% to 12.9% (with subsequent small fluctuations

---

[9]The actual figures – deduced by ourselves from data kindly made available by Bernard Aubry and Michèle Tribalat – are detailed in the Appendix (Table 5).

around 13% from 2003 to 2005). However, poverty is very unevenly distributed according to the origin of the householders. In France (Metropolitan Area) the poverty rates of households living below the 60% poverty threshold are [48]:

- 42.7% among African immigrants,

- 24.0% among European immigrants,

- 11.3% among non-immigrants.

In the absence of official statistics, we combine the numbers of youngsters in Isère according to their origin with the corresponding national poverty rates detailed above to estimate the proportions of minors with EU and AT origin living below the poverty threshold. We use these percentages irrespective of the census year, because the information is only available for 2007, and, as already mentioned, the demographic structure of poverty is persistent: it has not changed significantly since 1984.

The results are detailed in Table 4. Notice that they cannot be deduced by applying the percentages directly to data in Table 3: we have to consider separately the French and the European non-French populations (detailed in Table 5 of the Appendix) because the corresponding poverty rates are different.

The estimated juvenile poverty rates for all the juvenile population of the Isère department are reported on the upper part of Table 4. But the juveniles in our database live mostly in urban areas, where the immigrant populations are more densely concentrated. Estimations restricted to the urban population (under Police control, which surveys in France mainly towns and densely populated districts) are detailed in the middle part of the Table 4.

Table 4. Estimated percentages of children living below the poverty threshold in Isère according to their origin. The percentages of the EU population are the composition of the French children (11.3% living below the poverty threshold) and the EU non-French children (24% living below the poverty threshold). The values for urban areas are based on the juvenile population living in areas under Police control. The last lines of the Table are obtained by considering only the juveniles living in Grenoble – the Department's capital – and its surroundings

population type	origin	year		
		1982	1990	1999
all Isère	AT (%)	42	43	39
	EU (%)	58	57	61
urban areas under Police control	AT (%)	51	55	55
	EU (%)	49	45	45
Grenoble and sourroundings	AT (%)	53	56	57
	EU (%)	47	44	43

Another estimation, restricted to the juvenile population of Grenoble – the Department's capital city – and its surroundings, which concentrates 66% (1982), 63% (1990) and 62% (1999) of the Isère urban population (i.e. under control of the Police) is presented in the lowest part of Table 4. Notice that although the last two estimations do not differ crucially from each other, there is a slightly higher concentration of poor AT juveniles in Grenoble and surroundings.

Strikingly, despite the relatively small proportion of AT juveniles in the average population (less than 20% between 1982 and 1999), they constitute roughly 40% of the juvenile population living below the poverty threshold in Isère. Restricting to the population of urban areas alone, the poverty rate of AT juveniles is dramatically larger: they represent more than half of the juveniles living below the poverty threshold.

In one of the rare scientific publications addressing the question of child poverty in France, Legros [50] points out that the risk of poverty among children is 2.2 percentage points above the level in the population at a whole, and that poverty is persistent: a majority of children living below the poverty threshold in 2006 also lived below it in the preceding two or three years. Thus, our poverty rate estimations for children in Isère, based on the above percentages, probably underestimate the poverty level of youngsters. Also, due to poverty persistence, the possible error introduced by our generalization of the percentages of 2007 to the period 1985-2005 should not modify qualitatively our conclusions.

4. Delinquency and Poverty

Figure 5 summarizes our results. We represented the percentages of EU and AT delinquents in our database as a function of the year when the first sentenced crime has been committed[10]. Our representation is redundant for the sake of clarity, since we represented the two components (EU and AT) which are complementary (they add up to 100%). On the same figures we represented the estimated poverty rates of juveniles living in urban areas in Isère, given in Table 4 (with a linear extrapolation after 1999).

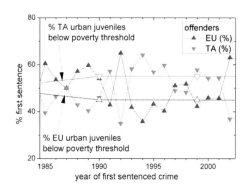 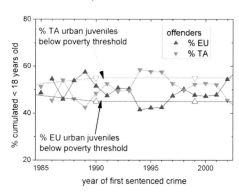

Figure 5. Proportions of AT and EU offenders (see text for the meaning of the two different representations), and proportions of AT and EU juveniles in urban regions in Isère living below the poverty threshold, as a function of the year when the first crime is committed.

Delinquents are counted using two different criteria, that give both similar results:

- left figure: we represent the number of first sentences (to avoid double counting of recidivists) as a function of the year of the corresponding crime. Thus, each juvenile

---

[10]We only consider crimes committed before 2003 to get rid of fluctuations imputable to the justice system (crimes committed after 2002 may not have been elucidated nor judged by 2005).

is counted only once, and appears in the representation the year of his/her first crime that has been sentenced.

- right figure: each sentenced juvenile is counted as a delinquent between the year of the first sentenced crime until his/her 18th anniversary. The corresponding data (labelled *cumulated < 18*), corresponds to the assumption that once a juvenile entered crime he/she remains a juvenile delinquent until majority.

Obviously, the second way of counting has less fluctuations than the first one. It is remarkable that both ways of counting criminals present very similar patterns: both EU and AT present fluctuations but remain close to the corresponding lines of poverty rates, some years below and others above these lines. These fluctuations are of the same order of magnitude as the small gap between the reference poverty rates.

5. Discussion and Conclusion

In this paper we investigated whether delinquents belonging to minorities are actually overrepresented in crime. Our study is based on 20 years (1985-2005) of sentenced serious crimes in Isère (France), that we split into delinquents belonging to the stigmatized minorities of African-Turkish origins (AT) or to the majority of European origin (EU) (section 1.1).

Our hypothesis is that the percentage of AT juveniles in the urban sub-population living below the poverty threshold (the reference population) is much larger than the percentage of AT juveniles in the overall population, not only because minority households have on average lower incomes than majority ones, but also because immigrant families have more offsprings than French ones, so that their income *per capita* (more precisely their *living standard*) is lower.

Our main result may be summarized in two steps:

Firstly, we showed in section 1.3 that the yearly number of EU and AT juveniles convicted of serious crimes are of the same order of magnitude. Based on information of the offenders' families composition, grasped from the corresponding judiciary files, we estimated (section 2) the living standards of the delinquents' population. They overwhelmingly belong to very poor families, mostly living in urban areas. More than 90% of them (precisely 85% of EU and 96% of AT) live below the poverty threshold.

Secondly, in section 3 we estimated the poverty rates of the Isère's juvenile population according to their origin, that we call the reference population, combining census data with economic poverty rates of the different subpopulations. Strikingly, when restricting to the juvenile urban population in Isère, the proportions of EU and AT youngsters living below the poverty threshold are similar, very far from the 20:80 ratio of TA:EU of the general population.

The percentages of TA and EU juveniles in the delinquents' database is similar to the composition of minority and majority youngsters living below the poverty threshold in urban areas: comparing similar socio-economic populations we find that there is *no evidence* of overrepresentation of the stigmatized minority among the juvenile convicted criminals.

Our analysis sheds some light on the long lasting and often emotional debate about the relation between immigration and criminality. More precisely, our data show that:

1. the number of sentenced offenses increases linearly through time, offenses committed by EU juveniles increase with a rate of about 1 per year while those committed by AT offenders increase at a rate of slightly more than 2 per year,

2. the larger rate of offenses committed by AT offenders is exclusively due to the activity of AT recidivists, that are more numerous than EU ones, since when we count offenders (and not sentences) both AT and EU youngsters are present in similar proportions in the course of the 20 years covered by the data,

3. the juvenile delinquents population is composed of about 50% of EU and 50% of AT offenders, without significative variations through time,

4. this ratio 50/50 is similar to the estimated ratio of EU and AT in the urban juvenile population of Isère living below the poverty threshold[11].

These conclusions are based on several hypothesis that seem quite reasonable, but would need further investigation:

1. our data correspond to very serious offenses, and it is unclear whether their statistics may be generalized to other types of crimes,

2. our data correspond to elucidated and punished crimes, which are a small fraction of all the crimes, whose number may be estimated according to victimization records; nothing can be said about authors of non-elucidated crimes,

3. our measure of recidivism is certainly a minorant because, as with the offenses themselves, it corresponds to past convictions, and not to past crimes. This drawback is systematic in all the criminological studies because only elucidated crimes are ascribable to the offenders. Unpunished crimes are thus not counted,

4. our evaluations of poverty levels in Isère (our reference population) are based on poverty percentages of 2007, that we have extrapolated to all the period under study; our estimations, difficult to verify because there is no other official statistics on the subject, are justified by the persistence of poverty [50],

5. our estimated poverty levels are probably underestimated because they do not take into account the fact that children average poverty is larger than that of adults [50].

An interesting observation grasped from our data is that recidivism is more frequent among the minority offenders. One has to keep in mind that our data, which correspond to *cleared* crimes, show that the proportion of first sentences meted out to EU and AT delinquents, as well as their corresponding ages, are roughly the same. This opens a new question: one may wonder whether AT juveniles – more numerous than EU ones among the recidivists – are intrinsically more active or whether the justice system selectively surveys minority delinquents when clearing new crimes.

---

[11] Note added in proof: Based on the TeO database, Michèle Tribalat (private communication) finds that 51% of the juveniles younger than 18 years old with a living standard of less than 11 606 euro/year (the 5% poorest population) are AT.

Table 5. Number of children according to their origin in Isère (global), and the composition of urban and non-urban areas. The number of children neither EU nor AT (other origins, excluded in our calculations of percentages) are detailed. Consistently with our definitions, the French population repatriated from the former colonies are included in the AT subpopulation

type of population	origin	year		
		1982	1990	1999
global	AT	45 688	45 908	38 748
	EU non FR	37 032	30 012	21 673
	EU	199 304	197 100	206 181
	excluded	1 912	2 696	3 219
urban	AT	21 544	19 848	16 950
	EU non FR	15 396	9 904	6 030
	EU	60 600	49 336	45 969
	excluded	1 184	1 212	1 504
non-urban	AT	24 144	26 060	21 798
	EU non FR	21 636	20 108	15 643
	EU	138 704	147 764	160 212
	excluded	728	1 484	1 715

The main conclusion of our study is that minority over-representation in crime is only apparent: poverty and urban environment are enough to explain it. When one compares populations with similar living standards, the proportion of juvenile offenders that belong to the discriminated minorities is similar to their share in the urban juvenile poor population.

This does not mean that poverty and urban environment are the unique determinants of violent criminality (needless to say that delinquents are a small fraction of the population – even among those living below the poverty level –), but rather that there is no need to invoke other determinants to explain minority over-representation. In other words, minority and majority criminality have similar determinants.

Interestingly, demographic statistics in USA present the same structure as in France. According to the 2011 census, 12.5% of non-Hispanic whites, 25.3% of Hispanics and 27.6% of Blacks live below the poverty threshold. Black and Hispanic minorities represent 55% of the poor. Poverty of children is even deeper: among the poor younger than 18 years old there are 12.5% of non-Hispanic whites, but 34.1% of Hispanics and 38.8% of Blacks. Since juveniles are responsible of a large proportion of crimes, it would be interesting to analyze to what extent minority overrepresentation in crime in the USA and in France might be similarly explained by poverty.

6. Appendix

6.1. Detailed Populations

The numbers of juveniles in Isère used in our estimations of poverty are detailed on Table 5.

EU		father		
		endogamous	exogamous	unknown
mother	endogamous	491		
	exogamous		45	108
	unknown		33	

detail endogamous

EU		father	
		FR	not FR
mother	FR	417	
	not FR		74

detail exogamous

EU		father		
		FR	not FR	unknown
mother	FR		26	97
	not FR	15	4	11
	unknown	27	6	

TA		father		
		endogamous	exogamous	unknown
mother	endogamous	574		
	exogamous		106	48
	unknown		54	19

detail exogamous

TA		father	
		EU	TA
mother	EU		70
	TA	19	17

Figure 6. Mixity of parental couples. Three upper tables: numbers of endogamic and exogamic couples, among the parents of EU juveniles ("unknown": origin unknown). Two bottom tables: the same for AT couples. Dark purple cells: impossible combinations.

6.2. Endogamy of Parental Couples in Our Database

The details of the composition of the offenders' parental couples in our database are given in figure 6. Clearly, endogamy (couples have both the same origin) is the rule.

Acknowledgments

We are grateful to Michèle Tribalat and Bernard Aubry for communicating us the data of the SAPHIR database, and Michèle Tribalat and Roberto Calemczuk for useful discussions and critical reading of the manuscript. The estimations and findings in this paper are those of the authors and do not necessarily reflect their views.

This work is part of the project DyXi supported by the joint program "Complex Systems in Human and Social Sciences" of the French Ministry of Research and of the CNRS. It has also benefited from support of the IXXI (Institut Rhone-Alpin des Sciences de la Complexité). M.B.G. and S.R. are CNRS members.

References

[1] Michael Tonry. Ethnicity, crime, and immigration. In Michael Tonry, editor, *Comparative and Cross-National Perspectives on Ethnicity, Crime, and Immigration*, volume 21, pages 1–29. Chicago, University of Chicago Press, 1996.

[2] Tushar Kansal. Racial disparity in sentencing: a review of the literature. Technical report, The Sentencing Project, 2005.

[3] Hugues Lagrange. *Le déni des cultures*. Paris, Seuil, 2010.

[4] G. Becker. Crime and punishment: an economic approach. *Journal of Political Economy*, 76:169–217, 1968.

[5] Kevin M. Beaver. *The Intersection of Genes, the Environment, and Crime and Delinquency: A Longitudinal Study of Offending*. PhD thesis, University of Cincinnati, 2006.

[6] Scott Sayare. French provocateur enters battle over comments. *The New York Times*, page A5, 2011, February 12.

[7] Vani K. Borooah. Racial disparity in police stop and searches in england and wales. *J Quant Criminol Published Online 13 Feb 2011*, 2011.

[8] Philippe Lombardo and Jérôme Pujol. Le niveau de vie des descendants d'immigrés. Technical report, INSEE, 2011.

[9] Alex R. Piquero and Robert W. Brame. Assessing the race-crime and ethnicity-crime relationship in a sample of serious adolescent delinquents. *Crime & Delinquency*, 2008.

[10] Donna M. Bishop and Charles E. Frazier. Race effects in juvenile justice decision making. *The Journal of Criminal Law and Criminology*, 86(2):392–414, 1996.

[11] Eileen Poe-Yamagata and Michael A. Jones. And justice for some. Technical report, National Council on Crime and Delinquency, Davis, CA., 2000.

[12] Brian D. Johnson and Sara Betsinger. Punishing the "model minority": Asian-american criminal sentencing outcomes in federal district courts. *Criminology*, 47(4):1045–1090, 2009.

[13] Marjorie S. Zatz. The convergence of race, ethnicity, gender and class on court decision making: Looking toward the 21st century. In *Criminal Justice*, volume The nature of crime: continuity and change, chapter Policies, Processes, and Decisions of the Criminal Justice System, pages 503–552. U.S. Department of Justice Programs, Washington DC, 2000.

[14] John Braithwaite. The myth of social class and criminality reconsidered. *American Sociological Review*, 46(1):36–57, 1981.

[15] Judith R. Blau and Peter M. Blau. The cost of inequality: metropolitan structure and violent crime. *American Sociological Review*, 47:114–129, 1982.

[16] Don Weatherburn and Bronwyn Lind. Poverty, parenting, peers and crime-prone neighbourhoods. Technical Report 85, Australian Institute of Criminology, 1998.

[17] Jan J.M. van Dijk. Determinants of crime. In Kristiina Kangaspunta, Matti Jousten, and Natalia Ollus, editors, *Crime and criminal justice in Europe and North America 1990-1994*, volume 32, pages 32–53. European Institute for Crime Prevention and Control (HEUNI), 1998.

[18] F. Bourguignon. Crime as a social cost of poverty and inequality: a review focusing on developing countries. *Revista Desarrollo y Sociedad*, 2009.

[19] Morgan Kelly. Inequality and crime. *The Review of Economics and Statistics*, 82(4):530–539, 2000.

[20] J. Ludwig, G. J. Duncan, and P. Hirschfield. Urban poverty and juvenile crime: Evidence from a randomizes housing-mobility experiment. *Quartely Journal of Economics*, 116:655–679, 2001.

[21] Lance Hannon and Robert DeFina. Violent crime in african american and white neighborhoods. *Journal of Poverty*, 3:49–67, 2005.

[22] Karen Heimer, Kecia R. Johnson, Joseph B. Lang, Andres F. Rengifo, and Don Stemen. Race and women imprisonment: Poverty, african american presence, and social welfare. *J Quant Criminol*, Published On Line, 2011.

[23] Moshe Levy and Sorin Solomon. New evidence for the power law distribution of wealth. *Physica A*, 242:90–94, 1997.

[24] Michal Brzezinski. Do wealth distributions follow power laws? evidence from "rich lists". *arXiv:1304.0212v1*, 2013.

[25] Edward L. Glaeser and Bruce Sacerdote. Why is there more crime in cities. *Journal of Political Economy*, 107(S6):S225–S258, 1999.

[26] Bohsiu Wu and Angel Ilarraza Fuentes. The entengled effects of race and urban poverty. *Juvenile and Family Court Journal*, pages 41–54, Spring 1998.

[27] Thomas McNulty. Assessing the race-violence relationship at the macro level: the assumption of racialinvariance and the problem of restricted distributions. *Criminology*, 39(2):467–490, 2001.

[28] Steven F. Messner, Lawrence E. Raffalovich, and Richard McMillan. Economic deprivation and changes in homicide arrest rates for white and black youth, 1967-1998: a national time series analysis. *Criminology*, 39(3):591–614, 2001.

[29] Thomas McNulty and Paul E. Bellair. Explaining racial and ethnic differences in serious adolescent violent behavior. *Criminlogy*, 41(3):709–748, 2003.

[30] María B. Vélez, Lauren J. Krivo, and Ruth D. Peterson. Structural inequality and homicide: an assessment of the black-white gap killings. *Criminology*, 41(3):645–672, 2003.

[31] Elizabeth Brown. It's urban living, not ethnicity itself': Race, crime and the urban geography of high-risk youth. *Geography Compass*, 1/2:222–245, 2007.

[32] John R. Hipp. Income inequality, race, and place: Does the distribution of race and class within neighborhoods affect crime rates? *Criminology*, 45(3):665–697, 2007.

[33] John R. Hipp. The role of crime in housing unit racial/ethnic transition. *Criminology*, 48(3):683–723, 2010.

[34] Lauren J. Krivo and Ruth D. Peterson. The structural context of homicide: accounting for racial differences in process. *American Sociological Review*, 65:547–559, August 2000.

[35] Pablo Fajnzylber, Daniel Lederman, and Norman Loayza. What causes violent crime? *European Economic Review*, 46:1323–1357, 2002.

[36] Kristiina Kangaspunta, Matti Jousten, and Natalia Ollus. Crime and criminal justice in europe and north america 1990-1994. Publication Series 32, European Institute for Crime Prevention and Control (HEUNI), 1998.

[37] Carl E. Pope and Howard N. Snyder. Race as a factor in juvenile arrests. *Juvenile Justice Bulletin*, pages 1–7, 2003.

[38] Sophie Body-Gendrot. Muslims: citizenship, security and social justice in france. *International Review of Law, Crime and Justice*, 36:247–256, 2008.

[39] S. Roché, S. Astor, and M-A. Depuiset. Socialisation familiale, délinquance et justice pénale. volume 2: La famille, la délinquance des mineurs et les décisions de justice. Rapport pour la CNAF et le GIP "Mission de Recherche Droit et Justice", 2008.

[40] Michèle Tribalat. Les concentrations ethniques en france. *Agir*, 2007.

[41] Catherine Borrel and Bertrand Lhommeau. Etre ne en france d'un parent immigre. *INSEE Premiere*, 1287, 2010.

[42] Cris Beauchemin, Christelle Hamel, Maud Lesné, Patrick Simon, and "Equipe TEO". Les discriminations : Une question de minorités visibles. *Population et Sociétés*, 466:1–4, April 2010.

[43] Bernard Aubry and Michéle Tribalat. Importance et évolution des concentrations en zone gendarmerie de 1968 à 1999. Technical report, Centre de Prospective de la Gendarmerie Nationale, March 2007.

[44] G. Kleck. Racial discrimination in criminal sentencing: a critical evaluation of the evidence with additional evidence on the death penalty. *American Sociological Review*, 46:783–805, 1981.

[45] Sebastian Roché, Mirta B. Gordon, and Marie-Aude Depuiset. Oxford handbook of ethnicity, crime, and immigration. In Sandra M. Bucerius and Michael Tonry, editors, *The handbook of ethnicity, crime, and immigration*, number 29, chapter Case study: Sentencing Violent Juvenile Offenders in A Color Blind Country: does ethnicity matter in France? HECI, 2013.

[46] Bernard Aubry. Database of juvenile demography in france. Technical report, INSEE, 1999.

[47] Bruno Aubusson, Nacer Lalam, René Padieu, and Philippe Zamora. Les statistiques de la délinquance. *Dossiers, France, Portrait social 2002/2003*, pages 141–158, 2007?

[48] Philippe Lombardo and Jérôme Pujol. Niveau de vie et pauvreté des immigrés en 2007. Technical report, INSEE, 2010.

[49] Itsván György Tóth, Terry Ward, and András Gábos. Child poverty and child well-being in the european union. Technical report, TÁrkI Social research institute (Budapest) - Applica (Brussels) - Report for European Commission, 2010.

[50] Michel Legros. Child poverty and child well-being in the european union. policy overview and policy impact analysis. a case study: France. Technical report, TÁrkI Social research institute (Budapest) - Applica (Brussels) - Report for European Commission, 2010.

INDEX

G

J

K

L

T

U